# Yoshida Shigeru

# The Library of Japan

*Labyrinth*
Arishima Takeo
Translated by Sanford Goldstein and Shinoda Seishi

*The Autobiography of Fukuzawa Yukichi*
Fukuzawa Yukichi
Revised translation by Kiyooka Eiichi

*Kokoro, and Selected Essays*
Natsume Sōseki
Translated by Edwin McClellan
Essays translated by Jay Rubin

*Konoe Fumimaro: A Political Biography*
Oka Yoshitake
Translated by Shumpei Okamoto and Patricia Murray

*The Spirit of Japanese Capitalism, and Selected Essays*
Yamamoto Schichihei
Translated by Lynn E. Riggs and Takechi Manabu

*Yoshida Shigeru: Last Meiji Man*
Yoshida Shigeru
Edited by Hiroshi Nara
Translated by Yoshida Ken'ichi and Hiroshi Nara

# Yoshida Shigeru
# Last Meiji Man

By
Yoshida Shigeru

Edited by
Hiroshi Nara

With translations from Japanese by
Yoshida Ken'ichi
and
Hiroshi Nara

ROWMAN & LITTLEFIELD PUBLISHERS, INC.
*Lanham • Boulder • New York • Toronto • Plymouth, UK*

A Pacific Basin Institute Book

To the memory of Frank Gibney, whose profound insights into Japanese politics and culture stimulated the creation of this volume.

ROWMAN & LITTLEFIELD PUBLISHERS, INC.

Published in the United States of America
by Rowman & Littlefield Publishers, Inc.
A wholly owned subsidiary of The Rowman & Littlefield Publishing Group, Inc.
4501 Forbes Boulevard, Suite 200, Lanham, Maryland 20706
www.rowmanlittlefield.com

Estover Road, Plymouth PL6 7PY, United Kingdom

British Library Cataloguing in Publication Information Available

**Library of Congress Cataloging-in-Publication Data**
Yoshida, Shigeru, 1878–1967.
  Yoshida Shigeru : last Meiji man / by Yoshida Shigeru ; edited by Hiroshi Nara ;
with translations from Japanese by Yoshida Ken'ichi and Hiroshi Nara.
    p. cm. — (The Library of Japan)
  Mostly excerpts from his Kaiso junen with the last 3 chapters added.
  ISBN-13: 978-0-7425-3932-7 (cloth : alk. paper)
  ISBN-10: 0-7425-3932-6 (cloth : alk. paper)
  ISBN-13: 978-0-7425-3933-4 (pbk. : alk. paper)
  ISBN-10: 0-7425-3933-4 (pbk. : alk. paper)
  1. Yoshida, Shigeru, 1878–1967. 2. Prime ministers—Japan—Biography.
3. Japan—Politics and government—1945–1989. I. Nara, Hiroshi, 1951–
II. Yoshida, Ken'ichi, 1912–1977. III. Yoshida, Shigeru, 1878–1967. Kaiso junen.
English. IV. Title.
  DS890.Y63A3 2007
  952.04'4092—dc22
  [B]

2006039038

Printed in the United States of America

⊗™ The paper used in this publication meets the minimum requirements of
American National Standard for Information Sciences—Permanence of Paper
for Printed Library Materials, ANSI/NISO Z39.48-1992.

To my late wife, Yukiko,
the memory of whose constant faith
in her country and her people strengthened and
inspired me during the years of crisis.

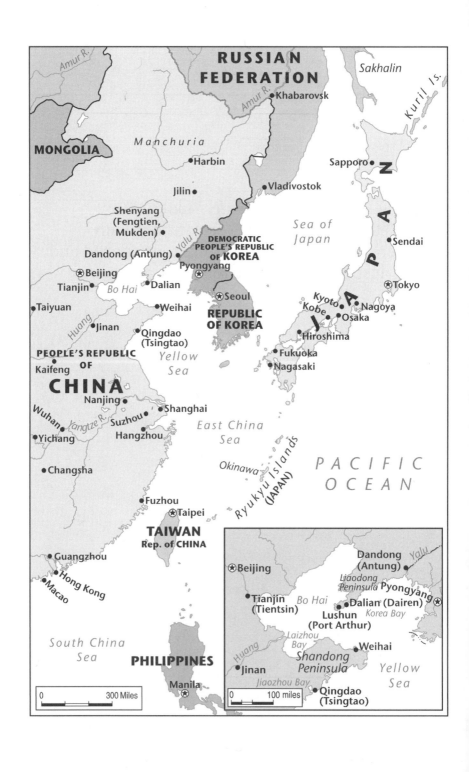

# Contents

**Part II: New Translation**

# Foreword to the New Edition

In April 1946, some months before his sixty-eighth birthday, a modestly retired diplomat named Yoshida Shigeru, thanks to an unlikely combination
of shattering military defeat, secret police imprisonment, and the offhand
directives of a new United States military occupation, stepped out on the
stage of history as the postwar prime minister of Japan. At the time, in a
country devastated and half-starving, its national spirit crushed by total failure, there were not many takers for the job. Yoshida, who had left his last
government post (as ambassador to Great Britain) in 1938, had quietly but
insistently opposed Japan's Pacific War—to the point where the army *ken-
peitai* police jailed him for several months because of his "pro-British and
American" sentiments. This made him persona grata to the American occu-
piers when he appeared as foreign minister in the end-of-the-war Higashikuni cabinet in 1945.

In May 1946, after the first choice, Hatoyama Ichirō, had been "purged"
by MacArthur for his wartime activities, Yoshida became, quite unexpectedly, an apparently transitional prime minister. To everyone's surprise but
his own, he took over his two posts (for a time he doubled as foreign minister) and made the job semipermanent. With more than seven years in
office—barring one period when his party was in opposition—before his
resignation in 1954, his was the longest stay in power since the great Meiji
era statesman, Itō Hirobumi.

Known to both friends and enemies as "One-man," Yoshida held the
reins of power tightly and confidently, rather in the manner of Itō and the
other autocratic leaders of that period. Born in the tenth year after the 1868
Meiji Restoration—his father was one of the young samurai reformers—he
was educated and became a diplomat in the shadow of modern Japan's

"founding fathers." His father-in-law, Makino Nobuaki, who later became Meiji's foreign minister, was the son of Ōkubo Toshimichi, the leading architect of the Meiji nation-state. Stationed in China during the beginnings of Japanese imperialism, Yoshida accompanied Count Makino to the Versailles negotiations in 1919 and strongly supported his country's close ties with the British. A firm believer in the emperor system and Japan's role as a peaceful world power, he was a crusty political conservative who took a dim view of popular democracy. At first dismissed by some historians as an anachronism, his strong loyalties to tradition and the Meiji mystique in the event armored him against social turmoil and intense political opposition.

Having been present in Japan during the Yoshida years, first as a navy officer with the occupation and later as a *Time* correspondent, I can bear witness to the controversy. For a generation of hopeful young reformers, the prime minister was all too close to the old *zaibatsu* big business establishment. He was unreasonably opposed to the new American-sponsored labor movement. Chants of "Break up the Yoshida cabinet—*Yoshida naikaku buttsubuse*" resounded at all the union rallies that I covered. Yet his agreement with many occupation reforms also antagonized some of the political old guard. For our part, occupation officers—most of us were ardent FDR New Dealers—criticized his government's back-door efforts to slow down our democratizing reforms.

At that, he had a tough row to hoe. Although the head of a parliamentary government, his party returned to office by free elections, he had to work under an all-powerful foreign occupation, whose directives—however much he filtered them—had to be observed. A reluctant partner in the occupation's early democratizing, he welcomed Washington's later "reverse course" that concentrated on building back Japan's economy as a key factor in the cold war containment of international communism. His own visceral anticommunism went so far as to suggest to occupation authorities (unsuccessfully) that some of the supreme commander's officials be removed because of alleged "leftist" sympathies. On the whole, however, he got along well with MacArthur, who was something of an anachronism himself.

As a parliamentarian, he was autocratic. He handled opposition much like an angry schoolteacher dealing with fractious pupils. "One-man" did not suffer fools gladly—and his definition of fool was distressingly broad. His shout of "baka yarō" (freely translated, "you damned fool") at an impertinent questioner became something of a trademark in a Diet whose debates, for all their intensity, were generally conducted in honorifics. Aided by a palace guard of protégés and sycophants, he ran roughshod over rivals whenever he could. This gave him an ample supply of political enemies. In fact, he was ultimately forced to resign because of gathering intraparty opposition.

Throughout his life he was a strong antimilitarist. Even after the outbreak of war in Korea, he resisted the American sentiment for expanding the newly founded National Police Reserve into a proper army. He heartily supported the antiwar Article Nine of Japan's made-in-America Constitution. To replace the purged militarist oligarchy that had brought the disastrous war on Japan, he sponsored the governance of career bureaucrats like himself. He supported the elevation of his one-time finance minister Ikeda Hayato to the prime ministership in 1960 and another former bureaucrat, Satō Eisaku, after Ikeda's resignation. "The Yoshida School" was the name given by Japanese to the succession of these and others, like Miyazawa Kiichi, following in his footsteps. The new four-lane highway to Ōiso, Tokyo wags of that time suggested, had been built to speed the way of politicians making the pilgrimage to his retirement home there to seek the old man's advice.

In September 1951 at the San Francisco Peace Conference, Yoshida had realized his longtime goal of restoring to Japan its independence—even if it came at the cost of an ancillary security treaty with the United States that over the years has proved something less than a blessing for both parties involved. I interviewed him at the time on one of the first big news shows on American television. I remember his comment: "Japan has regained political independence. Now we must see that economic independence is also achieved. For without this political independence has little meaning."

His statement encapsulated his policy of business, finance, and government bureaucracy collaboration—Japan, Inc., Americans called it—which led directly to Japan's high-growth era and created an economic superpower. In the process the nation's traditional political skills were transferred to the economic sector, with the Ministry for International Trade and Industry—the famed MITI—assuming the direction of an economic effort comparable to America's Pentagon in the security sector. Yoshida's guiding principles of governance—reliance on business-led progress, a resolutely supply-side economy, anticommunism, and national pacifism, buttressed by security and political commitment to the American alliance—became a virtual template for Japan's policy throughout the cold war period. It was perpetuated by the conservative Liberal Democratic Party, which succeeded Yoshida's original liberal organization.

A changing society, shifting international relationships, the disastrous "bubble" economy and the Liberal Democrats' own senescence and corruption have been transforming the political map of Japan for the twenty-first century. Even so, reformers and growing intraparty opponents have had their difficulties in dismantling the structure of bureaucratic governance that Yoshida left behind him. His name still towers over most of his successors.

The memoirs presented here are largely excerpts from a more detailed book, *Yoshida Shigeru: Kaisō Jūnen* (Yoshida Shigeru: Recollections over Ten Years), that was published in 1958, four years after Yoshida left public office. They comprise the closest to an autobiography that he ever wrote. The reader should remember, therefore, that these chapters, dealing with the history of Japan between the army's incursions into China in the 1930s and the end of the U.S. occupation in 1952, represent the history of those times, as Yoshida saw it. He was a man of strong opinion, generally unvarnished. The reader who wishes to see both sides of a story would do better to consult books by professional historians. Yet Yoshida's view of events in which he participated and his appraisals of the people he dealt with are much more than "the footnote to history" that the original translator's note claimed for them. As a memoir, they provide new light and insight on a period that, however rich in American comment, has offered to English-speaking readers only a few translations that give the Japanese side of the story. What most Americans know only as "MacArthur's Occupation" was also Yoshida's.

This is exactly why the original translator took pains to produce an excellent English rendition of a book previously available only in Japanese. Yoshida Ken'ichi, Shigeru's only son, was himself an interesting figure. An accomplished scholar of the Latin and Greek classics at Cambridge, he returned to Japan to build a reputation as an excellent literary critic and essayist. Like his English-speaking father, he was a man at home in two worlds. His originally selected chapters are supplemented by additional chapters dealing with Yoshida's early life and some famous mentors and acquaintances, as well as the author's reflections on patriotism and devotion to Japan's imperial mystique that tell us a great deal about his personal ideology. These have been ably translated by Professor Hiroshi Nara of the Japanese literature department at the University of Pittsburgh. Pittsburgh's Professor J. Thomas Rimer, one of America's most distinguished Asianists, has been kind enough to oversee the editing of this book.

As a longtime critical admirer of the senior Yoshida—and a friend of the late Ken'ichi as well—I have been privileged by the opportunity to write this brief foreword. Those of us in Tokyo's foreign press corps knew him only slightly—and we often criticized his "ultraconservative" policies in our reporting of those times. Yet as a person he drew our abiding respect. Immaculately turned out in his morning coat and striped trousers, with wing tip collars, pince-nez spectacles and, in his leisure moments, a trademark Churchillian cigar, he looked even in the Japan of the far-off fifties like a man from another world. Indeed he was. Like his postwar European contemporaries Konrad Adenauer and Alcide De Gasperi, he had come out of an older generation to rescue a new one.

Unlike so many of his Japanese fellow politicians, he was not afraid of the West, but regarded himself as a part of it. Like the Meiji statesmen he had grown up with, he thought in internationalist terms—one reason why he detested the chauvinist army militarists. But within himself he kept a fierce devotion to the Japanese emperor and the insular cultural tradition that he represented. Such contradictions of the spirit were part of the original Meiji paradox and the life of this classic Meiji man reflected them. His last written work, published in the year of his death, 1967, celebrated the "Decisive Century" that began on the eve of the Meiji Revolution just a century before.

Frank Gibney
Pacific Basin Institute

# Editor's Note

The present volume consists of two parts. Part I is the English text of *The Yoshida Memoirs: The Story of Japan in Crisis*, a translation of Yoshida's memoirs done by his son, Yoshida Ken'ichi, first published by Houghton Mifflin Company in 1962, and then reprinted by the Greenwood Press Publishers in 1973. The text in part I differs from the original English translation in some minor details. Changes are made to reflect current practices in the United States regarding capitalization, hyphenation, spelling of people and place names, format for dates and times, as well as some romanization conventions of Japanese words. Errors in spelling and grammar in the original edition have also been corrected. For the sake of accuracy, long vowels in Japanese words are indicated with a macron, except in those words that are considered to be sufficiently assimilated into English. The new translation in part II complements part I; the new translation permits the reader to take a closer look at the personality of this strong-minded politician.

The chapters in the present volume were selected for their enduring relevance to anyone interested in the history of Japan in the twentieth century, during which the nation witnessed tumultuous events of gargantuan proportions. Yet the combined translations do not completely represent the breadth and detail of coverage of the original memoirs penned by Yoshida Shigeru. The original translator, Yoshida Ken'ichi, produced a translation of only some chapters, some with considerable abridgement, and even with the new chapters translated for this volume, some topics in the memoirs have been left for the reader of the original work. These include the territorial question concerning the so-called northern territories and Okinawa, resumption of diplomatic relations with China and India, the issue of war

restitution, administrative restructuring, balanced budget and related issues, and postwar economic recovery, as well as the text of his addresses and
letters. Yoshida's own assessment of his experience as a politician, his view
on the postwar constitution, and his vision of Japan's future path have yet
to be translated into English.

Hiroshi Nara

# Preface to the Original Edition

The years between 1931—when the Japanese Army occupied Manchuria—
and 1945—when the occupation of Japan began—saw Japan abandon its
traditional foreign policy based upon close and friendly relations with the
United States and Great Britain and embark upon a perilous course of military expansionism that led directly to the nation's alignment with the Axis
powers, estrangement from the Western democracies, the Pacific War, and
subsequent defeat and occupation.

The history of those climactic years has been recorded in detail and by
many pens on the Allied side. This memoir portrays something of the
course of events as seen through the eyes of one who was close to developments on the Japanese side, and who eventually was cast for a prominent
role in the greatest crisis ever to confront his nation.

As such, this personal and "inside" account of Japan's miscalculation and
its tragic consequences, and of the occupation years as viewed by one who
was called upon to be the spokesman for a defeated Japan in dealings with
the supreme commander for the Allied powers, represents a footnote to the
history of a turbulent era.

# Acknowledgments

I would like to express my gratitude to Tom Rimer for first suggesting this translation and editing project to me some years ago. He also served as a communication pipeline between the Pacific Basin Institute and me on many administrative details. The completion of this project was made possible by the generous support of the Pacific Basin Institute, Pomona, California. Additional financial help was provided by the Japan Iron and Steel Federation endowment publication subvention fund and the Richard D. and Mary Jane Edwards Endowment Publication Fund of the University of Pittsburgh. I am grateful to Frank Gibney, then president of the PBI, for seeing this project through and providing the foreword for the volume, Tom Rimer and Brenda Jordan for reading a number of drafts and making helpful suggestions, and Xinmin Liu for checking on the spelling of Chinese place and people names. Obtaining photographs turned out to be time-consuming, and in this regard I am grateful for the help of Hans Palmer and Pedro Loureiro of the Pacific Basin Institute and of Robert L. Kirschenbaum of Pacific Press Service. I am also grateful to Hans Palmer for clearing all copyright issues for this book. Lastly my gratitude goes to the editorial and production staff of Rowman & Littlefield. In particular I want to express my appreciation to Susan McEachern for her eagerness to publish this book and to Becki Perna, Sarah Wood, and April Leo for their expert help and patience in the production of this book.

Hiroshi Nara

# I

# THE YOSHIDA MEMOIRS: THE STORY OF JAPAN IN CRISIS

# 1

## The Unfolding Tragedy

This personal account of the background of the climactic events which stemmed from the Japanese Army's expansionist policies in Manchuria and China in the thirties and led inexorably to Pearl Harbor and the Pacific War and its tragic aftermath, may appropriately begin by recounting a fateful warning addressed to me by Colonel Edward House, the famous personal adviser on international affairs to President Woodrow Wilson during the First World War, when I met the veteran presidential envoy while on an official tour of inspection of Japanese diplomatic missions abroad in 1932–1933.

Colonel House was at that time widely known and respected in Japan. Count Makino Nobuaki, my father-in-law, who had been a member of the Japanese delegation to the Versailles Peace Conference that ended the First World War, had become acquainted with him in Paris during the conference and had given me an introduction to him. Thus it happened that I was the recipient of a warning that, had it been heeded, would have saved my country and its people an infinity of human misery and loss.

At our meeting, Colonel House opened the conversation by saying that a people devoid of "diplomatic sense" could never get along. I took this statement to mean that a faculty to understand the international situation at any given moment was vital to the formulation of sound foreign policies. The colonel went on to say that shortly before the outbreak of the First World War he had visited Europe at the instance of President Wilson and there met with Kaiser Wilhelm. The kaiser was at the time reviewing the German grand fleet in the North Sea, and the interview took place on his imperial yacht. The colonel did his best to convince Germany's ruler of the dangers inherent in the belligerent policy that country was pursuing at the time and stated that so long as Germany avoided war she would continue to prosper as one of the world's great powers, but that, if international tensions were pushed to the point of hostilities, the result would not be war between Germany and France but a world war—a conflict in which Germany would be faced with encirclement by Great Britain and other powers that would come to the aid of France, and which might well mean the loss of the position which Germany had managed to attain in the world at the cost of so much effort. The kaiser and the Germans then in power, however, did not listen, and the result turned out exactly as Colonel House had foretold.

Before the war Germany had been a power to be reckoned with both economically and strategically, and a serious rival to Great Britain, and at the time when I met Colonel House, Japan occupied an international position akin to that of all eastern "Germany." The colonel, speaking with great earnestness, went on to say that he would like to give the same advice to Japan that he had given earlier to Germany—that should Japan become involved in war, that country would forfeit all the advantages of her status as a modern power which she had so painstakingly built up; whereas, if she chose to follow peaceful policies and made it her sole aim to maintain and extend the prosperity of the nation and its people, the future was bright indeed. Colonel House added that, as an old man of experience, he hoped the Japanese people would consider his words.

Following my return to Japan I did my best to convey the colonel's message to as many people as possible. When Prince Konoe, one of our leading statesmen of that time, in his turn visited the United States and saw Colonel House, the colonel repeated the same words of advice to him. Unfortunately, as had happened in Germany previously, the colonel's words were disregarded in Japan. Breaking away from the diplomatic policies which had been pursued ever since the days of the Meiji (1868–1912), Japan for no adequate reason embarked upon a major war and caused whatever had been achieved by her up to that time to be completely destroyed.

Before dealing with the question of our diplomatic policy during the years preceding the Pacific War, it is necessary to touch briefly on the historical aspect of Japan's relations with Great Britain and the United States of America.

It is common knowledge that it was the Americans who took the initiative in opening up Japan to intercourse with foreign nations, but during the Meiji days, and even in the following Taishō era (1912–1926), the country with which we actually had most to do was Great Britain. During that period the United States was busy developing its own internal resources, whereas Great Britain had extended its power and influence throughout the Far East, thereby making her relations with Japan increasingly significant. Following two world wars, the power of the United States has enormously increased and, particularly since the termination of the Pacific conflict, op-

erations in that ocean have been conducted chiefly by the Americans. I[
natural, therefore, that Japan's relations with the two Western powers
should appear to have been reversed. But Anglo-Japanese relations still have
not lost their meaning in international affairs and still remain one of the
determining factors in the field of diplomacy between the free countries.

Japan's statesmen of the early Meiji period carried out the task of establishing Japan's position among the nations of the world with a competence
and sureness of touch which even now command the admiration of my
countrymen, and the basic diplomatic policy as laid down by them was cooperation with Great Britain. This attitude was fully reciprocated by the
United Kingdom, inasmuch as it was to the advantage of that country, in
view of its vital interests in the Far East, to range itself on the side of a Japan
that had emerged as the victor in the Sino-Japanese war of 1894–1895. For
perhaps the same reason, Great Britain refrained from taking any part in the
triple intervention by Russia, France, and Germany which followed that
war, and which accounted for the fact that when Russia later obtained from
China by force a lease on the Liaodong Peninsula (which Russia had previously pressed Japan into returning to China) and proceeded to build bases
at Dalian and Port Arthur, and Great Britain countered this move of the
Czarist expansionists by demanding from China a lease on the port of Wei-
haiwei, the British government was careful to submit the matter to us beforehand for Japan's approval.

This pro-Japanese policy on the part of Great Britain finally took the
form, as Russian expansionism in the Far East became more marked, of a
proposal for an Anglo-Japanese alliance. After the conclusion of this pact
Japan, with the help of her British ally and the no less friendly assistance of
the United States, managed to weather the crisis of the Russo-Japanese War
and was thereby launched on the road to national prosperity.

What strikes one about these events is the unanimity with which the
Japanese government and people generally acted in those days, in contrast to
the dissensions concerning the attitude to be taken towards Great Britain
and the United States which were at a later date to mar our politics and policies. Looking back, I am impressed by the behavior of the Japanese people
at that time in matters affecting my country's relations with foreign nations.
At the time of the signing of the Anglo-Japanese Alliance, Great Britain was
at the height of her power and the mistress of the seven seas, while Japan was
an insignificant island-nation in the Far East which had only just begun its
rise from obscurity. The difference—in international significance and power
potential—between the two countries was far greater than the differences
which exist between Japan and the United States today. Yet the Anglo-
Japanese Alliance was welcomed by government and people alike, and no
one viewed that document as meaning that Japan was truckling to British
imperialism or in any danger of becoming a glorified British colony.

When I recall this historical fact, and then recall the way in which our so-called progressive intellectuals speak today of Japan as little better than an American colony and "the orphan of Asia" and so forth, it makes me wonder if these critics belong to the same race of people who only fifty years ago had acted with such decision and judgment, and without displaying any trace of what can only be termed a colonial sense of inferiority. I cannot help thinking, however, that the Japanese people as a whole are still the healthy race they were, and do not subscribe to the curious opinion of a noisy minority which seeks to equate alliance and cooperation with servitude.

From about the time of the First World War a subtle change occurred in Anglo-Japanese relations. Japan's victory in the Russo-Japanese War, which set the nation on the path leading to its emergence as a first-class power, may well have given the British the impression that here was a country that should be dealt with carefully, and when, during the world war that followed, Japan presented the famous Twenty-one Demands to China, thereby creating a major diplomatic stir in the chancelleries of the world, her desire to dominate the political scene in China must have been made more than clear to all concerned. Moreover, the time and manner of Japan's entry into World War I were not necessarily chosen solely with a view to aiding her British ally. Though some such action was demanded by the provisions of the alliance, Japan's declaration of war on Germany and her subsequent ousting of that country from Qingdao (Tsingtao) and the Shandong Peninsula could well be interpreted as a move primarily designed to strengthen Japan's position in China while Great Britain and the other major powers were fully occupied with the war in Europe.

In the meantime the United States had been steadily growing in power as a result of the same war, and when that country emerged from the conflict as one of the world's leading powers it was not surprising that she should have harbored her own suspicions concerning Japan's real intentions towards China and been constrained to make use of the Washington Disarmament Conference as a means of curbing Japanese policy by insistence on the principles of equal opportunity for all and the open door. It goes without saying that the limitation of naval armaments represented a useful step towards mitigating the evils of an unrestricted naval arms race such as had then just begun, and that the Nine Power Pact was not directed specifically against Japan. But the fact remains that these international agreements did have the effect of hampering Japan's actions in general, and there can be no doubt that the prime aim of the United States in persuading Great Britain to terminate the Anglo-Japanese Alliance was directed to the same end.

Even prior to these events—as far back as the time when the First World War began—there had already been talk in some circles in Japan, particularly among segments of the imperial army, of my country's allying itself with Germany to attack Great Britain, and although such an idea lacked the support necessary to influence the actual course of events, the stipulations contained in the Twenty-one Demands providing for the employment of Japanese political and military advisers by the Chinese central government, the supplying of specific types of arms by Japan to China or, alternatively, the setting up in that country of military arsenals under joint Sino-Japanese management, and so forth, had been included in Japan's demands mainly at the request of that segment of the army. It was to be foreseen, therefore, that the more extreme elements within the Japanese Army would regard the series of events from the Washington conference to the abrogation of the Anglo-Japanese Alliance as so many steps initiated by Great Britain and the United States with the aim of hemming Japan in and hindering her expansion on the Asian continent. Added to these developments, the worldwide depression of the thirties had the effect of intensifying international trading competition, resulting in the shutting out of Japanese goods from former markets, which in turn led to Japan's seeking to find remedies for economic difficulties through direct action, including allying herself with Germany and Italy and intervening in Manchuria and other parts of China. The upshot of that crucial foreign policy switch was the Anti-Comintern Pact between Japan, Germany, and Italy; the formation of the Triple Alliance; and, finally, Japan's entry into the Second World War on the side of the Axis powers.

In order to put these events into proper historical perspective, two points need to be borne in mind. First, it is clear that the path which the nation followed from the time of the Manchurian Incident in September 1931 to the outbreak of the Second World War represented a deviation from Japan's traditional line of action and interest; and, secondly, it is open to serious doubt whether either those in responsible positions around the imperial throne or the Japanese people in general desired to see the country aligned with the Axis peoples in opposition to Great Britain and the United States.

It should not be forgotten that during World War I, although Japan may have taken advantage of her geographical situation far from the central theatre of conflict to further our national interests in China, and although some short-sighted persons did at that time advocate taking the opportunity to support Germany, there can be no doubt that the sympathies of an overwhelming majority of the Japanese people lay with the British nation, to which we were then allied. It is equally clear that our government leaders were wholeheartedly committed to fulfilling the obligations imposed by the terms of the Anglo-Japanese Alliance; it is a matter of history that Japan acted as the guardian of British interests in the Far East throughout that war, and that its naval forces were sent across the Indian Ocean and as far as the Mediterranean to cooperate in affording effective protection to Allied shipping. Commenting upon Japan's role in World War I, Lord Grey, Great Britain's secretary of state for foreign affairs at that time, stated in his book *Twenty-five Years, 1892–1916*: "We found in the Japanese Government and

# 8

8 *Chapter 1*

its Ambassadors, honorable and loyal Allies. They understood, as in the case of the Bryan Peace Treaty with the United States, the difficulty in which we sometimes found ourselves, and they smoothed the path."

In the same volume Lord Grey conceded that Japan utilized the situation created by the war to strengthen her position in China, but says of that matter: "What Western nation with a population feeling the need for territorial outlets would have used such an opportunity with more or even with as much restraint?" which seems to me a fair and statesmanlike estimate of the situation. It is axiomatic that the conduct of international affairs must have its basis in mutual trust. That Japan should have achieved a leading position among the nations of the world by pursuing her policy of alliance with Great Britain and friendship with the United States throughout the Meiji and Taishō periods and then discarded that traditional diplomatic policy and chosen to throw in her lot with the distant Axis powers was not only a major strategic blunder but an action all the more regrettable in that it destroyed the trust placed by other countries in Japan as a nation. Recovery from this historic "stumble" will require years to complete, but it is the task before my nation today and it exceeds all others in importance. Japan cannot allow the work of our great national leaders of the Meiji and Taishō periods, who were the architects of modern Japan, to remain, as it now is, in ruins.

Since Japan's defeat, and throughout the years of predominantly American occupation, it was inevitable that the nation's policies, both foreign and internal, should have been largely dictated by our relations with the United States. This phase continued for so long that there are still those in Japan who seem to think that the nation is even today entirely dependent on the United States in the ordering of our actions and policies. Such a view is not in accordance with the facts. Japan's policies vis-à-vis the United States must change as the nation's economic position improves, with the consequent strengthening of the country's international status and self-respect, and such a change is already seen to be occurring. But the maintenance of close bonds of friendship with the United States, based upon a deep mutuality of interests, must be one of the pillars of Japan's fundamental policy and always remain so.

The same fundamental considerations apply to our policy towards Great Britain. In the world as it is today, Japan's relations with that country may not be quite as important as our relations with the United States. But if we take into consideration the close relationship which exists between Great Britain and the United States, and the position these two English-speaking countries occupy in world affairs, it follows that our relations with them form part of an indivisible whole and are not to be separated into two compartments. Moreover, from the point of view of international trade, the importance to Japan of Great Britain and the other countries of the sterling area remains unchanged. Japan is an island-nation in which a population in excess of ninety-one million must be provided with a civilized standard of life. This can only be accomplished through an expanding volume of overseas trade. That we should, to that end, pay special regard to our relations with Great Britain and the United States, two countries that are economically the most powerful, and technologically the most advanced, nations of the earth, and our dealings with whom go back deep into history, is a matter of prudent national policy unconnected with any considerations of political ideology.

In regard to the question of national defense, there is no need to point out the meaninglessness of what is called the principle of neutrality. Events in the Eastern European satellite states of the Soviet Union have demonstrated conclusively that the independence of a country provides no sure shield before an invasion by powerfully armed foreign forces. The situation of Japan might be different if the nation possessed sufficient armaments, and was favorably placed geographically to defend its neutrality. But Japan is in no such position. The nation can be defended in no other way than by a system of collective security based on the U.S.-Japan Security Treaty.

With these broad considerations in mind, it seems to me clear enough that we should follow a policy of cultivating good relations with the free world, and particularly with the countries of South-East Asia that are geographically and economically closest to us, insofar as is consistent with Japan's traditional and basic policy of friendship with the United States and Great Britain. This is not to say that Japan should disregard the importance of its relations with the countries within the communist orbit; I emphasize the point in view of the fact that some within Japan tend to place so much stress on the nation's relations with the communist world and the nations of South-East Asia that they at times appear to overlook—or forget—the more basic necessity, in formulating our national policies, of fostering close ties of friendship between Japan and Great Britain and the United States— and particularly the latter.

It is appropriate to remind ourselves here that, as I noted earlier, certain groups of people in Japan began to manifest antipathy to Japan's traditional diplomatic policy as early as the days of the Taishō era. The reasons responsible for the display of such sentiments were varied, ranging from simple envy of the wealth and power of Great Britain and the United States to opposition aroused by some of the actions taken by those countries in international affairs. But the most culpable among such critics of Japan's traditional foreign policies, in my opinion, were those who encouraged and exploited anti-foreign feeling in others in order to strengthen their own political position.

The most cogent example of this tendency was the attitude adopted by Japan's militarists at the time of the Manchurian Incident. As I have noted, the anti-American and anti-British feeling among segments within the Japanese Army sprang from differing causes, but it is clear that the primary objective of the various military cliques was the same—to gain power at the expense of those around the throne and those in responsible positions within the civilian government who advocated a policy of friendship with Great Britain and the United States. These uniformed politicians coupled their pleas for the adoption of anti-British and anti-American policies with enticing proposals to eliminate existing social and political evils at home, and to establish a new order of things in the Japanese homeland. In fact, the course of action to which they finally committed the nation drove Japan into the Axis camp and precipitated the greatest disaster ever suffered by the nation. For this—and the defeat and universal misery which their policies visited upon my nation—they must be held responsible.

If we look back into history, we see that the stirring up and utilization of anti-foreign feeling for political purposes is an indication of political immaturity. The Boxer Rebellion in China during the closing days of the Ch'ing (Qing) dynasty is one example; recent events in Egypt, where attempts were made to eliminate French and British influence through violence in the name of peace, is another. This sort of anti–foreign policy has as its motive the strengthening politically, within the country, of those who are its advocates. It could in the case of Egypt easily lead to closer relations with the Soviet Union simply as a method of offsetting British and French power. Which is precisely the line of action, and the political strategy, adopted by Japan's Army extremists in the days before Japan's entry into the Second World War.

Some comment here in regard to my country's relations with other Asian and African countries may not be out of place. Many of these countries gained their independence after the Second World War, and, while we Japanese sympathize with the nationalistic aspirations now prevalent in these nations in the light of Japan's own experience in the early days of the Meiji era, we should bear in mind the differences existing today between the position of Japan and most of the newly established nations of Asia.

According to some people, Japan too gained—or rather, regained—her independence in 1952 after nearly seven years of foreign occupation, and, our plight being therefore much the same as those of other countries of Asia and Africa, we should throw in our lot with them in opposition to such "colonial" powers as the United States, Great Britain, and France. Such a view seems to be completely at variance with the actual facts. Apart from the few years of foreign occupation following the termination of the Pacific War, Japan has been an independent state throughout its long history and we cannot conceive of our country occupying any other status than that of a completely independent and sovereign nation. In the fields of government, economics, industry, and social development, also, Japan is more Western than Asian—at least insofar as the levels attained by us in those spheres are concerned—whereas many of the other countries of Asia and Africa are still undeveloped, or under-developed, industrially and economically, and their peoples have still to attain the standards of living to which modern civilization entitles them to aspire. In short, they are what we are forced to recognize as backward nations, which as yet have little to do with international economic relations. In their present stage of development, their leaders are, in general, more concerned with the task of raising their countries politically and socially from their former status as colonies and dependencies of foreign powers than with problems connected with their economic relations with the outside world. Their major task is not to decide to which of the world's two great camps they will adhere, but simply the firm establishment of their respective countries as stable independent nations. It naturally follows, therefore, that the foreign policy which many of these new Asian and African nations favor is based upon a kind of negative neutrality. And although they couple that policy with more positive advocacy of the maintenance of world peace and fulfilling the role of mediator between the world's two power camps, the principles so advanced lack the economic and military backing needed to give force to what they preach. We can both understand and sympathize with their present policies, but that is not to say that we should rate them as being more important—internationally—than they actually are, and still less that Japan should model its foreign policy on their largely negative philosophy.

I have stated that we Japanese are in many respects more European than Asian; nevertheless, Japan is geographically an Asian nation and economically an integral part of that continent and, as such, better equipped than are most Western peoples to understand Asia. Racially speaking, also, other Asian and African nations tend to feel a greater sense of kinship towards Japan than towards the peoples of the West. This fact coupled with our superior economic development, should it seems to me, leave us in little doubt as to the role which Japan must play in international affairs in the future. An example of the kind of role which we Japanese are eminently qualified to play in the development of the new Asia is to so combine Western (and particularly American) capital with our own technical knowledge and industrial skills that both can be combined and used for the development of the South-East Asian area.

Many of the countries of Asia and Africa having long been under the domination of Western powers, it is only natural that they should, in some instances, feel distrustful of foreign capital. Where such sentiments persist, it surely behooves Japan to act as "go-between" and strive to allay whatever remaining animosity the nations concerned may still entertain towards the

West. It goes without saying that such a task is not likely to prove an easy one. But, in my opinion, it is one Japan should strive to perform. It is our duty to aid the peoples of Asia and Africa in their economic development and thus foster an awareness in the countries concerned that the political institutions and way of life of the free nations of the earth are best suited to bring prosperity to their nations and happiness to the peoples therein.

# 2

## The Crisis Breaks

Many years before the outbreak of the Pacific War, the uniformed politicians in the Japanese Army had labeled me as a member of the liberal pro-British and pro-American set within Japan and, accordingly, an opponent of the extremist policies they advocated.

This antagonism on the part of the militarists to me personally came to a head with the formation of the Hirota cabinet after the insurrection of young officers forming part of the Tokyo garrison on February 26, 1936. I had never taken any active interest in politics, and always avoided being mixed up in such matters, but on this occasion I was asked by Prince Konoe Fumimaro, who was at that time president of the House of Peers, to prevail upon Hirota Kōki to accept the premiership and, under those circumstances, could not very well decline to assist to some extent in the selection of candidates for the various posts in the new cabinet. There was also some talk of my becoming foreign minister.

The day following the completion of the task of choosing the members of the cabinet, General Count Terauchi Juichi, who was the candidate selected by the army for the post of war minister, accompanied by Major General (later General) Yamashita Tomoyuki and other members of the army general staff, visited the official residence of the foreign minister, where the deliberations on the formation of the new cabinet were being held, and stated bluntly that if newspaper reports were true, men were proposed for posts in the cabinet who were undesirable in view of the existing political situation and that the army protested in the strongest possible terms against the nomination of such people. It was clear that I was among those to whom the army objected, and I at once made it clear that I was unavailable for office and withdrew from the deliberations. It was learned later that

Ohara Naoshi, candidate for the post of minister of justice; Shimomura Hiroshi, for that of minister of education; and myself were the real targets of the army's protest, on the grounds that we three were liberals with known pro-British and pro-American leanings.

It was at about this time that a further incident occurred, which did not endear me to the military clique. I was taken by Mr. Hirota to a meeting of a society called the Tōa Renmei (East Asia League), or some such name, which included among its members extreme nationalities like General Matsui Iwane, who after the termination of the Pacific War was sentenced to death by the International Military Tribunal of the Far East. At the meeting retired army generals and university professors with extreme rightist sympathies made speeches attacking Great Britain and the United States. I was asked to speak, and could not graciously refuse. Wherefore I remarked that their talk reminded me of a scene in one of Quackenbos's books on American history in which the North American Indians discussed among themselves how they might best get rid of the white men. It was clear that the audience was not pleased by my words, and I was not invited to be present at the meetings of the society again; my unpopularity among these people probably dates from about that period when I declined to join the ultranationalist "chorus."

Perhaps by way of some compensation for my having failed to obtain the post of foreign minister, Premier Hirota nominated me for the post of ambassador to Great Britain, and I departed from Japan for London in April of the same year. At that time the Nazis, led by Adolf Hitler, were gradually gaining power in Germany, and the confrontation between the Axis powers, on the one hand, and the democracies led by Great Britain and France, on the other, was becoming more marked throughout Europe. Back in Japan, in the troubled state of the country immediately after the Tokyo military revolt of the previous February, the army went through the gestures of disciplining its subordinate elements, but was in reality taking advantage of the widespread feeling of unrest and apprehension to throw in its lot with the extreme nationalists and expansionists, while ever more openly declaring itself on the side of the Axis powers in matters of external policy.

It was at about this time that the question arose whether or not Japan should join Germany and Italy in an anti-Comintern pact. It seems that the government, under pressure from the army, made up its mind in favor of the step, but it was decided that before the decision was finished Japan's diplomatic representatives abroad should be consulted on the issue.

In common with other Japanese diplomatic envoys, I was asked for my opinion, and replied that I was opposed to the idea; an opinion which I repeated when, later, both Tatsumi Eiichi and Ōshima Hiroshi, the military attachés at Japan's embassies in London and Berlin respectively, visited me in an effort to prevail upon me to change my views.

I opposed the step because, although it was represented in army circles as involving nothing more than an ideological question of ranging Japan against communism, it was clear that the primary objective of those who sought to make Japan a signatory to the pact was to join forces with the Axis powers against Great Britain and France and so, inevitably, against the United States; an alignment which would inevitably lead—or so it seemed to me—to a political and military alliance with the fascist powers and a future for my country that I could not but feel would prove disastrous. The pact thus linking Japan with Nazi Germany was, nevertheless, signed. Italy subscribed to it, and, as I had foreseen, it later developed into the Triple Alliance.

I was recalled from my post in London, and retired from Japan's foreign service, in March 1939. From that time until I became foreign minister in the Higashikuni cabinet at the termination of the Pacific War, I was without an official position of any kind. During those six and a half years, people might reasonably have thought of me as a retired diplomat enjoying his leisure years in the same way as others whose careers had ended. The reality was somewhat different. The international situation was steadily worsening from day to day; the state of affairs within Japan was no more encouraging. And since it was not possible to remain out of touch with the world or ignore the way things were developing, I was forced, whether I liked it or not, to play my part in events to the best of my power.

The anticipated European war was precipitated by Hitler's invasion of Poland in September 1939, a few months after I had left the foreign service, and with the resignation of Prime Minister Neville Chamberlain and the formation of the Churchill cabinet in Britain in May 1940 it became increasingly apparent that, to meet the exigencies of the war as the situation deteriorated for the democracies, Great Britain would do her best to draw the United States into the conflict, while President Roosevelt seemed already to have made up his mind concerning the inevitability of his country becoming embroiled in the war and was stepping up American aid to the United Kingdom. Japan, on the other hand, was being led—mainly by an obstinate group of army men and more and more obviously ever since the Manchurian Incident—first into closer relations with Germany and Italy, and secondly deeper into hostilities in China, while a group within the imperial navy declared itself in favor of a policy of southward expansion: none of which developments helped to improve Japan's relations with Great Britain and the United States.

Prince Konoe, who had in the meantime become prime minister, was aware of the dangers inherent in this policy and since April 1941 had engaged in negotiations with the United States aimed at finding through peaceful means some way out of an increasingly threatening situation. But that fact did not prevent units of the Japanese Army from marching into

French Indo-China; both Great Britain and the United States freezing our
assets in those countries; and the United States banning the export of oil to
Japan. Under such circumstances the progress of the negotiations could not
be other than tardy. Against that somber background, Prince Konoe formed
his third cabinet, and in the middle of October 1941 tendered his resignation to the emperor and was succeeded as premier by General Tōjō Hideki.

From that point, Mr. Tōgō Shigenori, the foreign minister in the new cabinet, was in charge of negotiations with the United States, and some of us
who had served in the foreign office, such as the veteran Baron Shidehara
Kijūrō and myself, consulted together and decided to do what we could to
assist Tōgō in his endeavors for peace.

Baron Shidehara was of the opinion that the main stumbling block in
our negotiations with Great Britain and the United States was China, a
country in which the British had vital interests. Hence he viewed it as important that the China issue should be discussed, thoroughly and frankly,
with Great Britain. I agreed entirely with his views, and accordingly had repeated conversations with the British and American ambassadors, Sir
Robert Craigie and Mr. Joseph Grew, in an effort to discover some formula
for avoiding war.

Sir Robert Craigie was appointed ambassador to Japan specifically on account of fears entertained by the British government that my country might
throw in its lot with Germany, and since his arrival in Tokyo had been doing his utmost to promote better feelings in Japan towards Great Britain. I
had seen him two or three times since the end of October of that fateful
year, but when, in view of the deepening gravity of the situation, I visited
him at his house at the seaside resort of Zushi, south of Tokyo, towards the
end of November, he told me sadly that, as I must have realized from a recent speech by Prime Minister Winston Churchill, the mind of the British
government had been made up and that a point had been reached at which
there was nothing more that he himself could do to save the situation. The
speech to which he referred was one delivered by the British prime minister at the Mansion House in London on November 10, 1941, in which he
stated that Great Britain would declare war on Japan within one hour of the
commencement of hostilities between Japan and the United States, should
such a disaster happen. The impression which I received from the speech
was that in order to crush Nazi Germany and bring the war to a speedy end,
Great Britain was prepared to do almost anything to draw the United States
into the war.

The British ambassador having thus been forced to relinquish an active
role in the matter, it devolved on Mr. Grew, the American ambassador, to
continue the quest for peace. On November 27, if my memory is correct,
Mr. Satō Naotake, the present president of Japan's House of Councilors,
who was at that time an adviser to our Foreign Office, came to see me on

behalf of Tōgō, the foreign minister. Satō brought with him some paɪ English which he wanted to show to Count Makino, my father-in-law, anu although I can no longer remember whether they were what is now known as the Hull Note alone, or the text of that note plus the Japanese government's reply of November 20—an interval of seventeen years has passed since then—I took the papers to Count Makino, who was then living in a suburb of Tokyo.

The count read the papers in silence, and remained silent after he had finished. I remarked that if the foreign minister wanted him to read the documents, it must be because he desired to know the count's opinion on them. Count Makino sighed and remarked: "This is no way to word a note." He then went on to say that the question of peace or war was a grave one indeed; that he hoped above all things that the foreign minister would act at this critical time with all the discretion and sagacity that the occasion demanded; that the work of building up modern Japan was the fruit of the labors of the men of Satsuma such as Saigō and Ōkubo, who had selflessly served the Emperor Meiji in his great task, and that, should there be war between Japan and the United States and it should so happen that the achievements of the men of the Meiji era should thus come to naught, the foreign minister, as one of those responsible, would stand accused before the throne and the Japanese people—and that, moreover, it would mean that he had disgraced the work of the men of Satsuma province, of which he was a native. Count Makino added that, coming from the same province himself, he desired me particularly to stress the latter point.

The count could not have expressed his opposition to the idea of war more strongly, and I conveyed his sentiments verbatim to Satō, who seemed very much impressed. I showed the papers to Baron Shidehara also.

It was clearly stated in the Hull Note that it was "tentative and without commitment," and that it was an "outline of the proposed basis for agreement between the United States and Japan"; whatever may have been the real intention behind it, the document was therefore by no means an ultimatum. I went to see Foreign Minister Tōgō and, while reporting to him Count Makino's words, carefully drew his attention to that aspect of the note. At the risk of being considered too outspoken, I suggested to him that if he could not prevent a Japanese declaration of war on the United States he should resign, an act which would hold up cabinet deliberations and give even the army something to think about; and that if as a result of such a gesture he should be assassinated, such a death would be a happy one.

Shortly after this conversation—about November 29 as far as I can recall—I went to the Tokyo Club, where I found Mr. Grew awaiting me. The American ambassador took me to a room upstairs and immediately asked me if I had read the Hull Note. I could not very well say that I had, so I compromised by answering that I had heard of its contents. Mr. Grew went on to say that the document was in no way intended to be an ultimatum, but merely to indicate the basis on which further negotiations between Japan and the United States might be conducted; and that as he very much wanted to explain this to the foreign minister personally, he wished me to arrange a meeting between them. I was, of course, in entire agreement with the ambassador's views and immediately made his intentions known to Tōgō, but our government had by that date already decided for war and the foreign minister declined to see him. Mr. Grew then asked others among his Japanese friends, including Viscount Inoue Kyōshirō, to arrange a meeting with Tōgō, but the minister, having already made up his mind on the matter, continued to decline, and the meeting never took place. It was a pity that this should be so; the memoirs of Lord Grey disclose that Britain's secretary of state for foreign affairs went on seeing the ambassadors of Germany and Austria-Hungary every time he was requested to do so, right up to the eve of the First World War, and paid careful attention to what the ambassadors had to say. Lord Grey's example is one from which all those in the foreign service of any country can learn, and the same can be said of Mr. Grew's efforts to preserve amicable relations between his country and Japan up to the fifty-ninth minute of the twenty-third hour. Such fidelity to one's highest responsibilities is what should be expected from all those who are in the diplomatic service of their country abroad.

At that moment, units of Japan's grand fleet were already biding their time off the Aleutian Islands, as the final hours of peace ticked away, and it seems that, after a meeting of the Council of Elder Statesmen on November 29, final official arrangements for a declaration of war upon the United States were completed at a further meeting of the council, held in the imperial presence on December 1. I had at that time no knowledge of these events, and it was, I think, on December 2 that I visited Mr. Grew at the American embassy to convey to him Tōgō's reply to his request for a meeting. But for six days more—until December 8 when, with the declaration of war on the United States, he was sequestered within his embassy—Mr. Grew continued diligently to strive to do something to retrieve the situation.

As I recall, the Japanese government embellished the official translation of the Hull Note with certain touches of a nature calculated to excite popular feeling in Japan against the United States and then submitted the document to the Privy Council. I still retain a strong impression that was what occurred, though I have at the moment no concrete evidence to substantiate my statement. However, although I can no longer remember who was responsible, I do recall that there existed a memorandum written by someone concerning the Hull Note in which the words "tentative and without commitment" had been omitted.

The impression that has remained in my mind serves to remind me today of the rage which I felt at the time against the more reckless elements within the Japanese Army, which would have been quite capable of such a falsification of the facts. Foreign Minister Tōgō himself and all the men of any political importance with whom I conferred at that time were united in opposition to war. The majority of the Japanese people, too, probably never seriously contemplated such a war happening. But none of the men in responsible positions, although at heart opposed to war, gave direct expression to their opinions. It is perhaps a characteristic of the Yamato race not to say things when they need saying, and to be wise after the event. It is not so with the British. On the issue of armed intervention in the Suez Canal Zone, for instance, those members of the Eden cabinet who opposed the interventionist policy of the British government said so, and resigned from their posts to show where they stood. That is how one should act in democratic politics.

I would like, at this point, to digress briefly from my narrative to say a few words concerning Ambassador Joseph Grew. Not only those who knew him, but all who have read his book entitled *Ten Years in Japan* need no reminder that he had a deep understanding of Japan and its people, and although he departed from his Tokyo post nursing a hatred for our militarists, he maintained a sharp distinction in his mind between the army extremists and the Japanese people as a whole. The occupation of Japan following the termination of the Pacific War was mainly the responsibility of the American armed forces, and there is reason to believe that Mr. Grew figured prominently in the drafting of occupation policies. To cite one outstanding example, the Americans declared it to be their policy to respect the will of the Japanese people in regard to the status and position of the emperor, but they seem to have foreseen from the outset that the majority of the people were loyal to their emperor and to have decided to act accordingly. I cannot help thinking that the views and active advice of Mr. Grew figured prominently in that decision. Here at least we have someone whom one need have no hesitation in calling a true friend of Japan.

I must also say something more here concerning Mr. Tōgō Shigenori, who was foreign minister at the beginning of the Pacific War. That statesman had seemed to be very much impressed by the words of Count Makino which I have previously recorded, and when he again assumed the portfolio of foreign minister in the cabinet headed by Admiral Suzuki Kantarō, which was in office when the war ended, he worked tirelessly to aid the prime minister in bringing the conflict to a close. It is my belief that he acted thus within the last wartime cabinet from a sense of responsibility for his part as foreign minister at the time of the declaration of war. At the cabinet meeting called to consider whether or not to accept the terms of the Potsdam Declaration, Prime Minister Admiral Suzuki; Admiral Yonai, the navy minister; and Tōgō favored acceptance, while the army minister, General Anami, and others were for continuing the war to the bitter end. Thus split, the cabinet could not agree on a policy, and finally a further meeting was held in the presence of the emperor, at which he, the emperor, declared in favor of accepting the Potsdam Declaration and so terminated the hopeless conflict.

Foreign Minister Tōgō as a man was taciturn, expressionless, and singularly bereft of anything that could be described as personal charm. I can well imagine him going to that final cabinet meeting wearing his customary wooden expression. That the war ended at this time, thus preventing further devastation and loss of life, was due as much to him as to anyone else in the cabinet, not excluding Admirals Suzuki and Yonai, and we should not forget that fact.

As I have recounted, my attempts to avert the approaching war not only failed entirely, but had the effect of causing the militarists to regard me, along with Prince Konoe, as a dangerous person and one implacably opposed to their carefully laid plans. However, this fact did not at the time hamper my movements in my capacity as a private individual, and I accordingly continued to seek some means of restoring peace.

Early in 1942—some days after the celebration, on February 11 of *Kigensetsu*, Japan's national day, which commemorated the foundation of our country, and when the fall of Singapore was already considered only a matter of time—I heard that Marquis Kido, the grand keeper of the imperial seals, had been received in audience by the emperor and had informed His Majesty that, although Japan had the military advantage at the moment, great difficulties still lay ahead. So far as I remember, the gist of his report to the throne on the situation was that the enemy had not by any means lost spirit; that Japan would have to drain itself of its uttermost resources in order to fight the war to a conclusion; and that therefore it was advisable to make peace at the earliest possible opportunity. I myself was of the opinion that the fall of Singapore offered an opportunity for making peace overtures that should not be missed, since to capture that key port and its British naval base would place Japan in a commanding position in the Far Eastern war theatre. Utilization of the occupation of Singapore as the occasion for proposing peace negotiations to the enemy seemed to me the most effective means of bringing the war to an early end. Being of that opinion, I was much interested to learn from Marquis Matsudaira Yasumasa, the chief (private) secretary to the grand keeper, of Marquis Kido's audience with the emperor and that Kido held the same views as myself concerning the right moment for proposing peace negotiations.

I had been privately contemplating the possibility of our government sending Prince Konoe to Switzerland to send out peace "feelers" from that neutral country, and when I heard the gist of Marquis Kido's remarks in his audience with the emperor my hopes rose that perhaps my plan might be realized. Early in June came the news that our naval operations in the vicinity of Midway Island had ended in disaster, and, not wishing to wait any longer, I outlined my plan to Prince Konoe.

The prince indicated his surprise, but I pointed out that, in view of his position near to the imperial throne, should he make the trip to Switzerland he would attract notice in government circles in Europe merely by staying in that country; that if Great Britain should suffer military reverses there might be those in her government who would try to approach him, while if the tide of war turned against Germany, there might also be those in authority in that country who would want him to act for them. I went on to remark that, although travel by sea and air would be dangerous, it would not be difficult to reach Switzerland by the overland route through Korea and Manchuria and thence by the Trans-Siberian Railway. Prince Konoe asked me if I thought there was any likelihood that such a mission, if he embarked upon it, would succeed. I replied that no one could tell until the plan had actually been tried, but that, even if it were only to demonstrate to the Allied powers that Japan seriously desired to make peace, such a trip would be worthwhile. This statement seemed to make an impression on the prince, and he asked me to sound Marquis Kido on the matter.

That palace official, when I saw him, refrained from giving me a straight answer. I had heard that General Tōjō, then prime minister, was constantly urging upon the marquis the necessity of keeping Prince Konoe's actions under close official surveillance, and I guessed that fact was probably behind his reluctance to commit himself regarding the feasibility of the plan. There the matter rested, nor did I ever hear anything further from Marquis Kido. There is, of course, no telling whether, had the plan been realized, it would have produced any useful result, but the thought still lingers in my mind that perhaps something might have come of it.

In that connection, I recall how, in Japan's earlier wars with China and, later, Russia, our government and those around the throne were alert, throughout the hostilities, to recognize the right moment to end the conflict and not to let slip that opportunity. In the Russo-Japanese War, General Count Kodama Gentarō, chief of staff of the Japanese Army in Manchuria, returned to Tokyo from the front immediately after our victory over the Russian forces in the battle of Mukden and told the government that battle should be the last; while Prince Itō Hirobumi, Japan's senior elder statesman of that time, dispatched Count Kaneko Kentarō to the United States shortly after the outbreak of the war to pave the way beforehand for the American diplomatic overtures which eventually culminated in the Treaty of Portsmouth between Japan and Russia. It was largely because of this degree of foresight and clear thinking on the part of those in power in Japan in Meiji time that a small island nation in the Far East came in less than half a century to rank among the five great powers of the world.

I was myself approached in this matter of peace moves by a veteran diplomat named Akizuki Satsuo, who, since he married a sister-in-law of Count Makino, was distantly related to me. Akizuki telephoned me in April 1945, saying he desired to see me, and upon my visiting him at his house within the grounds of a temple in Tokyo, where he was lying ill, confided to me that the navy was secretly considering a plan to begin peace negotiations with the Allied powers through Great Britain and that, in his opinion, I was the man best qualified to conduct them. He added that the sooner the negotiations were begun the better; and asked me for my views on the matter.

Akizuki was a man prone to advance most unorthodox ideas at times, and when I asked him how one was to get out of Japan, which was at that time completely encircled, he answered "by submarine." I then asked him how it was to refuel on the journey, to which he replied that Admiral Ozawa, the vice chief of the naval general staff, knew all the details and suggested that I confer with that officer. He added the comforting remark that even if I should die on the journey, I could not ask for a better death.

Despite my reservations concerning the feasibility of the plan, I went to see Admiral Ozawa in the imperial headquarters and told him the story, only to be informed in return that the navy had no knowledge of such a plan. I imagined that this attitude might have been adopted for security reasons, so I informed the admiral that, in that case, I was returning to my house at Ōiso and I asked him to inform Akizuki. The next day I was arrested by the military police.

Previous to these events, Prince Konoe had come to my house to see me on the night of February 13, 1945. By then the American forces had already landed in the Philippines and were driving our armies back towards the hills, and the general impression in Japan was that the end of the war would not be long in coming. Since the beginning of hostilities, the emperor had not received in audience anyone except Marquis Kido, his close adviser, Generals Tōjō and Koiso, the two wartime premiers, and military and naval officers in responsible positions at imperial headquarters. His Majesty now summoned to the palace all the elder statesmen in turn, and Prince Konoe had come to visit me on the day prior to his being received in audience. Later, I learned that in the case of Prince Konoe and Count Makino, Marquis Kido was in attendance during the audience in place of Fujita Hisanori, the grand chamberlain, who was normally present on such occasions—a fact which indicated the importance which the emperor attached to the views of these two statesmen.

The prince, on visiting my house, showed me a draft of what he was going to say to the emperor the next day. It began with the words: "I regret to state that in my opinion defeat is now certain. What I am about to tell Your Majesty is based upon that assumption." He went on to outline detailed reasons for that view and to consider the possibility of a communist revolution after the war had ended in defeat. Another significant passage in the document declared:

> Defeat may lower our national prestige, but British and American opinion has not gone to the length of contemplating making changes in the structure of the Japanese State, so that defeat alone need not make us fear for the future of the nation. What we should fear most is the possibility of a Communist revolution following defeat. The radical elements in the Army may not necessarily be aiming at a Communist revolution, but the civilians and those in the civil service who are aligned with those elements definitely have that objective in view and are utilizing the simplicity and ignorance of the Army men to that end.

I was in complete agreement with Prince Konoe on all these points and we conferred far into the night on revisions to the draft; I made a copy after it was completed, to show, at the prince's request, to Count Makino. I had no idea then that the same copy was later to form part of the evidence against me after my arrest by the military police.

Prince Konoe visited the palace the next day and, after being received in audience, visited me again as he had promised. He was in good spirits and reported that, as Marquis Kido had been in attendance in the audience chamber, he had been able to speak his mind without fear of being misunderstood by third persons; that the audience had lasted about one hour; and that the emperor had asked him many questions. According to the details of what had transpired, as reported to me by the prince, the point on which the emperor was most anxious to hear his views concerned the opinion of General Umezu Yoshijirō, chief of the imperial general staff, that, since the United States was bent upon destroying Japan's structure of government and reducing the country to a heap of ruins, it was prudent to continue the war with the friendly cooperation of the Soviet Union (Japan's non-aggression pact with that nation still held good at that time)—a view which was diametrically opposite to that which the prince had expressed. Prince Konoe had then answered that to come to terms with the United States was the only course open to Japan in the circumstances and that it was his firm belief that, even if the nation surrendered unconditionally, the United States would not wish to alter the structure of the state as handed down to us by our ancestors. He left the audience chamber under the impression he had been able to convince the emperor on this vital point. The prince also informed the emperor that it was most important that the excesses of the army should be checked, to which end decisive action on the part of the emperor was needed more than anything else.

I was arrested by the military police in April 1945. During the journey from my house at Ōiso to Tokyo in a police car, I had imagined that the reason for my being taken into custody was Akizuki's idea about leaving Japan by submarine in order to attempt to initiate peace negotiations, but during the interrogation at the military police headquarters no reference was made to that plan, and I discovered to my surprise that what the military police were interested in, and wanted to hear from me, were details of Prince Konoe's audience with the emperor in February. On that point I declined to talk. Even under the old Japanese Constitution then in force, the privacy of personal correspondence was guaranteed, and there certainly did not seem to be any reason why I should divulge information about the contents of the draft which Prince Konoe had shown me. The military police had, of course, confiscated the copy of that draft which I had made, and which they found during their search of my house, so the contents were known to them. What they really wanted, and could not obtain from me, was information concerning the replies made by the prince to the emperor's questions, and details of what the prince and I had been discussing and planning at my Tokyo house the night before the audience took place. It appeared that the military police were particularly anxious to obtain the fullest possible information concerning the prince's talk with the emperor, as was indicated by the fact that, in addition to my interrogation on the point, I heard later that Baron Harada Kumao (who was secretary to Prince Saionji, Japan's genrō and senior statesman), during his lifetime, Count Kabayama Aisuke, and others were also closely interrogated by the military police on the same matter.

The military police also questioned me concerning my relations with the British and American ambassadors, Sir Robert Craigie and Mr. Joseph Grew. I was on particularly friendly terms with the latter diplomat, and during his period of confinement within the American embassy compound following the declaration of war, had sent him food and other supplies whenever there was an opportunity to do so. The police charged me with having planned to meet him secretly, and questioned me closely as to where the meeting was to have taken place and for what purpose. I had planned no such meeting and said so. Whereupon my interrogators announced that they had evidence to show that I had and, on my asking to see it, produced a copy of a letter I had written to the ambassador when I heard he was leaving Japan in the exchange ship. They would not accept my explanation that the letter—which had evidently been intercepted by the censorship—was merely an innocuous farewell message. Pointing to the words "some better days" contained in the letter, they asked me what they meant. I explained that the words merely expressed the wish that we might meet again when better days came round, but the military police refused to be convinced and continued their charges that the words were evidence that I was arranging to meet Mr. Grew in secret. I further explained, with what patience I could muster, that however the words might sound when translated from the English original, they were just a form of saying good-bye; I felt the whole incident was rather silly. However, my interrogators were obviously not convinced, and probably did not want to be.

I knew Admiral Suzuki Kantarō, who was at that time prime minister, and General Anami, the minister of war, quite well and did not think it likely that I would be condemned to death. When Anami was vice minister of war, his official residence was next door to my house in Tokyo and we had greeted each other in a friendly fashion when meeting on morning walks. It was probably thanks to orders given by General Anami that I was treated well at the military police headquarters, although the questioning was sustained and severe. My father, before my adoption by the Yoshida family, Takeouchi Tsuna, had been imprisoned in one of our northern provinces on a charge of having been in league with the rebels during the civil war of 1878, and it seemed to me that a taste of prison life might not be so bad for me either for a change. Buoyed up by that mood, I passed the first few days of confinement not too unpleasantly. No one was allowed to visit me except those of my immediate household, and the daily questioning by the military police was such as could be borne with patience. But the mood lasted for only a few days and I soon began to tire of this kind of life. Freedom has never seemed such a precious thing to me as at that time.

Two weeks after being confined within the military prison headquarters I was transferred, in the company of thieves and other similar people, to the Tokyo military prison. The cell allotted to me was clean, and I had the gratification of not being visited by fleas and lice. During my stay in this prison there was no questioning at headquarters, and I was permitted to have whatever food I wished sent in to me from my house. In fact, I got rather more than I wanted, and the surplus was distributed among those in other cells and to the prison guards, which added greatly to my popularity. (In the next cell to me at that time was Ueda Shunkichi, who later became the attorney general in one of my cabinets.)

Meanwhile the fire raids on Tokyo had been growing steadily more severe, and one night, when the entire neighborhood had been turned into a sea of flame by incendiary bombs, the military prison suffered a direct hit and began to burn. I was taken by one of the guards to a vegetable store in the basement, but our refuge quickly grew too hot for comfort, and just as I was thinking how unpleasant it would be to be roasted alive the guard apparently had the same idea, and, with me still in close attendance, took refuge in the outer gardens of the Meiji shrine. After that night I was lodged in a prison at Meguro, a Tokyo suburb, and when that building, too, was bombed, transferred to a primary school building in the same district. After spending a few days in this fourth prison I was informed that I had been released on parole and was free to go home. My prison life had lasted exactly forty days.

I had rested for about one week at my house in Ōiso, forty miles south of Tokyo, when I received a summons from my late jailers to present myself at the primary school in which I had last been confined. Upon answering the summons, I was informed that Judiciary Lieutenant-General Shimada was waiting to see me, which seemed to foreshadow a change in the attitude of the military police towards me. Nor was I mistaken. As soon as I entered the room where the general sat, he began addressing me as "your Excellency" and said: "There can be no greater patriot than your Excellency." This was a great promotion for someone who had been treated as a traitor to his country until that day. From his words and manner I gathered that I had been cleared of whatever charges and suspicions the military police had harbored against me, and said: "Thank you for everything."

The general was not satisfied to end matters thus, however, and asked me to listen to what he had to say. I was wondering what more was in store for me, when the general went on to explain that there had been a brisk debate within the army concerning whether I should be prosecuted or not; that General Shimada himself had favored dropping the case against me but others had been of the contrary opinion; and that finally it had been decided by General Anami personally that I should not be prosecuted. General Shimada had obviously wanted to show me the reasons why he should be thanked. However, it was a weight off my mind. This denouncement also made me curious as to just what the military police had achieved by my detention, and my refusal to answer their questions.

For some time after that incident there were no callers at my home. Then, one day, a man in a kind of uniform and wearing a military-type cap presented himself. Members of my household thought the military police had come again, but it turned out to be Prince Konoe.

"I hope there are no military police about," were the prince's first words to me.

# 3

# Aftermath of Defeat

On the day that the Pacific War ended, on August 15, 1945, I was confined to my bed at my Ōiso home, having developed an abscess, due possibly to malnutrition during part of my period of detention by the military police. It was recorded of one of the heroes of Chinese history that he was "so angry that an abscess developed in his back," which may or may not show that I was heroic at least as far as abscesses were concerned.

Because of this minor affliction, I listened to the emperor's historic broadcast to the Japanese nation, announcing the termination of hostilities, in my home, and later read in the newspapers the accounts of my country's formal surrender at the ceremony held aboard the USS *Missouri* in Tokyo Bay on September 2. As the world knows, those two events placed Japan under the control of the Allied Army of Occupation for the next six years and eight months, early in which period I quite unexpectedly found myself called upon to assume the responsibilities of the head of the Japanese government under the occupation.

It may be of service to students of Far Eastern affairs to give here a brief outline of the administrative structure of the Allied occupation, as revealed by documents in the archives of the Japanese Foreign Office.

Sitting at the apex of the Allied arrangements, and constituting the highest authority for the determination of occupation policies, was the Far Eastern Commission in Washington, comprising representatives of eleven countries: the United States, Great Britain, the Soviet Union, China, France, the Netherlands, Canada, Australia, New Zealand, India, and the Philippines. Under this international body there was the United States government, which functioned in the formulation and communication of directives, and the supreme commander for the Allied powers, with headquarters in Tokyo, whose duty it was to implement such instructions. There also existed the Allied Council for Japan, sitting in Tokyo and consisting of representatives of the United States, the Soviet Union, China, and the British Commonwealth (Great Britain, Australia, New Zealand, and India), which was intended to serve as an advisory council to the supreme commander.

The establishment in Japan of a general headquarters for the Allied powers had already been decided upon by the government of the United States prior to Japan's surrender, and the Japanese government was given notice of the appointment of General Douglas MacArthur as the supreme commander on August 14, one day prior to the emperor's broadcast which terminated the Pacific War. But the other two bodies which functioned on the Allied side during the occupation period—the Far Eastern Commission and the Allied Council for Japan—came into being later, some time after General MacArthur had landed in Japan and begun his administration of the defeated nation. They were instituted as a result of a conference held in Moscow and attended by the foreign ministers of the United States, Great Britain, and the Soviet Union in November 1945, at which meeting the decisions reached provided Allied sanction for administrative policies that were by then already in force, and it was natural under the circumstances that it should be the United States government, and the supreme commander in Tokyo in particular that actually formulated and put into effect the policies underlying the Allied occupation.

The general headquarters for the Allied powers, which was to become familiar to all Japanese as GHQ, was first established at Yokohama, then functioned for a time in the American embassy in Tokyo until, on December 2, 1945, it moved to permanent quarters in the Dai-Ichi Sōgo Building in the center of downtown Tokyo.

The feature of this headquarters that merits particular attention is that it was divided into two separate groups, one concerned with army staff work and the other with civil government. The first group consisted of four sections and originally comprised the general staff of the U.S. forces in the Pacific, commanded by General MacArthur, but later also handled part of the responsibilities connected with the administration of Japan. Within this group, the first section dealt with the personnel of the Army of Occupation and its internal administration. The second section was concerned with the translation and classification of Japanese records; matters concerned with demobilization and intelligence; communication with the missions of the Allied powers in Japan on matters other than diplomacy; and liaison with the Japanese government. The third section dealt with questions of strategy, the enforcement of the terms of surrender and directives to the Japanese government, the mass repatriation of Japanese nationals from abroad, and the entry and exit of combat planes and warships. The fourth section dealt with supplies, civil aviation, occupation expenditures, the material effects of the occupation, the supply and distribution of oil within Japan, and the disposal of materials and equipment belonging to the Japanese Army.

The second group within GHQ was not concerned with strategy or military matters and dealt solely with matters connected with the civil administration of the nation—the sections handling general affairs with civil government, public health, welfare, information, labor, education, religion, and the national economy; the economic and industrial sections with agriculture, commerce, fishing, industry, international trade, natural resources and science—all these sections being under the direction of the deputy chief of staff.

Of all the numerous sections that comprised this latter group, perhaps the two that became best known to us who were called upon to work with GHQ were the Government Section and the Economic and Scientific Section. Government Section, or "GS," controlled the position and internal structure of the Japanese government and its policies, and such questions as the screening of candidates for official positions and the revision of the Constitution came within its purview. The section therefore played an important role in the rebuilding of Japan's basic political structure following the end of the Pacific War, and had, therefore, the closest contacts with us Japanese, but, as I shall show later, its activities were curtailed at the end of the second stage of the various phases of occupation policy. The Economic and Scientific Section functioned precisely as its name implies and requires no explanation; it was a section within General MacArthur's headquarters that not only the government but Japanese in general had close contacts with throughout the occupation.

A few words may not be out of place here concerning the provincial administrative structure of the Army of Occupation. Apart from the separate U.S. naval administration based upon the naval port of Yokosuka, south of Tokyo, the provincial structure was, until the end of 1949, under the orders of the U.S. Eighth Army, and its duties had mainly to do with vigilance and information. Provincial offices were established in all parts of the country where detachments under the command of the Eighth Army were stationed, but later these were reduced to a provincial office for Hokkaidō located at Sapporo; for the Tōkohu area at Sendai; for the Kantō area at Itabashi; for the Tōkai and Hokuriku area at Nagoya; for the Kinki area at Osaka; for the Chūgoku area at Kure; for the Shikoku area at Takamatsu; and for the Kyūshū area at Fukuoka. When, in 1950, the Eighth Army was relieved of duties connected with the civilian administration of Japan, these provincial offices were placed under the direct orders of the supreme commander and absorbed into the Civil Affairs Section within GHQ, under which auspices they continued to function until the end of the occupation in April 1952.

At the time when the Japanese government was informed by the Allied powers of the establishment of an Allied GHQ in Japan, it was required of us to create an office of the Japanese government to deal with matters having to do with the occupation and for the purposes of maintaining close contacts with GHQ. Wherefore, prior to the arrival of the first units of the occupation forces in Japan in August 1945, a Central Liaison Office was created and housed in a corner of the Foreign Office premises in Tokyo. Later, after I had assumed the post of foreign minister in the Higashikuni cabinet, the decision was reached to enlarge the functions of the Central Liaison Office, and among some structural changes its chief was raised to the status of president, with two vice chiefs under him. It was then thought that someone of greater stature than the foreign minister should be named to preside over the office, and the choice originally fell on Mr. Ikeda Seihin, a privy councilor who was a former minister of finance. Mr. Ikeda had already signified his acceptance of that post when it was found that GHQ was opposed to his nomination on account of some question concerned with his past political record and so, on Mr. Ikeda's own recommendation, Mr. Kodama Kenji, a former president of the Yokohama Specie Bank and president of the Central China Industrial Company, was sought out and eventually nominated. Later, however, further changes were made in the structure of the office, one of which provided that the foreign minister should hold the post of president, and so from March 1946 onward I came to occupy that position.

It is said that at the time of the inception of the Central Liaison Office there was some debate whether it should be placed directly under the orders of the prime minister or function as a department of the Foreign Office, and in January 1948, after I had left office at the end of my first term as prime minister, it seems that it was made a department in the Office of the Prime Minister under the new name of the Liaison and Coordinating Office. It became a department of the Foreign Office again during my third cabinet, was renamed the International Co-operation Bureau prior to the signing of the San Francisco Peace Treaty, and has continued down to the present as a department within our Foreign Office charged with handling liaison work on matters concerning Japan's relations with the United States and the U.S. Security Forces in Japan.

The occupation of Japan continued until the coming into effect of the San Francisco Peace Treaty on the basis I have outlined above, but looking back on those years it seems to me that the policies underlying the occupation underwent two varieties of change before it came to an end with the regaining of national independence. One, which was obvious to all, consisted of the fact that the occupation, which had at first been conducted along lines of great severity, became progressively more lenient in policy as time passed and before its end had been transformed and afforded all feasible aid to Japan. This change was marked by three distinct phases of which I shall write later. At this point I wish to dwell on the other sort of change.

This was concerned with the basic policy of occupation as formulated in the United States prior to the landing of American troops in the Japanese islands, which would seem to have undergone drastic alteration very soon after the occupation actually began. The American government apparently arrived at a plan for occupying Japan after that country's surrender long before that event actually took place, and appropriate arrangements for implementing the decisions taken were prepared. After Japan's surrender, however, it was discovered that the actual situation within that country was somewhat different from what had been anticipated, and it is my conjecture that the plan had to be revised in important respects in order to meet the conditions then existing. But although this was done, not all the original arrangements were changed; some were carried out in their original form, which would account for what may be regarded as certain excesses that occurred during the early phases of the occupation.

To give one example, it is known that the Army of Occupation had intended originally to forbid the use of Japanese currency and substitute for it their own military currency; to suspend our law courts and have all cases tried by courts-martial before their own judges. These measures were dropped at our request. This occurred before I assumed office as foreign minister; it does not seem to me likely that these plans of a military government were withdrawn merely because we so requested, but more probably because the occupation authorities themselves had come round to the view that they were not necessary or desirable.

The reasons prompting such changes in the occupation pattern were probably varied, but one was the fact that the Americans had, before their arrival in Japan, overestimated the power of resistance of the Japanese people. Mr. Walter Lippmann, the American commentator on political affairs, has said of the American policy of occupation that the United States made two great mistakes in regard to Japan—the first being to underestimate that country at the beginning of the Pacific War, and the second to overestimate Japan at the end of it and that this criticism applies not only to the actual fighting power of my nation but also to other psychological factors involved.

During the period of hostilities the Americans—despite the unquestionable superiority of their armament and equipment—had, no doubt, valid reason to respect the fighting qualities of the Japanese as demonstrated at Guadalcanal, Saipan, Iwo Jima, Okinawa, and elsewhere in the Pacific theatre. Later, when I came to know the generals on the staff of GHQ, they were unanimous in their praise of the Japanese as ranking among the finest fighting men in the world. They also told me that, in the event of an Allied invasion of the Japanese home islands taking place, they had calculated to lose at least half a million men in the operation, which indicates the extent to which they had overestimated and feared Japan's strength in the final stages of the war. The Americans were not alone in making that mistake. The British had suffered severe reverses in the early stages of the war in Malaya and the fear and hatred which they felt towards the Japanese had grown in proportion. All these factors contributed to the Allied blunder of assessing our military strength at rather more than it was actually worth; a fact which caused them to agree to pay the high price demanded by Stalin at the Yalta Conference for the Soviet Union's entry into the war against Japan. The Western powers could not imagine the Japanese—for so long and loudly advertised by the ultranationalist elements as "unbeatable"— surrendering without a last-ditch bitter struggle.

The same idea colored their thoughts and expectations concerning the kind of reception the Allied forces would receive from the Japanese people even if they managed to effect a successful landing in our home islands. They envisaged the possibility that a part of the Japanese Army might retreat into the mountainous interior of the country, with the emperor in their midst, and there continue to put up a desperate resistance; even if such a development did not occur, it is not difficult to imagine them thinking that in all probability the majority of the Japanese people would put up a solid resistance to the invading forces. In the light of such an estimate of the situation, it would be only natural that the occupation policy as formulated prior to our surrender should have been one of extreme severity. In other words, the Americans must have prepared plans intended to be implemented in enemy territory; hence the provision for a military currency to replace the normal civilian currency, and the intended suspension of our law courts and their replacement by Allied military courts. But in the event the surrender was effected by the Japanese government without a single serious incident, and nothing occurred later to justify the fears entertained by the Allied governments. This should have convinced them that there was in fact no need to establish a rigorous military government. Whether this conjecture accords with the facts or not, it is known that the decision to scrap the plans for a military currency and for the suspension of our law courts was reached before the formal surrender ceremony took place on board the USS Missouri on September 2, though I have no doubt that the efforts of Mr. Shigemitsu Mamoru, then foreign minister, and of Mr. Okazaki Katsuo, the chief of the Central Liaison Office, played no small part in causing that decision to be put into prompt effect.

Another mistake made by the Americans concerned their conception of the Japanese people as a whole. Mainly, no doubt, because of their experience with us before and during the war, they had come to the conclusion that Japan was basically a militaristic and ultranationalistic nation and the vast majority of its people deeply imbued with such sentiments. Given this premise, it was inevitable that the occupation authorities should make it their first business to eliminate anything and everything pertaining to militarism and—to use a favorite word of theirs—to "liberate" the Japanese from nationalistic pressures and practices as the first step on the road to liberalism and democracy.

Such a conception of the task ahead would account for the lenient attitude adopted by General MacArthur's headquarters towards Japan's communists during the first phase of the occupation, and the protection given to the revived trade unions, the legislation concerning labor, and so on—all of which were obviously inspired by the desire to speed the process of democratization. At the same time, however, it is also possible to see in these acts a desire to enlist the sympathies of the workers and the more radical elements within the country in favor of the occupation; it is also, and equally, possible to interpret the occupation-sponsored land reform—with its provisions that operated with particular severity towards landowners—as being in the nature of an attempt to win the support of the peasantry in the same way.

Quite apart from the changes in attitude on the part of the occupation authorities towards Japan's native communists, there are reasons for believing that in their handling of the renascent trade union movement GHQ initially allowed its members a degree of freedom in political activity that was not warranted by any actual economic need. This circumstance later led to much violent labor agitation with political undertones, which caused no little concern within GHQ and eventually forced the occupation authorities to purge Tokuda Kyūichi and other leaders of the Japan Communist Party who had been freed from prison after the surrender at the express insistence of GHQ.

The seeming contradiction cannot be explained away by any simple theory of democratization nor solely by changes that were occurring in the international situation. The real reasons for these initial shifts in occupation policies seem to me to be deeper and more cogent to the Japanese scene and concerned with the differences between the ideas current in the Allied nations before the surrender concerning the condition of the country and the situation as it actually turned out to be when the occupation got into its stride.

Apart from the changes in emphasis which occurred at the outset, the successive changes in occupation policy arising from the passage of time and new developments in the international sphere may be divided into three stages.

The first stage was concerned with the tasks of demilitarization and democratization and found its most concrete expression in the new Constitution with its renunciation of war and its emphasis on the rights and freedoms of the people.

In the matter of demilitarization, the complete disarming and demobilization of the nation's fighting forces; the abolition of all military organization; the trial and punishment of those proved guilty of war crimes; the

Chapter 3

disbanding of all ultranationalistic organizations; the prohibition of ultra-nationalistic education and propaganda; and—although the step seems to me to have been without much sense—the disestablishment of the Shinto religion were carried out in quick succession by order of the Supreme Commander for the Allied Powers (SCAP). Further, all existing facilities for the manufacture of armaments were listed for early destruction.

In the interests of hastening the democratization of Japan, there occurred the purges of undesirable persons from public life; the abolition of all forms of political surveillance; the extension of the suffrage to women, and other reforms. At the same time SCAP also enacted the land reform, the dissolution of the *zaibatsu* trading interests, and the elimination of excessive concentration of economic power, although these "reforms," undertaken as they were with the express object of speeding the democratization of the country, did not always seem to fit the actual facts.

By and large, these may be classified as the sort of idealistic reforms that usually accompany bloodless revolutions of the sort witnessed in Japan following the surrender, though there may also have been political considerations behind them such as I mentioned earlier. The occupation reforms that had the most significant consequences were the policy of toleration extended to the Japanese communists during the first stages of the occupation, and the undue degree of encouragement given to the trade unions, aimed at fostering their power, which included the promulgation of measures such as the Labor Standards Law. There was nothing inherently wrong about the general intention behind these reforms, but the fact remains that they were widely utilized by the destructive left-wing elements in the country, enabling them to stage demonstrations and engage in labor disputes of a political character, which intensified the general social unrest prevailing in Japan after defeat. This fact, as well as the changes in the international situation in the late forties, must be taken into account in considering the next phase of occupation policy.

The second stage may be said to have begun with the recognition of the need to provide Japan with a healthy and autonomous economy. It would appear, at least, that the growing antagonisms separating the free world from the Soviet bloc made a revision of occupation policy necessary and caused that policy to veer towards the strengthening of Japan economically in order that it would serve as a buttress against the infiltration and growth of communist influences.

The first public indication of this new emphasis came in speeches, delivered by Mr. Kenneth Royall, the U.S. secretary of war, in San Francisco, and by Mr. Frank McCoy, the U.S. representative on the Far Eastern Commission, before a meeting of that body in January 1948. As a direct result of the change in policy, such measures as the provision of financial aid to promote

Japan's overseas trade, the supply of raw materials under the Foreign Aid Acts, and the cancellation of interim plans to dismantle and allocate factory equipment for the settlement of war reparations were put into effect during that year and the next. In addition, the provisions of the Elimination of Excess Concentration of Economic Power Law and Anti-Monopoly Law (the law concerning prohibition of private monopoly and methods of preserving fair trading), which had been imposed on Japan by directives issued by GHQ, were also relaxed to some extent, thus removing at least some of the shackles impeding the revival of the Japanese economy. The importance of this change may be judged when we remember that, at the beginning of the occupation, it had been stressed in one of the directives addressed to General MacArthur by the U.S. government that the reconstruction and reinforcement of Japan's economy were not among his responsibilities.

These developments did not mean, of course, that the economic recovery of Japan was effected solely by reason of American aid. The increase in American assistance was accompanied by an American demand that Japan should do her full share in the task of speeding the national economic recovery. In December 1948, shortly after my second cabinet was installed in office, a repetition of that demand, couched in pressing terms, was addressed to our government by GHQ, the contents of which came to be widely known as the Nine Economic Principles. The following year Mr. Joseph Dodge arrived in Japan in the capacity of economic adviser to GHQ, with the diplomatic rank of minister, and various stringent measures aiming at economic retrenchment and deflation, along with the economic policies which were known as the "Dodge Line," were proposed and put into effect.

The third phase of occupation policy covered the period from the outbreak of the Korean War to the signing of the peace treaty in San Francisco. If the second phase was one of economic reinforcement, this final stage may be termed one primarily concerned with questions of security. The main change marking this third stage was the creation, after the outbreak of the Korean War, of a National Police Reserve of seventy-five thousand men—a fighting force organized at the instance of SCAP to reinforce the ordinary police force already in existence—and the reorganization of the Maritime Safety Board and its reinforcement by an additional eight thousand men. These measures were intended to fill the gap left by the dispatch of part of the U.S. occupation forces in Japan to the Korean battlefields, but since Japan's present land, sea, and air Self-Defense Forces grew out of the reserves raised at that time, we must regard the event as one of the most significant to occur during the final years of the occupation era.

At the same time Japan's factories for the manufacture of war materials, which at an earlier stage of the occupation had been either ordered to be destroyed or earmarked for reparations payments, were also set to work again. After these changes the occupation continued without any further major shift in emphasis—and assumed ever more, in General MacArthur's words, "the friendly guidance of a protective force"—until, with the coming into effect of the San Francisco Peace Treaty on April 28, 1952, it passed into history.

# 4

# Blueprint for an Occupation

When we come to examine the actual manner in which the work of the occupation was carried out within GHQ, the fact immediately emerges that the men charged with administering the edicts of the supreme commander belonged to differing groups, some of which were subtly antagonistic to each other in their attitude towards the tasks with which they were confronted.

In the beginning, the men staffing General MacArthur's headquarters were composed of those who had followed that soldier in his campaigns preceding his arrival in Japan, and others who had been sent from the United States for the express purpose of assisting in the tasks of the occupation. The two sets displayed interesting differences, the former group being real soldiers, while the latter—particularly those in upper ranks—though in uniform, were actually civilians who had, until their arrival in Tokyo, been lawyers, salesmen in department stores, editors of provincial newspapers, and so on. The two contrasting groups could be easily recognized, the men from the United States by their zeal in trying to speed the work of democratizing Japan as planned, and the soldiers for their greater concern to make a success of the occupation as such. We might say that the former group were idealists and the latter more practical.

As I have previously pointed out, there is every reason to believe that the work of the occupation was, during the early phase, pressed forward according to a plan that had originally been conceived before the actual surrender, and in accordance with a definite line of thought that lay behind the plan. The more idealistic among the men within GHQ required of the Japanese government that the plan should be followed to the letter, and were comparatively uninterested whether the measures they proposed were sound in their relation to the actual conditions existing in Japan, or were likely to succeed. Moreover, when suggestions were made from our side concerning the method of putting these measures into effect, they were— even if advanced with a view to ensuring the smooth working and effectiveness of the measures concerned—regarded by the idealists within SCAP as constituting so much resistance offered to the occupation authorities and even, in some cases, as outright obstruction.

A typical example of the difference in attitudes of the two groups within SCAP towards the tasks of the occupation may be seen in the matter of the reform of the police system.

Japan's police system went through major changes in the course of the occupation years—and also major readjustments to these changes. The police reform also constituted an issue in which the mistakes of the occupation were apparent to a marked degree in regard to the actual effectiveness of the measures taken and which demonstrated most forcibly the contradictions which often existed between the democratic ideals which SCAP sought to foster and the practical needs of government. In this matter of police reform, those who clung most tenaciously to the democratic ideals were the men of Government Section within GHQ, while those who supported us in our suggestions for amendments designed to serve the practical needs of maintaining law and order were the men in the Public Safety Department of the Second Section of the U.S. Army Staff.

The Government Section, as I have already explained, was the department within General MacArthur's headquarters charged with the task of supervising the implementation by the Japanese government of the reforms demanded by the occupation authorities. It was, therefore, natural that the men in the Government Section should at times have appeared to be too much attached to ensuring that the reforms were put into effect precisely as planned; on the other hand, the men on the U.S. Army Staff just as naturally placed major importance on the maintenance of law and order as the primary requisite for the smooth operation of the occupation administration. The antagonism which on occasion arose between these two sets of occupation officials, stemming from differences in the nature of their tasks, was therefore quite comprehensible.

However, although this antagonism existed, it was Government Section which was in charge of the work of actually directing the Japanese government, so that, willy-nilly, it was with this section that we had most to do. But the Army Staff men usually supported us, for the reasons already outlined, and their Second Section helped to temper the, at times, rigorous demands made by the Government Section not only in the matter of police reform but on such questions as the purging of people from public life. I may add that when the National Police Reserve came into being, it was placed under the control of the Public Safety Department of the Second Section of the staff, probably on account of the similarity of the tasks with which both it and the section were concerned. It was also General Charles Willoughby, chief of the Second Section, who was most active in urging that the Japanese Communist Party should be declared illegal, although that step was never actually taken.

The policies advocated by the occupation came in this way to be progressively relaxed with the passage of time, and it goes without saying that we Japanese, for our part, never lost an opportunity to demand the revision and readjustment of those occupation policies which we judged to be impractical and not suited to the actual conditions existing in Japan.

The amendment to the Anti-Monopoly Law which was passed by the fifth Diet session may be cited as an example of this fact. The release of persons from the disabilities imposed by the purge ordinances was a subject of constant negotiations with GHQ and, at the end of October 1949, persons so affected were de-purged in large numbers, including all those who had been officers in Japan's armed forces. In regard to the police, our proposals for closer relations between the national police force and the police of (local) autonomous agencies—and the absorption into the national police of such of the local police as it was found difficult to maintain from local funds—were agreed to by GHQ, and confirmed by the National Diet in 1950. Many of the controls placed upon the Japanese economy were also relaxed, either by directives issued by SCAP or with GHQ approval, in 1949 and 1950.

General Douglas MacArthur was relieved of his duties as supreme commander for the Allied powers by President Truman on April 11, 1951, and he left Japan five days later. On the same day Mr. John Foster Dulles, who was at that time an adviser to the U.S. State Department, arrived in Tokyo, and on April 18, I went to see Mr. Dulles and General Matthew B. Ridgway, the new supreme commander, at GHQ. At that meeting I told General Ridgway that although my country had surrendered unconditionally, Japan had at least not capitulated in any craven fashion; that we had stood by our obligations and would continue to do so, and that General MacArthur had trusted us on that point; that, however, it did not prevent us from submitting proposals which General MacArthur may at times have found disagreeable, and that I had to warn General Ridgway that we should continue to do so. The general and Mr. Dulles appeared to accept all this with good grace. The fact was that I had been urging on General MacArthur the necessity of revising many of the reforms effected by the occupation which were at variance with the actual needs of the country and the customs and traditions of its people and had obtained his consent in principle. I had in consequence prepared a memorandum embodying all the revisions desired, and had just been on the point of submitting it to the supreme commander when he was recalled. I had taken it with me to the meeting with General Ridgway and handed it to him in the presence of Mr. Dulles.

On May 1, 1951, on the occasion of the fourth anniversary of the promulgation of the new Constitution, General Ridgway issued a statement in which he made it clear that the control of the country by the occupation authorities was to be relaxed in preparation for the restoration of Japan to her position as an independent and sovereign nation, and that he was about to give the Japanese government the power to consider the revision of laws framed in accordance with the Potsdam Declaration.

The government thereupon began a thorough survey of the vast array of laws which had been enacted during the occupation, and to this end an informal committee was created to serve as an advisory body to the prime minister.

The men who comprised this committee were Kimura Tokutarō, former minister of justice; Nakayama Ichirō, president of Hitotsubashi University; Maeda Tamon, former minister of education; Obama Toshie, an adviser to the financial newspaper *Nihon keizai shinbun*; Ishizaka Taizō, president of the Toshiba Electric Company; Itakura Takuzō, president of the newspaper *Jiji shinpō*; and Hara Yasusaburō, president of the Nihon Kayaku (Chemicals) Company. To these were added later Professor Tanaka Jirō of Tokyo University and Mr. Ishibashi Tanzan, president of the *Oriental Economist*. The committee, which was to discuss the questions on hand informally and from an absolutely free and untrammeled standpoint, had no name, though it later came to be called the Ordinance Consultative Committee in the newspapers. Its first meeting was held on May 14, 1951, and it continued to meet until the beginning of national independence in the following year, doing much good work in releasing persons who had been purged from public life and in planning the revision of laws relating to labor, agricultural land, economic controls, and education. It also proved itself of great value in the framing of laws preparatory to the coming into effect of the peace treaty.

# 5

# General MacArthur and His Aides

General Douglas MacArthur's name is as well known in Japan as in the United States and other countries, and since an extensive range of memoirs and records exists concerning the great American soldier, I shall confine myself here to some personal impressions gathered during years when I had occasion to consult with him frequently in his capacity of Supreme Commander for the Allied Powers and the man responsible for the administration of occupied Japan.

On the occasion of my initial meeting with him, I was surprised to learn that General MacArthur's association with Japan was no new development and that he had a considerable knowledge of my country and the Japanese dating back over forty years. His father, Lieutenant-General Arthur MacArthur, had, when commander of the U.S. Forces in the Philippines, paid a visit to the Japanese forces at Port Arthur and Dalian during the Russo-Japanese War, and his son—then a lieutenant—had accompanied the elder MacArthur as his aide-de-camp and met such Japanese national heroes as Admiral Tōgō and General Nogi, who had, it appeared, left a very strong impression on him as men who were remarkable not only in their respective fields of action but as individuals. It seemed to me that General MacArthur had come to judge the Japanese people as a whole on the basis of those early meetings, and I once pointed out to him that men like Tōgō and Nogi were exceptional types such as no longer existed in the Japan of today, but he refused to be convinced, replying that it was strange that I, as a Japanese, should seek to denigrate my own people and adding that, if one considered the farmers working in the fields from early morning until late at night—not only men but also women and young girls—and, further, remembered the achievements of the Japanese in various fields of scientific research, it was clear that as a race they were inferior to none in the world.

This estimate which General MacArthur had formed of us never changed; throughout many discussions which I had with him on the subject, he held fast to his own view as to our merits as a race. This reminds me of the stir in Japan when, upon his return to the United States, General MacArthur addressed Congress and was reported in the Japanese press as saying that the Japanese as a race were, in terms of political maturity, only twelve years old. But a careful reading of the whole speech will show that all the general meant to imply by the statement was that the Japanese people were still immature where liberalism and democratic government were concerned; in the same speech he went on to remark that, in view of their traditional and original culture and their intrinsic qualities of character, there was much to be expected from the Japanese in the future.

In addition to this innate friendliness, which might be taken as stemming from a genuine understanding of the country and its people, I found the supreme commander remarkably quick in sizing up a situation and acting on it. When as foreign minister in the Higashikuni cabinet I met him for the first time, he gave me the impression of being straitlaced, a poseur even; this initial feeling soon wore off, however, after I had seen more of him, giving place to a warm appreciation of his other qualities and character.

I have already noted that those within GHQ could be roughly divided into idealists and realists. General MacArthur was a realist not only in his capacity as a soldier but also as an administrator faced with the involved and complicated tasks of the occupation. For instance, the decision not to place the country under military law obviously rested with the supreme commander, and he could only have reached it through his quick perception of the actual state of affairs in Japan after the surrender, which was not of a nature to require a military government to maintain order.

The same qualities were at work in his attitude to the throne. He seems to have acted on a belief that it was necessary to enlist imperial aid in order that the nation might implement the terms of the surrender without any outward friction, and he must clearly have thought that, since the surrender had been successfully negotiated by means of the imperial rescript and resulted in the emperor's historic broadcast to his people, it was desirable to have the cooperation and sympathy of the emperor in order that any subsequent unnecessary bloodshed should be averted.

In his assessment of the situation General MacArthur was right, and he has reason to be proud of the fact that this was the only case in history in which an enemy country was occupied without a single shot being fired, or the life of a single soldier lost.

The emperor first visited General MacArthur on September 27 of the year of the surrender. I had then just assumed the post of foreign minister, and when I heard that it was the emperor's wish to meet the Supreme Commander for the Allied Powers, I came to the conclusion, after much thought, that such a meeting was desirable and calculated to have good results, and conveyed the imperial wish to the general. General MacArthur answered that his position prevented him from visiting the emperor at the imperial palace, but that if the emperor would come to his residence he would be delighted to meet His Majesty. At the meeting thus arranged, General MacArthur seems to have been much impressed by the emperor and told me later that he had never met a person who behaved so nobly and naturally. This first meeting was followed by several more, and the emperor, too, seems to have become completely at ease with the general in their conversations together. At each meeting, the tall form of the general would appear in the doorway of the U.S. embassy to welcome the emperor and again to bid him farewell, towering above His Majesty.

In the course of the Tokyo war-crimes trial conducted by the International Military Tribunal for the Far East, when Pu Yi, the ex-emperor of Manchukuo, was summoned as a witness, it was proposed by the Soviet representative in the Allied Council for Japan that the emperor of Japan should also be summoned to appear, and it was the supreme commander and the chief prosecutor, Mr. Joseph Keenan, who opposed such a step: General MacArthur, as the supreme commander, was obliged to pay due heed to the wishes of the council, but the decision lay with him, and the proposal did not materialize. The general had come to have a great respect for the emperor, and even told me once that, although Japan had lost the war, the throne was still important to the Japanese people and the reconstruction of Japan depended on the people rallying to the imperial symbol. It was this attitude towards the emperor which must have dictated General MacArthur's policy in regard to the Tokyo war-crimes trial; at any rate, the fact remains that the respect and understanding shown by the general towards the throne, and his decision to exculpate the emperor from all and any relationship with war crimes, did more than anything else to lessen the fears of the majority of the Japanese people in regard to the occupation and to reconcile them to it. I have no hesitation in saying that it was the attitude adopted by General MacArthur towards the throne, more than any other single factor, that made the occupation an historic success.

Another instance of the supreme commander's quick grasp of a situation was in the matter of the continued use of the trade names of those financial groups that had been ordered to be dissolved. GHQ had ruled that the new business firms that arose as a result of the dispersal of the so-called *zaibatsu* combines should be prohibited from adopting the former trade names such as Mitsui, Mitsubishi, and Sumitomo. But calculations indicated that if the new firms were obliged to adopt new trade names, the expense involved would total a staggering sum in the neighborhood of fifteen million yen—while, further, the losses incurred in our export trade before

new names would become well-known in world markets would come to
even more.

I explained this dilemma to General MacArthur, reminding him that a
general election was approaching and the Liberal Party, of which at that
time I was president, would inevitably lose if we were forced to take a step
resulting in such a catastrophic loss to the financial world, and that this
would be considered as an indirect interference by GHQ in Japanese politics. General MacArthur thought over my words for some time and then
said in that case he would postpone enforcement of the step for one year.
In fact, the matter was never raised again.

Two more matters concerned with General MacArthur merit mention
here. One was that he was in favor of ending the occupation as early as practicable, holding firmly to the opinion that the longer a foreign army remained in occupation of a country the greater was the mischief. I recall once
having occasion to see him over an incident in which members of the occupation forces had misbehaved and caused damage to Japanese. After listening to me, he explained that in the first months of the occupation the members of the occupation force were mostly those who had seen combat service
during the war and these veterans, contrary to a widely held opinion, were
usually well behaved. But the veterans had by that time, the general explained, been largely replaced by newcomers arriving directly from the
United States and in many cases they did not take a particularly serious view
of their jobs; it was no longer so easy to maintain discipline among them—
a fact which he cited to indicate there was all the more reason why the occupation forces should depart from Japan at the earliest possible date. There
was a tone of sincerity in his voice as the general said this, and I am certain
that his conviction that the occupation should end as early as practicable
had much to do with the peace treaty becoming a reality as soon as it did.

The second matter illustrates the fact that General MacArthur was not
only quick to perceive, but also quick to reach a decision, though the two
perhaps come to the same thing; I heard the story from the general himself
when I visited him in New York some years ago. It appears that the Soviet
Union, bent upon making as much out of the Allied victory as possible, had
offered to provide a Russian military force as part of the Allied Army of Occupation, with the suggestion that the Red Army units thus made available
to General MacArthur should undertake occupation duties in Hokkaidō,
Japan's northernmost island. General MacArthur flatly declined the offer.

I had myself at the time heard rumors of this proposed partition of Japan,
and my anxiety had been intense. Countries like Czechoslovakia and
Poland, which had not originally been communist nations, had succumbed
to communism through the Soviet Union sending its armed forces into
them and bringing off a coup d'état. The native communists alone were not
strong enough to do this, but had Soviet forces been permitted to enter

Communism

Hokkaidō, there can be no doubt that Hokkaidō would today have been another East Germany or North Korea, and Japan would have been divided—a loss compared with which the loss of the Kurile Islands is a small one indeed. For preventing this, if for nothing else, the Japanese people have abundant reason to be grateful to General MacArthur.

Negotiations with GHQ involved questions which, though they may appear trivial today, caused us a good deal of trouble at the time. This could, upon occasion, develop into downright anxiety on our part, particularly when the issues involved concerned food and other vital matters: particularly as we were not sure at first of the occupation authorities' intentions. Such difficulties and apprehensions lessened as time passed and we got to know the supreme commander, the chief of staff, and others within GHQ, and they became aware of conditions in Japan; in due course it became possible to work with them with far greater smoothness than might have been expected.

However, although we established perfectly friendly relations with General MacArthur and his chief of staff, such was not the case with some of the other members of GHQ, among whom were some quite peculiar types, and it often happened that after seeing these people we found it necessary to go direct to General MacArthur himself in order to straighten out difficulties. I should like to dwell briefly here on this point, and on the men who filled the upper ranks of the supreme commander's headquarters.

From the nature of the occupation administration, it was natural that the department with which we Japanese had most to do was the Government Section. General Courtney Whitney, the chief of that section, became in time a well-known figure throughout Japan, as also did Colonel Charles L. Kades, who was the vice chief under him. General Whitney was by profession a lawyer, had been associated with General MacArthur ever since the time when General MacArthur was the military adviser to the Commonwealth of the Philippines, and had accompanied the general to Japan. During the occupation years he was on the same footing as the others on the staff of the supreme commander, but he was not a soldier in the strict sense of the word.

If a personal note may be permitted, I have reason for believing I was not much liked by General Whitney and others within Government Section—a fact illustrated by the active opposition within that section to my forming my second cabinet. The reasons for this dislike can, of course, only be a matter of conjecture: one reason may well have been that I hardly ever put in an appearance at Government Section. In the early days of the occupation, after seeing General MacArthur about some matter I would say that I would go round to the Government Section, or whatever section was concerned with the matter on hand, and discuss matters further, and frequently General MacArthur would reply that there was no need as he would have the men concerned come to see us. He would then call General Whitney, or General Marquet, chief of the Economic and Scientific Section, and give his orders, to which all they could answer was, "Yes, sir."

Such a procedure expedited business, but it is possible that the officials concerned did not particularly enjoy having to stand to attention in my presence. Another factor contributing to my lack of popularity in some SCAP quarters may have been that Government Section would on occasion inform the Japanese Foreign Office that certain designated persons were failing to show a proper spirit of cooperation towards occupation policies and should be discharged or purged. To all such insinuations, I made it a rule to reply that we preferred to have such directives communicated to us in writing and not transmitted orally. That usually took care of the matter, as they well knew that if the submission were in writing I would take the papers round to General MacArthur and thrash out the matter with him personally. Looking back on that time, it was perhaps not surprising that they came to dislike me.

Not only in the Government Section, but in all sections outside the general staff, there seems to have existed a good sprinkling of radical elements—what might be called "New Dealers"—among the younger members, particularly at the beginning of the occupation. These belonged to the group that I have classified as the idealists, and traces still remain of their having sought to utilize occupied Japan as an experimental ground for testing out their theories of progress and reform. They included elements that were rather more than radical, and which made friends with Japan's own left-wingers and, in some cases, worked on them for their own purposes. Gradually, however, they were recalled to the United States, where it seems some were questioned by the Congressional Committee on Un-American Activities, no doubt in regard to their activities in Japan.

I once referred, in a conversation with General MacArthur, to the general character of the men within GHQ, not necessarily confining my remarks to these progressive people, and I recall his remarking to me that, the United States being on the whole a progressive nation, with no lack of lucrative jobs for promising young men, it was difficult to attract them to come and work in Japan.

If I did not get on very well with the Government Section, or with those within GHQ whom I have called idealists, I did for some reason or other establish many friendships among the men who were professional soldiers, and often received good and wise advice from them. Though they were military men, many had cultured backgrounds and, what was more to the point, they were people who placed the actual effects of the occupation administration above theories, so that, once convinced that a proposed measure had practical value, they were prepared to help and encourage us without troubling themselves with what had gone on before. General Charles A. Willoughby, the chief of the Second Section of the general staff, was one of these, and General Robert Eichelberger, who first commanded the Eighth Army under General MacArthur, was another. Holding the sort of positions they did within the occupation set-up, they helped us on every occasion to maintain order in the country and to deal with the native communists, when these people again became active in the country. They even went to the length of providing me with escorts when I toured the provinces during elections, and sent me sandwiches and other food on journeys because, they said, they knew it was in short supply. These might be classed merely as acts of personal friendship; but there can be no doubt that these men, through their efforts both directly and indirectly to smooth over difficulties concerned with occupation administration, did a great deal indeed towards improving relations between the occupation and the Japanese people, and so, ultimately, between the United States and Japan.

A word here may not be out of place concerning the men on the Allied Council for Japan, the structure of which I have already explained. The council had its offices in a building adjacent to General MacArthur's head-quarters in the center of downtown Tokyo, but relations between GHQ and the council were, from its inauguration, of a nature best described as deli-cate. GHQ appointed an American representative to the council, who also acted as its chairman, and General MacArthur presided over its first meet-ing in person. But the Soviet representative, General Kuzma Derevyanko, had so much to say at this meeting in support of communism, and so ob-structed proceedings generally, that it was thought undesirable that the supreme commander should be drawn into the discussions in person at fu-ture meetings, and subsequent sessions of the council were presided over by Mr. George Atcheson, the diplomatic adviser to SCAP.

Mr. Atcheson was a career diplomat who had been stationed for many years in China and had a reputation in the U.S. State Department as a spe-cialist on Far Eastern questions. He was a man of sterling qualities and, since he lived in the former mansion of the Sumitomo family quite near to my official residence during the time that I was foreign minister, we became very friendly. It was most unfortunate that he died in an airplane accident near Hawaii while making one of his periodic trips back to the United States. His place as American representative on the council was taken by Mr. William Sebald, who succeeded him as chief of the Diplomatic Section within GHQ, and who is now one of the assistant under-secretaries in the State Department.

Both Mr. Atcheson and Mr. Sebald, following General MacArthur's policy, had a strenuous time in discussions with the Soviet representative and oth-ers at meetings of the council—discussions in which the American repre-sentative kept the interests of Japan and the Japanese people well to the fore. This attitude was not necessarily welcomed at that time by the other Allied powers, but General MacArthur and the American representatives car-ried through their policies none the less.

The Soviet representative, General Derevyanko, came to Tokyo with a staff numbering several hundred people and the intention, apparently, of being most active. But his demand that the Soviet forces be permitted to occupy Hokkaidō met with General MacArthur's firm refusal and, apart from taking a certain part in directing the activities of the Japanese Communist Party and doing some propaganda work, the Russians were not able to accomplish very much. General Derevyanko had, on the contrary, to sustain some hard rejoinders from General MacArthur concerning the failure of the Soviet Union to repatriate Japanese surrendered personnel held in that country, and it seems that the activities of his staff were considerably curtailed.

At the meetings of the Allied Council, and also in the Far Eastern Commission sitting in Washington, there was at first a great deal of discussion of a harsh nature concerning Japan, including such questions as the responsibility of the emperor in regard to the Pacific War. The attitude of General MacArthur's headquarters towards occupied Japan came in for considerable criticism, and the fact that GHQ was nevertheless able to carry through its policies must have been largely due to the wholehearted support given at that time to General MacArthur by President Truman. It remains true, however, that the attitude taken by General MacArthur did excite a measure of ill feeling among some of the other Allied powers—a fact which may very well have been one of the reasons for his recall by President Truman.

I recall receiving reports concerning the sessions of the Allied Council from people in the Central Liaison Office. Japanese were not permitted to use the front entrance to the building where these were held; officials of the Liaison Office, newspaper reporters and all who had business there had to use a side entrance, and were only allowed to go as far as the gallery. And as I have already indicated, the severest measures against Japan were in the meantime under discussion within the Council chamber. It has been said that to sit and listen to these discussions made one realize better than anything else that Japan had been defeated and there was no altering the fact.

However, in Japan's own House of Representatives the situation was reversed. With all pressure from the nation's militarists removed and complete freedom of speech regained, the liveliest argument went on between members, and the fact of defeat at times appeared to have been forgotten. Even Communist members of the Diet were clamoring for rearmament, declaring that an independent country without arms was unthinkable. The atmosphere of the National Diet presented a sharp contrast with that of the Allied Council proceedings, and it seems to me that the two added up to a more or less accurate picture of the country as it really was on the morrow of defeat.

I assumed office as foreign minister in the Higashikuni cabinet on September 17, 1945, on the same day that General MacArthur's GHQ was transferred to the Dai-Ichi Sōgo building across the street from the imperial palace. A few days later I visited Admiral Suzuki Kantarō, who had been prime minister at the time of the surrender. Before accepting that office, the admiral was for many years grand chamberlain to the emperor, and I had come to know him intimately in this connection through Count Makino, my father-in-law. Admiral Suzuki had been burned out of his home during a wartime raid and was then living in a friend's house. I told him I had been appointed foreign minister and said I had come to seek his advice as to how to set about my work: he replied that it was important to be a good winner in a war but equally important to be a good loser, and that he wanted me to remember carefully that cardinal fact. It was good advice, and I decided then and there to follow it throughout in my dealings with GHQ.

Being a good loser does not mean saying yes to everything the other party says; still less does it mean saying yes and going back on one's word later. It was obviously important to cooperate with the occupation authorities to the best of one's power. But it seemed to me that where the men within GHQ were mistaken, through their ignorance of the actual facts concerned with my country, it was my duty to explain matters to them; and should their decision nevertheless be carried through, to abide by it until they themselves came to see that they had made a mistake. My policy, in other words, was to say whatever I felt needed saying, and to accept what transpired.

This was an attitude which General MacArthur seemed to understand perfectly, but others within GHQ seemed to consider it as one of resistance and obstruction. At least, they showed signs of regarding me as an unmanageable person; and the loss is theirs. Of course, now that the occupation is a matter of history, we hear people boast of how they resisted the Americans during those years. But it seems to me that one should give words like "resisting" and "resistance" a definite meaning and use them according to the sense thus defined. Thus Gandhi resisted the British while they ruled India, and one may legitimately speak of the resistance which the French put up against the Germans while France was occupied during the Second World War. But resistance of that sort was not carried on by us during the occupation of Japan. Our object was to remonstrate, or to explain, whenever that was deemed necessary, because we thought that such a course was for the good of the occupation authorities and ourselves, and I believe we were justified in so thinking.

At the time of the surrender our greatest fear was that perhaps Japan might remain under occupation for an indefinite number of years. Actually, we regained our independence after only six years and eight months, and it seems to me that we were able to attain our objective so quickly through being good losers.

When we come to consider individual cases, however, the record cannot be said to have been kept up throughout. There were two sorts of Japanese who were particularly obnoxious. One consisted of those who, because they wanted to obtain some advantage through the good graces of GHQ, made extravagant presents to the men in it, or gave them lavish dinner parties, so either incurring their contempt or succeeding in actually spoiling them. Presents and dinners may be the normal outcome of the Japanese love of hospitality, but there are surely limits to such practices; and when it is a question of expecting something in return, it does not bear speaking of further. It was this kind of person who also, during the occupation years, took whatever GHQ said, in whatever circumstances, as law, whether out of an inordinate respect for foreigners, or from a comic sense of being helplessly Japanese. It was not edifying and I hope there are fewer such people about now.

The second sort were those who, being what are called "progressives" or radicals, made assiduous pilgrimages to GHQ, particularly at the beginning of the occupation, to denounce and report on their fellow Japanese, no doubt activated by the desire to rid the country of what they considered were undesirable elements. They played an active part in the purges, particularly purges connected with the press and the publishing world generally. And since, as I have pointed out before, there was a good deal of the leftist element within GHQ itself at the start of the occupation, the two groups got together and made use of each other for the greater glory of their peculiar ideals. Our progressives and radicals might now say they were merely cooperating with the occupation, but the fact remains that their cooperation had as its main object the promotion of those of their own set, to the indiscriminate detriment of other citizens, and, objectively considered, their actions cannot escape the censure of disloyalty and downright treachery. But enough has been said of these people.

There are some now in Japan who point to similarities between the Allied, and predominantly American, occupation of Japan, and our occupation of Manchuria, China, and other countries of Asia—the idea apparently being that, once an occupation regime has been established, the relationship between victors and vanquished is usually found to be the same. I regret that I cannot subscribe to this opinion. Japan's occupation of various Asian countries, carried out by army officers of no higher rank than colonel and more often by raw subalterns, became an object of hatred and loathing among the peoples of the occupied countries, and there is none to dispute that fact. The Americans came into our country as our enemies, but after an occupation lasting little less than seven years, an understanding grew up between the two peoples which is remarkable in the history of the modern world.

Criticism of Americans is a right accorded even to Americans. But in the enumeration of their faults we cannot include their occupation of Japan.

# 6

## My Political Apprenticeship

The coming of peace found me indisposed and confined to my home at Ōiso, on Japan's "Riviera" south of Tokyo. I therefore did not participate directly in the events of the first climactic hours following the emperor's broadcast to the nation.

From what I heard later from Marquis Kido, then the grand keeper of the imperial seals and principal adviser to the emperor, it seems that Prince Konoe had, before the outbreak of the war, favored prevailing upon Prince Higashikuni to accept the premiership when he himself had resigned from office and before General Tōjō Hideki had been appointed prime minister.

It had at that time been the opinion of Prince Konoe, one of the nation's senior statesmen, that nothing short of the authority of a prince of the imperial blood at the head of the cabinet could curb the excesses of the militarists. But Marquis Kido and others held the contrary view that, although such a plan might work were the Japanese government intent upon following a peaceful policy, it would only bring opprobrium on the imperial house to invite Prince Higashikuni to head the government at a time when those in authority had to reckon with the possibility of the nation being plunged into war; for this reason the choice fell on General Tōjō, whose cabinet led the country into the conflict. With the termination of hostilities, however, a different situation presented itself, and Prince Higashikuni had been asked to form a cabinet and exert the authority of his position to override any objections which the army might have to carrying out the measures made necessary by the circumstances in which the war came to a close.

On September 17, 1945, shortly after the arrival in Japan of the first units of the U.S. Army of Occupation, I received a telephone call from the late Ogata Taketora, who was then chief secretary to Prince Higashikuni's newly formed cabinet, informing me that the prince desired to see me on urgent business and requesting me to come to Tokyo without delay and to take formal morning dress with me. I assumed that the "business" on which the prince desired to consult with me was probably connected with General MacArthur's headquarters, and went to Tokyo the same evening in a car sent to fetch me to the prince-premier's official residence.

On arrival at the prime minister's official residence, however, Ogata told me that Shigemitsu Mamoru, the foreign minister, who had earlier in the same month signed the surrender document on behalf of the Japanese government on the deck of USS *Missouri* in Tokyo Bay, had been obliged to resign, and it was suggested that I was the person best qualified to take his place within the cabinet. I had been out of touch with public affairs for some considerable time, and as, in my view, it was important that someone with an established reputation, both within Japan and abroad, should occupy the post of foreign minister at that juncture, I urged the appointment of either Mr. Ikeda Seihin or Baron Shidehara Kijūrō, both of whom were still alive and in good health at that time. But Ogata brushed my suggestions aside, and as he informed me that Prince Higashikuni was awaiting me, I left the official residence for the villa of the Sumitomo family, which had been assigned as the temporary residence of the prince.

When I was in the presence of His Highness, the prince stated he was depending on me to accept the post. I outlined to the prince the same views that I had advanced to Ogata, mentioning the names of Ikeda and Shidehara. But it was difficult for me to be as outspoken in the presence of His Highness as I had been with Ogata, and I finally agreed to conform to his wishes and accepted. Whereupon, although the evening was already advanced, the investiture at the imperial palace was held that day.

Such an event had been far from my mind when I had left Ōiso earlier in the evening, and in my haste to obey the prince's summons I had forgotten to take with me black shoes to wear with morning dress. Ogata inquired what I had done with my shoes; I told him that although he had asked me to bring formal attire, no mention had been made of shoes to match. In the circumstances, there was nothing to be done but borrow shoes, and as the only pair available were too large for me, I had great difficulty in walking and preventing my footwear from emitting strange noises while in the presence of the emperor. In this manner I made my first bow on the Japanese political scene.

That hurried journey from Ōiso to Tokyo brings to my mind an incident that occurred on another such trip early in the occupation. My car was passing through a deserted avenue, lined with pines, on the Tōkaidō Highway between the towns of Fujisawa and Totsuka, when two American GIs suddenly appeared and signaled my driver to halt. I imagined them to be on some kind of marauding expedition, but they turned out to be soldiers returning to Tokyo who had lost their way, and they politely requested a lift, if only for part of the way, should I be traveling in that direction. Relieved that their intentions were strictly honorable and benevolent, I invited them into the car and we had not proceeded far before they were pressing chocolates, then chewing gum, and finally cigarettes upon me. The incident surprised and pleased me; feelings which were probably shared by the majority of the Japanese people in their initial contacts with the men of the occupation forces. I recall thinking at the time that it was this natural way of acting on their part, and the inherent good nature of the average American, which enabled the occupation of Japan to be completed without a shot being fired.

Shortly after these events, on October 4, 1945, General MacArthur issued a directive known as the Memorandum on Removal of Restrictions on Political, Civil and Religious Liberties, the purpose of which was, first, to repeal all laws restricting the freedom of citizens, such as the Public Peace Maintenance Law and Peace Regulations, and, secondly, to abolish the Police Bureau of the Ministry for Home Affairs and the Special Service Section in all prefectures. The directive also required the immediate dismissal by the Japanese government of nearly five thousand officials in the departments concerned, beginning with the home minister, director of the Police Bureau and the superintendent-general of Metropolitan Police, and reaching down to every prefectural chief of police and the special service sections. In retrospect, such a step appears quite natural and, in all the circumstances, only to be expected. But at that time our government had not yet become acclimatized to the stringent requirements of the occupation authorities, and the cabinet resigned the following day.

This raised the question of a successor to Prince Higashikuni as prime minister. Marquis Kido, in his capacity as grand keeper of the imperial seals, decided that Baron Shidehara Kijūrō was the most appropriate choice and sent his secretary, Marquis Matsudaira Yasumasa, to me with a request to convey his decision to the baron.

Baron Shidehara had been foreign minister in the days when I was vice minister. Considerably my senior, and a doyen of Japan's foreign service, he had, like me, the reputation of being a pacifist and was therefore almost as unpopular with the army as I had been. For this reason, he had retired from public life and was living almost as a recluse.

After journeying to his house on the outskirts of Tokyo, I informed him of Marquis Kido's wishes. The baron was not pleased; he made immediate objections, and continued to make them. I repeated to him exactly what Ogata had said to me when I had been offered the post of foreign minister: that this was no time to shirk responsibility and that the situation had to be taken firmly in hand, and so forth. But Baron Shidehara declined to be swayed, and after about an hour's discussion I had to admit myself beaten and left.

Reporting back to Marquis Kido, I expressed the opinion that the only course remaining was for him to speak to the baron personally, adding that I had told Baron Shidehara before leaving him that he might expect a summons from the palace in the very near future. My assessment of the situation proved correct. The marquis sent for him and set about the task of winning him over, saying the emperor was most anxious that a new cabinet be formed immediately in view of the prevailing situation. It seems that the marquis had previously obtained the emperor's acquiescence in the procedure to be followed at the meeting, and had arranged for lunch to be brought to him and the baron from the imperial household kitchen while the talk was in progress. The baron finally agreed to accept, and when Marquis Kido reported this to His Majesty, the usual form for imperial audiences was abandoned and the baron was given a seat in the imperial presence and addressed by His Majesty in person. Shortly thereafter I was deputed to visit the Allied GHQ in order to obtain General MacArthur's consent to the baron's nomination as premier.

I well remember that visit. I was discussing the nomination with Lieutenant General Richard K. Sutherland, the chief of staff, when General MacArthur came into the room and inquired what we were talking about. I told the general I had come to obtain his consent to the nomination of Baron Shidehara as prime minister. General MacArthur asked me how old he was, and when I answered that he was a little over seventy, replied that this seemed terribly old. General MacArthur then inquired whether the baron could understand English. The baron had always prided himself on his English and this question from the supreme commander was one which I certainly did not propose to forget. I answered that he spoke English well, and made a mental note to tell the baron some day about the general's question.

General MacArthur's consent to the baron's nomination as premier being forthcoming, the task of lining up a new cabinet began. Headquarters for the task was the official residence of the foreign minister, where I was living, as at that time there was no suitable alternative. The actual task of calling in candidates for the various posts and interviewing them fell to Mr. Tsugita Daisaburō, who was later appointed chief secretary to the new cabinet; I too provided some assistance by advising the baron whenever consulted by him. The task was made easier by the fact that the army had ceased to exist except in name and there were yet no political parties worth speaking of. Time was needed to obtain GHQ's approval to the nomination of each minister, but even so the list was completed within two days.

There still existed in those days the posts of ministers for the army and navy. At my suggestion, General Shimomura Sadamu and the late Admiral Yonai Mitsumasa were respectively named for these posts, and these men deserve to be remembered for the fine work they did in preventing the armed services from getting out of hand, and in carrying out all arrangements relating to the army and navy which had been made necessary by Japan's surrender. I myself was retained in the new cabinet as foreign minister, but the title had become a misnomer—in fact the Foreign Office now existed only in name. On October 25, shortly after the new cabinet was formed, all diplomatic and consular work was suspended by a directive issued by Allied GHQ, after which all such work, including any communications between the Japanese authorities and the various foreign liaison missions established in Tokyo, had to be relayed through the Diplomatic Section of General MacArthur's headquarters, and my work as foreign minister was restricted to communication with GHQ on important matters connected with our government.

One such matter for negotiation remains in my mind. A SCAP directive, issued by GHQ, ordered the dismissal of fifteen prefectural governors. Baron Shidehara, the prime minister, was confined to his bed with pneumonia at the time and he instructed me to try to get the directive reviewed and, if possible, cancelled. I therefore visited General MacArthur at the American embassy and urged him to reconsider the matter, pointing out that such a wholesale dismissal would throw the prefectural governments into confusion. General MacArthur listened, smiled, and asked me what was the population of Japan, walking around me in circles the while, as he usually did on these occasions. He then said that there were tens of millions of Japanese and he found it difficult to believe that the dismissal of fifteen of them could possibly result in the disruption of prefectural government; there must be any number of ambitious men serving under the governors concerned who would be glad to be given a chance to prove themselves, and, further, that in an overpopulated country such as Japan it was important that young men be provided with opportunities. The loss of fifteen men represented no cause for worry, and the general added that such a view was merely common sense.

I could think of no reply to this line of argument—it even occurred to me that it might not be such a bad idea to get rid of some of the old men and promote younger men to replace them. And so, indicating my agreement, I left the embassy. Later, when I reported the conversation to Baron Shidehara, the prime minister had not much to say either.

I have previously commented, and shall do so in greater detail later, on General MacArthur and his GHQ in Tokyo during the occupation years. But at this point would like to correct a serious error in a volume entitled *MacArthur* written by General Courtney Whitney, who was the chief of Government Section within GHQ during the occupation. It is not my purpose to criticize books written by others, but the passage in question concerns me personally in my capacity as Japan's foreign minister at the time mentioned, and the incident is considered sufficiently important by the author to be described in the volume concerned as follows: "There were times when MacArthur had to make it clear that he intended to use his authority if it became necessary. An early instance came when he issued a so-called 'purge' directive."

The book is an account of General MacArthur's career as a commander during the Second World War and as Supreme Commander for the Allied Powers and Commander-in-Chief of the U.S. Forces in the Far East and Japan during the years following the war. In the second section of the volume, entitled "Japan," it is stated that government during the occupation years was conducted for the most part through the medium of the Japanese government, but that the commander-in-chief was directed to act on his own authority whenever he thought necessary in pursuance of his duties.

An episode detailed in the volume to illustrate this fact seems to have taken place at the time when the SCAP directive ordering the so-called purges was issued and several members of the Shidehara cabinet were named among those to be debarred from public posts. This would indicate that the episode is presumed to have happened a little after January 4, 1946. According to General Whitney's volume:

> Evidently misguided by the reasonableness of MacArthur's early occupation policies, all of the cabinet members decided to resign *en masse* as a form of protest. The Prime Minister at the time was Baron Kijūrō Shidehara, who, because of illness, sent his Foreign Minister, Shigeru Yoshida, to announce this decision to MacArthur. He also announced the decision to the press, which proclaimed it by banner headlines before Yoshida's call.

It is further stated in the book that General MacArthur saw me at once and listened to me in cold silence while I informed him that it was our intention to hand in our resignations to the emperor and to beg His Majesty to name Baron Shidehara again for the post of prime minister. And the author goes on to add, after a short note to the effect that this was the procedure followed when a cabinet resigned in Japan under the Meiji Constitution then still in force, that the general then said to me:

> Mr. Minister, I have the highest regard for Baron Shidehara, and I know of no one better qualified to carry out the terms of my directive, but if the cabinet resigns *en masse* tomorrow it can only be interpreted by the Japanese people to mean that it is unable to implement my directive. Thereafter Baron Shidehara may be acceptable to the Emperor for reappointment as Prime Minister, but he will not be acceptable to me.

I do not personally remember any such episode as this ever having taken place. If, in fact, the Shidehara cabinet decided on resignation at that time, the decision was reached without my knowledge—without the knowledge, that is to say, of the foreign minister. Nor do I have any recollection of ever having heard General MacArthur speak of Baron Shidehara in any such scene as is described in the book. The only occasion on which I spoke to General MacArthur concerning Baron Shidehara was when I went to obtain his consent to the baron's nomination as prime minister after the resignation of the Higashikuni cabinet. However, the passage in question is written with the dramatic veracity of a supposed eyewitness, and it is difficult, therefore, to believe that the episode is based upon something no more tangible than a mere flight of imagination. It is possible that such a scene did actually take place between some person other than myself and the supreme commander, and that General Whitney is confusing the circumstances.

# 7

# The "Yoshida Era" Begins

If I remember correctly at this distance in time, it was during my period in office as foreign minister in the Shidehara cabinet that Hatoyama Ichirō joined with Andō Masazumi, Ashida Hitoshi, and other members of the Diet belonging to the prewar Seiyūkai group to form the Japanese Liberal Party, and soon after this other members of the Diet who had mostly belonged to the old, rival, Minseitō group got together to form the Japanese Progressive Party. I had never felt any particular affinity with political parties, or had close connections with the prewar groups, and was not invited to join either of these new groupings. Nor did I take any particular interest in them. The only time I had anything to do with them, before I was most unexpectedly forced into the position of accepting the presidency of the Liberal Party, was when I had a share in urging Baron Shidehara to become president of the Progressive Party.

At the time when the Shidehara cabinet was formed, the revived political parties had hardly come into existence, and although there existed a Diet composed of members elected during the Pacific War, legislative activity in those days was largely confined to enacting measures in accordance with the wishes of the supreme commander, so that no urgent need existed for the establishment of close connections between the political groups and the cabinet. Moreover, a special session of the Diet convened to legislate on these measures requested by GHQ—including the introduction of women's suffrage, the framing of a labor law aimed at encouraging the development of trade unions, and the reform of the Agricultural Land Adjustment Law to provide land holdings to tenant farmers—was dissolved towards the end of 1945 as soon as these measures had been enacted. And as the resultant general election, the first of the postwar era, was delayed on account of the time needed to screen candidates under the provisions of the GHQ directive concerned with the "purges," and the new House of Representatives did not meet until April 10 of the following year, there was no point until then in establishing close contacts with the political parties.

The Progressive Party, composed largely of Diet members considered to have been sympathetic towards Japan's war-time government, was deprived of a number of its key figures as a result of the purge directive and the screening of its candidates before the election, after which only some ninety of its members were returned compared with more than one hundred and thirty Liberals. Thus it became the second strongest group in the new Diet, barely ranking ahead of the third, the resurgent Socialists. The late Mr. Machida Chūji, who had been named president at the inception of the party, had been purged, leaving the group without a leader, and the prominent figures within the party, such as Machida and Ōasa, must have had a difficult time trying to find a way out of a confused situation.

At about this time, the men around Shidehara were of the opinion that the baron should join the Progressive Party and become its president, both in order to resolve the situation in which the party found itself and because, unless the baron meant to retire from public life upon the completion of his tenure as prime minister, it would assist him to continue to serve his country in a manner commensurate with his abilities were he formally to join a political party, and even contest a seat in the House of Representatives during the coming election.

The same idea had also occurred to me, and so, shortly before the election campaign opened, I went to see the baron and broached the subject, saying that the days of government by civil servants were over; that he himself may have been nominated for the post of prime minister by the emperor, but, from now on, it would be the head of the political party with the largest number of seats in the Diet who would form the cabinet; and that in these circumstances the wisest course would be for him to join the Progressive Party and become its president. I pointed out that the party was at that time without a leader, and that Mr. Machida, the former president, was at a loss to find a successor, and that, since he and Mr. Machida, having in the past served in the same cabinet, were on good terms, there could be no better choice. But on that occasion, as on a previous one, the baron voiced objections to my advice and I could not prevail upon him to act on my suggestion.

Mr. Machida Chūji had served as minister of agriculture and forestry in the Hamaguchi cabinet at the time when I was vice minister for foreign affairs, and I had remained on intimate terms with him ever since. I therefore went to see him, and outlined my ideas, emphasizing that Baron Shidehara had, on several occasions, served as foreign minister in Minseitō cabinets and thus could not be said to lack ties with the Progressive Party, which was the successor of that prewar group. Mr. Machida expressed complete agreement with my ideas, but told me he had already made overtures to the baron and similarly failed to move him. Whereupon I sought a further interview with the baron, taking Mr. Ōasa Tadao with me, and after much persuasion from Mr. Ōasa the baron finally capitulated and agreed to our proposal.

Before we parted, Ōasa asked me about my own political intentions. I informed him that I personally had no particular interest in political parties and so was not contemplating joining either of the new groupings. To which Ōasa indicated his dissent, stating that if he had exerted himself to entice the baron to join the Progressive Party, it had been with the object of drawing me into the party as well. I countered this by saying that, once having ensured that the baron would be installed as president of the party, the question of myself joining or not joining was of no importance, and left it at that.

Thus Baron Shidehara became president of the Progressive Party. The election results became known hard on the heels of that event and made it clear that the Liberals were to be the strongest group in the new Diet. It was generally assumed that Mr. Hatoyama Ichirō, the president of the Liberal Party, would inherit the premiership after the resignation of the Shidehara cabinet. So widespread was this view that the fact of the baron accepting the presidency of the second largest party in the Lower House seems to have been interpreted in some quarters as a move on his part to continue in office by forming a coalition cabinet with the Liberals. Even some members of the Shidehara cabinet may have accepted this conception of the baron's strategy, but at the time I remained in ignorance of that fact as well as of a host of other things that were apparently going on behind the scenes during the period between the holding of the general election and the bombshell announcement that Hatoyama Ichirō, the president of the largest group in the new House of Representatives, had been summarily purged by order of the supreme commander.

This event, the most dramatic to occur on the political stage in Japan during the occupation years, happened only a few hours or days before Mr. Hatoyama was expected to be named the new prime minister, and came as a complete surprise to me. From what I subsequently learned, the contingency seems to have been hinted at to various persons within the government for some time before it happened (though I never learned from what quarter), and there are reasons for believing that Mr. Narahashi Wataru, chief secretary to the cabinet, and Mr. Mitsuchi Chūzō, minister for the interior, had been keeping such a possibility up their sleeves. In an effort to propagate the idea that the Liberals, although the largest group in the new Diet, need not necessarily be invited to form a government, those still in office began to circulate views that seemed to ignore the accepted concepts of constitutional government, and only when popular disapproval was aroused were rumors started that Mr. Hatoyama was about to be purged. It seems that Mr. Hatoyama himself received warnings not to assume a prominent role in politics as the possibility of his being purged existed. However, he took no notice of such reports and actively sought a coalition with the Japanese Social Democratic Party through the intermediary of the late Mr. Miki Bukichi. His failure to achieve such an understanding between the two minority parties in the Diet coincided with the announcement of his actual purging from public office by the occupation authorities. I myself was one of the victims of the resulting situation, since the elimination of Mr. Hatoyama from the public scene was the immediate cause of my casting my lot with a political party, something I had never previously contemplated, and being named its president.

Mr. Hatoyama's summary purge made havoc of the plans for a new cabinet, which were then well advanced. Baron Shidehara had already tendered his resignation and everything was ready for the investiture of the new cabinet except the cabinet itself. I received a message from Mr. Hatoyama asking me to agree to be nominated as the president of the Liberal Party, but I had never had any inclination for a political career, nor did I have any experience of domestic administration. And as my father-in-law, Count Makino, advised me against acceptance, I declined Mr. Hatoyama's offer—recommending instead that the same offer be made to Mr. Kojima Kazuo, a man very much my senior in the tangled world of domestic politics.

Mr. Hatoyama next asked me to sound Mr. Kojima. I did so, and Mr. Kojima's answer was that, as an old man of nearly eighty, he had no intention of taking an active role in politics. Reporting the result of this interview to Mr. Hatoyama, I next suggested Mr. Matsudaira Tsuneo, a former minister of the imperial household and a veteran diplomat, and Mr. Hatoyama again requested me to conduct the negotiations.

Mr. Matsudaira's reaction did not seem to me to be too completely negative, so I urged Mr. Hatoyama to approach him directly. However, shortly thereafter I received a visit from Hatoyama, who surprised me by saying that he had just visited Mr. Matsudaira to inform him that the idea of his becoming president of the Liberal Party was impracticable; I taxed Mr. Hatoyama concerning the reasons for this abrupt change of attitude in the matter, but he replied merely that party affairs would not develop smoothly were Mr. Matsudaira to be appointed president, and I sensed that for some unexplained reason he had encountered strong opposition to the proposal from within the party. Mr. Hatoyama thereupon once more invited me to accept the post of president, and we were back where we began.

Time passed; and meanwhile we members of the Shidehara cabinet had to function as "caretakers" with no indication when a new cabinet would come into existence. The newspapers variously reported that I was to become adviser to the Liberal Party, or that I had been approached with a view to becoming its next president. One day, after a meeting of our "lame-duck" cabinet, the late Dr. Matsumoto Jōji, then a minister of state, asked me why I did not end the speculation by accepting the proffered post of party president, remarking that we were all awaiting the formation of a new cabinet that never seemed to materialize and the situation was most unpleasant for all concerned. I replied by reminding him that I was not even a member of the Liberal Party and therefore did not see any reason why I should accept its presidency, but that Mr. Ashida Hitoshi, a veteran Diet member who was at that time minister of public health in the cabinet, was a member of the new party, and therefore a more appropriate candidate for its leadership. Baron Shidehara had listened to this exchange, and asked me to join him in his office when other ministers had departed. When I did so, he urged me to accept. I pointed out that he himself had complained at length of my share in inducing him to become president of the Progressive Party, and all the unpleasantness which that post entailed, and it seemed to me strange that he should now be wanting me to taste the same sort of unpleasantness—on which note the conversation ended.

Shortly thereafter, however, Baron Shidehara invited me to confer with him again, and on that occasion was far more pressing in his demand that I agree to assume the leadership of the Liberal Party. Nothing had happened in the meantime to improve an involved and deteriorating political situation. In addition to the maneuvering inside the Liberal and Progressive Parties of the political Right, the Socialists and Communists were indulging in complicated moves among themselves, and the Communists were displaying much activity in the propaganda field, thereby aggravating the already widespread postwar unrest and confusion.

Early in April, shortly after the general election, a mass meeting had been held in Tokyo's Hibiya Park to protest about the continued existence of the Shidehara cabinet, after which many thousands of demonstrators, led by the Communists, had marched to the official residence of the prime minister across the street from the Diet building. On that occasion the police had been forced to fire on the crowd, and armored cars and jeeps of the occupation forces had been mobilized to patrol the area. From that time until the Shidehara cabinet's exit from the political scene, such demonstrations before the prime minister's official residence took place almost daily. May Day celebrations, in abeyance during the war years, were revived and on May 1, 1946, hundreds of thousands of workers assembled in Hibiya Park; similar rallies were staged in all parts of the country, and the newspapers reported that Japan had been submerged under a sea of red flags.

Under such circumstances, the ending of the political deadlock and stabilization of the situation became an urgent necessity, and I began to think that maybe I should have to accept the presidency of the Liberal Party after all. I therefore invited Mr. Hatoyama to see me and had a final talk with him. At that meeting I put forward three conditions governing my acceptance of the post: the first of which was that I had no money and did not intend to collect any for the party; the second that Mr. Hatoyama was to have no say in the selection of ministers to the new cabinet; and the third that I was free to resign whenever I reached the conclusion that I had had enough of politics. Mr. Hatoyama agreeing to all three conditions, I finally indicated my willingness to accept the presidency. Mr. Hatoyama probably imagined that my tenure as president of the Liberal Party would last only until the opportunity came for him to re-enter public life and resume that position; I myself certainly had no idea at that time that I should retain the presidency of the party, and the premiership, for very long.

My acceptance was only the first step. I was next told to join the Liberal Party formally and to become the chairman of the executive committee. This was in order to represent the party in that capacity, as a president could only be elected at a general meeting of the party and, in fact, some months were to elapse before I was duly confirmed in the presidency by the votes of the party. The next step was to set about forming a cabinet, a by no means easy task. I had previously participated in the formation of two Japanese cabinets—the prewar Hirota cabinet and the Shidehara cabinet that followed the surrender—but it was my first experience at forming my own cabinet. Plans governing the formation of the new administration had already been laid down by my new party, and in general I followed these, but difficulties arose over the choice of a minister of agriculture and forestry. It was my idea that the reconstruction of the country after the ravages of war should best begin with the rehabilitation of the rural areas, and also that, in deciding the future basis of the country, major emphasis would have to be placed on agriculture. With these views in mind I rejected the candidates for the post of minister of agriculture and forestry put forward by the party and decided to select a candidate on my own initiative. I consulted with Baron Ishiguro Tadaatsu, who had occupied the same position at the end of the war and was a recognized authority on agricultural matters; he recommended Professor Tōhata Seiichi of Tokyo Imperial University, whom I personally approached with the offer of the post, but because of various complications he eventually declined. Professor Nasu Hiroshi, formerly of the same university, was the next name on my list of prospects, but General MacArthur's headquarters withheld consent to his nomination and negotiations again fell through.

I had begun to lose heart, and was thinking of throwing up the whole business when Baron Ishiguro took pity on me and suggested Mr. Wada Hiroo, who was then director of the Agricultural Administration Bureau in the Ministry. There was some objection to this proposal from members of my party, but the emperor himself had expressed his anxiety over the political situation and there had already been more than enough delay, so I persisted and Mr. Wada was appointed minister. This nomination of a man new to politics for an important post in my first cabinet caused some comment at the time; later everyone came to know Mr. Wada as one of the ablest leaders of the Socialist Party.

Those were stirring, if slightly uncomfortable, times. Communists, led by the late Mr. Tokuda Kyūichi, surrounded the prime minister's official residence, which was our headquarters, and, finding the gates closed against them, swarmed over the walls and would not be driven out. Others adopted similar tactics, and the longer the delay in completing the list of ministers, the more those who were opposed to my forming a cabinet used every such means to defeat the fulfillment of the task. Mr. Hayashi Jōji, who was our spokesman and nominee for the post of chief secretary, was on one occasion confined to a room by a crowd of agitators and forced to remain there for six hours. Under such conditions, it was fortunate that we were able to form a cabinet at all. But in the fullness of time we managed that feat, and the first Yoshida cabinet came into being on May 22, 1946, one month after the resignation of Baron Shidehara's administration. Four members of the Progressive Party, including Baron Shidehara himself, who accepted the post of a minister of state, entered the new cabinet, so bringing about a coalition between the Liberals and Progressives.

# 8

## My First Cabinet

The period in which I took office as prime minister for the first time was one marked by general unrest following the destruction and sufferings of the war years, aggravated by widespread scarcities, particularly of food and raw materials, which made life hard for all—a situation not improved by the constant propaganda carried on by subversive elements bent upon utilizing the unhappy conditions then prevailing to further their own ends. There were frequent street demonstrations to demand more food, which was understandable, and the mob entered the imperial kitchens in an attempt to unmask the continued use of luxuries, indicating that such acts at least were being deliberately planned by men with definite political interests. Incidents of that nature, and a growing tendency to lawlessness, formed only part of the situation with which the new cabinet had to cope. Inflation was growing worse day by day, and we were so heavily engaged in the task of meeting and seeking to alleviate this condition and enabling the country to regain a measure of stability that, looking back on those days, I do not recall the cabinet doing anything tangible enough to merit recording here in detail. In truth we were leading a kind of hand-to-mouth existence, counting ourselves fortunate to see the end of each day.

There were at that time not enough food and not enough houses. In addition, several millions of Japanese—the remnants of our armed forces and Japanese residents from overseas—had been repatriated and must be provided for. Railways, roads, bridges, and port facilities were in urgent need of repair; order had to be kept, and, above all else, food for the people obtained somehow. Moreover, we remained completely in the dark concerning the intentions of the Allied powers towards Japan and had to deal with the directives issuing from General MacArthur's headquarters as they were received. In this situation, our main problem was to stabilize the economy and put industry back on a working basis. To achieve this, we began to feel an increasing need for a coalition cabinet which would include not only representatives of the Liberal and Progressive Parties, but Socialists as well.

Baron Shidehara was strongly in favor of such a step, and although I myself had at that time very little experience of politics, it seemed to me that such a move might be a powerful help in finding a way out of an almost impossible situation. To that end, I had several talks with men in responsible positions in the Socialist Party such as Mr. Nishio Suehiro and Mr. Hirano Rikizō, and, initially, considerable progress was made towards the formation of such a coalition cabinet. But, despite the efforts of all concerned, the plan had in the end to be discarded.

There were many reasons for this failure, but, so far as I was personally concerned, the negotiations and their unsuccessful outcome made me realize as I had never done before that there exist within each of our political parties traditional trends and characteristics which are far more deeply rooted than anyone not on the inside would imagine. A party may call itself the Liberal Party, but it is still, in fact, the old prewar Seiyūkai Party. The postwar Progressive Party was to all intents and purposes the old Minseitō Party. And so on. The traits that originally distinguished these groups are handed down and, instead of disappearing with time, come to the surface as strongly as ever when such proposals as the formation of a coalition cabinet or the merging of two groups are mooted. This condition was not confined to the conservative parties; just as much rivalry existed between the left and right wings of the Japanese Socialist Party. And there is not much sign of any remedy even today, which is a pity. Democracy consists of the rule of the many, and if members of political parties do not follow the advice of their leaders on plans supported by the majority, but reach decisions and act in the interests of the particular faction within the party to which they happen to belong, it is difficult to expect democracy to operate smoothly and produce good results.

The food situation at that time was so serious that the government was advised that ten million persons could be expected to die of starvation; however, the remnants of wartime food stocks together with supplies forthcoming from the occupation authorities were sufficient to tide us over the immediate crisis.

I recall, during our efforts to obtain sufficient food, visiting GHQ and informing the occupation authorities that unless Japan could import four and a half million tons of foodstuffs, many of our people would face starvation. The figure I quoted had been supplied to me by the Ministry of Agriculture and Forestry; actually, however, imports of only seven hundred thousand tons of food in that first year following the surrender were sufficient to ward off any starvation, and I had to listen to considerable and pointed criticism from members of General MacArthur's GHQ regarding the inaccuracy of Japanese statistics. Apparently, the ministry had arrived at the figure given me by estimating the size of that year's domestic harvests as conservatively as possible in order to obtain the maximum amount possible from the occupation authorities, a circumstance which was understandable in view of the fact that Japanese government officials had become accustomed during the war to handle statistics in a manner most suited to their own purposes.

General MacArthur himself later brought up this matter in a conversation I had with him, saying our government agencies were apt to be far too casual in their calculations. I replied that if we had not been, we would in all probability never have embarked on such an ill-considered conflict, or, having begun it, might have won. With this line of reasoning the general could only agree. However, this episode concerning the amount of food needed from abroad to meet the nation's immediate needs impressed upon me the necessity for being more careful in the compilation of statistics, and I accordingly asked a number of experts to review and reorganize the methods by which our figures were compiled, and this was done.

During the weeks and months that followed, the food crisis eased. Labor unrest, on the other hand, became more widespread and an increasingly serious problem. In a New Year message to the nation issued in 1947 I alluded to some of those responsible for the unsettled state of the nation as "renegades," a remark which called forth a storm of protest from many quarters. I had meant the word to apply to the professional agitators who were at that time taking advantage of existing confusions to foment discontent among the workers and aggravate the general national unrest; however, not only the agitators and their accomplices, but responsible newspapers and radio commentators chose to interpret my remark as being applied to Japan's workers as a whole, from which fact one can judge the excitable state of the public mood in Japan at that time. I considered, and told some of the officials in General MacArthur's headquarters that these labor troubles were one result of the excessive protection accorded the revived trade-union movement by GHQ. And, as I pointed out earlier in this volume, there was ground for believing that some within GHQ were actually in touch with the organized labor movement and had assisted in bringing about the existing unhappy state of affairs.

On the other hand, some of the leading officials in GHQ—particularly those who were professional soldiers—had decided early in the occupation on the need to take steps to discourage the kind of labor agitation that had little to do with the economic needs of the workers. It was most important, however, that the right moment should be chosen for instituting such measures, in view of the reactions which this course might be expected to cause within the Far Eastern Commission and the Allied Council for Japan. The representatives of the Soviet Union on those bodies, for example, welcomed rather than otherwise the existing social unrest in general, and labor disputes in particular, and were bent upon deterring Allied headquarters in Tokyo from taking any action in the matter. It was therefore necessary that GHQ, while recognizing the need for imposing checks upon irresponsible agitation, should hold its hand until the moment arrived when further inaction would make it impossible to maintain public order.

The psychological moment for action came with the calling of a general strike for February 1, 1947—this was a blow at Japan's tottering economy which was banned by General MacArthur. Even so, the prohibition of a stoppage of work, which would have had incalculable consequences for the nation, was protested against by the Soviet representative in the Allied Council for Japan, but his motion was rejected. Had GHQ not acted, and had the projected general strike been allowed to take place as planned, I cannot conjecture what would have been the subsequent course of my nation.

Looking back on that time, and remembering the revival of my country since then (one of the most spectacular events of the postwar era anywhere), I feel that the Japanese nation owes a profound debt of gratitude to General MacArthur for the decisive action he took. When, later, I visited West Germany, I was told by government leaders in that country that its workers had put the reconstruction of their country before all other interests, and done their best to avoid any strikes or actions that might retard the attainment of that goal, a fact which, it seemed to me, goes far to explain the position which the West German Republic has achieved in the world since the war.

On February 7, 1947, after events had made it clear there existed little hope of our being able to form a national cabinet and the threatened general strike had been averted by intervention from General MacArthur's headquarters, I received a communication from General MacArthur:

February 6, 1947
Dear Mr. Prime Minister:
 I believe the time has come for a general election. Momentous changes in internal structure, in economic outlook and in the whole fabric and pattern of Japanese life have occurred since the last general election nearly a year ago. It is necessary, in the near future, to obtain another democratic expression of the people's will on the fundamental issues with which Japanese society is now confronted. In this way, we will once more advance in the process of democracy which now governs this state. The exact time and details are matters which I leave to the discretion of the Japanese Government, but the election should take place as soon as practicable after the close of the present session of the Diet so that a new legislative body may initiate and synchronize with the introduction and effectivation of the new Constitution. The past year has been one of accomplishment. I look with equal confidence to the future.
Very sincerely,
[signed] Douglas MacArthur

The Diet then in session was accordingly dissolved on March 31, and 92nd Imperial Diet, the last of Japan's parliaments to be elected under the Meiji Constitution, came to an end.

At the general election that followed on April 25, 1947, the Japanese Socialist Party won 143 seats and became the majority party in the House of Representatives; the Liberal Party was the second largest party with about ten fewer seats; and the Democratic Party (successor to the Progressive Party), which numbered among its leading members Mr. Ashida Hitoshi and Baron Shidehara, the former president of the Progressive Party, was in third place with 120 seats.

Although the Socialists were the first party in the Diet, they still lacked the number of seats necessary to command a majority, whereas the rival conservative parties could easily do so if they were willing to cooperate in forming a government. The resulting delicate situation gave rise to proposals that the Liberals should form another coalition cabinet with the Democrats participating, or even that we should attempt to inveigle sufficient members of the Democratic Party into our own Liberal ranks and become the majority party. However, I decided that the proper course was to turn over the government to the Socialists and thus establish a sound precedent in democratic politics.

When the results of the general election became known, old Mr. Kojima Kazuo, who was then still very much alive, came to my official residence to see me, and expressed the opinion that under the circumstances the correct course would be for me to resign. I replied that that was also my appraisal of the situation, which seemed to please him, and he left. I heard later that, upon departing, he had announced to newspaper reporters waiting at the entrance: "Yoshida's going," and then hurried away. That was typical of Kojima; it is a pity we no longer have men of his caliber these days.

My tenure of office had lasted just one year—from May 1946 to May 1947—but a number of important legislative measures had been enacted by the 90th, 91st, and 92nd Diets held, under the old Constitution, during that period. Not only was the Constitution revised, but the war-time compensation payments were discontinued and, in this connection, the Enterprises Reconstruction and Reorganization Law, the Land Reform Law, the Triple Labor Laws, the Property Tax Law, the House of Councilors Election Law, the Fundamental Law of Education, the Local Autonomy Law, the Anti-Monopoly Law, and other measures were enacted, all of these being directly concerned with the rebuilding of postwar Japan and the reform of the entire body of our laws. But what remains most vivid in my memory are the events of May 3, 1947, when the new democratic Constitution went into effect and His Majesty attended in person the ceremony held in the outer grounds of the imperial palace to commemorate that momentous event.

# 9

# In Opposition—and
# an Election Victory

Immediately before my formal resignation as prime minister I received a visit from Mr. Katayama Tetsu and Mr. Nishio Suehiro, respectively chairman and secretary-general of the Socialist Party. Mr. Katayama first came to my room alone and indicated that in the coming coalition cabinet of Socialists and Democrats he would like to include some members of the Liberal Party as well, adding that he did not imagine that I myself would care to enter the new government.

By way of reply, I inquired what was the policy of the so-called left wing of the Socialist Party. Whereupon Katayama called in Mr. Nishio, who had been waiting in an anteroom. Mr. Nishio spoke at some length, but what he had to say all boiled down to the fact that the left wing of the majority party favored cooperation with the Japanese Communist Party.

I pointed out bluntly that in that case any idea of including members of my Liberal Party in the new cabinet could not be considered, as that party had always been opposed to any dealings with the Communists. And if two groups of people, one for and the other against cooperation with the Communists, came together to form a cabinet, the result would inevitably turn out to be a sorry one, even for the Socialists. We parted on that understanding.

Shortly thereafter, however, some twenty or thirty of the leading members of the Liberal Party who had got wind of this conversation came to see me and informed me that if we did not accept the Socialist proposal and turned the government over to the Socialists, it would not be possible to maintain unity in Liberal Party ranks. I pointed out that a political party was guided by certain principles, and to form a coalition cabinet with a party that did not share the same views of political philosophy merely in order to remain in power represented the negation of solemn principles; that they could thus repudiate the principles of the Liberal Party if they so wished, but I would not do so; and that, as an important matter was involved, it would be fitting and proper to refer the whole question to a full meeting of members of our party in the Diet and reach a considered opinion. At the meeting, held the next day, I expressed the same views. There was some applause, and that was the end of the matter so far as the Liberal Party was concerned. At the meeting of the Diet called to nominate the new prime minister, held on May 23, all members of the Liberal Party present voted for Mr. Katayama, and the Katayama cabinet—first in Japanese history to be headed by a Socialist and Christian—came into being.

At the preceding general election of April 1947, I had contested, and won, a seat in the House of Representatives as a Liberal Party candidate. This was the first time in my life I had ever run for parliament, and previously I had no thought of doing so. But it was incumbent upon me, as a member of a political party, to have a seat in the Diet, and the new Constitution expressly stipulated that, as prime minister, I must be a member of the legislative body of the nation. Thus the question arose as to which electoral district I should select for my candidacy. My preference, an obvious one, was Kōchi, on Shikoku Island, where my family had originated and which prefectural constituency had elected my father to the first imperial Diet and my brother and brother-in-law to subsequent parliaments. There was, however, also some talk of Kanagawa prefecture, near Tokyo, where I had lived most of my life. Before finally deciding I consulted with Mr. Yamazaki Takeshi, then the Speaker of the Lower House, on the matter. He dissuaded me from choosing the Kanagawa district, saying I would probably be elected on a first attempt but sure to be defeated the next time. I was not, Mr. Yamazaki pointed out, the sort of person who went out of his way to be nice to electors, or who would put himself out when voters came to visit me, so that it was too much to hope that I would maintain my popularity with them for long, whereas if I chose Kōchi, I would not be the target of so much criticism even if I did not put in an appearance in the constituency very often— Kōchi being far away from the center of things. And, for the same reason, there would not be so many Kōchi electors coming up to Tokyo, and when they did, my cousin, Mr. Hayashi Jōji and others could receive them and my unamiable manners would pass unnoticed. He was quite right!

The Katayama cabinet, and the succeeding one headed by Mr. Ashida Hitoshi—both of which were formed of coalitions between the Socialist and Democratic Parties—lasted from May 1947 to October 1948, during which time we of the Liberal Party formed the opposition in the Diet, and both the party and myself personally gained considerable experience as a result.

Although a Socialist-dominated cabinet had come into existence, conditions in Japan, especially in regard to the lives of the people, did not noticeably improve, and we of the opposition appealed to the two conservative parties to join in forming a new national party that, with the resultant majority in the Diet, would be in a position to carry out the policies that we judged were needed to cope with the situation. Some members of the Democratic Party at that time, including Baron Shidehara, who did not approve of the coalition with the Socialists, supported this proposal, but the majority of the Democrats did not, whereupon those favoring such a step seceded from the party.

At about this time the Katayama cabinet resigned, and was succeeded by the Ashida cabinet, another coalition of Socialists and Democrats. This development was not generally popular, and that fact was instrumental in bringing about the birth of the new party that we had in mind. Thirty-six members of the Democratic Party who had "bolted" that group to form the "Democratic Club" decided to throw in their lot with us, and on March 15, 1948, the merger took place and we made a fresh start as the Democratic Liberal Party, of which I was elected president.

In October of the same year the Ashida cabinet resigned and I, as the president of the opposition party, should have been nominated automatically to form a new cabinet. Such a smooth and normal transfer of power was, however, complicated by an incident that may be of interest as illustrating one aspect of Japan's political situation as it was during the occupation.

The incident in question seems to have originated at General MacArthur's GHQ, where—and I have the Government Section particularly in mind—I have reason to think I was not too well liked. These people raised no objection to the Liberal Party returning to power, but harbored a natural disinclination to my resuming the office of prime minister; and a rumor was circulated in the quarters concerned to the effect that GHQ was averse to my forming another cabinet.

I have mentioned earlier that some of Japan's politicians at that time regarded everything said by the men at GHQ as law and attached an exaggerated importance to both the smiles and the frowns of the occupation authorities. So the rumor was given credence and seeming authority, and before long some people were saying that, in view of the fact that GHQ would surely object to my nomination as prime minister, it would be better to find someone else. Thus a movement got under way to have Mr. Yamazaki Takeshi, then chief secretary of the party, named in my stead.

I was confined to my home at Ōiso by illness at the time, which did not, however, prevent my receiving visits from people who told me that indications were that there was no hope of GHQ consenting to my nomination, to which I answered that we would have to see about that when it came to the point, and there was no need to take rumors into consideration beforehand.

On or about October 7, if I remember correctly, an extraordinary meeting of officials of the party was held, at which I pointed out there existed no grounds for believing the rumors that were circulating and that political decisions should not be swayed by considerations of personal likes and dislikes. At a further meeting of party members of both houses of the Diet the following day, I stressed the importance of our party, at that juncture, setting an example—not so much for the sake of getting into power but in order that democratic procedures should be established in our country. I added that members of the party should unitedly disregard such things as rumors, which ran counter to the spirit and concepts of democratic government. My stand was approved, and Mr. Yamazaki, who until that meeting had remained undecided in his mind as to the correct course of action, resigned from the Diet, so putting a decisive end to the movement in his favor. I then visited General MacArthur, informed him of my resolve to head the next government and obtained his approval. At the session of both houses of the Diet held on October 14, 1948, I was nominated prime minister, and my second cabinet came into being on October 19.

The cabinet was in office, but the Democratic Liberal Party did not hold sufficient seats in the House of Representatives to command a majority. To attempt to remedy that state of affairs, I intended to dissolve the Diet and appeal to the country at the earliest opportunity. However, complications arose before that decision could be put into effect. We of the Democratic Liberal Party insisted on the right of the government to dissolve Diets under Clause 7 of the new Constitution, which decrees that such a right rests with the cabinet in office. The opposition contended that Clause 7 merely concerned a formality by which a cabinet obtained imperial consent to its dissolution, and that Clause 69, which states that: "If the House of Representatives passes a non-confidence resolution, or rejects a confidence resolution, the Cabinet shall resign en masse, unless the House of Representatives is dissolved within ten (10) days," actually governs the circumstances under which a dissolution may take place. Reports circulated that it was the intention of the opposition parties to abstain from voting should the government party propose a vote of confidence, in order to prevent its being rejected (thus opening the way for a dissolution under the terms of the Constitution); we also received "inside" information suggesting that GHQ favored the same interpretation as the opposition regarding Clause 69.

There followed a good deal of coming and going in political circles as the arguments for and against the conflicting opinions were discussed, but finally, on October 28, it was arranged that the opposition should, in accordance with a recommendation from GHQ, propose and carry a vote of non-confidence in the government and so permit the dissolution of the Diet, and after some further obstruction on the part of the opposition parties the Diet was dissolved on December 23. It seems that General MacArthur, upon hearing of the government plight, had reversed those who were supporting the claims of the opposition, and agreed to a dissolution.

At the election that followed, the Democratic Liberal Party won an overwhelming victory, securing 264 seats in the House of Representatives. The Japanese Communist Party won 34 seats, compared with 4 in the previous Diet, but the Democrats and Socialists—the so-called middle parties—suffered severe losses, which may be accounted for by the desire of Japanese voters for a stable government with moderate policies. The result of this general election, held in January 1949, laid a solid foundation for the Democratic Liberal administration that lasted for six years, during which time much was accomplished in the reconstruction of the nation, and our efforts to regain our sovereign independence were finally crowned by the signing of a peace treaty at the San Francisco Conference in September 1951.

# 10

## The Last Three Yoshida Cabinets

No particular difficulties arose in connection with the formation of my third cabinet, but I took some time over the details because I wanted not only the Democratic Liberals but all conservative factions who subscribed to our basic policies to come together in the government and thus make possible a stable administration—and my negotiations with the opposition Democrats took longer than was at first expected.

The bid to create a coalition cabinet of all the conservative groups was unsuccessful, but two prominent members of the Democratic Party who favored such a coalition, Mr. Inagaki Heitarō and the late Mr. Kimura Kozaemon, joined the cabinet. After the completion of the cabinet I continued my efforts to bring together all conservative elements into one political party, and in February 1950 we managed to win over to our ranks thirty-five Democratic members of the House of Representatives and five in the Upper House, and thereafter our party was known as the Liberal Party.

The third Yoshida cabinet which thus took office was my longest, lasting for nearly the maximum of four years permitted under the Constitution. Since the cabinet possessed an absolute majority in the House of Representatives, no serious fear of political instability existed, but the country itself was still far from a state of well-being, either economically or socially. Numerous incidents instigated either by Communists or left-wing elements added to the unrest and gloom. Mr. Joseph Dodge, the president of a Detroit bank, had arrived in Japan as financial adviser to General MacArthur's headquarters, and was sponsoring a stringent policy of retrenchment (known as the "Dodge Line") in economic and financial fields. One result of this policy was the reduction of personnel in Japan's civil service by 260,000 employees, a step that provoked the almost physical opposition of the parties of the Left in the Diet and even more violent appeals to direct action outside parliament, particularly from extremist elements within the National Railway Workers' Union. Such a reduction of government personnel in hard times was not calculated to lessen social unrest, but we were forced to take the step in order to meet budget deficits and reconstruct the national finances on more healthy lines.

An additional complication confronting the government was the fact that many of the promises we had made at the general election of January 1949 were found to be incompatible with the economic policies espoused by Mr. Dodge. The national budget compiled under his direction in that year was of a most rigidly balanced nature in which even the funds needed for the control of food and foreign exchange were to be appropriated from the general revenue, contrary to the usual custom; all government subsidies were curtailed; and the whole budget designed to provide a surplus of revenue. This fact made it impossible to carry out pledges to reduce taxes, or even to increase grants for public works. And members of our own party were among those who voiced their discontent. It was only in the sixth and seventh Diets held in the autumn of that year, after we had passed measures for personnel reduction and financial reform in the fifth (special) Diet earlier, that the Liberal Party was able to enact a measure providing for a substantial reduction in taxes amounting to some ninety billion yen.

While on the one hand we were thus able to achieve a measure of economic stability, on the other depression followed the postwar inflation, the number of unemployed increased, and certain political elements were active in stirring the social unrest precipitated by current conditions. Japan's Communists came out openly for revolution by force, and held what was termed a "rally for the rising of the People" in the outer grounds of the imperial palace in Tokyo, in the course of which several officers and enlisted men of the U.S. occupation forces were injured. This incident seriously alarmed both the Japanese cabinet and General MacArthur's headquarters, and resulted in Mr. Tokuda Kyūichi and some twenty other leading members of the Japan Communist Party being purged from public life and the banning of *Akahata*, the Communist Party newspaper. Shortly afterwards the Korean War began, transforming Japan's situation so far as economic depression was concerned, because of the sudden upsurge of orders for war materials, which lasted until a further depression developed during my fifth cabinet.

In 1951, the third year of my third cabinet, the peace treaty was signed at San Francisco—while in Japan those who had been purged from public life during the occupation had their rights progressively restored, a process which lasted from June till August of that year. Men like Mr. Hatoyama Ichirō and Mr. Ishibashi Tanzan, who had been directly and specifically purged by order of GHQ, did not regain their full status until August.

General MacArthur's headquarters—in the course of our negotiations which preceded the de-purging of those affected—admitted that the purges had in some respects been too sweeping. But though GHQ raised no objection to the lifting of restrictions on others, difficulties were present in the case of Mr. Hatoyama, who had been purged at the instance of the Soviet government, and Mr. Ishibashi, whose economic policy was considered to have been in open opposition to that of GHQ. The government persevered in its efforts, however, and finally secured GHQ's consent to the restoration of all rights to Mr. Hatoyama in August. Unfortunately, Mr. Hatoyama suffered a serious stroke in June of that year, and, with the San Francisco peace conference scheduled to take place in September, it was out of the question for me to hand back the presidency of the ruling party to him as some members of the party apparently expected me to do.

On April 28, 1952, the San Francisco treaty came into effect and Japan regained its sovereign independence. But the activities of the disaffected elements within the nation continued unabated. Specifically, since U.S.-Japanese relations had now been clearly defined by the peace treaty and the U.S.-Japan Security Pact, Communist propaganda began to take on a more definite anti-American flavor. It therefore became necessary to enact laws to deal with political actions calculated to endanger public safety, but it required three months to secure the necessary Diet approval—and then only after disorders within the nation's parliament, of which I shall speak later. In the meantime, members of the Liberal Party who had gathered around Mr. Hatoyama as he recovered from his illness began making trouble within the ruling party, with the result that it became progressively more difficult to secure the smooth operation of business within the Diet itself. And so, although the term of office of members of the House of Representatives was not due to expire until the following January, I deemed it prudent, in view of the differences within the party, to dissolve the Diet and appeal once more to the country.

Although personal and public attacks made upon me by disaffected members of our party complicated the task of conducting the campaign, we still managed to retain a majority of seats in the Lower House in the following election, and I set about the task of organizing my fourth cabinet, completion of which task was delayed by the fact that the pro-Hatoyama faction within the party insisted on naming him as head of the party and next prime minister. We were eventually able to arrive at an understanding, but the members concerned, numbering more than twenty, next formed a rival group within the party, which subsequently represented a serious menace to the solidarity and unity of the Liberal Party and a source of instability in the general political situation that followed the organization of the new cabinet.

Although the Liberals held more than half the seats in the House of Representatives, the difference in the strength of the government forces and the opposition was no more than ten seats; therefore the disaffected group within our own party had only to absent themselves from their seats to leave the government at the mercy of the opposition during voting. As events transpired, when the opposition on March 14, 1953, proposed a vote of nonconfidence in the government, some thirty members of our own party voted with them, and I was forced to dissolve the Diet after only five and a half months.

The result of this further appeal to the country was that the Liberal Party retained its position as the largest party in the House of Representatives, while the Democrats (who were now called the Progressives) lost more than ten seats, and the disaffected Liberals as much in proportion. The outcome was that, though we were still called upon to form a cabinet, we would not be in a position to command a majority in the House unless a coalition was effected with one of the other parties or groups.

I myself felt more than ever the urgent need for the establishment of a stable conservative government; I therefore invited Mr. Shigemitsu Mamoru, president of the Progressive Party, to cooperate with us. I knew that among the Progressive Party there now existed a strong current of discontent, in the light of the election results, at the idea of continuing to cooperate with the Socialists who had nothing in common with them in regard to basic policy. But the members of that party were still insisting on Mr. Shigemitsu heading the cabinet instead of myself, so that Shigemitsu himself was not in a position to promise me anything beyond a readiness to discuss with us all important questions and issues that might arise in the Diet. However, although we were unable to arrange for any of the Progressives to join the cabinet, the desirability of conservative cooperation came to be better understood by them in time, and we managed to implement most of our important projects during the following year with their support and that of the "separatist" Liberals of the Hatoyama camp. Among these projects was the enactment of a measure to prevent strikers from causing stoppages of electric power and miners from damaging coal pits by the withdrawal of safety men—this act being passed despite violent opposition from the Social Democratic Party.

This unofficial conservative coalition also functioned during the following Diet, and two bills proposed by the government concerned with educational reform, two more concerning defense arrangements, and yet another for the reform of the police all became law during the year 1954.

The two educational reform acts prohibited teachers connected with compulsory education from indulging in political activities or introducing politics into classrooms. The two defense acts were concerned with the raising of the National Police Reserve to the status of a Self-Defense Corps and the establishment of a National Defense Agency. And the police reform act dealt with the abolition of the regional police and the merging of the whole force charged with the preservation of law and order into one nationwide organization.

The Socialists, as usual, offered violent resistance to all these measures. In the case of the police reform, in particular, they went to the length of forcibly stopping the Speaker from entering the House of Representatives on the night of June 3, the last day of the session, in order to prevent him from proposing the prolongation of the session, and thus prevent the bill from coming up for final debate. At the same time they introduced gangs of ruffians into the precincts of the House to intimidate anyone who might oppose them, and not only the normal Diet guards but also the police force might never have been realized.

Despite this carefully ordered violence, however, the Socialists did not succeed in their intentions. The session was prolonged, the vote duly carried amid confusion, and although both left and right groups of Socialists declined to appear in the House the following day, public opinion forced them to present themselves to the Diet later, an apology addressed to the people was issued in the name of all the parties, and the Police Act was duly passed and became law on July 1. There were some, at the time, who advised me to abandon the attempt to pass the Police Act in order to avoid political confusion, but I still think that my decision to go ahead with it, despite the Socialist opposition, was correct. Had I not done so, the abolition of the regional police system, which had not worked satisfactorily in the conditions existing in Japan, and the improved organization of the nation's police force, might never have been realized.

During my fifth cabinet we were called upon to deal with a number of problems concerned with foreign affairs, in addition to the purely domestic matters discussed above. With the materialization of a project to obtain arms from the United States under the Mutual Security Act, it became necessary to expand Japan's police reserve into a defense force, and to add to its allotted duties the defense of the country against external aggression. To enact this measure it was necessary to again secure the support of conservatives outside the Liberal Party. I therefore had another talk with Mr. Shigemitsu, the leader of the Democrats, and succeeded in reaching agreement with him concerning the addition of defense duties to other tasks of the police reserve after its transformation into a defense force, and the gradual expansion of the defense program.

The case was different with Mr. Hatoyama and those of his followers who had left our party with him. Mr. Hatoyama favored revising Japan's new Constitution to permit the nation to rearm; to this step, as I shall write later, I could not agree. Mr. Hatoyama has since come to speak less of rearmament and the revision of the Constitution, particularly after he formed his own cabinet, but I continue of the opinion that I was right in not agreeing with him at that time. A serious question like rearmament, with all its implications in the matter of the financial burden imposed upon the nation and people, should not, in my view, be taken up lightheartedly, and the maintenance of a defense corps along the lines of our system of collective security with the United States seems to me, even today, the best means of defense. However, a desire became apparent among the group led by Mr. Hatoyama to return to the fold of the Liberal Party, and talks to that end were begun, which lasted from the summer to the autumn of 1953. Something had to be done about these differences of opinion, and so the Constitution Research Council and the Diplomatic Council were set up within the party, resulting in the return to the Liberal ranks of most of the dissident group, including Mr. Hatoyama himself. We now numbered 229 members in the House of Representatives, or very nearly half the total membership, and were able to enact the defense bills in the next Diet.

The Diet also saw the passing of the law providing for a government subsidy to reduce interest rates for financing the construction of ocean-going merchant vessels. It had originally been proposed by the Progressives, but it was obvious to all that such an act was needed to assist in the reconstruction of our shipbuilding industry, which had suffered so much during the Pacific War. Nevertheless, it came to be linked with financial contributions made to the Liberal Party by those in the shipping industry and precipitated what were then termed the shipbuilding scandals. These so-called scandals, and the wild charges that arose at the time, have remained to this day one of the most disagreeable memories of my whole political career, and a few words concerning the incident may not be out of place.

That the system of government grant for payment of interest for shipbuilding provided for in the act represented a timely measure for aiding the reconstruction of the country's mercantile marine, and improving its international financial relations, affords little ground for dispute. But contributions made to Liberal Party funds by shipping men at the time of the passage of the act came under suspicion of bribery. Various people were implicated, including Mr. Satō Eisaku, then the chief secretary of the Liberal Party, whose arrest for interrogation by procurators became imminent.

I have never been able to fathom the whole affair, but, from what I was able to learn concerning Satō's supposed complicity, I understood that a court of law might take up the question of whether or not there had been a breach of the law concerning the Regulation of Political Funds and Expenditures, but never was an explanation advanced by the procurator's office why Mr. Satō had to be arrested. The act itself was one of national importance, and, as such there could not have been—and never was—any question of its passage or rejection being influenced by money; contributions to Liberal Party funds were arranged by responsible men in financial circles, and members of the shipping industry were by no means the only people who responded to the party's appeals. The procurators who demanded the arrest of Mr. Satō must have wanted to question him concerning the form in which the contributions from shipping sources had been made; whether the donations had been solicited by members of our party, or whether they were forthcoming to thank them for passing the act. There was no other explanation possible and none was forthcoming.

All investigations for the detection of alleged criminal acts or irregularities should have for their aim the collecting of objective evidence, but the methods employed by the procurators on that occasion seemed not yet entirely free from the traditions of the Edo period of Japanese history, during which great importance was attached to confessions elicited from the suspects themselves; this practice easily leads to forms of questioning being adopted which one can only term medieval. It was this analogy which at once came to my mind when I was asked to consent to Mr. Satō's arrest.

I am reminded in this connection of an episode in the case of Burgess and Maclean in Great Britain. Both were members of the British Foreign Service, and questions were asked by Labor members of the British House of Commons why stricter security measures had not been instituted in their case before the pair managed to make their getaway. The reply of the British government was that though these two men had both been under surveillance for a long time, they were not arrested because there was not sufficient material evidence and that the arrest of citizens without such evidence was an offense against the rights of man. There is much that we can learn from such an attitude.

The question of Mr. Satō's arrest came up at a time when proceedings in the House of Representatives had reached a crucial point, and even if his arrest would not have constituted a positive breach of correct judicial procedure, no reasons advanced were strong enough to authorize the serious interruption of government business his arrest would have entailed. I accordingly consulted with Mr. Ogata Taketora, the deputy prime minister, and had Mr. Inukai, the minister of justice, instruct the public procurator-general to postpone Mr. Satō's arrest until the end of the Diet session, then only a little more than ten days away. This step, however, was seen as an attempt by the government to put illegal pressure on the investigation being conducted by the procurators and produced a storm of criticism from all sides, although, when the session ended and Mr. Katō R. (who had meanwhile became minister of justice in Mr. Inukai's place) informed the procurators' office that they could proceed with Mr. Satō's arrest, they refrained—for their own inscrutable reasons—from taking any action.

What distressed me even more than the behavior of the procurators in this matter was the way in which some of Japan's politicians, who well knew the actual circumstances connected with the incident, chose to utilize the affair as a political weapon with which to bludgeon me, purely from motives of self-interest—and in doing so received the plaudits of the public, as though they were heroes who had risen up in defense of the martyred procurators.

This reaction poses a problem for the future of democratic government in Japan.

# 11

## The West Revisited

On September 26, 1954, I departed from Tokyo's Haneda Airport on an extensive tour abroad which took me to Canada, France, West Germany, Italy, Vatican City, Great Britain, and the United States, the first such extended visit to the West to be made by any Japanese leader since the regaining of national independence in 1952. It had been my original intention to include India and the countries of South-East Asia in my itinerary, but, because of the prevailing political situation in Japan, the whole trip had first to be postponed, and when I finally set forth it was found that time did not permit me to include Asia in my travels.

I had long wanted to revisit the West, where the Second World War had brought about major changes, not only in international relations, but also in the internal affairs of the countries concerned. These nations had all adopted new policies to meet the postwar situation, and it was desirable that we should study such changes at first hand in order to assist Japan in forming and implementing its own policy for national reconstruction, particularly as we Japanese had been subjected to the unprecedented circumstance and attendant changes of having suffered defeat in war for the first time in our long history.

I had broached the possibility of my visiting the United States and other Western countries in conversations with Mr. John Foster Dulles and other representatives of the United States government who had visited Japan, and it appeared that my words had been reported to President Eisenhower, for I had received a personal message from the president saying he would welcome me if I was seriously contemplating a trip to Washington. If such a visit were to materialize, it seemed to me equally important that I should also visit Great Britain. At that time various diplomatic questions were pending between that country and Japan, and it was my wish to contribute in every way possible to the promotion of better understanding by going to London personally.

With these major purposes in mind, my departure was scheduled for the beginning of June. Unfortunately, just as I was due to depart, unrest in the Diet came to a head, and I found it necessary to postpone my departure. Viewed in the light of the disorderly and unseemly conduct of certain legislators, as outlined in the previous chapter, it could not be said that democratic concepts of government had yet been established in Japan, and it would have been meaningless, in my view, to go abroad in such circumstances as the representative of a government under such strong attack at home. My departure, therefore, was postponed on my insistence. Mr. Ogata Taketora, the deputy prime minister, and other leaders within the ruling Liberal Party urged me to reconsider, stating that in my absence they would ensure the passing of the Police Law and the solution of other political problems then facing the cabinet. With members of the Diet behaving in a scandalous way, I rejected this advice and spent the next four months attempting to achieve some sort of stability in the political situation. A measure of success having attended my efforts, I eventually set forth in September of that year, traveling by a chartered CPAL plane to Vancouver via the Aleutian Islands.

Arriving at Vancouver after a flight of little more than twenty-five hours, I was met at the airport by Mr. James Sinclair, the Canadian minister of fisheries; Robert Mayhew, retiring Canadian ambassador; T. C. Davis, Canadian ambassador; A. R. Menzies, chief of the Far Eastern Division, Canadian Foreign Office; Mayor Fred Hume of Vancouver; and other dignitaries. After a brief rest at the Hotel Vancouver, we made a tour of the St. Henri Park and the university, and I placed a wreath on the cenotaph in the park commemorating Canadians of Japanese descent who had died in the First World War. The weather was fine, and a large assembly of Canadians of Japanese ancestry had gathered for the occasion, and I was invited to speak to them after the wreath-laying ceremony. In a brief statement—my first public words on North American soil—I remarked that it was sad beyond words that so many gallant men who had fought for Canada in the 1914–1918 War should have lost their lives in battle, but that it was also a fine tribute that they had been prepared to do so for the country of their adoption; adding that, whatever their racial origins or descent, it was incumbent upon those listening to my words that they also should think of themselves always as Canadians and strive to be good Canadian citizens.

It has always seemed to me that the Japanese people, as a whole, tend to have too narrow a concept of the world, and need to broaden their horizons and to regard themselves more as citizens of a world containing many countries and races, rather than just Japanese. Once Japanese adopt a foreign nationality, it is only right and proper that they should be ready and willing to live and die for the country of their adoption. Without such freedom of spirit, it would be difficult for Japanese to be welcomed in other lands in which they may settle, and be afforded those opportunities for useful activity which their own overpopulated land cannot offer.

Leaving Vancouver late that evening on a plane placed at our disposal by the Canadian government, we arrived in Ottawa the next morning. Mr. Louis St Laurent, the prime minister, came to meet me at Rockcliffe Airport, greeting me with great cordiality. The prime minister had visited Japan earlier that year, and had apparently formed a favorable impression of my country. Maybe because of this, the reception accorded me and my party wherever we went in the dominion was most encouraging.

On the day of our arrival in Ottawa I paid an official call on Prime Minister St Laurent and had an hour's conversation with him, which turned mainly on economic problems. Japan's trade with Canada was practically a one-way affair—my country was at that time buying extensively from Canada, particularly wheat, but selling almost nothing in return. We would have liked to buy even more of the excellent Canadian wheat, but without an increase in Japanese exports to Canada this was not possible. This fact was in the forefront of my mind when I told Mr. St Laurent that Japan was a small country deficient in natural resources, with many former markets abroad virtually closed to her; that, in a word, Japan was everything that Canada was not, and that although we desired to buy more from her, we could not do so unless Canada bought from us as well. I added that we were doing our best to manufacture superior-quality goods from raw materials purchased abroad, and that if Canada would buy these we could purchase more from Canada in return. To this, Mr. St Laurent replied that Canada had no objection to buying more from Japan, but that the goods must be really superior in quality for the Canadian market and not the kind of cheap merchandise that found its way into Canada via the United States, and that prices, if they were competitive, did not matter so long as the quality of the commodities offered justified them. In reply, I naturally promised the prime minister to have goods sent from Japan that would be both good and expensive. I later quoted the gist of the conversation in a letter to a friend of mine back in Japan who was in the export business, and it appears he followed up the prime minister's formula, much to his advantage.

The following day I talked with Mr. Malcolm MacDonald, then the British high commissioner for South-East Asia. It had been part of my plan, when I set out on my tour, to take the opportunity to discuss certain ideas which I held concerning South-East Asia with those occupying responsible positions in the British and American governments, and Mr. MacDonald was one of the people I had in mind in this connection. A son of the late Ramsay MacDonald and a statesman early known for his considerable talents (he was colonial secretary in the Baldwin cabinet at the age of thirty-five), I had first met him when, during my tenure of office as vice minister for foreign affairs in prewar days, he had come to Japan to attend an international conference held at Kyoto. Young as he then was, I had been much impressed by the active interest which he displayed in Japanese affairs. Subsequent to that meeting, I had been sent to Great Britain as ambassador, and Mr. MacDonald had later served for several years in Singapore as high commissioner for South-East Asia, and we had ample opportunity to see each other over the course of the years. His wife was Canadian, and by good fortune he happened to be visiting that country when I arrived.

The main point of the policy towards South-East Asia that I had in mind, and to which I still adhere, is that countries such as the United States, possessing large reserves of capital, should invest it in the region on a large scale, while Japan should contribute her technical knowledge; and that, with other countries such as Great Britain, France, and the Netherlands, with their traditional ties with the area, also contributing men and material, a center for the development of South-East Asia should be established at Singapore under the direction of men of experience and ability such as Mr. MacDonald. Such a coordinated international effort on the part of the free countries of the world to develop South-East Asia economically and to increase the wealth and well-being of its peoples would not only open new and expanded markets to the free countries, but would act more powerfully than any other measure to combat the menace of communism. Any country or people would prefer to be rich rather than to remain poor and reduced to the status of a satellite state, which in my opinion represents the equivalent of some of the former colonies. Even the Chinese living in the area would support such a scheme, since they would be free to make money, which they would not be permitted to do under the communist system. Through them, communication might very well be established with the people of mainland China.

I spoke on these lines to Mr. MacDonald, telling him frankly that, in my view, he was the man best suited for the job of directing operations should such a scheme be decided upon, and adding that it was my intention to urge the scheme upon others in the governments of the countries I was about to visit. Mr. MacDonald seemed greatly taken with the idea and we promised to meet again after I returned from my trip. But, unfortunately, I was forced to resign shortly after getting back to Japan, and the plan came to nothing.

From Ottawa I journeyed by train to New York, where, on September 29, I boarded the *Queen Elizabeth* bound for France. The five days needed to reach Cherbourg were a rest-cure which I greatly enjoyed. Occasionally I took my meals with the newspapermen who had accompanied my party from Japan. After the manner of their kind, they all wanted to talk politics, a practice of which I disapprove because politics at the dining table tends to spoil one's appetite! But still the subject would come up again and again before I could stop them, and it was so obvious that it was professional eagerness that caused them to transgress that I found myself answering them from time to time with whatever thoughts and ideas came into my head.

The main thing they appeared anxious to discover was whether I had any intention, upon my return to Japan, of resigning my office in favor of Hatoyama Ichirō, the former president of the Liberal Party. This appeared to me a strange question, even if their job caused them to ask it. According to all democratic precedent, I could not resign the premiership if circumstances did not permit it. On the other hand, I would obviously have to, whether I was personally so inclined or not, if upon my return I found circumstances against me. For the rest, I myself naturally intended to continue with my work after my return; otherwise I would not have set forth on the tour to study conditions abroad.

Everything depended upon the political situation following my return, and it was silly of the newspaper reporters to expect me to be able to give any other answer. The idea of my handing or not handing the government over to Mr. Hatoyama was equally extraordinary. In these days, governments are not handed from one person to another as if they were gifts. If Mr. Hatoyama was found to have recovered completely from his recent illness, and was viewed as the best available man to head the Japanese government, it would have become a part of the policy of all concerned to elect him to that position; if he was not, there was nothing I could have done about it. And it was even stranger that these newspaper reporters, and presumably the readers of the newspapers which they represented, should be so greatly concerned with the question of who was to be the head of the government, instead of with the larger issue of in which direction, and with what degree of success, the government was heading, which should be all that matters in democratic politics.

The *Queen Elizabeth* reached Cherbourg early on October 4, and we departed immediately for Paris in a special train. It was a fine day, and the French countryside, which I had not seen for so many years, formed a pleasing picture, with its lush meadows and fruit-laden apple orchards giving an impression of plenty quite different from the vast stretches of land in Canada.

Upon reaching Paris, we were met at the St. Lazare station on behalf of the French government by M. Jean Bertoin, the minister of national education; the commandant of the military region of Paris; and other officials. Our stay in France was scheduled to last nine days, so we were not pressed for time, but official visits had to be paid as soon as possible. The next day began with my entering my name in the visitors' book at the Elysée Palace and ended with a dinner given us by M. Pierre Mendès-France, the French prime minister. In between, I laid a wreath on the grave of the Unknown Soldier beneath the Arc de Triomphe, called upon the presidents of the National Assembly and the Council of the Republic; M. Edgar Fauré, the vice premier and finance minister; the president of the Assembly of French Union; the president of the Economic Council and others, and received their calls in return.

The main object of my visit to France was to discuss current world problems with the French premier, M. Mendès-France. In addition, I also welcomed the opportunity to meet and talk with President René Coty and M. Fauré, the vice premier. On the evening of October 6, I paid a formal call upon President Coty to express Japan's thanks for the welcome extended to our crown prince by the French nation on the occasion of His Highness's visit to France the previous year. My call also afforded me an opportunity to exchange views with President Coty on the current international situation.

Premier Mendès-France was extremely busy at the time and he was also suffering from a cold caught while attending the Nine Power Conference in London, so I did not see him until towards the end of my stay in France. The day before my visit, the French Socialist Party, at a national council, had approved by an overwhelming majority the Nine Power Agreement concluded in London, making victory for the Mendès-France government certain in the no-confidence debate then pending in the French Chamber of Deputies, and on the evening of October 12, the day I talked with the premier, the cabinet won approval for its policies, supported by the Radicals, the Socialists, and the de Gaullists.

I had always thought the bickering and back-biting rampant between contending groups were the curse of the Japanese political world, and I could sympathize with the French premier when I learned of the equally complicated state of affairs existing in France, with so many small political parties contending for power. I therefore congratulated M. Mendès-France on the expected government victory, which seemed to please him. We then went on to discuss the problem of communism.

I left Paris by plane the same afternoon, and reached Düsseldorf in West Germany—the next stop in my itinerary—in less than two hours. It occurred to me at the time that for two countries to be geographically so close together presented problems from which Japan—with the seas separating it from its neighbors—is fortunately free. Geographical propinquity helped one to understand the sensitivity displayed by the French towards such questions as West German rearmament, as well as that country's regarding this as unreasonable inquisitiveness on the part of the French. I talked with leading men in both governments during my tour, and in retrospect recall a certain reserve in their attitudes whenever they were talking of the other country. It seemed to me at that time that in the case of France, with so many small parties confusing the political scene, the business of governing the country must have been a very difficult matter; I was therefore all the more impressed when Herr Konrad Adenauer, West Germany's chancellor, told me at our first meeting that only a strong government can govern a country well—a statement which echoed my own sentiments.

After a short rest at the Hotel Breidenbacher Hof in Düsseldorf; an exchange of visits with Herr Dr. Karl Arnold, the governor of Westphalia; and my attendance at a tea-party given by Japanese residents in West Germany, we left for Bonn, the West German capital, and arrived at the Japanese embassy there that evening. The next day I signed the visitors' book at the official residence of the president, and then called on Herr Adenauer.

During my stay in West Germany I was much impressed by two things: the first, the economic recovery effected by the German people, and the second, my meeting with Herr Adenauer, which turned out to be one of the most pleasant experiences of my tour. I saw Herr Adenauer four times during that first day at Bonn, and each time we met we understood each other better, so that by the evening, when we met together for the fourth time at an official dinner-party, we found ourselves exchanging opinions and confidences as though we had known each other for years. Perhaps our characters had something in common. The courses taken by our careers certainly coincided. I had never thought of myself as being older than middle-aged, but in fact both of us were over seventy; both of us had been called to head the governments of our respective countries while they were under foreign occupation; both our countries had suffered defeat in war and both had faced the same problems of reconstruction. This similarity between our experiences had perhaps even tended to mould our respective characters after the same pattern—though in appearance Herr Adenauer is very tall and it would be very difficult to say that I am! However, the West German prime minister gave me the impression of a man of purpose on whom one could rely, and I hoped that in this respect we were perhaps alike.

I called upon Herr Adenauer for the first time at 11:30 a.m. on October 13, and the prime minister returned the call at noon. Both were official visits and our brief talk was concerned for the most part with political matters. Discussion continued at a lunch given us by President Theodor Heuss, and also at a dinner at night. We would probably have gone on with our talks the following day had I not been suffering from an attack of indigestion due to an overindulgence of the excellent food of France. The symptoms persisting, I was forced to agree to a doctor, recommended by Herr Adenauer, being called in, and on the advice of both doctor and prime minister it was arranged that I should take a complete rest for one day.

I had met and talked briefly with President Heuss before the beginning of the official lunch-party given by him on the thirteenth. Herr Heuss, who had been reelected at a presidential election held the previous July, was also over seventy years of age. Formerly a journalist of standing and a university professor well known for his liberal views, he was the author of a book entitled *Hitler's Way*, which had so incensed the Nazis that they had burned it. It was difficult to visualize this, however, when confronted by the gentle, white-haired old man.

First of all, upon meeting, I thanked President Heuss for the manner in which our crown prince had been received in West Germany during his tour abroad, and conveyed to the president messages from the emperor and empress. President Heuss replied in most courteous terms, and then said there was something he wished to show me. Thereupon he produced a Japanese book, which was a translation in Japanese of a volume dealing with currency written by the president's father-in-law, Herr Georg Friedrich Knapp, and which he described as one of his most prized possessions.

President Heuss went on to say that Germany and Japan had shared the experience of foreign occupation, but that Japan had been fortunate in having been occupied only by the United States, whereas Germany was occupied by three other countries. I replied that Japan had actually been occupied by eleven countries, but that it was certainly fortunate for her that the United States had played the leading role throughout the occupation period. The president then remarked on General Douglas MacArthur's sterling qualities, and said that I must, nevertheless, have gone through some trying times negotiating with the army of occupation.

While in West Germany, I also talked with Herr Ludwig Erhard, the economic minister, Herr Dr. Karl Arnold, the governor of Westphalia, and many others whom I met at various functions. I was anxious to find out from these officials how the financial recovery of West Germany had been accomplished; how, in particular, a substantial prosperity had been achieved in so short a time; why West Germany had no strike problem; and what measures were being taken to combat communism. I was informed that, as a result of the war and defeat, Germany had found herself completely impoverished and the German people rendered penniless. There had been no time for squabbling. The people, faced with dire poverty, could only come together to do what they could to hasten national recovery and had set themselves to work to that end. Strikes were ruled out as being meaningless, for people knew work stoppages only injured both the national interests and their own. I received the impression from my talks that, with the vast majority of the people in that frame of mind, the influence of communism upon national production was negligible, a truly enviable state of affairs. However, the Germans seemed to think that Japan too was forging ahead with the work of national reconstruction, and I was often told that the Japanese were famous throughout the world for their industry. I must confess that I could not at the time bring myself to agree with this view; from the way the Japanese trade unions were then behaving, industry was not the outstanding characteristic of my countrymen as I saw them. I

have been told since that both the Japanese trade unions and the Japan Socialist Party have become more realistic, than which nothing could be more
desirable for the future of the country. In my time, and particularly during
the first half of my tenure of office, the workers tended to think more of
their rights than of their responsibilities—especially their responsibility to
work for the restoration of their nation; and even civil servants, considering
themselves to be workers in the ordinary sense, were only too ready to
strike, to the detriment of the public welfare.

I outlined the actual situation existing in Japan to the German leaders as
follows: that the prime cause of industrial unrest lay in errors of occupation
policy, notable examples of which were the basic labor laws which the occupation authorities forced us to enact; that it was all to the good that the
freedoms and rights of workers had thereby been vastly increased, but that
some workers took advantage of the resulting situation to make exorbitant
demands that gravely retarded production; that, on the other hand, Japan's
major financial concerns having been splintered (also by order of the occupation authorities), there was not enough capital available to enable producers to plan sufficiently in advance, so that it was difficult for them to
manufacture goods of suitably high quality with which to compete with
other industrial countries in the international market; that this state of affairs naturally adversely affected Japan's exports, which in its turn reduced
correspondingly the incentive to work.

The German leaders listened to this explanation with apparent deep interest, but the fact remains that the Germans were also for a considerable
time under occupation by foreign armies, so that, actually, some other explanation must be found for the differences in the tempo of economic recovery between the two nations.

Concerning the subject of strikes and disturbances caused by communist
agitators, West Germany's leaders were unanimous in their answers, typical
of which was that given me by Herr Arnold, the governor of Westphalia. The
reason for the absence of strikes and manifestations of communist agitation, Herr Arnold declared, was very simple—that every day numbers of
refugees crossed from Soviet-occupied East Germany into West Germany,
and told the people the truth of what it was like to live under a Communist
regime and how, whatever the Soviet Union or the Communists of East Germany might say concerning the merits of their system, the facts were actually quite the opposite; and that so long as the people of West Germany
were being given this evidence every day by refugees who had escaped from
the "blessings" of Communist rule there existed no likelihood of their being taken in by Communist propaganda.

With economic recovery proceeding at a brisk pace, and no chance of
Communist infiltration, it was clear to me that the Germans had come out
winners in the battle for national survival. Before my visit I had heard a

great deal about West Germany's achievements, but I had my doubts, since it seemed to me that being split into East and West Germany was calculated seriously to complicate the internal situation of the West German Republic. But in Germany I had to believe the evidence of my own eyes. Thus I told Herr Adenauer in one of my conversations with him that, in view of the fact that both of us had been placed at the head of our respective governments at more or less the same time and under similar circumstances and conditions, I had always regarded him as my rival; that it had been my ambition all along to succeed in putting Japan back on its economic feet before he could do likewise with West Germany, but that—seeing and hearing all I had since coming to Germany—I now realized that the game was over and I no longer had any hesitation in taking off my hat to him. Herr Adenauer laughed a good deal at this and replied that if he visited Japan he would probably find himself obliged to say the same thing to me. Whereupon I begged him on no account to consider making such a visit, since it would be a most disagreeable experience for me. Which provoked us both to more laughter.

I found myself in complete agreement with West Germany's leaders as to the proper attitude to be adopted towards the Communist bloc. Since the United States and the Soviet Union, the two major powers, are in opposition to each other, one supported by a group of free countries, the other by satellite Communist nations, the only logical policy for both West Germany and Japan to adopt in foreign affairs is cooperation with the United States as members of the group of free nations.

At the same time, both West Germany and Japan stand on the frontiers of the group; for these two countries to maintain their freedom requires the defense of the freedom of the whole group, while their proximity to the Communist countries brings them constantly into contact with these Red-dominated countries, with increased opportunity for negotiations of all kinds with them. It was the opinion of the West German leaders that, though it would be foolish not to utilize our respective positions to promote friendship with the Communist nations as much as possible through trade and other peaceful means, it was essential that all such efforts on our part should not in any way contribute to the isolation of the United States, which was the ultimate aim of Soviet Russia. The realization of such an aim would mean the weakening and possibly the eventual collapse of the whole group of free nations. The West German leaders thought, as I myself have always done, that since today's world is divided into two rival camps, one led by the United States and the other by the Soviet Union, it was only natural that Soviet Russia should seek to entice other free countries away from America—and unthinkable that the free countries should permit such a maneuver to succeed.

What I have said might, perhaps, lead people to think that I found ___ self in agreement with the leaders of West Germany about everything, but there was one point on which I could not see quite eye to eye with them. This was on the issue of rearmament. They expressed interest in Japan's attitude towards this question. I told them that, for the present, rearmament for Japan would have the opposite effect to that desired—that it was obviously necessary and desirable to possess a certain amount of armed strength, but to go beyond that point, on a scale that warranted the name of rearmament, would place too great a burden upon our people, would provoke national unrest and only serve to aid Communist propaganda and infiltration. The West German leaders did not seem disposed to agree with this contention: they stated that they were paying 9,000,000,000 marks annually for occupation expenses, which was enough to maintain an army of half a million men, and that they were going to rearm as soon as the result of the Nine Power Conference in London had been made clear. My visit to them took place shortly after the conclusion of that conference in London, held to reach decisions on the question of German rearmament; the Paris Agreements, evolved as a result of that conference, were later signed and the rearmament of West Germany became a fact in 1956.

On the question of the attitude of the German people towards the various armies in occupation of West Germany, someone summed it up this way: the Americans were liked, the British known for their stolidity, and the French liked least of all. This appeared to express prevailing feeling in West Germany most succinctly.

We left Frankfurt for Rome during the afternoon of October 15. Traveling in Europe for the first time in many years, I was much impressed by the extent to which air communications had been developed and the high standards of the roads in all the countries we visited; which in turn reminded me of the poor quality of the roads back in Japan. It is difficult to claim a high degree of civilization when the road network is in the condition still existing in my country.

The state of a nation's roads is not only a question of communication but one that directly affects industry and production and living standards in general. I noticed that many of the Italian roads are routed to run along the tops of hills, a practice which not only offers fine views of the country but also obviates the risk of roads being flooded. There is the added advantage of not having to take arable land out of production for the purpose of road-making, so that the authorities need to expend less money in reimbursing the owners across whose lands the roads are to pass. It seemed to me that for a country like Japan, which bears a close resemblance to Italy geographically, this idea of routing main highways to follow high ground instead of skirting the hills required to be looked into.

Another problem in which I had long been interested was that of Italian emigration. Italian immigrants, unlike our Japanese immigrants, appear to adapt themselves easily to the ways and customs of the countries in which they settle, and so are to be found flourishing in all parts of the world, forming in themselves, by reason of their remittances to relatives in Italy alone, an economic asset to their mother country. Seeing the Italians in Italy with their staid and contented outlook and demeanor, in spite of the lack of natural resources and arable land, confirmed all I had heard concerning the benefits of immigration, and I was sorry I did not have the opportunity to study the question more closely.

I met and talked with Signor Mario Scelba, the Italian prime minister, and Signor Caetano Martino, the foreign minister, in a room in the Villa Madama which commanded a magnificent view of Rome. I was told that this was the room in which cabinet meetings were held whenever they took place at the villa. It was rather like the room in which cabinet meetings are held in the official residence of the Japanese prime minister in Tokyo, except for the difference in the view from the windows, but then, of course, it was for the view that the villa was originally placed there.

After our talk Signor Scelba took me out on to the veranda and pointed out to me the various landmarks of the city. It was an impressive panorama, making one conscious of the twenty or more centuries of history which Rome has shared with the world. I also met other members of the Italian government besides the prime minister and foreign minister, and the talks followed more or less the same lines as those I had previously enjoyed with leaders in France and West Germany. One point which I stressed in the discussions with the men of the Italian government was the need for their cooperation in obtaining the agreement of the nations concerned for the early release of Japan's war criminals, and I was pleased to receive their assurance that they were prepared to do everything in their power to achieve this. I have always doubted the wisdom of the policy of continuing to incarcerate war criminals in jail over long periods of time. It only serves to perpetuate in the minds of the people the memory of the horrors of a nightmarish war, and the enmity which the vanquished feel towards their victors. It may even have the effect among the ignorant of making martyrs and heroes of the war criminals concerned. From the humanitarian point of view also, I felt that the men concerned should be released, since one may be safe in assuming that they have, by their confinement, more than atoned for whatever they have done.

The Italians have taken the view that it was now time that all matters pertaining to past history should be closed and proclaimed a general amnesty, so that there was at that time no one held in prison on such charges in Italy. However, there were still at that date fifty thousand Italians in Soviet Russia whose fate was unknown. About sixty thousand Italians had disappeared into the Soviet Union during the Second World War, of whom only ten thousand had been repatriated; the remaining fifty thousand had not been accounted for. This is not a large number compared with that of our own people who have perished or are still languishing in Soviet Russia (and who also have not been accounted for), and the Italians promised us their aid in the event of Japan's undertaking some such project as endeavoring to send a commission of inquiry into the fate of the missing surrendered personnel. I need not add that I found myself in complete agreement with the Italian leaders over the question of the attitude to be adopted towards the enigmatic Soviet Union.

On October 20 I was received in audience by Pope Pius XII at Castel Gandolfo, the papal villa on the outskirts of Rome. His Holiness had just recovered from a severe illness, but seemed in excellent spirits. I congratulated him first of all on his restoration to good health, and then thanked him for the kind reception given by the papal court to Japan's crown prince Akihito on the occasion of His Highness's visit. Replying, the pope inquired after Japan's imperial family and, upon my answering that they gave us Japanese nothing but cause for rejoicing, said that he prayed for their continued well-being.

I then brought up the question of Japan's war criminals and told His Holiness that there were at that time some seven hundred convicted war criminals still held in Tokyo's Sugamo prison; that holding them in further custody only served to prolong memories of the war and was unwise even from a purely political point of view; that it was my intention to approach the British and American authorities on the matter during my trip, but that I particularly desired the active support of His Holiness in view of the enormous moral prestige which he enjoyed in the world today. The pope promised to extend his support to my purpose, and I withdrew from the audience with an impression of him that did not belie the great international prestige that he enjoyed.

# 12

## Old Friends in Britain and the United States

I departed from Rome airport on the afternoon of October 21 after exchanging farewells with Prime Minister Scelba, his wife, and other Italian officials who came to see my party off. The plane taking us to London, the next stop on my tour, was a turbo-prop of the "Discovery" type, then the pride of the British European Airways. It was new, clean, and comfortable. Clouds obscured our vision as we rose into the air and continued to do so throughout the flight to London, where we arrived at about six in the evening. But there was no end to the people I was able to see during the next week that I spent in Britain's capital, which I had not visited since prewar days.

During a week crowded with appointments and talks, one engagement stood out: I was given the opportunity to address some hundred members of both Houses of the British Parliament in the palace of Westminster on the afternoon of October 26. I spoke for about thirty minutes, and said that, as in the days of the Anglo-Japanese Alliance, both Great Britain and Japan were again faced with a common menace—this time the menace of international communism; that it was clear that the aim of Soviet Russia was to add South-East Asia to the circle of her satellites, and that it was my desire that Great Britain and Japan should achieve a closer relationship and work together to remove this common menace. I added that if there were anything that might be thought to deter such a spirit of cooperation from being achieved, it was the fears entertained by the British towards the Japanese as possible rivals in the field of world trade, but that a closer inspection of actual economic conditions in Japan should show that a state of rivalry need not, by any means, exist between the two countries even in the delicate matter of trade and world markets. After my speech, questions were asked concerning the payment by Japan of an indemnity to British war prisoners, communist China, Japan's labor laws, and other issues, but I felt that in the main the questions were advanced in a friendly spirit and from a genuine desire to understand the actual state of affairs in Japan. One lady member of Parliament, who had, I gathered, just returned from a tour of inspection of Japan and its textile industry, posed some questions which could have been taken to infringe on what might be termed the limits of ordinary friendliness, but I could see that she was given friendly advice from other members present to desist.

On October 27 I was entertained at dinner by Sir Winston Churchill, the British prime minister. The speech which he made at the end of the meal has remained in my memory. He said that he had heard that I had a reputation in Japan of being a somewhat tough character, but that he was glad that the dinner had given him the opportunity of seeing for himself that I possessed other and more respectable qualities as well; that he was sure that he was not alone in welcoming me to Great Britain, since there were present at the dinner representatives of the opposition and British trade unions besides members of the government and the Conservative Party. He went on to say that he had no intention of discussing the merits or demerits of the abrogation of the Anglo-Japanese Alliance, since he was not in the cabinet at that time, but that he could at least say that if the alliance had continued in existence, world history would have taken a different course.

Sir Winston continued in the same vein, but what struck me most was the way in which Britain's prime minister gave such free expression to his own opinions. I had heard that to refer to the former Anglo-Japanese Alliance was taboo in British political circles, but such inhibitions appeared to offer no obstacles to Sir Winston Churchill. No doubt he was adept at receiving foreign politicians and diplomats, but I could sense that his attitude towards us had nothing of formality or show about it but was based on kindness, pure and simple. For instance, he asked me after dinner whether I knew Mr. Clement Attlee, then the leader of the British Labor Party, and when I said I did not, immediately brought Mr. Attlee over and introduced us. This gesture I admired from another point of view: democratic government may consist of controversy between opposing political parties, but can be carried on successfully only if there exists a basic understanding between the rival parties as to the final aims of government, the happiness of the people, and so forth, and if the men forming the parties are free to mix with each other, to dine together, and to form friendships transcending party politics. In this matter the dinner given by Sir Winston Churchill gave me some idea of the workings of British politics as well as of the personality of our host.

I had previously spent some years in London as a young diplomat and later had been assigned there as ambassador, and I have always entertained

towards the British capital a feeling of friendly intimacy. It was a great pleasure, therefore, during my visit to be able to renew acquaintance with many
old friends, including Lord Hankey, Sir Robert Craigie, Sir Edward Crowe,
General F. S. G. Piggott, and others who had either served for long periods
in the British Foreign Service in Japan or whom I had met during my years
in the United Kingdom. Worthy of special mention was the audience given
me by Queen Elizabeth II at Buckingham Palace on October 26. Only Sir
Anthony Eden, the foreign secretary, was in attendance, and I recall being
very much impressed by Her Majesty's manner, in which a natural dignity
and youthfulness of appearance seemed so well blended. I was also impressed by Sir Anthony's behavior towards the queen; there was in it a mix-
ture of respect and affection, which I am told the British people universally
entertain towards their sovereign, and seeing Her Majesty in person made
me realize why this was so. I was also glad of the opportunity which my
visit afforded me to see once again Mrs. Neville Chamberlain, the widow of
the former prime minister. We Japanese should remember that Mr. Neville
Chamberlain, prior to the outbreak of the Second World War, placed greater
importance and emphasis on Anglo-Japanese relations than on British relations with Germany, and had relieved Sir Robert Craigie of his diplomatic
assignment to the United States expressly to send him to Japan to see what
could be done about improving Anglo-Japanese relations.

In actual truth, while I had been looking forward to renewing old friendships in London, I had not felt entirely happy about undertaking the trip in
an official capacity, there being at that time many questions, mainly of an
economic nature, pending between the two countries. I quickly discovered
upon my arrival that my fears in that connection were unfounded. Friends
were still friends even where economic issues and public affairs were concerned, and their kindly intervention gave me hardly an unpleasant moment during my entire stay. I recall my meeting with General Arthur Ernest
Percival, who had been the commander of the British garrison at Singapore
at the time of its surrender to the Japanese forces. General Percival came to
see me as a representative of the Ex-Prisoners of War in the Far East and
urged a speedy settlement of the claim for compensation for British prisoners of war who had suffered at the hands of the Japanese Army, as provided for under Article 16 of the San Francisco Peace Treaty. Japan had originally intended to meet such claims out of our funds deposited in the Bank
of Switzerland, but the Swiss government—which had represented Japanese
interests during the Pacific War—declined to take the necessary steps to re-
imburse the claimants, on the ground that there were payments due to
them from Japan for previous advances made to the Allied powers on our
behalf. I could therefore only assure General Percival that payment of damages had been guaranteed by the Japanese government as part of the obligations imposed on my country by the peace treaty, and that we would do

everything in our power to see that restitution was made. Sir Norman Roberts had meanwhile been sent to Tokyo by the British Foreign Office with the rank of minister to deal with the question, and I am glad to add that the resultant negotiations between the two governments ended to the full satisfaction of Sir Norman Roberts shortly after my return to Japan.

There were other matters which needed attention. These consisted mainly of grievances against Japan or the Japanese such as unfair trade competition by our manufacturers; allegations regarding unethical use of British industrial designs and trademarks; excessive Japanese government aid to shipping, shipbuilding, and other industries connected with exports; the establishment of shipping routes without the sanction of the Japan-Homeward Freight Conference; and so forth. To these complaints and charges my reply was that, with postwar legislation regarding the conditions of Japanese labor making it obligatory for our manufacturers to provide a high standard of welfare for our workers, the dumping of goods and other forms of unfair trade competition were no longer possible, and that even in cases such as textiles, where competition between the two countries might seem unavoidable, British and Japanese manufacturers should cooperate in developing markets through a judicious arrangement of the outlets and types of goods to be reserved to each country.

At a meeting called for the purpose of hearing such British grievances, Foreign Secretary Eden, in introducing me, remarked that I had come to London as Japanese ambassador shortly after his own appointment to the post of foreign secretary before the Second World War, and that we had remained friends ever since. Mr. R. A. Butler, then the chancellor of the exchequer, rose to say that at a time when the foreign currency reserve in Great Britain was in an alarming state of depletion, the Japanese government had deposited £20,000,000 in the Bank of England as guarantee for the payment of the capital and interest of Japanese loans raised in the United Kingdom, and that I was at the head of that government. These words by the two respected statesmen did much to improve the atmosphere of the gathering, so that the following talk was conducted in a spirit of friendly persuasion. Speaking of Sir A. Eden, I recall paying a visit to him at the Foreign Office and newspapermen crowding around anxious to get a photograph of the two of us together, whereupon Sir Anthony became exasperated and shouted to them to go away, which reminded me of similar experiences that had befallen me in Japan,

I departed from Great Britain aboard the *Queen Mary* on October 28, bound for the United States and the last stage of my tour, and during the five days that elapsed before we reached New York on November 2, I was able to recover completely from the fatigue engendered by my crowded days in Europe. The ship's newspaper, the *Ocean Times,* on October 30 carried the news that Japan had been granted the right to negotiate with other countries concerning trade and tariff agreements, which was a first step towards being admitted to GATT, and this naturally pleased me. Upon our arrival in New York we were immediately taken to the house of Mr. John D. Rockefeller III outside the city. It was the sort of residence that one would find hard to duplicate, or even to think of, in Japan. It covered so many acres that I was told it took Mr. Rockefeller more than half an hour by car to visit one of his relatives living within the grounds. Included in this spacious domain were pastures where cattle grazed, milking cattle and beef cattle confined to separate pastures. They seemed very contented in such beautiful surroundings and I suggested to Mr. Rockefeller that I would like to be one of them, upon hearing which he laughed and remarked that if I cared to go down to the cellar of the house, I would find them hanging from the ceiling in the form of beef.

Mr. John D. Rockefeller III is, of course, the grandson of the great John D. Rockefeller, and since he has accepted the position of president of the Japan Society in New York City, numerous Japanese business men and politicians of note, including such prominent public men as Mr. Hatoyama Ichirō and Mr. Shigemitsu Mamoru, have been placed under an obligation to him as the kindest and most genial of hosts. He and his wife have visited Japan on several occasions, and cultural enterprises in my country—including one of such scale and scope as the founding of International House in Tokyo—are indebted to him for his generosity and support.

On November 5 a dinner was given to welcome me by the Japan Society at the Waldorf-Astoria Hotel, to which some fifteen hundred people were invited, with speeches by, among others, Senator Alexander Wiley, chairman of the Senate Foreign Relations Committee, and Senator J. William Fulbright. I was told that Japanese residents of New York had never before been present at a dinner-party of such distinction and magnificence, and it was clear that the occasion had been made possible only through the prestige and personal efforts of Mr. Rockefeller III as head of the Japan Society.

It was also a personal pleasure to me to be able to meet General Douglas MacArthur again during my stay in New York. Now president of the Remington-Rand Company, the former Supreme Commander for the Allied Powers in Japan was as interested in Japan as ever, and was most sympathetic when I outlined to him the progress achieved on the work of reconstruction and rehabilitation there. I also had the opportunity of discussing old times with General Charles A. Willoughby, who had been an assistant chief of staff under General MacArthur in Japan. Lunches were given me by Mayor Robert F. Wagner of New York City, and Mr. Thomas E. Dewey, then the governor of New York State—occasions when I was able to meet and talk with many influential leaders of American opinion. Mr. Sawada Renzō, Japan's ambassador to the United Nations, also gave a cocktail party. I further delivered a speech before the Council of Foreign Affairs, and made a broadcast for the Columbia Broadcasting System. After which busy day in New York, I left with my party for Washington on November 7.

The prime object of my visit to the nation's capital was to meet leaders of the Eisenhower administration, and not so much to talk with them with reference to any specific question or issues as to explain to them the actual political and economic state of affairs in Japan and so, I hoped, promote better understanding between our two countries. However, a few weeks before my visit, a group of officials headed by Mr. Aichi Kiichi, Japan's minister of international trade and industry, had arrived in Washington to discuss such problems as the purchase of surplus agricultural products from America, and the settlement of our obligation to the United States incurred through the so-called GARIOA funds, with the government authorities concerned. This procedure was adopted because, my own stay in Washington being necessarily short, it was thought desirable that these experts should precede me and get through a certain amount of preliminary work connected with questions likely to be raised in the course of my talks with high-ranking officials of the U.S. government. Actually, the advance party had done their work so well that discussions of the questions with which they were concerned had already got past the preliminary stage by the time I arrived.

I was able, while in Washington, to see President Dwight D. Eisenhower; Vice President Richard Nixon; Mr. John Foster Dulles, the secretary of state; Mr. Charles E. Wilson, the secretary of defense; Mr. George M. Humphreys, the secretary of the treasury; Mr. Sinclair Weeks, the secretary of commerce; Mr. Harold Stassen, the foreign operations administrator; and other leading members of the U.S. cabinet. I also met Mr. Eugene R. Black, president of the World Bank, and was able to have talks with the British and French ambassadors in Washington. Most fortunately, I was given the opportunity of meeting Senator Jose P. Laurel of the Philippines Republic, who happened to be in Washington, and was able to discuss with him the question of Japan-Philippines reparations. I would add that no feature of my visit comforted me so much as meeting Mr. William Richards Castle and Mr. Joseph C. Grew again, both former U.S. ambassadors to Japan, who welcomed me with the same kindness I had always remembered.

While the gist of my conversations and discussions with members of the administration was given in a statement issued jointly by President Eisenhower and myself, I was given the opportunity to present my views concerning the development of South-East Asia at a luncheon at the famed National Press Club in Washington. This was attended by some three hundred newspapermen from all parts of the world, and many questions followed my speech. However, owing no doubt to the masterly manner in which the proceedings were conducted by the chairman, I received a good deal of applause, and there was none of that cantankerous feeling in the air such as is inseparable from meetings with the press in Japan. The text of my address will probably be found in the relevant archives.

So far as my joint statement with President Eisenhower was concerned, I wanted above all to outline a policy whereby the United States should recognize Japan's status in Asia as an independent country, with the two nations cooperating on an equal footing for the maintenance and promotion of peace in Asia. Next, I desired to make it clear that Japan was ready to do all in her power to contribute to the economic development of the free countries in Asia and also that our two governments had reached an understanding to the effect that the economic welfare of Japan was a question of importance to the free world in general, so that while the United States would be ready to consider any means for the improvement of the economic status of the Japanese people, Japan herself would do her best to promote overseas trade and strengthen her economic position in the world. In short, we hoped to indicate in the statement that the economic development of Asia was the best means of defending the freedom and peace of Asia.

Negotiations in regard to the purchase of surplus agricultural products from the United States were brought to a satisfactory conclusion through the efforts of Mr. Aichi and his party and the authorities concerned on both sides. On this point the position was clear: there was a surplus of agricultural products in the United States, while Japan was in need of foodstuffs to supplement her domestic production. It was most desirable that Japan should be able to purchase the necessary basic food without depleting her scarce foreign currency reserve; but, at the same time, since the purchase of U.S. products had to be included in the normal quota of goods imported into Japan, it was feared that it might affect imports of rice and other foodstuffs from South-East Asia. However, it was eventually found that this would not be the case, and since the negotiations were going so well, I decided to take the step of closing with the American offer.

At the end of a fortnight's stay in the United States, I returned to Japan on November 17. Apart from many pleasant memories garnered along the days and miles since I had left my country, and a considerable gain in knowledge, one thing stood out from all the rest of the impressions received during the journey. That was the way in which I had been met everywhere by demands for the payment of money due—rather in the manner, I felt, of the president of a shady company. In France it was the question of an old loan which the city of Tokyo had raised in France; in Italy, the return of her holdings frozen in the Yokohama Specie Bank; in Great Britain, the indemnity due to British prisoners of war; and in the United States, the GARIOA funds.

I have always held that foreign debts must be paid at no matter what sacrifice to my country. Japanese credit once ranked with that of Finland as among the highest in the world. It would never do to let that credit be impaired after it had been built up through so many years of labor and sacrifice by our predecessors. For that reason I always answered inquirers by saying that Japan would pay whenever such just demands were presented to me, and I am happy to say that at least the indemnity to British prisoners of war was taken care of shortly after my return. Before I could devote my attention to the rest, I found myself out of power.

# 13

## The Postwar Constitution

I now propose to review in some detail the reforms and changes that took place during my tenure of office in the occupation era and the period immediately thereafter. Some of these have already been touched upon in preceding pages, as they necessarily had to be in order to complete the outline of my postwar career and unfolding events, but this could not be done at any length if the narrative were to present a coherent whole. At the same time, however, to omit the details of the many important changes which came to Japan in the wake of the Pacific conflict would give an incomplete picture of a climactic period in my country's history, and convey an impression wanting in exactitude, not perhaps of my own part in events but of the history of the Allied occupation, a defect which I now wish to remedy.

One of the factors on which sufficient emphasis was perhaps not placed in earlier chapters was the attitude of the American occupation authorities towards Japan and their task in that country. As I have already made clear, there was no room for doubt concerning the goodwill which they bore towards the Japanese people; nevertheless they did have very definite ideas concerning the policy to be pursued in the occupation of my country. This fact did not arise from individual tastes and convictions. That policy had already been determined by the Allied powers as represented by the United States, which had given authority to members of the U.S. forces to occupy Japan to the end that the policy agreed on should be carried out. From which it follows that whatever attitudes and courses the policy might dictate, the men within General MacArthur's headquarters in Tokyo had no option but to conform. With Allied policy in itself, as outlined in the document entitled "United States Initial Post-Surrender Policy for Japan" issued by the American president to the Supreme Commander for the Allied Powers on August 29, 1945, we Japanese—or, in fact, any postwar Japanese government in its senses—had no cause to quarrel. The ultimate objectives of the Allied occupation of Japan, as set forth in Part I of that document were:

> (a) to ensure that Japan will not again become a menace to the United States, or to the peace and security of the world;
> (b) to bring about the eventual establishment of a peaceful and responsible government which will respect the rights of other States and will support the objectives of the United States as reflected in the Charter of the United Nations. The United States desires that this government should conform as closely as may be to principles of democratic self-government, but it is not the responsibility of the Allied Powers to impose upon Japan any form of government not supported by the freely expressed will of the people. . . .

These objectives were, in essence, our own, from the moment the war had ended. Thus the fact emerged that, from the point of view of objectives, at least, we Japanese and the occupation were in agreement.

There was, however, the relationship between the occupation authorities and the Japanese government to be considered. As stated in Part II of the document cited above, the Japanese government was permitted, under instructions from the supreme commander, "to exercise the normal powers of government in matters of domestic administration." But this was purely through the "desire of the United States to attain its objectives with a minimum commitment of its forces and resources," and it did not "commit the Supreme Commander to support the Emperor or any other Japanese governmental authority in opposition to evolutionary changes looking toward the attainment of United States objectives"; the policy being "to use the existing form of government in Japan, not to support it." Moreover, it is further stipulated in the same paragraph of the document that

> changes in the form of government initiated by the Japanese people or government in the direction of modifying its feudal and authoritarian tendencies are to be permitted and favored. In the event that the effectuation of such changes involves the use of force by the Japanese people or government against persons opposed thereto, the Supreme Commander should intervene only when necessary to ensure the security of his forces and the attainment of all other objectives of the Occupation.

In other words, the Japanese government was not sure of protection by the occupation forces even in the case of revolution, should it happen that those concerned in it could convince the occupation authorities that it was all in line with occupation policy: The Japanese government under the occupation was, therefore, simply there on sufferance.

It should be admitted at once, however, that there was in the main nothing in the presidential instructions issued to the supreme commander to which anyone could take exception. The limitations on self-government were common-sense precautionary measures that any armed forces in occupation of enemy territory, charged with the overall administration of such territory, would be wise to impose and which had probably always been taken by such a force in similar circumstances, whether set forth in instructions or not—with the sole difference, perhaps, that no such force had up to that time been charged with the task of democratizing the territory concerned according to its own lights. On the other hand we, as the Japanese government, were not in office simply because we were permitted by the occupation to exist; we had our task as a government for which we were answerable alike to our emperor, our people, and our history. In a sense, we might have found the task confronting us considerably easier had we found our own aims to be diametrically opposed to those of the occupation, so that we could concentrate our efforts on thwarting occupation policy at every turn. As events turned out, the difficulties experienced by both sides sprang mainly from the fact that our aims were the same.

One might say that there is no shortcut to success in any sort of work that is worth undertaking. The occupation, with all the power and authority behind its operation, was hampered by its lack of knowledge of the people it had come to govern, and even more so, perhaps, by its generally happy ignorance of the amount of requisite knowledge it lacked. A great deal had been written about Japan by American experts during the war and during the occupation years, and, as in similar cases, expert opinion was considered sufficient. We, on our part, could do nothing without the prior approval of the occupation authorities, and here again, as so often happens, our experience was found to clash with the expert knowledge possessed by the occupation. It was also obvious that to act with the aid and approval of the occupation authorities was, besides being the only way, the quickest to effect any measure desired and so, through long series of negotiations, the work of reform—whether idealistic or not from the American point of view—progressed.

We did not find much to propose to the occupation authorities, for the zeal of the men and women of the occupation took care of practically everything, so that it was sufficient (and rather more than sufficient) for us to take the directives as they were issued one after another, and to strive to assert ourselves, as the government, whenever they seemed to err on the side of impracticability. The impetus came from the occupation; for the final form that was given that impetus, we at least did what we could to realize what seemed best, according to our views at that time.

The revision of the Constitution was perhaps the most important single reform undertaken after the termination of the Pacific War. That the need for it would arise sooner or later became clear the moment Japan accepted the Potsdam Declaration. But, at the time I entered the Higashikuni cabinet as foreign minister, the state of mind in which everyone had been left by the surrender, the directives flowing from GHQ, and the general business of winding up the war, left no one in a condition to give thought to a matter of such major consequence to the nation as revision of the Constitution.

Eventually, shortly after the formation of the Shidehara cabinet in October 1945, Prince Konoe was given a post in the office of the grand keeper of the imperial seals, and it became known that the office was about to begin work—with the assistance of the prince—on preliminary studies necessary for the revision of the Constitution, a development reportedly due to a suggestion made to Prince Konoe by General MacArthur when the prince was minister without portfolio in the Higashikuni cabinet, but of this nothing certain is known. There existed a feeling that such an important matter of state as the revision of the Constitution was clearly within the province of the government and not of the Office of the Grand Keeper of the Imperial Seals, which existed solely for the transaction of business connected with the palace; at any rate, since it was now clear that the office had embarked on the work of preparation, it was thought that the government should also institute similar preparatory steps, and a decision to form an informal committee to report on the question of constitutional revision, to be formed within the cabinet, was decided upon at a cabinet meeting on October 13, with Dr. Matsumoto Jōji, minister without portfolio, as minister in charge.

The reaching of this decision was influenced directly by a suggestion to the same effect given by General MacArthur to Baron Shidehara during a conversation which took place between them when the latter paid his first official visit as prime minister to the supreme commander on October 11. The work of revision proceeded from that date until November 3, 1946, when the new Constitution was finally promulgated under my first cabinet—a period of a year and one month during which a great deal of discussion took place within the committee and with GHQ, and the issues concerned were debated point by point by the Privy Council, the House of Representatives, and the House of Peers, involving numerous alterations to the original draft.

When the committee was first formed under the Shidehara cabinet, however, the idea was not so much to begin work with the immediate revision of the Constitution in view as to examine points in the old prewar Constitution that called for consideration, so that when the necessity for revision should arise the government would be prepared for it.

The Constitutional Problem Investigation Committee came into being on October 25, 1945, in accordance with the cabinet decision of October 13, and its first meeting was held on October 27. Its members were Dr. Miyazawa Toshiyoshi of Tokyo Imperial University; Dr. Kiyomiya Shirō of Tōhoku Imperial University; Dr. Kawamura Matasuke of Kyūshū Imperial University; Mr. Narahashi Wataru, the director of the Bureau of Legislation;

Mr. Irie Toshio, chief of the first section of the bureau; Mr. Satō Tatsuo, chief of the second section; and Mr. Ishiguro Takeshige, chief secretary of the Privy Council, with Drs. Shimizu Kiyoshi and Minobe Tatsukichi of the Imperial Academy and Dr. Nomura Junji, professor emeritus of Tokyo Imperial University, as advisers.

As I have stated, it was clear from the moment we accepted the terms of the Potsdam Declaration that Japan would be required at some time to revise the Constitution. But the general feeling in government circles was that a change of such importance should be brought about with all requisite and proper care and study; or in other words that undue haste in the matter was not only unnecessary, but clearly to be avoided. Given the condition of unrest prevalent in the nation at that time, this was obviously the sensible attitude to adopt. The government formed a committee to take up the preparatory work for the revision of the Constitution in order to indicate our willingness to consider the matter, and in view of the demand for revision which one sensed was gaining strength within GHQ and among certain sections of our people. It quickly became apparent, however, that we were not to be allowed to take too long a time over the task, so that the discussions on the question gradually came to take on less the character of inquiry and more that of actual drafting. Even so, the aim of the government at that time continued to be to introduce no more changes than were thought absolutely necessary.

This attitude on the part of the government was made clear by Dr. Matsumoto, the minister in charge, in the budget committee of the House of Representatives on December 8 of the same year. On that occasion he emphasized certain points, which were at that time termed the Four Principles of Revision. These were: (1) that no change was to be made to the principle of sovereignty residing in the emperor; (2) that the powers of the Diet were to be increased and certain restrictions imposed on whatever was, until then, considered the imperial prerogative; (3) that ministers of state were to be held directly responsible to the Diet and for all matters connected with the state, instead of to the emperor, and only for matters of state within their particular province, as formerly; and (4) that the rights and liberties of the subject were to be given more protection, and stronger safeguards were to be erected against their infringement. In brief, it was the desire of the government to satisfy the clauses in the Potsdam Declaration dealing with the democratization of Japan without altering the fundamental principles of national government laid down in the Meiji constitution.

Several drafts were drawn up by the committee along those lines. Meanwhile, political parties and other such groups were producing their own versions of a revised constitution, but Dr. Matsumoto had his final draft ready by January 1946, based upon the findings of the committee of which he was in charge, and referred this to the cabinet. I do not remember all the details of his draft version, but it was a modified form of the Meiji constitution, in which, for instance, the clause stating that "the person of the Emperor is sacred and inviolable" had been changed to "the person of the Emperor is most exalted and inviolable," and so on. Dr. Matsumoto explained that, since a great deal of alteration was bound to be demanded from all sides once the draft was made public, it was prudent to introduce as little change in the original draft as possible. This draft was forwarded to General MacArthur's headquarters in February 1946.

Possibly prompted by the fact that this draft was widely reported in the Japanese press, General MacArthur instructed General Courtney Whitney to prepare a draft constitution in the shortest possible time. The occupation authorities must have thought that, since our draft did not differ very conspicuously from the old Meiji constitution, the only course was to prepare another, incorporating their own ideas, and show it to us as an example of the kind of thing they wanted. The work of drafting the GHQ version took one week.

On February 13, officials of GHQ came to see us by appointment, at the official residence of the foreign minister. There were present, on the Japanese side, myself as foreign minister, Dr. Matsumoto, and Mr. Shirasu Jirō, who was then deputy chief of the Central Liaison Office. The GHQ officials were headed by General Courtney Whitney and included Colonel Charles L. Kades, among others. General Whitney informed me that GHQ was not satisfied with the Japanese draft of the revised constitution, and that he had brought with him a model draft, blueprinted within GHQ, and that he wanted us to turn out a version based upon this draft as soon as possible. He then handed us several copies of the draft and went on to say that it would meet with the approval both of the U.S. government and the Far Eastern Commission; that General MacArthur had given much thought to the question of the position of the emperor, which could best be safeguarded by revising our constitution along lines laid down in the model version drafted by GHQ; and that if this was not done, GHQ could not answer for whatever might happen to the emperor. He added that this was not an order, but that GHQ desired most earnestly that the Japanese government should forward to General MacArthur's headquarters as soon as possible a draft constitution incorporating the basic principles and form of the GHQ model version.

After this statement, the GHQ officials went for a walk in the garden in order to give us time to look over the draft thus presented to us. Dr. Matsumoto began reading it with great attention, and I too had a look. The document began with the words "We, the Japanese people," indicating that it was the people who were framing the constitution and not the emperor. And it was stated in Chapter 1 that the emperor was "the symbol of the State." Also, in this original draft, the Diet was to be composed of one chamber only. After they returned from the garden, Dr. Matsumoto asked the GHQ officials some questions, and then informed them that we would read over the contents of the draft carefully and give our considered opinion later. General Whitney and his companions then left.

As indicated by the few words already quoted, the GHQ draft was of a revolutionary nature. The government was not prepared to frame a new constitution based upon such a model and started negotiations with GHQ to see if there was not some means of coming to a compromise. General MacArthur's headquarters remained adamant, however, regarding the basic principles of revision. This being the position, Dr. Matsumoto gave a detailed explanation of the situation at a cabinet meeting on February 19, at which various members of the cabinet expressed their views; two or three being absolutely opposed to acceptance of the GHQ version of the constitution as a working model. No solution being found, it was finally decided that Baron Shidehara should visit GHQ personally and discuss the matter, after which the cabinet would consider again what was to be done.

Baron Shidehara accordingly paid a visit to General MacArthur on February 21 to ascertain the supreme commander's own views concerning the question of revision. From the account of the interview given by the prime minister at a cabinet meeting held the next day, it seems that the general had stated that the welfare of Japan was foremost in his mind and that, particularly since he had met the emperor, it had been one of his primary concerns to safeguard the position of the throne; but that feeling within the Far Eastern Commission towards Japan was still of unwonted severity, most of the countries represented—especially the Soviet Union and Australia—being apprehensive that Japan might become powerful enough in time to make reprisals against the Allies; that one of the purposes of the revised constitution, as drafted within GHQ, was to secure the throne against the possibility of drastic reforms being proposed and put into effect by the Far Eastern Commission; and that the two main points to be stressed in the draft were the definition of the emperor as the symbol of the state and the renunciation-of-war clause. Having thus reported, Baron Shidehara stated he had received the impression that, apart from these two points, there might still be room for compromise on others.

However, when Dr. Matsumoto went to see General Whitney at GHQ on the afternoon of the same day to ascertain to what extent alteration in the text of the GHQ version was permissible, he was told that the version formed a coherent body of laws and that, except for the substitution, if necessary, of a bicameral for the unicameral system of parliament, alteration in part of the text would affect the whole. General MacArthur's headquarters was taking a far stiffer line in regard to the GHQ version than was expected by us, and there was little to be done about it. Dr. Matsumoto accordingly set to work to frame a constitution based on the GHQ model with the assistance of the councilor of the Bureau of Legislation. But it then appeared that GHQ wanted this task finished in about the same time that had been needed to produce their model version, and a completed Japanese draft was accordingly submitted to GHQ on March 4, without an English translation, which there was no time to prepare. The new Japanese version was then gone over in the Government Section of General MacArthur's headquarters by American and Japanese experts, the work taking all night and the best part of March 5. The cabinet met on the morning of the fifth, and Dr. Matsumoto gave his report of what had taken place the previous day. The final draft of the new constitution, as finally approved by GHQ, reached us in batches while the cabinet was meeting, and we discussed it point by point. It contained much that the cabinet as a whole could not bring itself to agree to, particularly regarding the position of the emperor, and many members expressed themselves freely on the point. It was only when it had been ascertained that His Majesty had been heard to say that it would be unwise to delay the cabinet decision concerning the revised constitution more than was unavoidable, and that there seemed to be nothing particularly wrong about the definition in it of the position of the emperor, that even dissident members were forced to withdraw their opposition and the conclusion was reached that we should have to accept the final version sent to us from GHQ, which was regarded as the only means of preserving the throne. After the meeting Baron Shidehara was given audience by the emperor and received the imperial assent to the draft, as also the permission for the issuance of an imperial rescript regarding the revision of the constitution. As it was known that GHQ wanted the draft published as soon as possible, the Bureau of Legislation worked throughout the night to prepare a summary for publication, which we went over at a cabinet meeting held the following day.

The question of why GHQ was in such haste to complete steps for the revision of the constitution remains unanswered. To my thinking, one of the main reasons for this was a sincere desire on the part of General MacArthur to make secure the position of the throne. It was clear from what the general told me himself that he had been very much impressed by the personality of the emperor. But, apart from this, he was fully aware of the fact that it was solely due to the prestige enjoyed by the emperor among the Japanese people that the Allied forces had been permitted to make a bloodless landing on the Japanese mainland and he made no secret of being a warm supporter of the imperial regime. This fact would naturally cause him to be apprehensive of possible moves in the Far Eastern Commission by countries like the Soviet Union and Australia, and he must have wanted all the more to have ready a new constitution for Japan which would be beyond criticism, even by the representatives of those countries. His haste can be understood when we remember that the Far Eastern Commission had come

into being as a result of a foreign ministers' conference held in Moscow towards the end of the year before, and that its first meeting took place at
Washington on February 26. The point was stressed whenever a difference
of opinion occurred between the Japanese side and GHQ over questions of
the prerogatives or functions of the emperor in drafting the new constitution: we were told time and again that it was to the advantage of His
Majesty, in the event of the draft being laid before the Far Eastern Commission, for us to comply with the wishes of GHQ.

There was also the fact that a general election was due on April 10 of that
year, and GHQ must have been understandably anxious to have the draft
published as early as possible in order to give the Japanese people time to
think over the terms of the new constitution and to express their opinion of
it by their votes. The Potsdam Declaration stated that the government of
Japan was to be established according to the freely expressed will of the
Japanese people. And the general election must have seemed an excellent
opportunity to consult that will—especially so in the case of General
MacArthur himself, who had always favored an early peace and termination
of the occupation, for which he declared in March of the following year that
Japan was ready. All of which leads one to think that the first postwar general election of April 1946 was to MacArthur the appropriate moment to
hear the opinion of the Japanese people on the proposed new constitution.
The fact remains, however, that there was a good deal of the American spirit
of enterprise in the undertaking of such a fundamental piece of reform as
revision of the constitution within two months of Japan's defeat; as for
wishing to see that reform realized in so short a period as half a year or a
year, one can only put it down to that impulsiveness common to military
people of all countries. We should remember that there were all these factors at work at that time, as a result of which, as well as others, the Japanese Constitution was revised in the way it was.

Thus it came to pass that on March 6, 1946, a summary of the draft of the
proposed revised constitution was published. In actual fact, what was proposed was not anything in the nature of a revision of the Meiji constitution
but the substitution of a completely new constitution for the old, or, as was
stated in the imperial rescript issued for the occasion, "a fundamental revision." But the procedure followed was that laid down in Article 73 of the
old Constitution for the revision of that document, according to which the
bill is referred to the imperial Diet by imperial command. An imperial rescript was accordingly issued, following which the government prepared to
submit the bill for revision to the Diet. The summary of the draft was published in the newspapers on March 7 and, in view of its contents, the public commotion it aroused was only to be expected. The definition of the emperor as the symbol of the state was one of the points most debated, as it
had been during meetings of the cabinet, and, as I have already stated, it

was only because we had heard that the emperor had himself expressed the view that there was nothing in it to which exception should be taken that we had brought ourselves to accept it.

The next point most discussed was the clause concerned with the renunciation of war. I myself was in favor of it, for the reason that, since it was an accepted idea among the Allied powers that Japan was a militaristic nation, it was most necessary to take steps indicating that it was not, for which purpose the insertion of the renunciation-of-war clause in the new constitution seemed to me one of the most effective. It has been said by some that it was Baron Shidehara, the prime minister, who first proposed the clause, General MacArthur also seems to have testified to the same effect before the U.S. Senate on his return, but I have the impression that it was General MacArthur who suggested it to the baron in some conversation between them, to which Baron Shidehara could very easily have replied with enthusiasm.

To go back a little, the first general election to take place in Japan following the Pacific conflict was held, as planned, on April 10, 1946. It was distinguished from all former elections by the fact that many men belonging to conservative groups had been purged from public life by order of GHQ and so prevented from taking any part; the vote was given to women for the first time, and the age limit for voters lowered, so that some twenty-three million new electors were added to the fourteen million persons previously enfranchised; and, lastly, that Japan's Communists were permitted to participate freely in a general election for the first time in our history and made use of this newly acquired freedom to attack the throne.

The results of the election gave the Liberal Party 140 seats, making it the largest party in the Lower House; the Progressives 94 seats; the Socialists 92; and the Communists only 5. It is to be noted that all the above-mentioned parties, with the exception of the Communists, as well as other political groups which were formed in various parts of the country to take a hand in the election, favored the continuance of the throne, in marked contrast to the Japanese Communist Party.

After the election, Baron Shidehara became the president of the Progressive Party, but his cabinet resigned on April 22, and my first cabinet came into being one month later on May 21. Thus it happened that the task of revising the constitution became one of my main responsibilities during the opening months of my tenure of office as prime minister.

The bill providing for the revision of the nation's basic law was placed before the House of Representatives on June 25, 1946. Following my speech introducing the measures, questions were immediately forthcoming, all of which centered upon possible changes in Japan's imperial structure of government as a result of the provision vesting sovereign power in the people instead of the emperor, and the clause renouncing war. Diet members of both the Right and Left focused their questions mainly on these two points in the document throughout the subsequent debates. On the one hand, the Socialists wanted the fact that sovereign power resided in the people stated more emphatically in the new constitution; on the other, many members of the Liberal and Progressive Parties had during the election campaign committed themselves not to change the structure of the state and sought guarantees that none would take place.

In my first reply to questions in the House, I stated that we had all come to regard the Meiji constitution as an immutable set of laws to be accorded all the respect that was due through the ages, but that the spirit of that basic law had, unfortunately, become distorted with the passage of time, leading to the national calamity with which the nation was faced. I added that, from the point of view of the Potsdam Declaration, the constitution as it then stood was found to be inadequate for the government of the country. I further said that, in order to enable Japan to preserve its traditional system of government and the happiness and well-being of its people despite the disaster that had befallen us, it was necessary to remove the misunderstanding then current among other nations of the world that the Japanese national structure in its traditional form represented a menace to world peace; and that, in order to achieve that aim, it was most important that we should frame the new constitution along the lines of democracy and pacifism.

In regard to the question of the imperial structure of government, as it existed in Japan, I pointed out that the Meiji constitution had originated in the promises made to the Japanese people by the Emperor Meiji at the beginning of his reign, and there was little need to dwell on the fact that democracy, if we were to use the word, had always formed part of the traditions of our country, and was not—as some mistakenly imagined—something that was about to be introduced with the revision of the Constitution. As for the imperial house, the idea and reality of the throne had come into being among the Japanese people as naturally as the idea of the country itself; no question of antagonism between throne and people could possibly arise; and nothing contained in the new constitution could change that fact. The word "symbol" had been employed in the definition of the emperor because we Japanese had always regarded the emperor as the symbol of the country itself—a statement which any Japanese considering the issue dispassionately would be ready to recognize as an irrefutable fact. Concerning the renunciation of war, I pointed out that the right of self-defense was not specifically denied in the draft of the new constitution, but that since both the right of belligerency and the maintenance of all forms of war potential were renounced in Article 9 of the new Constitution as drafted, it followed that war as a means of self-defense was also renounced. This provision, I indicated, was desirable because self-defense had been the excuse advanced by both sides in most wars waged in recent years, while Japan had come to be widely regarded as a militaristic nation, liable to embark upon a war of retaliation the moment the country had recovered sufficiently from the losses of the Pacific conflict. The renunciation of war, even in self-defense, was therefore a necessary step in order to rectify this wrong impression, held by other nations, of our aims and intentions.

Such was the gist of my replies to questions put to me by Mr. Hara Fujirō, but Mr. Nozaka Sanzō, of the Japanese Communist Party, later asked whether Japan should not rather limit the kind of war to be renounced to wars of aggression, since wars of self-defense obviously could not be classified, ipso facto, as evil. To this suggestion I replied that to admit the possibility of war in self-defense would, in itself, provide an incentive to embark on other types of conflict, it being a well-known fact that practically every war in recent years had been undertaken on that plea. However, it is interesting to look back on that time and to be reminded that in those days Japanese Communists supported war, even if limited to wars of self-defense. I further made it clear, in a reply to a question from Mr. Hara Fujirō, that a distinction should be made between wars of self-defense and the fundamental right to defend one's country, which should not, however, extend to embarking on war in the name of that right.

The next step consisted of referring the revision bill to a committee composed of members of all political parties, with Dr. Ashida Hitoshi as chairman. This body sat from July 1 to August 21, 1946, through the heat of the Tokyo summer, which the serious nature of the questions discussed did not allay. I attended the meetings of the committee from time to time, but the presentation of the government's case was entrusted to Mr. Kanamori Tokujirō, a former director-general of the Bureau of Legislation, who had entered my cabinet as minister of state in charge of the revision of the constitution in place of Dr. Matsumoto.

General MacArthur's headquarters maintained in general an attitude of watchful silence throughout the discussions in the Diet, but GHQ did intervene once or twice in regard, for instance, to the question of sovereignty. The occupation authorities carefully studied the reports of the discussions in progress and at one point indicated that Mr. Kanamori's replies in the Diet suggested that the conception of the new constitution did not differ fundamentally from that of the old; and that, from the nature of the questions asked, it seemed to them that the vagueness of the wording of the draft might give rise to some misunderstanding, so that it was thought desirable that steps should be taken to make it clear in the draft bill that sovereign power resided in the people and not in the emperor. There was some truth in this view, inasmuch as the words "sovereign will of the people," as contained in the draft handed to us by GHQ, could not be translated accurately enough into Japanese to mean the "will of the people which was sovereign"; therefore they were changed at the suggestion of General MacArthur's headquarters to "the will of the people with whom sovereign power resides," and translated into Japanese accordingly. Other such exchanges occurred both with GHQ and in the Diet, but the bill finally passed the Lower House on August 24 with only eight dissident votes.

The bill then went to the House of Peers. Both during the tenure in office of Baron Shidehara's cabinet and since I had formed my first administration, we had been preparing for that contingency by having as many men who were authorities on legal matters as possible included in the lists of imperial nominees for the Upper House. And I may add that the entire Upper Chamber applied itself resolutely to the task of revision of the Constitution as its last service to the state, since, under the terms of the new constitution, the peerage was to be abolished and the House of Peers pass out of existence.

The debates in the Upper House, both in committee and in full session, occupied about a month and a half, the last full session being held on October 6. On that occasion, in addition to changes voted for in committee, amendments were proposed concerning the powers of the emperor and the need for additional emphasis on the dignity of family life. The one concerning the powers of the emperor was proposed by Yamada Saburō and Takayanagi Kenzō, and had for its object the alteration of clauses in the bill under which the emperor would merely attest the ratification of treaties and the granting of full powers and credentials to ambassadors and ministers for the performing of these acts in his own right, with, in addition, the power to grant general and special amnesties. The reason for this was that, if the throne were to remain the throne, it was contrary to international custom for the cabinet to ratify treaties and send out ambassadors and ministers with the emperor merely attesting that these actions were taken, and that such a situation would be detrimental to national prestige abroad. The two members concerned came to see me and stated that they had already obtained the assent of GHQ to the proposed amendment and that they most earnestly desired the government to accept it. However, perhaps because of replies already given in the Lower House, Mr. Kanamori was opposed to the change and, possibly for other reasons as well, it was finally rejected.

The amendment concerned with the dignity of family life was proposed by Dr. Makino Eiichi, who reasoned that, as only the question of marriage was taken up in the bill as drafted, and nothing specific said about the relationship between parents and children, there was a danger of people coming to overlook and disregard the obligations of family life and something should be done to prevent such a development. This proposal was also rejected.

In the end the bill passed the Upper House with only a few minor amendments and with only four dissident votes. It was then sent back to the House of Representatives to obtain its assent to the amendments, and passed the Lower House in full session on October 7, 1946. It received the imperial sanction on the advice of the Privy Council and, in due course, became law.

# 14

## Critics of the New Constitution

The new Constitution thus enacted came into effect on May 3 of the following year. We hear a great deal of criticism in these days that the document was forced on the Japanese nation by the occupation authorities: criticism which keeps pace with and reflects the growing demand in some quarters in Japan for the Constitution to be again revised. Speaking from my own experience as one of those responsible for its drafting, I cannot entirely agree with the statements that this postwar Constitution was forced upon us. It is quite true that, at the time of its initial drafting (and due to circumstances about which I have already written), General MacArthur's headquarters did insist, with considerable vigor, on the speedy completion of the task and made certain demands in regard to the contents of the draft. But during our subsequent negotiations with GHQ there was nothing that could properly be termed coercive or overbearing in the attitude of the occupation authorities towards us. They listened carefully to the Japanese experts and officials charged with the work, and in many cases accepted our proposals. When it happened that our discussions with them reached a deadlock, they would often adopt the attitude that we were perhaps too steeped in the ways of the old constitution to look at the problems in any other light; we might at least give their suggestions a trial and then, if they did not work, we could reconsider the whole question at the proper time and revise the necessary points. And they meant it.

This point should be emphasized. In a letter addressed to me in my official capacity as prime minister and dated January 3, 1947—that is to say, four months before the new constitution was to come into effect—General MacArthur told me that the Far Eastern Commission had come to the decision that the Japanese people were quite free to take up the question of the new constitution a year or two after its coming into effect and to make whatever revisions were considered necessary, for which a plebiscite might be instituted and all other such requisite steps taken; that the Allies did not desire that any doubt should exist as to the new constitution having been chosen by the free will of the Japanese people; that a people obviously had the right constantly to watch over the constitution of their country and to make alterations whenever considered necessary. The general told me of the decision of the Far Eastern Commission as he thought it important that I should be kept abreast of current developments.

The decision of the Far Eastern Commission to which General MacArthur referred had been reached on October 17, 1946, ten days after the new constitution had been approved by the Japanese Diet, and General MacArthur's letter was written some months before its coming into effect on May 3 of the following year—which are facts that should interest those who hold the coercion theory. The general's letter was made public in Japan on May 27, 1947, but at that time both government and press were more intent on disseminating knowledge concerning the nature of the new Constitution, and, perhaps for that reason, the contents of the letter did not attract much attention.

Later, in the summer of 1948, during the period in office of the Ashida cabinet, Mr. Suzuki Yoshio, then minister of justice, received suggestions from GHQ that the Constitution be reexamined in the light of later experience. Mr. Suzuki accordingly gave instructions to officials of his ministry to begin investigations; at the same time apprising the Speakers of both Houses of the Diet of that fact. As a result of this development, there was some talk of setting up a committee of inquiry. However, shortly afterwards the Ashida cabinet resigned, and after the formation of my second cabinet the Diet was dissolved and nothing more was heard of the project.

The following year, 1949, was the year in which the period of a "year or two" mentioned in General MacArthur's letter terminated, and the question of possible revision excited a certain amount of public interest: to the extent, at least, that various legal bodies published tentative drafts in periodicals and so on. But for some reason, the general public was not stirred. On April 30, 1949, it was reported that the Far Eastern Commission had decided not to issue any further directives in regard to the Japanese Constitution. And there the matter rested.

This, however, was not the whole story. After the draft of the new constitution had been completed, it was submitted for discussion to the Privy Council, the Lower House of the Diet and the House of Peers, the members of which official assemblies included Japan's foremost authorities on law and administration. And, despite the fact that the nation was at that time under foreign occupation, these men were able to give free expression to their opinion without any restraint whatsoever. So far as the new Constitution is concerned, therefore, it is correct to say that the best informed elements among the Japanese people had a hand in shaping it, a point which is in these days too easily and too often ignored.

There are those also who lay emphasis on the fact that the Constitution was framed immediately after a disastrous war and when the country was under the military occupation of foreign powers. But if we consider the constitutions of other countries, the fact emerges that most of these, too, came into being in time of war or some period of national stress, and few in a time of peace and stability. There exists little reason for being sensitive to the circumstances in which Japan's present Constitution was drawn up. It is far more important to consider whether or not that document actually operates to the advantage of the Japanese people. It seems to me a question not so much of what we should do about the Constitution as of what we should do with it, and of what we are prevented from doing because it is as it is. And, in my opinion, there is little that we are debarred from doing that is important enough for us to feel impelled to demand any change.

Many of the arguments advanced by the revisionists are not incompatible with the present form of the Constitution. Thus, in regard to the position of our emperor, for instance, he is defined, as the Constitution stands at present, as "the symbol of the State and of the unity of the people," which is what Japanese emperors have always been. Legally speaking, sovereign power has passed from the emperor to the people. But we have only to look back on the history of our country to know that our emperors have never been identified with autocratic power. People have always rallied to them to resist tyranny. Whatever the vicissitudes of legal phraseology, the conception that we Japanese have of our emperors has never changed.

In regard to the question of rearmament I shall have something to say later. Here I will content myself by pointing out that, as the head of the government responsible for the forming of the Constitution, I have always held the view that Article 9—the renunciation-of-war clause—does not need to be amended. And I still adhere to that view. It is difficult to see how one could do otherwise when one considers the burden of national expenditure that the people of Japan already have to bear, and the international situation as it still remains today. There are some other points on which the revisionists would like to see the Constitution amended, but the fact remains that such a step as the revision of the Constitution of a country is not one to be taken lightly, much less made the platform of a cabinet or single political party. Obviously, there exists no reason why revision should not come in the long run. And it is equally obvious that the people should always be watchful and vigilant regarding its operation. But the actual work of revision should only be undertaken when public opinion as a whole has finally come to demand it, and then only after listening to all that the people have to say on the issue. It should be a matter of long years of patient experiment and the product of much disinterested thought—factors which lie outside the scope of a single cabinet or a single political party.

# 15

## The Purges

The system of purges instituted by the occupation authorities still arouses bitter memories in the minds of many Japanese who occupied official positions in national and local government prior to, and at the time of, the termination of the Pacific conflict.

In pursuance of the stipulation contained in the Potsdam Declaration that "there must be eliminated for all time the authority and influence of those who have deceived and misled the people of Japan into embarking on world conquest," an initial directive setting forth the procedure for barring those held responsible for the war from holding official positions issued by the supreme commander on January 4, 1946. On February 28 of the same year the Japanese government (under the Shidehara cabinet) issued Imperial Ordinance No. 109 and the relevant cabinet and Home Office ordinances, and the "purge" began.

From the point of view of the Allied powers at the time of the arrival of the occupation forces in Japan, the nation was an ultra-militaristic police state, in which liberal and democratic ideas were suppressed and the people regimented for the waging of wars of aggression. It was therefore necessary to destroy the influence of all those in leading positions who had brought about this situation, and thus to liberate the Japanese people and encourage them to embrace liberalism and democracy. In other words, it was the aim of Allied policy to democratize Japan; but, together with other occupation measures such as the disintegration of major financial groups and the punishment of war criminals, the "purges" were also the expression of a desire on the part of the Allied powers to retaliate against the leaders of the nation they had defeated, so that—at least during the early phase of the occupation—they formed an important place in occupation policy. As one looks back at this distance of time, however, the system of purges thus instituted may not have been anything of which the occupation felt particularly proud, but rather an episode which those responsible do not wish to recall. For instance, in an account of the occupation written by General Courtney Whitney, who was the officer in charge of implementing the purges and their most ardent promoter, they are dismissed in a matter of two or three lines. If the purging from public life of tens of thousands of Japanese is in fact an unpleasant memory for those responsible, it is equally so with us. I myself have a vague childhood recollection of a government order issued in early Meiji days whereby a number of "undesirable" politicians, including my father, were required to leave Tokyo and forbidden to come within a radius of a certain number of miles of the city. Since that time, the purges ordered by the occupation authorities were the first to take place in Japan and were, moreover, on a scale seldom paralleled in any country outside the Communist nations. It was understandable therefore that the SCAP directive of January 4, which committed so many leading figures in the nation to banishment from public life, came as a major shock to us.

As foreign minister in the two successive cabinets of Prince Higashikuni and Baron Shidehara, I was opposed to the purges from the first, and for good reason. For it was by no means true that all of those formerly holding responsible positions in Japan were militarists or ultranationalists. One feels almost foolish to have to make such a self-evident statement, for many of those concerned were leaders holding liberal and democratic views, whose courage to act on such ideas had given us modern Japan. And if, for a relatively brief time, the militarists and their supporters had their own way in the country, it was false to conclude that such had always been the case.

In this matter, as in many similar issues, a certain amount of knowledge of the history of the country is necessary if hasty conclusions are to be avoided. Hence I was opposed to the attitude displayed by the occupation authorities of taking what had been a temporary phase as being a permanent and fundamental state of affairs, and then driving people from their position in the light of arbitrary standards based upon a misreading of history. I frequently expressed my views to officials within GHQ, but they had been so convinced beforehand that Japan was a militaristic police state, and that liberal and democratic ideas did not exist even among civilian leaders of the nation, that it was difficult to make them listen. In the event, the dragnet spread, as time passed, beyond all expectation, and entangled within its meshes the good and bad alike.

The first group to be purged, in accordance with the initial GHQ directive of January 1946, was composed of those in national political circles and the upper ranks of the bureaucracy, and the number was not large. But it seems that the Far Eastern Commission in Washington—and particularly the Soviet representatives—were not satisfied, and the objection was raised that

General MacArthur's headquarters was proving too lenient in its methods. Whether or not this report was correct, from that time onwards the occupation officials responsible for implementing the purges in the Government Section of GHQ began constantly to complain to our own officials concerning the small number of purges, especially when compared with similar purges being conducted in Germany.

This seemed to me a most unreasonable attitude. The object of the purges, viewed in the light of the Potsdam Declaration, was to rid Japan of the authority and influence of those who had been really responsible for precipitating the nation into war, and their number, therefore, could only be a result and not a standard of the "screening." Moreover, Japan had not been placed under a totalitarian regime controlled by a nationwide organization of men of the same political persuasion, as in the case of Germany, so that it was meaningless to assert that the number of our purges compared unfavorably with the total in Germany. I instructed the officials of our Central Liaison Office to stress these points in their discussions with GHQ, and did so myself on many occasions, but our efforts were fruitless.

General MacArthur's headquarters further displayed, from the beginnings of the purges, a pronounced prejudice against the leaders of Japan's financial world. This sprang from what one might call the left-wing conception that the nation's capitalists had lured the politicians and militarists into an imperialistic and aggressive war in pursuit of personal profits; the extent of which prejudice could be gauged from the fact that initially a considerable number of our financiers were listed with those to be detained in Tokyo's Sugamo Prison to answer charges of war crimes before the International Military Tribunal of the Far East at the Tokyo war trials. It is most probable, therefore, that GHQ had been intent from the outset on including Japan's financial figures within the scope of the purge.

This fact reminds me of an incident that occurred some months before the purges began. As was the case within GHQ, foreigners generally in Japan in those days entertained feelings of animosity towards our financial leaders and there was already much talk among them of the coming disintegration of the trading "empires" which had been built up. So it came as no surprise when, at a press conference with foreign correspondents held shortly after the formation of the Shidehara cabinet in October 1945, with myself as foreign minister, I was confronted with the kind of questions one might expect. The general purport was that, since the financiers had been behind the war, the strictest measures should be taken against them. I answered that it would be a great mistake to regard Japan's financial leaders as a bunch of criminals: that the nation's economic structure had been built by such old-established and major financial concerns as Mitsui and Mitsubishi, and that modern Japan owed her prosperity largely to their endeavors, so that it was most doubtful whether the Japanese people would benefit from the disintegration of these concerns.

I explained further that the so-called *zaibatsu* had never worked solely for their own profit, but often at a loss, as, for instance, during the war when they continued to produce ships and planes on government orders regardless of the sacrifices involved; that the people who had actually joined hands with the militarists and profited from the war were not the established financial groups, but the new rich, who were alone permitted by the military to conduct business in Manchuria and other occupied territories to the detriment of the old-established concerns; and that those who had most heartily welcomed the termination of the Pacific conflict were the leaders of these old-established concerns who had laid the foundations of their prosperity in times of peace and had never felt at ease in their relations with the military clique who had become the masters of the nation for the duration of the war. After I had concluded my statement, a Chinese correspondent, whose name I cannot now recall, asked me if I were a relation of the Mitsuis. I am not, but it was an unexpected tribute to the opulent appearance I no doubt then presented.

Apparently my remarks on that occasion received a good deal of attention in Allied—including Soviet—circles. But when I held another press conference in May of the following year, after I had formed my first cabinet, I stated in answer to questions from correspondents that I still believed the reply I had made as foreign minister regarding Japan's financial concerns to be true. And I still do so today.

In regard to the implementation of the purge in the case of the press and writers generally, two important factors need to be taken into consideration. First, General MacArthur's headquarters was naturally concerned, in the course of its activities, with examining closely newspapers, magazines, and books published in Japan before and during the Pacific War, which fact would in any case have raised the question of purges in that sphere. Secondly, many Japanese belonging to what is known as the "progressive" element, particularly those with Communist affiliations, made strong representations to GHQ, supported by data which they had themselves compiled, urging a thorough overhaul of the publishing and writing worlds, and there were some within Government Section of GHQ who established close contacts with such Japanese. This fact was not, of course, restricted to the fields of writing and publishing, or to the question of purges only; we find such Japanese, either genuine Communists, fellow-travelers, or opportunists turned left-wing overnight, paying constant calls upon Government Section in the guise of advanced democratic thinkers anxious to proffer advice on measures aimed at the democratization of Japan. Their activities, coupled with the ignorance of the Americans at that time in regard to the real state of affairs in my country and the nature of the Japanese Communist Party and its activities, exercised an actual influence within GHQ to the extent that it served to foster a view of Japan that was far from the truth.

This was the background to the next stage of the purge story, which opened, so far as I can remember, about the middle of September 1946, with Government Section handing us an official memorandum stating it was the policy of GHQ to extend the scope of the purges to the financial world, provincial authorities, and the press, and requiring the Japanese government to prepare and present to the occupation authorities a plan to that end.

At that juncture the implementation of the first series of purges, and the disintegration of financial concerns and decentralization of economic power, as well as the pressures being exerted on the press by radical labor unions, were already causing a disturbing amount of unrest. In addition, the purges were supposed to affect only those who had been actually responsible for the war. For both these reasons, I instructed the officials of the Central Liaison Office to make a strong protest to Government Section, which was rejected. I further wrote personally to General MacArthur to acquaint him with the actual state of affairs. Matters remained in abeyance, no action being taken on our part to present a plan as suggested in the memorandum, when in November Government Section informed us unofficially of a plan for the extensive purges which GHQ had prepared. This plan turned out to be even wider in scope than we had at first been led to expect, though it covered only the financial world and the provincial governments and did not include the press. That was to come later.

Concerning the application of the purge directive to the provinces, the GHQ plan designated as purgees all those who had been heads of any administrative group at any time during the period from the beginning of the China Incident in 1937 to the end of the Pacific War, from the governors of prefectures to mayors of cities and towns, headmen of villages, and even heads of block associations. The plan further called for the purging of people connected with the Imperial Rule Assistance Association, such as all heads of district branches in prefectures, cities and villages, advisers, councilors, and so forth; which meant, that institution being what it was, practically everyone of note in every part of Japan.

Most of the prefectural governors had been included among those who had been purged earlier, but to hold mayors, the headmen of villages, and the heads of block associations directly responsible for the war solely because they had been in office at some time during the specified period had no relation to actual facts whatever. If the idea had been to permit the people to choose new leaders in the light of changed conditions in the postwar world, the edict would have been more understandable. But in that case, measures other than purging the previous occupants of those offices, with all the disabling conditions that purging entailed, should have been taken. To brand these people as having been responsible for the war by the application of quite arbitrary standards, without any reference to their past actions, was not only contrary to the spirit in which the purges were supposed to have been instituted, but a sure means of aggravating the already disordered condition in the provinces and thus a legitimate cause for grievance on the part of the inhabitants in general. And we said so. General MacArthur's headquarters seems to have felt the force of our protests, or at least the earnestness with which they were proffered. Though GHQ by no means changed its fundamental policy in the matter, it did agree to exclude the heads of block associations from those to be purged. The occupation authorities were adamant, however, on the question of purging mayors and headmen of villages, and when we sought permission to screen these people individually, rejected that request also.

A further subject of concern to us was the inclusion of people who had been connected with the Imperial Rule Assistance Association. We explained to GHQ that, unlike the German Nazi organizations, this institution was so created that mayors, village headmen, and other community leaders were automatically appointed as heads of its branches; that apart from special cases, offices like those of advisers, counselors, and councilors, were purely honorary and, owing to the ambiguous nature of the institution, difficult to refuse when offered, so that were the purges to be enforced in the manner prescribed by GHQ, the result would be the banning from any part in further public activity of the most moderate and reliable elements in the country and consequent crippling of provincial self-government. However, in this case also we were unable to make GHQ see reason, and it was agreed only to make certain concessions in regard to advisers and counselors.

The GHQ plan for extending the purge to Japan's financial world was also of a most comprehensive nature. Had it been enforced to the letter, it would have played havoc with our national economy, which was perhaps not surprising when we consider the extent to which, as I have explained, GHQ held our financial leaders responsible for the war, and how that view was supported outside General MacArthur's headquarters by the Soviet Union and certain other Allied powers. It seems that two persons within GHQ had played particularly important roles in the drafting of the purge plan, a Mr. Thomas Arthur Bisson, who had been in Japan before and was an enthusiastic New Dealer with advanced views regarding ways and means of democratizing our financial world, and a Miss Eleanor M. Hadley. Miss Hadley had also been in Japan before and was known for her researches into our financial concerns. She had taken a particular interest in the relationship between big business and the war and, as a result, acquired a rooted conviction that it was necessary for the successful democratization of Japan to systematically disintegrate the larger commercial groups—by which she did not mean only the *zaibatsu* concerns, such as Mitsui and Mitsubishi, but all others where she considered too much capital had been accumulated, or the products of which enjoyed too great a share of the market. She had apparently written books on this subject since her return to the United States and continued to disseminate her views in the form of articles and lectures.

The details of the plan drawn up by these two officials were disclosed to the Japanese government in December 1946. The specifications for firms to be included within the scope of the purge were: (1) firms with a capital of 100,000,000 yen or more, (2) firms whose products commanded more than ten per cent of the market, (3) enterprises engaged in the manufacture of war materials or other activities calculated to aid war and aggression, (4) enterprises that had taken part in the economic development of colonies and occupied territories, and (5) firms that were a force in the economic world irrespective of the amount of their capital.

Firms that answered this description numbered some 240 to 250, and all who had been directors (presidents, vice presidents, managing directors, and ordinary directors) of such commercial units during the period specified in the purge edict were to be purged, and, in addition, auditors and others who, though not directors, were held to have exerted much influence. This definition meant that virtually all important commercial firms in Japan came within the scope of the purge edict, and that all who had occupied positions of consequence in such firms were to be purged. This was something which the Japanese government could not, of course, lightly accept, and we not only made our representations and protests directly to Government Section, but also put our case before the Economic and Scientific Section, which had by that time begun to realize the need for the economic recovery of the nation and strove to mitigate the conditions of the purge.

Despite our efforts, however, we succeeded only in securing some concessions in the case of relatively small concerns. All Japanese commercial enterprises of any consequence were included, and our plea that reservations should be made in favor of firms engaged in purely peaceful industries was disregarded. In view of the mentality of those who had drawn up the plan, what was involved was in the ultimate analysis a difference of philosophy or ideology, and in these circumstances our views could not prevail. It still remained true, however, that if ordinary directors of commercial companies were all to be automatically purged, the Japanese economic world would be deprived of virtually all those with experience of company management, and any hope of economic recovery would receive its death blow. Something had to be done, while GHQ, for its part, appeared equally determined to concede nothing. The date set by General MacArthur's headquarters for putting into effect this second series of purges was January 4, 1947, the anniversary of the issuing of the GHQ directive ordering the initial series. At a cabinet meeting held the day before, it was decided that our officials in charge of the matter should obtain the exemption of ordinary directors of companies at whatever cost. The ensuing negotiations between government representatives and GHQ lasted four hours, at the conclusion of which time we were informed that Government Section of SCAP had at last conceded the point and our men had succeeded in obtaining General MacArthur's consent to the proposed amendment.

One episode connected with these events may be worth recording. The original GHQ plan, as handed to us, called for the purging of "standing directors" as well as others occupying top positions. This was translated into Japanese by our side as "managing directors." Strictly speaking, however, a "standing director" could be interpreted as one who functioned regularly in a company, which would have included most ordinary directors. We held to our interpretation that "standing directors" were, in fact, managing directors, and by so doing were able to save many ordinary directors who might otherwise have been so classified from the purge. Which shows that upon occasion mistranslations serve their turn.

As I briefly indicated earlier, the background to the purges in the realm of writing and the press was composed of a combination of elements. The occupation authorities had been determined from the outset not to allow anyone to escape who had taken an active part in shaping Japanese public opinion in the direction of war, whether as individuals or in the capacity of officials of publishing organizations, but, at the beginning, standards by which such guilt would be measured had not been decided upon.

The fact that later a most detailed and comprehensive plan of purges to be carried out in this sphere was outlined to us by GHQ may be attributed to three causes: first, to the persistent campaign conducted at GHQ by our own left-wing elements with a view to monopolizing newspapers, publishing, broadcasting, the cinema, and all other communications media for themselves; secondly, to the existence within GHQ itself of elements who were in sympathy with that attempt; and thirdly, to the desire on the part of Government Section to purge specific persons.

The plan, as handed to the Japanese government by GHQ, required us to conduct a thorough examination of all newspapers, magazines, and film and radio scripts that had appeared or were used between August 7, 1937, when the China Incident began, and December 8, 1941, when Japan declared war upon the United States, and to report all items uncovered that either preached or supported militarism, ultranationalism, or aggressive wars. This was an impossible assignment to complete with our limited resources within the time limit stipulated, but General MacArthur's headquarters directed us to hire extra researchers for the task, to make special grants of money available for the purpose, and to push ahead with the job at all costs. The government, therefore, hired a large number of students to do the reading, and a committee of scholars and journalists was formed to consider and decide upon the items presented.

In undertaking this task, we were specifically ordered by GHQ to investigate the *Tōyō keizai shinpō*, a magazine dealing with economic affairs edited by Ishibashi Tanzan, who was then Japan's finance minister, and a magazine, *The Diamond*, similar in character. The *Tōyō keizai shinpō* was known to us all as a liberal and anti-militaristic periodical, but our researchers made a careful examination of its contents, as ordered, and the result was that twenty-five or twenty-six items were discovered that answered to the specifications, but at the same time we unearthed twenty-seven or twenty-eight of a nature which made us wonder how they had got past the censors at the time.

Our officials, and the committee also, decided on the strength of these findings that the *Tōyō keizai shinpō* did not come under the provisions of the purge, but Government Section would not agree with this judgment—a decision arising from the fact that, as I shall explain later, it had from the first been the fixed intention of that section within occupation headquarters to purge Mr. Ishibashi. To achieve their aim, GHQ insisted that the *Tōyō keizai shinpō* could not be exonerated, and in support of that attitude ruled that the publication of one article of a militaristic nature was sufficient to inculpate a periodical, no matter how many other articles of a contrary nature it might have printed. Having shot someone with a poisoned arrow, argued Government Section, no amount of medicines will bring him back to life again—a piece of reasoning which under other circumstances would have sounded just plain silly. However, the ruling was given, and as a result of the investigation of the *Tōyō keizai shinpō*, newspapers and magazines had to be completely free of all obnoxious material in order to be judged innocent and exonerated, which, in practice, meant that all Japanese newspapers and magazines became objects of the purge.

The next question to arise was to what extent the men in these publishing companies and organizations should be purged. We were told it was to be everyone down to heads of departments, a ruling which, if carried out, would have stopped the organizations concerned from functioning altogether. Endless negotiations were conducted with Government Section on this point. January 4, the date set for the purge, came and went without any decision. Finally, by the time the purge was put into effect, about two months later, considerable concessions had been made by Colonel Charles L. Kades, deputy chief of Government Section, including the exemption of the heads of departments, and we were able to reduce the scope of the purge as it affected the press and publishing to a workable minimum. By such negotiations and processes, the purges initiated by the GHQ directive of January 4, 1946, gradually took definite shape and were implemented, until by May 1948, when a halt was called to the operation, some two hundred thousand people had been purged.

Henceforth, we had to cope with GHQ directives concerning the movements of this army of purgees. Japanese were not wanting who were prepared, and even pleased, to furnish General MacArthur's headquarters with information purporting to show how purgees were giving directions to their former followers and subordinates, or going to their former places of work to influence their successors by their presence, and such testimony was not without its effect upon GHQ. As a result, we were required to issue a series of orders of a most peculiar nature, such as prohibiting purgees from engaging in activities of a political nature or exerting their influence on people in official positions, and, again, prohibiting them from entering buildings housing their former places of work—culminating in an order prohibiting the kin of purgees within the third degree of consanguinity from holding positions formerly occupied by the purgees. In the case of financial concerns, this last prohibition may have been understandable as a measure to prevent the sons and brothers of purgees from becoming presidents and directors of their former companies, but so far as civil servants and others were concerned very definite rules existed governing promotion, which operated quite independently of whom any person might be related to. In addition, to visit in this way the sins of the purgees, if sins they were, upon their relations to the third degree smacked of something out of feudal history and ran completely counter to the requirements of common humanity. We argued at length with GHQ over these measures, but their minds were made up and they could not be moved from the position they had taken, and so we had finally to give in. In the case of the order concerning relations within the third degree of consanguinity, I found this to be so intolerable that I wrote personally to General MacArthur on the matter, but to no avail. Thinking about that order in retrospect, I still feel it to have been a senseless measure.

However, despite some excesses, if the purges are considered dispassionately and as a whole, we have to admit that they did exert a considerable influence in bringing about the democratization of all spheres of activity in Japan. Most of the former leaders in the walks of life concerned were removed from the national scene; new men were promoted to key positions in their stead, and this new personnel, operating new systems, caused a complete break with things as they were before and during the war, making it impossible, at any rate, for "the authority and influence of those who have deceived and misled the people of Japan" ever to return. There are those who refer to this operation as the moral disarmament of Japan and a bloodless revolution, and some of the aspects presented by the purges certainly deserve that description.

On the other hand, however, it is equally certain that, viewed from some other angles, the purges had a most injurious effect upon the national life. One aspect of the matter that caused me particular anxiety at the time was the way in which the excesses that occurred were beginning to show signs of constituting a positive hindrance to fresh activity in all spheres. In the economic world, for instance, nothing was more urgent than increased exports, and the improvement of Japan's position in world markets, but there existed a serious lack of available men experienced in such matters because of the large numbers eliminated by the purge. In the political world new men were certainly welcome, but there were among those who had been purged many with long training and experience in parliamentary government whose presence was much missed. These members of the old Conservative and Socialist Parties had gone through untold hardships to maintain the tradition of parliamentary government through the Taishō and Shōwa eras in the face of the pressures from military and rightist opinion. There were other men in the provinces who were now debarred from taking part in local government. The absence of these men represented so much loss to the healthy development of democracy in Japan. And, for the moment, there was no remedy.

Furthermore, the purges had been instituted under the occupation regime by order of the supreme commander, and their operation was bound to be mechanical. The standards of screening were arbitrary and stereotyped, and it was impossible to take into consideration more than a given amount of evidence in the short time allowed for making decisions. It followed from this that many cases occurred in which the result turned out to be unjust or unfair, and the Japanese habit of reticence caused most of the victims to remain silent even then. Moreover, although the original aim of these purges, as planned by GHQ, was to keep those purged out of official positions, because of the social unrest existing in those days, a purgee from some official position frequently found difficulty in obtaining work in private concerns, even though no legal barrier existed to such a step, and, in extreme cases, even in starting a small business of his own. Finding employment and sustenance in the period immediately following the termination of the Pacific War was in any case a most difficult matter, and to have to cope, in addition, with the disabilities attendant upon being purged must often have presented insurmountable obstacles. Thousands must have been driven to the direst poverty, so that, in the last analysis, we were faced with problems that lay far removed from the effect originally intended when the purges were instituted.

In this connection, we should also remember that, unlike the French, who took up the question of collaborators on their own initiative and vented their feelings on these people after the war, we Japanese had no particular desire to prosecute and judge those who were, or might have been, responsible for our miseries. Hatred of the military was strong, but there arose no move amongst us to form, for example, a people's court to call even the men of the army to account.

Thus Japan was confronted on the one hand by the trial of former war leaders before the International Military Tribunal of the Far East in Tokyo, and on the other by the drastic occupation-ordered purges, accompanied by undesirable repercussions on the national life to which I have already referred. All of which contributed to the general gloom in Japan at that time and caused me to fear that, as any open criticism of the policies and actions of General MacArthur's headquarters was quite out of the question in the circumstances, these happenings would later furnish the pretext and material for the growth of anti-American sentiment in my country.

No such anti-American feeling then existed in Japan, but by 1949, when the war-crimes trials virtually ended, it was natural that our people should demand a review and reassessment of the whole question of the purges and their consequences. The conclusion of a peace treaty ending the occupation of Japan was no longer something that lay in the remote future, and the time had arrived for efforts to bring the purges to a conclusion, since a system that banned so many experienced leaders and men from national and public affairs was not one that could continue indefinitely.

Machinery for the review and cancellation of individual purge decisions was not altogether lacking even during the enforcement of the purge directives. On March 3, 1947, during my first cabinet, a Public Office Qualifications Appeal Board had been formed to take up cases of those who considered themselves unjustly purged and furnished evidence supporting that fact, and to arrange for their rescreening. But out of a total of more than a thousand cases which were approved for rescreening, occupation headquarters consented to cancel the purge charges of only about one hundred and fifty, and the board itself went out of existence at the time of the announcement of the last list of purgees. However, since some two hundred thousand persons had by then been purged, the handicap arising from such a large number of men of ability being debarred from useful activity began to make itself strongly felt, both in the national life and on popular sentiment in the country. Immediately after the general election held in January 1949, during my second cabinet, I paid a visit to General MacArthur and requested permission to set up a second appeal board. I was not quite sure how this suggestion would be received, but the supreme commander readily consented, and the news, when announced, was most favorably received, not only by the purgees themselves, but by the country generally.

However, although General MacArthur had no objections to the step, and was indeed most cordial about it, the attitude of some of those within GHQ was not so accommodating once the new board began its work. Thus, when Mr. Tanimura Tadaichirō, the chairman of the board, paid his first visit to

General Courtney Whitney, the chief of Government Section, he was informed by General Whitney that the board had been permitted to come into existence as a special favor and that Government Section would not consider any relaxation of the standards fixed by the purge ordinances; that the board should only consider cases where there had clearly occurred an error of judgment, or those involving some glaring instance of unfairness, such as might cause the purge ruling to be canceled in special cases. In the event, our subsequent negotiations with Government Section proved to be fully as arduous as during the period when the purges were in progress.

The board met on 119 occasions during the next eighteen months, each time reporting its findings to GHQ. But we were unable to obtain any information from Government Section, and remained completely in the dark as to what the reply in any individual case might be. Repeated efforts to ascertain decisions were made in vain. In the meantime, the board and officials in charge of conducting the purges in all parts of the country were being flooded with inquiries from anxious purgees wanting to be told the outcome of their appeals as early as possible.

In these circumstances, I was once more forced to appeal directly to General MacArthur, and wrote the supreme commander a letter setting forth the precise situation, with the result that, contrary to our expectations in view of the attitude of GHQ up to that moment, the findings of the board were accepted by General MacArthur's headquarters in practically every case. Out of some thirty-two thousand cases reexamined, over ten thousand persons were exonerated. Later some of the standards set forth in the original purge ordinances were also relaxed, and in October 1950, 3,250 former young officers of the army and navy who had enrolled at the military or naval academies after the outbreak of the Pacific War were released from the purge.

It is possible to imagine several reasons why GHQ, which had been so unhelpful when the board had been set up, and continued for so long to ignore its findings, thus showed such a complete change of front at the last minute. The patient efforts of the Japanese government to secure consideration of our case probably had some effect in persuading the men within GHQ to consider the matter in another and more favorable light, but the changes then taking place in the international situation—and particularly the outbreak of the war in Korea—also played their part. The Korean War, especially, completely transformed the scene in the Far East. The basic policy of the occupation of Japan was abruptly switched from having the demilitarization and democratization of the country as its main objectives to the relaxation of controls placed, until then, upon the Japanese nation.

In my view, one is justified in assuming that this fact also influenced GHQ's attitude towards the purges. After the departure of a substantial portion of the U.S. occupation forces in Japan to Korean battlefields, GHQ needed to think about the problem of the maintenance of public order in

Japan and, in consequence, the movements of public opinion in that country. GHQ must have felt apprehensive concerning the dangerous condition to which our local government structure had been reduced because of the nonavailability of experienced men to carry on the work, and the opportunities which that fact offered to extremists to engage in their subversive activities; or, again, the need for men possessing managerial ability at a time when it was vitally important for Japan to effect and complete its economic recovery in preparation for the signing of a peace treaty and the competition with other countries in world markets which was bound to follow. I recall having pointed out these considerations in my letter to General MacArthur.

At that time, as I have emphasized, there existed in Japan no trace of anti-American feeling. Consequently, GHQ was not required to take that factor into account when considering the purge question. But if the persons concerned had not been released from the purge and the nation at large had continued to be weakened and irked by the restrictions thereby imposed by the purge ordinances, the anti-American sentiment which came into being later would have gained far more ground, and with reason. Looking back upon those days, I feel it was fortunate, both for Japan and the United States, that the persons concerned were exonerated from the purge at that moment.

In such circumstances, the second board brought its task to a satisfactory conclusion and was abolished at the end of March 1951. It was followed by the setting up of the Public Office Qualifications Examination Committee, which was established in June 1951 and effected the release from the purges of 177,000 persons; after which an appeal committee was created in November of the same year and added another 9,000 to the number. Five months later, on April 28, 1952, the San Francisco Peace Treaty came into effect, and all laws and ordinances relating to the purges were abolished, thus putting an end to the whole vexed question.

Before concluding my memories on this subject, I would like to add a few personal reminiscences relating to the purge issue. There existed, as part of the purge machinery, a special procedure, in which the Government Section within SCAP headquarters presented the government with a special memorandum informing us that such and such a person was to be purged. There were altogether some twenty such cases, including those of Mr. Hatoyama Ichirō and Mr. Ishibashi Tanzan, and in the last stages of our dealings with GHQ over the purges we were told that, although the Japanese government was free to cancel the case of any person who had been purged through the usual channels, it was for GHQ to decide on the cases of those who had been purged by special memorandum.

When I visited General MacArthur to secure his permission to set up the second appeal board, the general gave me his consent with the proviso that

Mr. Hatoyama and Mr. Ishibashi should be excluded from the list of those the board would consider. General MacArthur added that, in the case of Mr. Hatoyama, the Soviet Union had insisted strongly on his being purged and it was difficult for the U.S. government alone to reach a decision on the matter. In this connection, I may have been partly to blame for getting Mr. Hatoyama into the Soviet Union's bad books. Shortly after the termination of the war, when Mr. Hatoyama was actively planning the formation of the Liberal Party, he came to see me and the talk had turned on the political program to be adopted by the new party. On that occasion I stated that Communism was going to pose problems everywhere, both in Japan and in the world at large, and that it might be a good idea if the new party were openly to advocate an anti-Communist policy and make it one of its chief features. Whether influenced by my remarks or not, Mr. Hatoyama adopted an anti-Communist policy, coupled with support for the throne, as two of the main planks of the Liberal Party, which may well have incensed the Soviet Union and caused them to object to the last to his being de-purged. Mr. Hatoyama may have changed his opinions since that time.

In the case of Mr. Ishibashi Tanzan, he is an expert on economic questions with original ideas of his own, and a man with faith in his ideas. He served as finance minister in my first cabinet and held firmly to his own views in all negotiations with GHQ. Perhaps for that reason, the men in the Economic and Scientific Section of GHQ seem to have received the impression that he was out to resist the occupation. However, he continued to stick to his line, and in the end, I was informed by GHQ that, in their opinion, I would be well advised to request Mr. Ishibashi's resignation. I replied that if a minister was to be sacked each time he objected to something said within GHQ, it would be impossible to carry on the government of the country; that this was clearly a case involving interference in the internal affairs of the country, and therefore contrary to SCAP's declared policy, and left it at that. So, later, GHQ purged him as a "memorandum case."

From what was subsequently reported to me by officials in charge of purge matters at our Central Liaison Office, Colonel Charles Kades of Government Section had been overheard saying, long before the event, that GHQ was afraid Mr. Ishibashi might emerge as the ringleader of an antioccupation faction and that, although the attention of the Japanese government had been unofficially drawn to this alleged fact, the government had taken no action. Which would seem to show that, as I have stated in earlier passages dealing with the purges of the press, GHQ had made up its mind, if other forms of pressure failed, to purge Mr. Ishibashi by finding fault with the *Tōyō keizai shinpō*, which he edited—a fact which was further made abundantly clear by the attitude GHQ took in their screening of that magazine. Such being the case, it was impossible to do anything about Mr. Ishibashi, or about Mr. Hatoyama's purging, so long as the occupation lasted.

These two examples serve to demonstrate that the "memorandum" method of purging persons was utilized by GHQ in order to get rid of specific people whom General MacArthur's headquarters considered undesirable. The case of Count Kabayama Aisuke was another instance of this technique. The count was, as everyone knows in Japan, the president of the Japan-American Society in Tokyo, and a man who may justly be said to have spent his entire life in the cause of Japanese-American friendship. For some obscure reason, however, GHQ desired that he be purged and, it seems, began saying so quite early in the occupation. The ostensible reason given for this was that the count had been connected with a steelworks at Muroran in Hokkaidō. That fact did not, however, explain the urgency with which GHQ wanted him purged, and each time the matter was raised I instructed our officials in charge to ignore it. There the issue rested for the duration of my first cabinet; the count was eventually purged during the tenure of office of the next, Socialist, cabinet headed by Mr. Katayama Tetsu.

Yet another case concerned Mr. Hōketsu Kōta, who was director of the Bureau of Research in the Japanese Foreign Office at that time. It seemed he did not listen attentively enough to some advice given by General MacArthur's headquarters, which thereupon issued instructions he was to be purged on the ground that he had been a secretary of the Supreme War Council. The demand being repeated on a number of occasions, I told our officials to request GHQ to present it formally and officially in writing, with the intention of raising the matter with General MacArthur personally as soon as we received instructions in written form. They never came.

I recall having frequent recourse to this procedure, and in no single case did we receive the written instructions asked for. For that reason, I think I can justly claim that, in no single instance, was any member of the Foreign Office, which was my particular domain, unjustly purged or forced to resign. But in other ministries, and particularly in provincial offices under the jurisdiction of the local military government, many officials seem to have been purged or got rid of for such reasons as alleged recalcitrance, or not being sufficiently cooperative, or on other grounds advanced by Japanese informers, and many sound men and fine administrators were thus forced out of their jobs. The occupation certainly claimed its toll of victims, especially in the early stages.

# 16

# Educational Reform

As I indicated earlier, the Allied forces came to Japan imbued with the fixed idea that we were a nation of ultranationalistic militarists. To liberate the Japanese people by introducing and spreading liberalism and democracy throughout the country became one of their main aims during the first stages of the occupation. The Americans must have been deeply impressed by the stamina displayed by our fighting men during the Pacific campaigns, which had enabled them to put up such a gallant fight against the overwhelming superiority in arms enjoyed by the U.S. forces. And the British had suffered too much at our hands during the early stages of the Malaya campaign to be able either to forget or forgive easily. Given these factors, it is not difficult to understand that, immediately after Japan's unconditional surrender, the Allied powers were not content merely to consign the nation's leading militarists and ultranationalists to Tokyo's Sugamo Prison as war criminals, but went on to purge so many others from public and business life, and to introduce fundamental changes in our laws designed to reform the Japanese people. Educational reform was a vital phase of this policy, and so we were required to put it into practice as a matter of urgency.

The formalization of occupation plans for educational reform coincided with the arrival in Japan in March 1946 of a U.S. educational mission sent at the request of GHQ. At that time the Shidehara cabinet was in office, with Mr. Abe Yoshishige as minister of education. The American mission conferred with Japanese education experts, studied plans for reform, and returned to the United States after submitting a report to GHQ. After the formation of my first cabinet in the same year, an Education Reform Council was created as an advisory body to the prime minister to study the report of the American mission. That document had been written in the spirit of such basic concepts as the rights of man and equal educational opportunities for all, and was, on the whole, sensibly inspired and sound. It contained, however, some points which required careful consideration if they were to be applied to Japan, which was why the council was brought into being to review the report and advise us. The council did so, furnishing the cabinet with its own report and concrete plans for educational reform.

The central theme of both American and Japanese plans was what is now known as the 6.3 system, by which it is made compulsory for all Japanese children to receive six years of primary and three years of middle school education, instead of only six years of primary school education as formerly—with further provisions designed to enable all possessing the necessary aptitude to go to a university later. There was nothing basically wrong with this idea of equal opportunity for all. A similar plan had been proposed back in Meiji days by Dr. Kikuchi Dairoku, then president of Tokyo Imperial University. The question had been taken up again by a private group charged with the study of national policy gathered around Prince Konoe during the Pacific War. It was, in fact, precisely because we had put it into practice to the extent permitted by the state of our national economy that Japan had been able to catch up so rapidly with scientific and industrial progress and in other fields.

But before attempting further improvements to our school system, we had to consider, first of all, what was the aim of the new system and, more important still, how the 6.3 system was to be financed. Even when Japan was at the height of her prewar prosperity, compulsory education covering six years of primary school was the maximum that could be attempted. A bill providing for eight years of compulsory education had been enacted by the Diet during the Pacific conflict, but it remained a dead letter. To implement, at that moment, a plan providing for nine years of compulsory education in the impoverished condition in which we found ourselves after defeat seemed to me, if not a near impossible feat, at least one that would lay a far too heavy burden upon an already sadly harassed people. I, therefore, indicated that, while I agreed with the aim, I was of the opinion that we should proceed gradually towards putting it into effect.

At about this time, however, both educationalists and public opinion in Japan began to demand the immediate execution of the plan, whatever the cost. The pro-reform elements were supported by well-meaning, but not always very thoughtful, younger officials within GHQ, and by Japanese progressives eager to seize any pretext to make themselves heard. Still, the reformers represented public opinion, and I was well aware of that fact. But one can make too great a sacrifice to public opinion, and so I stuck to my view that there should be no undue haste in the matter. Mr. Tanaka Kōtarō, the minister of education, and Mr. Yamazaki Kyōsuke, the vice minister, were of the same opinion and they must have had a hard time trying to prevail upon the occupation authorities not to be too precipitate.

The tide of opinion was running strongly in favor of the occupation viewpoint, and GHQ reached the decision that the 6.3 system should be put into effect at all costs in 1947. The minister of education and those around him were thus placed in an unenviable position. As I have said, there was nothing wrong with the system itself; the only question was how such an undertaking was to be financed in the impoverished condition of Japan. The sensible way of implementing the reform would have been first to re-fashion the primary schools according to the new model visualized in the reform plan, and next the middle schools, and so on up to the universities. To reorganize all schools from bottom to top simultaneously so that the new system would be in working order within three years from 1947, which was what General MacArthur's headquarters demanded, was something that no one seriously interested in education, and informed regarding the condition of the country, could consider. Both Mr. Tanaka and Mr. Ya-mazaki resisted the demand, and when I felt they could really do no more, I advised them to retire and take a rest, deciding that further resistance was useless and would only result in harming our relations with GHQ. The new system was duly introduced in the manner demanded, a step concerning which we should remember the price paid by those who were required to carry it out, rather than measure the degree of success attained.

One problem that presented itself in connection with the implementing of educational reform was how we were to secure a sufficient supply of efficient teachers. I held frequent conferences on this point with the education minister, but we were not able to arrive at any solution. Nor, in my opinion, has a solution been found to this day. Thus, the three points on which it seemed to me we had to concentrate in regard to the introduction of educational reform were the spirit in which education is conducted; the organization of the schools; and the training of the teachers. I stressed these aspects so far as I was able to all those concerned.

It is still my view that the track along which the new Japan is now traveling—or at least the nation's basic course—was charted during my first cabinet. The new Constitution was drafted and promulgated. In the field of education, a system having as its aim the training of democratic citizens, with opportunities for all who possess the necessary qualifications to go to a university, was decided upon and introduced. At this point, the Liberal Party, which I headed, lost a general election and we had to leave educational and other problems to the Socialists, who had become the largest party in the House of Representatives and formed a cabinet under Prime Minister Katayama.

I returned to office and formed my second cabinet in October 1948. In the meantime social conditions, and particularly the education issue, had taken a decided turn for the worse. Little had yet been accomplished towards the reconstruction of the country from the ravages of war. Japan still had far to go. Yet the nation had become prey to destructive communistic tendencies, which were responsible for mounting labor troubles and strife, and such excesses as primary schoolteachers and students going on strike. The new educational system, such as it was, seemed to be taking exactly the direction I had originally feared. The lack of funds was painfully apparent, but even had that defect been remedied, the "new" education seemed strangely lacking in content and aim.

Teachers, in many cases, appeared not to know of what their work fundamentally consisted. Democracy and education are concepts which anyone can express in words, but when it came to the question of how to set about educating young Japanese as the future citizens of their country, teachers were without what may be termed any guiding spirit to inspire them in their task. Primary schoolteachers and university professors were both, therefore, teaching without much confidence in their work. And the counterpart of this attitude was to be found among the students, many of whom regarded it as democratic to despise their teachers and make light of their elders generally. Before the war, patriotism and reverence for the throne ranked high among the qualities of the Japanese people. To discard these in planning a new program for education may have been considered necessary in view of the fact that events before and during the Pacific War had demonstrated that patriotism could foster ultranationalism, and reverence for the throne could become a tool in the hands of the militarists; but democratic education as an abstract concept did not make up for the loss involved.

Moreover, Japan seemed to have an increasing number of teachers who did not appear to have any idea what education was about and was intended to accomplish. Whether university professors or primary schoolteachers, many tended to pamper their pupils and truckle to their juvenile views from the mistaken idea that to do so was being "progressive," instead of going about their work with a certain firmness, and encouraging their charges to form their own opinions and standards of judgment independently of whatever happened to be the latest fashionable view. Teachers' trade unions had also come into being. There is nothing inherently wrong with that fact in itself, but when these unions behave—as in Japan ours did and still do on occasion—exactly in the manner of those labor unions that have apparently forgotten the true and legitimate functions of trade unions and spend their time in political agitation with scant regard for their professional duties as teachers, then it is permissible to question the validity of such unions and their activities. Democracy is founded on understanding and magnanimity. But these teachers' unions, like so many other similar bodies in postwar Japan, made a point of never understanding any views but their own, and insisting only on what they considered their own rights. Thus we found ourselves faced with a state of near anarchy in a field which could not be left to the mercies of time and the teachers' unions.

We had gathered together a group of distinguished men of learning in the Education Reform Council, and if these scholars had wielded more influence and authority over public opinion, it would have helped considerably, but, the country then being in the troubled state it was, the people did not know to whom to listen. Later, during the term of my third cabinet, I had another committee formed of educationalists whom I respected, attached directly to the prime minister's office, to advise me personally on matters connected with education. This was called the Education Council, and later became the Round Table Conference on Education. Dr. Takase Sōtaro was then the minister of education, and the council's first members were Abe Yoshishige, Amano Teiyū, Watsuji Tetsurō, Hasegawa Nyozekan, Takahashi Seiichirō, Suzuki Bunshirō, Itakura Takuzō, and Baba Tsunego, to whom were later added Koizumi Shinzō, Suzuki Daisetsu, and Nakayama Ichirō. I myself attended the council's meetings as frequently as other duties permitted, and we reviewed and discussed all problems concerned with education. It quickly transpired that we all held much the same views concerning the pressing problems of the day, such as the decline in public morals, the need for curbing excesses arising from a misunderstanding of the meaning of freedom, the neglect into which respect for the nation and its traditions had fallen due to mistaken ideas of progress, the biased political outlook prevalent among university students, the marked falling off in the quality of scholarship in evidence at all stages in the country's schools, the need for raising the standards of teachers and so on. We considered the possibility of issuing some sort of manifesto in which the points that were obviously most important in the educational field might be set forth and stressed, but were then faced with the question of whether this should be issued by the government or the Diet, and also by other technical aspects of the problem. And since it was generally agreed that any error in handling would only have the opposite to the desired effect, we came to the conclusion it would be wiser not to go on with the project.

Meanwhile, the situation continued to deteriorate. Communism gained more ground in the universities among professors and students alike; teachers' unions were becoming increasingly leftist in tendency, to the extent that many were being taught in schools that it was undemocratic to entertain feelings of loyalty towards one's own country. A subject had been added to the curriculum in the lower schools called a civics course and based upon the American system of education; this so faithfully copied its model that it taught children nothing of the social structure of their own country. Japanese history and geography were no longer taught, or if they were, it was in such a manner that our imperial house was invariably represented as an unbroken line of tyrants. What astonished me most was the discovery that a great many teachers were opposed to the singing of Japan's national anthem and the hoisting of our flag on ceremonial occasions on the ground that such observances were feudalistic. The teachers were indeed teaching Japan's children to become good democratic citizens of their own country!

Things having reached such a sorry pass, I finally prevailed upon Dr. Amano Teiyū, whom I greatly respected, to assume the post of minister of education in May 1950, after he had refused the post several times on the ground that he was not suited to a political career. Clearly something had to be done. When a second American educational mission came to Japan at about that time, even they noted in their subsequent report that although praiseworthy efforts were being made to introduce new methods in education, more attention needed to be paid to the ethical aspect. Dr. Amano held consistently to the view that before and during the war too much stress had been laid on whatever concerned the state and not enough on the individual; whereas since the termination of the Pacific conflict, the individual had become everything and the state nothing. He wanted, therefore, to emphasize the importance of the middle way, and to teach people how difficult it is to actually keep to it. I was completely in agreement with this view and wanted him to reconstruct Japan's educational system along those lines.

Dr. Amano issued a statement, in the same year, concerning November 3—a national holiday which had before the war been celebrated as the anniversary of the Emperor Meiji and was now "Culture Day"—to the effect that there was no reason why the national anthem should not be sung and our flag hoisted on that day. He also conceived the idea of getting together a code of ethics, a sort of moral minimum which should be acceptable to all, and publishing this, not with the intention of forcing it upon people, but to serve as a reference. This was entitled the National Code of Conduct, and the general reaction to the document as well as to Dr. Amano's statement regarding "Culture Day" was, at least so far as the attitude of the Japanese press was concerned, one of uniform disapproval.

The objection to the singing of our national anthem and hoisting of the flag was that such observances would mark a revival of the old militarism. That raised in regard to the National Code of Conduct did not concern itself with the contents of the document, but denounced the whole project as being feudalistic and forcing a standard of morality upon the people, which was just what it was not meant to do. The minister had also advocated the addition of "ethics" or morals as a subject on the curriculum of high schools; this was objected to for the same reasons.

In connection with the question of hoisting the national flag, it may be mentioned that, during the early occupation days, this was prohibited by the occupation authorities. No directive or memorandum was ever issued to that effect, but many cases were reported of members of the occupation forces ordering flags to be lowered when hoisted on national holidays and other occasions, and there is an instance on record of a man having been sentenced to six months' imprisonment with hard labor by the Yokohama Military Tribunal for disobeying such an order. The attitude of GHQ in this matter, as shown by their replies to our official inquiries regarding such occurrences, was equivocal, and remained so until it was made clear in a directive issued on January 6, 1949, that General MacArthur's headquarters had no objection to Japan's flag being flown anywhere within the limits of our own territory. No doubt GHQ had misgivings at first that the sight of our national colors might have the effect of exciting anti-occupation feeling among our people, so strong and natural is the assumption that the flag is a symbol of the country and that everyone loves one's country. If so, GHQ need not have harbored any such fears in regard to our educational circles and teachers.

Upon my return from San Francisco after signing the peace treaty in 1951, the condition of our education had become a major national problem. By then, it had become more widely accepted than ever that democracy consisted of asserting one's rights without being feudalistically conscious of obligations. Teachers were so instructing their pupils, and, even more reprehensively, behaving in a manner that suggested their prior loyalty belonged not to their respective schools but to their unions. Soviet Russia, instead of the United States, was now being held up by them as the model nation to emulate, and the activities of these teachers were such as to lead one to suppose that what they desired was a revolution along the lines of the Russian revolution of 1917. Nor was I alone in such apprehensions; many parents and the public at large were beginning to be similarly disturbed.

In August 1953, Mr. Odate Shigeo, at that time minister of education in my fifth cabinet, visited me at my house in Ōiso to make a detailed explanation of the situation. Later, on January 14 of the following year, at a meeting of the Round Table Conference on Education held at the official residence of the prime minister, the minister spoke at length on the urgent need to get rid of teachers who were using the schoolrooms for the propagation of their extremist ideas and engaging in other subversive activities, and outlined to us the drafts of two bills designed to achieve that result. My feeling was that the government had withheld action long enough and could not wait further, and at the opening of the 19th Diet session I particularly stressed the need for the spring cleaning of our educational system and made clear my intention to introduce new legislation to that end. Two bills were subsequently presented to the Diet—one prohibiting teachers engaged in compulsory education of the young from taking part in political activities, and the second banning all overt political education forced on teachers by their unions. These measures met with violent opposition from a minority in the Diet, the teachers' unions, and a section of the press. Strenuous efforts were made within the Diet to obstruct discussion of the bills and for a time it appeared doubtful when we should be able to bring them to a vote. Mr. Odate displayed remarkable courage throughout the bitter debates that followed, and both bills finally became law in May 1954.

# 17

# Police Reform

Another important reform which we were ordered by the occupation authorities to initiate was the reform of the nation's police set-up and the establishment of two separate police systems—one national-rural, and the other based upon local autonomous forces—each independent of the other. This development occurred while the Liberal Party, of which I was president, was out of power, and even after my return to the premiership and the formation of my second cabinet, I was for some time not certain how the new system worked in practice until a succession of events which called for police action caused me to become aware of the peculiar nature of the new set-up.

According to the new police system sponsored by the occupation authorities, each city, town, and village in the country had its own police force, while, in addition, there existed the "national" police. I was originally under the impression that the latter had jurisdiction over the whole country, but I learned this was not so; the national police had authority only in those districts where there existed no local autonomous police. Furthermore, the government possessed no powers of any kind over either the national or local police forces.

Such a system contained weaknesses, a fact which GHQ no doubt thought would contribute towards the democratization of the nation's police system. It did, but as Communist disturbances attained ever more serious proportions, the inefficiency of the new police system made itself increasingly felt. For instance, cases were reported where Communists in small towns and villages took possession of police stations and occupied municipal offices and the local police were powerless to deal with the situation. Strikers occupied factories in the same way and began operating

144

them for their own profit. The police had, in truth, ceased to mean much as a force entrusted with the maintenance of law and order, and when Koreans in the port city of Kobe started rioting throughout the city, General Eichelberger, who then commanded the U.S. Eighth Army, had to fly to Kobe personally and place the city under martial law before order was restored. I have always considered police work to be one of the most important branches of administration, for which the cabinet must accept the fullest responsibility; however, the cabinet should also be given adequate powers of control over police activities. This was not the case in regard to the Japanese police at the time I formed my second cabinet.

Riots were occurring in different prefectures throughout Japan, to which acts of violence were added a number of cases of train wrecking and the discovery of the dead body of the president of the Japan National Railways on a railroad track in the suburbs of Tokyo on the eve of the announcement by him of a substantial reduction in railway personnel. I called in Mr. Saitō Noboru, who was then head of the national police, and asked why he did not himself go to the scene of these incidents and assume direction of operations, only to be told that the national police could not intervene unless the local police requested their aid.

Even in the case of the May Day rioting before the imperial palace in 1952, which the Tokyo Metropolitan Police managed to put down with some difficulty, the government could give no direct orders to the police. It is inconceivable that there should exist any other country in the world in which all control of the police was handed over to the towns and villages within its boundaries. This was the police system forced upon us following the recommendations of a special advisory mission sent from the United States to Japan. It must therefore have been based on the American system, in which state police and city police function independently of the federal government; but in the United States there is the FBI which operates directly under federal orders and takes care of cases that cannot be left to state or city police, or which lie outside their jurisdiction.

We particularly felt the need for some overall police organization of that type at a time when disturbances that were by no means local in character were taking place up and down the land and against which even the comparatively strong police forces in the large cities could do very little. I therefore instituted investigations to find a way to remedy matters and, as a result, was able to arrange for the establishment, during my tenure of office, of the present system of national police divided into prefectural units, but not before a great deal of preliminary and patient negotiation had taken place. Apart from this step, there was eventually established a separate police force—initially known as the National Police Reserve—acting under the direct orders of the government as a reinforcement of the ordinary police in any emergency (which later was expanded and developed into the present

Defense Force). However, the main theme of this chapter is the reorganization of the police forces after they had been reformed under the previous cabinet.

According to the original occupation reform, all towns and villages with a population of more than five thousand inhabitants were required to raise and maintain their own police. Under this requirement, more than sixteen hundred such police units, each operating independently of all others as separate forces, came into being, of which more than fourteen hundred policed small towns and villages. Such districts as did not raise their own forces were grouped together under the jurisdiction of the national police, and although theoretically each local force could ask others to cooperate, or apply for additional aid to the national police, such action was made difficult by the professional and sectional jealousies to be found in all such groups and there were very few cases in which the national police had been called in without causing friction. Furthermore, the fact that the police were financed by the municipality made it all too easy, especially in the case of small towns and villages, for people of influence in the place to establish special relations with the custodians of law and order.

As I have said, dividing up the police system into feeble, small, and self-contained units did not contribute to making them a body dedicated to serving the interests of the people, but did obliterate all traces of the kind of political and ideological police supervision that had existed up to the end of the Pacific War. But now the fact that the police had become so feeble had become a serious drawback. And to that problem was added another: many towns and villages were finding it financially difficult to provide funds for maintaining their own local police and were beginning to complain on that score to the government. None of these factors augured well for the new system, and less than one year after its establishment there were already demands from many quarters that, without necessarily changing the whole system again, at least the local forces in comparatively small towns and villages should be amalgamated with the national police.

The labor troubles and train wreckings which were featured in the news from 1949 onwards served to strengthen such demands. At the same time, however, the agitation for change also served to stiffen those of the opposite opinion, who held that any such step would carry the threat of a return to the old form of political and ideological police, such as existed in Japan in prewar times. In this matter, also, the conflicting views of the Government Section within General MacArthur's headquarters and of G2, the section of the U.S. Army concerned with security matters, reflected the controversy within the nation itself. The Public Safety Division of G2 had been opposed to the establishment of small autonomous police units at the time of the original reform, and so were well disposed towards the suggestion that these small units be amalgamated with the national police. On the other hand,

Government Section had been responsible for sponsoring the new system, and was, moreover, charged with the specific duty of democratizing Japan. It was natural, therefore, that those within Government Section should frown on any plans for a second reform that would change in any way the basic lines of the first, particularly if amendments suggested the least possibility of a return to the former police system. In fact, Government Section may well have suspected the Japanese government of wanting to revise the police law in order to recover the right of appointing the chief of police, as a necessary step towards attaining the sort of police who would heed its wishes and orders. Under these circumstances, we found it awkward to present proposals to GHQ from our side for the revision of the Police Law. Added to which, the Public Safety Division of G2, which seemed at first to favor the abolition of small police units, now displayed a change of front, due perhaps to some warning given by those higher up within GHQ, and informed us that it would not be advisable to contemplate a revision of the law until at least two years had elapsed from the date of the original reform.

However, following the incidents of 1949 to which I have previously alluded, Communist activity within Japan began to take on the character of attempts to bring about a revolution by force. Imperialism once more became the declared enemy of the native Communists, and American policy was attacked at every turn, with the obvious aim of causing a rift in U.S.-Japan relations. It seems that the more moderate policy adopted until that time by the Japanese Communist Party had come under criticism in Moscow, and that this change of tactics was the result of a new policy dictated from outside. From that time, the attitude of General MacArthur's headquarters towards the Communists became correspondingly more severe. Then came the most noteworthy event of the year 1950—the outbreak of war in Korea—raising fears that Communist activity in Japan would increase still more with the advance of the North Korean army into South Korea, and giving further ground for anxiety regarding the ability of our enfeebled police force to maintain order in the country. In these circumstances, the Supreme Commander for the Allied Powers issued a directive calling into being a new organization to be called the National Police Reserve, thus providing our government with a police force taking orders directly from the cabinet. This new force was placed under the supervision of the Public Safety Department of G2, while the ordinary police remained under the control of Government Section within GHQ. There was some talk at the time among cabinet members of making the new force a national police under the control of the government, but GHQ regarded it more in the light of an embryonic army, and it continued to expand along those lines until it became the Self-Defense Force of today.

It had become quite clear by that time that the two weakest points of the reformed police system consisted, on the one hand, of the inefficiency of small independent police units and, on the other, of the impossibility of employing the police on a national scale. Various proposals for remedying the situation were suggested, both by the Government Section of GHQ and our own authorities, but none of them solved the crucial question of the feeble local units. And to add to the already existing complicated structure our own version of the American FBI, as envisaged by some of the plans, seemed merely to make the police an even more unwieldy organization. Finally, in 1951, we arrived at a solution whereby provision was to be made for the local autonomous police to be abolished by plebiscite, and their duties taken over by the national police; a second feature of the proposed reform being that the national police was given the right to function in an area under the jurisdiction of the local police, should the governor of the prefecture concerned request such action. This reform was enacted and found to be effective. There were 1,400 police units in towns and villages at the time of the change, and only 127 remained by 1954. No case occurred during the same period of the governor of a prefecture resorting to the national police.

I was still not satisfied, however. The system was not yet of a nature which permitted the government to assume full responsibility for the work of the police, and I had yet another police bill introduced into the Diet, which, owing to the dissolution of the legislature in May 1953, unfortunately did not pass. The same bill was reintroduced in the next Diet in 1954 and, with the cooperation of the Progressive Party, became law. Its main points were the abolition of the local autonomous police and the reorganization of the national police by prefectures with the unification of powers of command and appointment. The right to appoint the chief of police and the general management of the whole system was entrusted to the Public Safety Commission as before, this being a valuable feature of the postwar reform. I may add that, before becoming law, the bill met with the same sort of opposition, involving resort to violence by a minority in the Diet, as did the two educational bills previously—the opposition declaring that the bill was reactionary and aimed at the revival of the prewar police state. Time has proved to the Japanese people, however, that there was no substance in such charges.

# 18

## The Self-Defense Force

In July 1950, shortly after the outbreak of the Korean War, I received a communication from General MacArthur; it was urgent official business, with orders for measures to be taken to assure the maintenance of order in the Japanese islands, including the establishment of a National Police Reserve force to consist of seventy-five thousand men, and an increase in the size of the Maritime Safety Force by eight thousand men. The necessary steps to implement these decisions were to be taken by the Japanese government without delay.

I had long felt grave concern over the inefficient state of our police under the postwar reform set-up and had been seeking means of remedying the situation, so that this directive from SCAP seemed to me the opportunity. I therefore immediately called together the officials concerned and began discussions regarding the measures to be taken. The purpose of the directive was clear enough: it was to strengthen our police force in a manner that would fill the gap left by the transfer of U.S. troops from occupation duty in Japan to the Korean battlefronts, and to meet the danger of Communist invasion in areas outside Korea. What we were not quite clear about, however, was the character to be given the new force and its relation to the existing police. Moreover, the establishment of the new police force was certain to provide an occasion for detailed questioning of the government during the special session of the Diet that had just been convened, so we lost no time in entering into negotiations with GHQ to ascertain their exact views on the matter. As a result of talks at headquarters, we were able to state, in reply to questions in the Diet, that the new force was to be organized separately from the ordinary police and under the direct orders of the government, although it would maintain close relations with both the national and provincial police with the object of reinforcing these whenever such action might become necessary.

In reply to questions whether the creation of the National Police Reserve did not constitute a step in the direction of rearmament, we stressed the fact that the new force was designed purely for the purpose of maintaining order within Japanese territory and bore no relation to anything in the nature of rearmament. This particular point, however, came up for discussion more and more as plans for the gradual strengthening of Japan's means of self-defense progressed.

The question of the character and purpose of the new force having been thus decided, we had now to set about completing its organization. To handle this task a committee was formed—with Mr. Ōhashi Takeo, minister of justice, and Mr. Okazaki Katsuo, chief secretary to the cabinet, as its leading members—to discuss the matter. Mr. Masuhara Keikichi, who was then governor of Kagawa Prefecture, was chosen as the person most suitable to direct the new force, and Mr. Eguchi Midoru, the vice minister of labor, was later asked to join the committee. I knew Mr. Masuhara well, and we were able to secure his services as chief of the National Police Reserve when the new force was inaugurated, with Mr. Eguchi serving as deputy chief. Needless to say, we at all times kept in touch with GHQ, and were able to come to agreement with General MacArthur's headquarters on such basic principles as placing the force under the orders of the prime minister. The chief was to be appointed and would be in command of the entire force; the country was to be divided into a given number of districts; and the force was to have such equipment as was necessary for the performance of its duties and functions as an auxiliary police force charged with the maintenance of order in the country.

The National Police Reserve came into being on August 10, 1950, a month after my receipt of the supreme commander's directive.

With the appointment of the chief and deputy chief, we set to work to raise the men for the new force. In view of the generally censorious attitude adopted by the public towards the new reserve, and the sort of ideas then prevalent among our younger generation, there were some who were pessimistic about the number of possible volunteers; in the event, the result exceeded all our expectations and we found ourselves coping with 382,000 applicants, or five times the actual number of men required. Those who were accepted were put into police schools under the control of the national police to undergo their preliminary training. Apprehensions had also been voiced concerning the likely quality of the applicants. These, too, proved to be groundless: we were not only able to get fine men, but the quality of the applicants seems to have been kept up through the years, so that I was told last year by one of the chiefs in the Kyūshū district that he was particularly impressed by the officers now being turned out by the camps.

We thus met with little difficulty in the selection of men for the new force, but the initial task of getting together officers qualified to command was not easy. The obvious solution would have been to employ men who had commanded in the old imperial army and navy, a plan which, however, was accompanied by equally obvious drawbacks and which I myself desired to avoid resorting to if possible. General MacArthur's headquarters was also against any such step, and, as we had already begun recruiting men, the issue became urgent. We had first of all to reach a decision on who was to be placed in actual charge of the operational side of the force, a post which, according to the new regulations, was to carry the title of chief of general group. Our choice for the post was Mr. Hayashi Keizō, who was then deputy director-general of the Imperial Household Agency, and we had no reason to regret it later. In the case of other officers, these would rank high in the normal grades of members of the civil service, and as it would have been impossible to obtain so many men of such senior rank by the usual procedures provided under civil service regulations, we changed the rules so far as the new force was concerned to permit the nomination of officers.

But the question of where to find the officer material still remained, and also the companion question of by what standards they should be selected. It was impossible to arrive at any hard and fast rule in this matter, so we decided to do without fixed rules and rely upon recommendations made from all quarters, judging applicants on their individual merits. In this way we finally managed to obtain two hundred approved men. In addition to that number, we still needed a further six hundred officers to serve under the two hundred; these were selected by examination from some twelve thousand applicants. We also promoted men from the ranks, and so, at last, were able to furnish the National Police Reserve with the necessary first quota of officers needed.

We now had both officers and men, but the question of pay came up next—or, to be more exact, had been troubling us from the first. It was my belief that, in order to get good material and not give the men grounds for discontent, we should fix the pay as high as possible, and I had issued instructions to that effect to those concerned with the raising of the force. This course, however, met with objections from GHQ—our tentative plan was to fix the pay of "second patrolmen," the lowest rank in the force, at 5,000 yen (14 dollars) monthly plus a round sum of from 50,000 to 100,000 yen (140 to 280 dollars) upon discharge. The Government Section of GHQ opposed this proposal on the ground that, since the men would be completely provided for by the state, their monthly pay need be no more than necessary for pocket money; that the bonus to be paid upon completion of their term of service—which had been fixed at 60,000 yen (168 dollars) after negotiations with GHQ—should be regarded as deferred regular pay; and that 5,000 yen monthly was, in any case, excessive remuneration by comparison with the standard earnings of members of Japan's civil service, which at that time were roughly about 6,300 yen monthly.

A difference of opinion on this question of pay also existed between Government Section and G2 within General MacArthur's headquarters. G2, in charge of the new force, was in complete agreement with us on the pay issue, being aware that we were being called upon to create a body of seventy-five thousand men with the greatest possible speed, and that a high rate of pay, fixed without reference to the corresponding rates of remuneration in other government services, was the only means at our disposal for attracting the kind of recruits we wanted. The Government Section was not without reasons, however, for objecting to this course. The ordinary police forces were under their control, and the men within Government Section feared that a big difference in pay might cause men of ability in the ordinary police to resign their posts and enlist in the National Police Reserve. The argument continued with Government Section remaining adamant, while, in the meantime, men were being enlisted whom we could not pay because the sum had not been fixed. It was a situation that was bound to influence the morale of the new force adversely, and also of those who might otherwise be induced to enlist. Thus the government was faced with a crisis. As a last resort, it was decided that I should appeal personally to General MacArthur, which I did by letter early in October 1950. This led to the proposal that we should consider the question from the economic viewpoint of what the nation could afford. After discussions between Mr. Okazaki, the chief secretary of the cabinet, and General Marquat, head of the Economic and Scientific Section of GHQ, the pay of second patrolmen was finally fixed at 4,500 yen monthly plus a bonus of 60,000 yen per man upon completion of service. Certain other minor difficulties having been surmounted, we were at last able to endorse the scheme at a cabinet meeting held on November 10, 1950, three months after recruiting for the new force had begun. Thus the new force, as an auxiliary force to supplement the functions of the ordinary police, came into being. Although officially certain preliminaries still remained to be completed, the buildings that had formerly housed the Fisheries College were taken over as the headquarters of the National Police Reserve, and I inspected the men there for the first time in December 1950.

The personnel of the Maritime Safety Board (Japan's embryo coastguard) had also to be expanded by eight thousand additional men. To accomplish this, ships were necessary, and we had none worth speaking of at the time apart from a few patrol boats used by the Maritime Safety Board to assist vessels in distress, the largest of which was only 700 tons. However, as it was out of the question to build new ships at such short notice, it was decided to make shift with what patrol vessels were available for the time being and begin by recruiting the additional men, which was done.

The establishment of the National Police Reserve and the increase in the personnel of the Maritime Safety Board contributed to the strengthening of Japan's police forces, but it remained obvious that, once a peace treaty was signed with the Allied powers and the nation regained its independence, such forces would be far from adequate for the defense of the country. Recognition of this fact led to the decision to invite the U.S. forces to remain in Japan after the signing of the peace treaty, and to the signing, at the same time as the treaty itself at San Francisco, of a U.S.-Japan Security Treaty.

Although thus named, in fact the burden of the defense of the Japanese homeland was actually laid entirely on the shoulders of the Americans, and the United States naturally did not desire that this should be a permanent arrangement any more than we did. The question therefore arose, early in the talks between the two nations to decide on the wording of the pact, of the desirability of Japan's gradually increasing its defensive power in order to assume a share of responsibility for the security and defense of our country. The obligation to do this was written into the pact, and became one of the important problems confronting Japan after the nation regained its independence.

To briefly outline subsequent developments, the strength of the National Police Reserve, which started out with 75,000 men, was increased to 110,000 at the time the peace treaty came into effect in April 1952. In August of the same year, the National Police Reserve and the sea force, which until that time had been under the control of the Maritime Safety Board, were brought together and jointly placed under a newly created government agency, the Security Board, which took its orders directly from the cabinet: at the same time the ground force was re-christened the Security Force (Hoantai), and the sea force the Maritime Security Force (Keibitai); the prime task assigned to both forces being the maintenance of tranquility and order in the country and the protection of lives and property. In regard to the problem of ships for the Maritime Security Force, it was thought that the only practical means of procuring these was on loan from the United States. This question had been discussed at an early stage in our negotiations with GHQ, and after many such informal talks I finally addressed a letter to General Matthew B. Ridgway, who had succeeded General MacArthur as Supreme Commander for the Allied Powers in April 1952, requesting the loan of American vessels, and stating that Japan possessed at that time only three patrol boats of 700 tons each, twenty-two of 450 tons, and twenty others of 270 tons, a total quite inadequate to guard a coastline extending over some nine thousand miles in length; and that, to remedy this situation, we would appreciate the loan of at least ten frigates and fifty landing craft.

Special legislation was necessary before the U.S. administration could accede to such a request, and this was enacted in the following July. The law then passed authorized the loan of ships not only to Japan, but also to countries such as the National Republic of China in Formosa and the Republic of Korea, both of which had also asked for ships. The terms and other conditions of the loan having been laid down in the law, negotiations were opened with the U.S. government, which resulted in the Charter Party Agreement between Japan and the United States being signed in Tokyo in November 1952, providing for the loan to Japan of eighteen frigates of 1,500 tons each, and fifty landing craft of 250 tons. This agreement was ratified by the Japanese Diet and became effective late in December.

At about this time the U.S. government decided to group all forms of aid extended to foreign countries under one law, and so the MSA, or Mutual Security Act, came into being. The proposed loan of vessels to Japan came under the new law, and so in May 1954 a second U.S.-Japan agreement was signed for the loan of U.S. naval vessels to Japan, whereby Japan obtained, in addition to the ships already mentioned, two destroyers of 1,600 tons each and two of 1,400 tons.

These developments created other problems for us. In order to benefit from the provisions of MSA, Japan had to undertake to fulfill the obligations set forth in the law. And this had been primarily designed to apply to countries possessing an army and navy, to which Japan alone happened to be an exception. Something needed to be done to bring Japan into line with the law's requirements if my country was to be granted full MSA status, and, as the situation also, both in Japan and abroad, required some such step to be taken, it was decided to include among the duties of the new Security Forces that of repelling foreign invasion, and to frame a new law for that purpose.

To enact such a law, it was necessary for me to obtain the support of the conservative opposition in the Diet—the Progressive Party and certain Liberals who had seceded from my own party. Therefore in September 1953 I visited Mr. Shigemitsu Mamoru, the president of the Progressive Party, at his home in Kamakura and came to an understanding with him; first, regarding the gradual reinforcement of our defensive power to compensate for a gradual reduction in the strength of the U.S. security ground forces in Japan; and secondly, on legalizing the decision to make it a duty of Japan's Security Forces to repel foreign invasion. However, there existed other points that needed discussion in our negotiations with the two conservative opposition groups, and so the talks continued until March 1954, when we were at last able to reach a full understanding, at about the same time as the signing of the MSA agreement. Thus assured of the necessary support, the government introduced two bills into the Diet, the Defense Agency Establishment Bill and the Self-Defense Force Bill. These, as expected, met with the usual violent attacks from the leftists, on this occasion with the additional imputation that the bills were unconstitutional. However, both laws were enacted and became effective on July 1, 1954.

*Posing for a photograph after his return from Italy, where he served as ambassador, 1932.*

*Leaving for a diplomatic mission in Turkey, 1932.*

*The smiling, cigar-smoking Yoshida is the image best remembered by the Japanese, 1942.*

*Tokyo, 1948.*

*Walking on Ōiso beach close to his home, 1948.*

*Yoshida listens to an open letter of inquiry regarding the bribery scandal involving his government and the textile industry, 1948.*

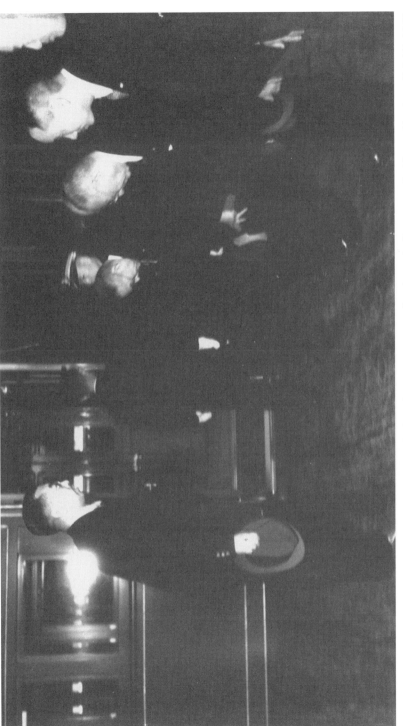

*At Tokyo Station, Yoshida (bowing most deeply) and other high-ranking government officials send off Emperor Hirohito on his trip to Kyūshū, 1949.*

*Meeting John Foster Dulles, on left, and William Sebald of the United States to discuss strategies for the upcoming San Francisco Peace Conference, 1951.*

*Yoshida yells, "Fools!" and makes other disparaging remarks to his political foes in a speech to a budget committee meeting of the House of Representatives, 1953.*

*Famous for disliking cameramen, Yoshida wards them off with his walking stick, 1954. In 1952 he splashed water on an approaching cameraman while giving a speech.*

*Yoshida pays a visit to President Dwight Eisenhower in the White House, 1960.*

*Yoshida relaxing with a cigar. He once received cigars from the emperor, who knew about his smoking preference, 1964.*

Under the new laws, the Security Board became the Defense Agency; the Security Force the Ground Self-Defense Force; and the Maritime Security Force the Maritime Self-Defense Force, to which was now added the Air Self-Defense Force; and the Self-Defense Force as a whole became an officially recognized force charged with the defense of the peace and independence of our country. I resigned office in the following December, but have continued to feel a strong concern for the force over the establishment and development of which I had thus presided, and nothing has pleased me more than the reports reaching me which show that the force has continued to become steadily more efficient, not only in regard to its equipment, but also in the quality and training of its men.

Some reference is perhaps in order here to the attitude of the Japanese public at large towards the new Defense Force, at the time of its inception. The general reaction was, quite simply, that the step involved something illegal and unconstitutional, which was given a specious pretext for existence by laws enacted by a reactionary government, and although such a view was perhaps inevitable in view of the trend of public sentiment, which was strongly pacifist at the time, it was nonetheless to be regretted. Moreover, the force was viewed with disfavor by many of those who had seen service in the former imperial army and navy, on the ground that there was little to be expected from a body of men from the formation and training of which they themselves had been excluded. I was apprehensive that such a cold reception from both the political Left and Right, so to speak, might have adverse effects upon the young men in the force, and searched for some means whereby to encourage people to look upon the new uniformed men with affection and respect. To this end, I issued instructions to the authorities concerned to turn out the force to undertake rescue work whenever floods, typhoons, or major fires occurred—calamities to which we Japanese are only too frequently subject—in order to foster a closer relationship between the men of the force and the inhabitants of the districts where they were stationed. I also had them parade in formation through the streets of large cities, such as Tokyo, so that the people might have the opportunity of being stirred by the sight. I cannot say to what extent these and other measures actually influenced public sentiment, but it appears that in the provinces, at least, the Self-Defense Force has since come to be regarded with a more friendly feeling than formerly.

Another matter which caused me concern was the education of officers. This had been an important problem in the days of the former imperial army and navy, when many academies and institutions existed for that purpose. The problem that we now faced was to remedy the shortcomings of the former method of imparting military education as practiced in the prewar institutions and to ensure that the men, as members of a defense force forming part of a democratic system of government, had a sound knowledge not only of the technical aspects of their work, but also of the world at large: to turn out, in other words, officers who would be sensible citizens as well.

This matter had been in the forefront of my mind ever since the establishment of the National Police Reserve, and I had consistently urged the importance of raising the various educational centers to their proper level. To this end, the Public Security University was founded in 1952 under the direct control of the Security Board, and the first students were enrolled in April 1953. It was originally suggested that this university should be housed at the site of the former Naval College near Kure, in the Hiroshima Prefecture, but I objected to this step because it seemed to me doubtful whether we should be able to get competent professors to work at such a distance from Tokyo, and also because I considered it desirable that the college should be established in some place near the nation's capital in order that students should be able to acquire a sound sense of values through contact with the trends of the present-day world at home and abroad.

A suitable site was eventually found at Kurihama, and the name of the institution changed to the Defense University, in line with the change in the status of the force. We were fortunate in securing, through the kind offices of Dr. Koizumi Shinzō of Keiō University, Mr. Maki Tomoo as its first director. Four years after its foundation, in March 1957, I was invited as the first director-general of defense to the first graduation ceremony held at the college, and the bearing of the 337 graduates for the land, sea, and air services that day was for me a moving experience. They and their successors must not be cast in the mould of the officers Japan had before. To know nothing but the art of waging war may make men efficient in actual combat, but it causes them to be totally lacking in general knowledge and the behavior proper to sensible citizens, which, in turn, leads them to meddle with assurance in fields beyond their ken. The Pacific War, and the years leading up to that tragedy, were rich in such examples of uniformed politicians. The vision inculcated by a liberal education alone can save soldiers from that danger.

The establishment of the Defense Agency and the Self-Defense Forces, perhaps inevitably, aroused argument in many quarters that these acts were in contravention of Article 9 of the postwar Constitution renouncing war, and were, in fact, so many steps towards rearmament—a controversy that has continued to this day. I myself have consistently opposed rearmament, and said so throughout my tenure of office. On no occasion did I contemplate taking such a step, and I would like, before closing this chapter on Japan's Defense Force, to restate my personal views on the issue.

To me, the idea of rearmament has always seemed to be one verging on idiocy. A nation such as the United States may possess sufficient arms and equipment to call herself armed, but this is made possible by the untold wealth of the American people and the impetus given to the perfection of her armaments by the Second World War.

For Japan to attempt anything which could be considered as rearmament, even on the smaller scale warranted by the differences in national wealth and products between our two countries, is completely out of the question. Rearmament, for Japan, is simply a word with which politicians and others may conjure, but which to anyone with the slightest knowledge of the subject can never be anything more than a word. The necessary wealth is lacking, and, even more than wealth, the necessary psychological background, which is the desire of the people to rearm, is just not there. The miseries and destruction of the Pacific War are still actualities for a large majority of the Japanese people; they remember only too vividly what war is like and they want none of it again.

The proposal that Japan should rearm was first advanced in earnest immediately before the outbreak of the Korean War. The American government had begun seriously to consider the question of concluding peace with Japan, and that fact gave rise to the problem of the defense of the country after a peace had been concluded and the Allied forces had been withdrawn. The international situation made it out of the question to leave Japan sovereign and naked—and without defense—and it was in that way that the subject of Japanese rearmament first came to be discussed. I objected to the suggestion for reasons already outlined, and we compromised, at least at that juncture, by arranging that the disused facilities of the former imperial army and navy be restored to operation, to cooperate with the U.S. forces. Soon after this decision the Japanese government received General MacArthur's directive to establish a National Police Reserve (with the outbreak of the Korean War), and thus the first step towards the provision of some means of defense for Japan by the Japanese was taken at the instance of the occupation authorities.

That directive was dated July 8, 1950, and the eighth special session of the Diet had been convened for the twelfth of that month, so that the proposal to create the Police Reserve came in for a good deal of questioning during the session, and much criticism that the step was unconstitutional. In reply to interpolations in the Diet, I stated that the purpose of the new force was restricted to the maintenance of law and order within the country, and that no such thing as a step towards rearmament was being contemplated. And that, in fact, the National Police Reserve could not, by any stretch of the imagination, be regarded as an army. The controversy as to whether a Self-Defense Force is, in fact, an army or not, and therefore unconstitutional, dates from that time.

All government replies to Diet questioners in such circumstances are the result of discussion between the various departments concerned, and made either by the prime minister or the minister in charge. In this case, Mr. Ōhashi Takeo, then minister of justice, replied to questions on the issue of constitutionality by pointing out that the Constitution forbade the maintenance of forces capable of conducting war, with all that step means in modern times, but that it was permissible to devise means of national defense with forces that were not equipped to conduct wars. To questions as to what we would do if the United States demanded that Japan rearm, I myself answered that we must obey the constitutional ban on rearmament, and would decline to take such a step, even if such a demand were received.

This was, in my view, common-sense policy and, given the position in which Japan was placed, the obvious and sensible next step was to make common cause with the United States for the defense of the country. But this step too, or, to be more exact, the text of the U.S.-Japan Security Treaty, also became the subject of questions and target of attacks when the document was submitted, together with the San Francisco Peace Treaty, for ratification by the Diet at the twelfth session in October 1951. The charge was made that even the stationing of foreign troops in Japan would infringe on Article 9 of the Constitution, to which we replied that, as anyone can see who can read, while "war as a sovereign right of the nation and the threat or use of force as a means of settling international disputes" were renounced in Article 9, the U.S.-Japan Security Treaty represented a means of maintaining the peace and independence of Japan, and, further, that every nation possesses the right to defend itself. This did not satisfy our radical interlocutors, however, and debate on the subject has been going on both within and outside the Diet ever since.

On the other hand, it should be remembered that there were those openly in favor of rearmament, and who held either the view that such a step was not unconstitutional, or that the Constitution should be revised to make rearmament possible. These persons were also vocal in the Diet debates, though it is possible that some of the questions put to me were asked in the hope of unmasking me as a crafty politician who was apparently suspected of denying the existence of plans for rearmament while promoting them under cover.

To make my own position crystal-clear on this point, I declared in my policy speech delivered at the opening of the fifteenth session of the Diet, following the formation of my fourth cabinet in October 1952, that Japan should naturally reinforce its defensive power as the nation's economy recovered, but that the time had not yet arrived, by any means, to consider rearmament. To subsequent questions I replied that, if rearmament was to be undertaken, it would have to be achieved with the acquiescence of the Japanese people.

The trouble with all such questions was that there was so little reality behind them. It was the same with discussions about the possibility of our forces being sent overseas, which to this day continue to fill columns in Japan's newspapers. Such fears no doubt have their origin in the Korean War, when many countries sent their troops to form contingents of the United Nations' forces in Korea. They may also have been influenced, and inflamed, by a report that President Eisenhower stated during the presidential election of 1952 that Asia should be defended by Asians, or words to that effect. Again, questions were asked in the Diet, to which I answered that cooperation with the United Nations was only possible for Japan insofar as it was compatible with our Constitution, treaty commitments, and the laws of our country in general; that beyond that point, the United Nations could not ask us to undertake any commitments, nor did we have any obligation to do so. In short, any such step obviously lay outside the competence of the government of Japan.

What struck me forcibly about these questions concerning the sending of our forces abroad was the all too clear intention behind them of giving the Japanese people, and the men of our Self-Defense Forces particularly, the impression that the sort of contingency might easily arise, and that our new forces and our nation as a whole might be made the tools of American imperialism and aggression—to borrow for once the phraseology of Japan's "progressive" intellectuals. The insinuation was as misleading as it was groundless, and I stressed that fact in my replies in the Diet. No country in the world today is in a position to defend itself unaided against aggression—even the powerful United States relies upon the collective power of the free countries as a major means of defense. It was this fact, and the same need on our side, which gave birth to the U.S.-Japan Security Treaty. Or, rather, in our case it was the inescapable outcome of four historical forces: defeat, occupation by foreign armies, the regaining of independence, and the threats to which we found that independence exposed us. Our national interests coincided with those of the United States in that matter, and I continue to believe that allying ourselves with the United States remains the best means of providing for the defense both of the United States and of ourselves.

# 19

## Agricultural Reform

The reform of agriculture was another major objective of occupation policy. Viewed from the standpoint of the Allied powers, the Japanese land system was not only feudalistic, but also weakened the national economy while providing the militarists with one of their firmest bases of support. The agrarian half of the nation represented a reservoir of soldiers and cheap labor. Rural landlords impeded the democratization of Japan equally with the militarists, the financiers, and the bureaucracy. To end this state of affairs by liberating the agricultural classes and raising their living standards was, therefore, regarded by the occupation authorities as a vital step in bringing about the demilitarization and democratization of Japan.

We had, indeed, anticipated that would be the case. The agricultural problem had been a major issue confronting successive Japanese cabinets since the early years of the century. Furthermore, agricultural controls enforced during the Pacific War had the effect of placing small farmers in a specially favored position in the country, so that by 1945 the existing state of affairs, whatever the outward form might suggest, differed to a marked degree from what was widely imagined abroad from available textbooks on the subject. It was true that the change had been occasioned by the need to maintain the food supply during the period of hostilities. But that objective became even more pressing with the end of the war, so that Japan's agricultural system would in any event have had to be reconsidered in order to bring it closer in line with the actual situation.

That circumstance led to the passing of the first agricultural reforms at the time of the Shidehara cabinet, when Mr. Matsumura Kenzō was minister of agriculture, and before any SCAP directive had been issued on the subject. The plan then prepared had been drawn up by Mr. Wada Hiroo, at that time director of Agricultural Administration and later minister of agriculture in my first cabinet, and its two main points were the substitution of payment of farm-rent in money, instead of in kind as previously, and the restriction of individual ownership of agricultural land to three *chō* (one *chō* being approximately 2.45 acres), beyond which amount the plan made it compulsory for landowners to turn over the land to the tenants, a revolutionary step at the time.

This Japanese plan was doubtless evolved with knowledge of GHQ's intentions to seize the opportunity of solving the agricultural problem that had been troubling the nation for so long. But even so it met with a chorus of objections when it was originally outlined at one of our cabinet meetings. In particular, the compulsory acquisition of agricultural land by tenants was a revolutionary idea never before proposed in Japan, and, as the session of the Diet during which the bill was to be introduced—the first to be convened after the termination of the war—was to last for only two weeks, many members of the cabinet were of the opinion that such an important measure might well be delayed until later, when there would be more time for debate. Some compromise appeared necessary. In the event, the plan was endorsed by the cabinet after the limit of individual holdings had been raised from three to five *chō*, and was published in the press on November 23, 1945, after which date it was declared illegal for landowners to effect any change in regard to their agricultural land holdings—this to prevent them from forcing tenants to agree to alterations in their leases or contracts before the reform could be put into operation.

Although, as I have mentioned, agricultural land reform was one of the more important occupation objectives, both the Allied Council for Japan and General MacArthur's headquarters adopted a somewhat more leisurely attitude to this question than towards other problems and appeared disposed to give the question serious consideration before proceeding to take any definite steps. This was, no doubt, because reforms and changes connected with farm land had invariably been accompanied by a good deal of trouble and rural unrest, and sometimes even by bloodshed, in other countries. Thus it happened that the first plan for agricultural reform proposed by Mr. Matsumura must not only have furnished GHQ with a practical blueprint for carrying out the reform, but also have been instructive in indicating to the occupation authorities, at the time of its publication, that, while some objected to it as being too radical, the number of those in Japan who expressed a contrary opinion—that the plan did not go far enough—was by no means small. It is therefore most probable that the Matsumura plan encouraged GHQ to push forward with a plan of its own, which later became the second agricultural reform.

The bill embodying the Matsumura plan was introduced in the lower House of the Diet on December 6, 1945, and, as was to be expected, met

with stiff resistance. On December 11 a GHQ directive concerning agricultural land reform, dated December 9, was read to the House committee to
which the bill had been referred. This did not differ materially in content
from the bill proposed by the government, but its wording—including a demand for the raising of the living standards of the Japanese farmers who
had been "enslaved . . . for centuries of feudal oppression"—left no doubt
as to the real intentions of GHQ. This document transformed the atmosphere in the Diet towards the government measure, and the bill passed both
Houses with only slight modifications. It may therefore be said that the directive facilitated the passage of the bill, but the directive itself said little beyond pointing out the necessity of enacting agricultural reform as a step in
the democratization of the Japanese economy, and requiring the Japanese
government to present not later than March 15, 1946, a practical plan of reform embodying certain points, which were indicated only in general and
abstract terms. In other words, the main purpose of the directive seemed to
be to show the Japanese government that GHQ was very much interested in
the question.

The law based upon the Matsumura plan was promulgated before the
end of 1945 and became effective from February 1946. That part of the
measure dealing with the compulsory transfer of land was not enforced because General MacArthur's headquarters thought the provisions of the law
on that point could be improved upon; wherefore land ownership remained unchanged until the implementation of the second agricultural
land reform.

Officially, GHQ was waiting for the Japanese government's reply to be
submitted by March 15, 1946, but, unofficially, the occupation authorities
had early indicated to the Ministry of Agriculture flaws which they had de-
tected in the details of the first agricultural reform. These were made public
for the first time at a press conference held by William J. Gilmartin and
Wolf I. Ladejinsky, the experts within GHQ in charge of the reform, on
March 12, 1946, just before the deadline fixed for the government's reply to
SCAP, and consisted of two points: that the maximum holding of five *chō*
was too large and would leave too many tenant farmers in the same position as before, and that, in order to ensure that land transfers were carried
out and to shorten the period for this to be accomplished, the government
itself should act as agent instead of transfers being direct between landlords
and tenants. However, a general election had already been ordered at that
time by a directive from GHQ, and Mr. Matsumura had in the meantime
been purged from public office. Therefore the outgoing government, not
having the time to make fresh plans, presented a reply to GHQ based, in its
essentials, upon the first reform.

General MacArthur next referred the question to the Allied Council for
Japan. As a result of the deliberations of this body, agreement was for once

reached between the American, British, Soviet, and Chinese representatives, and their conclusions were submitted to General MacArthur on June 17. It seems that during the meetings both Mr. W. Macmahon Ball, the British Commonwealth's representative, and General Kuzma Derevyanko, representing the Soviet Union, presented individual plans, and the one finally adopted broadly followed the lines suggested by the British representative. This did not differ materially from the plan that had emerged from discussions between GHQ and officials of our Ministry of Agriculture, except on one point—the Allied Council plan contained a clause that would have limited the average area of land to be transferred to a tenant farmer to one *chō*. This clause, no doubt based upon ignorance of actual farming conditions in Japan, would have played havoc with agricultural production had it been adopted. Fortunately we were able to make this clear to GHQ and the suggestion was dropped. The Soviet representative favored the confiscation from the owners of all tenant-worked lands without compensation, and the knowledge that such a proposal had been advanced probably helped in reconciling the landowners to the actual terms of the second land reform.

The final details of the reform measure were decided upon in the course of our negotiations with GHQ, and then brought together and communicated to the Japanese government, not officially as a directive, but more privately in the form of advising us of their opinion. Apparently General MacArthur took that step because he thought that such an undertaking as agricultural land reform—affecting as it did the fundamental economic structure of our society—could only bear fruit if it was planned by the Japanese themselves and of a nature genuinely acceptable to the Japanese people. I think that the methods employed in this matter of land reform, at least, enabled GHQ and the Japanese government to work well together, which was not always the case.

The general election was held on April 10, 1946, as a result of which the Shidehara cabinet resigned on April 22. By that time the food shortage had become acute and social unrest had grown. What was called "Food May Day" was held on May 19, following the usual May Day observance on May 1, and the political scene at the time appeared mainly composed of masses of red flags and demonstrators. In such an atmosphere, I found it a difficult matter to form my first cabinet, but the appointment of Mr. Wada Hiroo as minister of agriculture finally completed the list of members and the first Yoshida cabinet came into being on May 22, with agricultural land reform now a matter of pressing importance.

The population in the rural districts had in the meantime remained relatively calm in the face of the mounting unrest in the cities, and gave the impression of eyeing the burgeoning agitation in the urban areas with distrust and disapproval. One does not care to think what would have happened had events taken another course and if the farmers had made common cause with the city crowds. Again, if at that time the government had failed to carry out a thorough agricultural land reform, and aroused discontent in the rural areas, the result would have been incalculable. Fortunately Mr. Wada, the new minister of agriculture, had not only planned the first reform, but had been in charge of all subsequent negotiations with GHQ. There was nothing he did not know on the subject, and I could safely leave matters in his hands. As the minister concerned, and acting as my representative, he was handed, towards the end of June, the GHQ communication concerning agricultural reform based upon the report of the Allied Council. The government set to work to examine the details and, after further negotiations had taken place with GHQ on some minor questions involved, the cabinet finally decided on the plans for the second agricultural reform at a meeting on July 26, 1946.

The major points of the reform as finally agreed upon were that all agricultural land belonging to landowners who did not reside in the districts where the land was located, and which was being tilled solely by tenants, was to be transferred to the tenants; and that individual ownership of tenant land was to be limited to the average of one *chō* (four *chō* in Hokkaidō); that the total amount of agricultural land to be owned individually, including tenant land, was to be limited to three *chō* (twelve *chō* in Hokkaidō); that it was to be made compulsory for land beyond that limit to be sold to the government for resale to tenant farmers; and that payment to landowners for their requisitioned land was to be made in government bonds. A bill embodying these provisions was introduced into the Lower House of the Diet on September 7, 1946, and passed both Houses without amendment on October 11, 1946.

As a result of the outcome of the general election of April 1947, my first cabinet resigned and power passed to the Socialists. The date for the completion of the transfer of farm land had been set for the end of 1948, and so when, after the terms in office of the Katayama and Ashida cabinets, I came to form my second cabinet in October 1948, the transfer operation was still incomplete. And as it was realized by all concerned that the redistribution of land was a permanent measure, and one to be conducted smoothly and efficiently, the completion date was postponed until July 1950.

The final result was that two million *chō* of agricultural land were requisitioned from some 1,500,000 landowners and turned over to those who had previously been tenant farmers, numbering around four million persons. In addition to which operation, 450,000 *chō* of pasturage and 1,320,000 *chō* of uncultivated land were also disposed of in the same manner. Tenant-tilled land, which until that time had accounted for 46 per cent of Japan's agricultural land, diminished to 10 per cent. The tenant farmer practically ceased to exist, while the great landowners of the old days and absentee landlords passed into history.

The effects of such sweeping changes on Japan's agriculture as a whole are, of course, incalculable. The agricultural land reform was, in fact, a revolutionary measure, and to have carried it out without any major friction, and certainly without anything in the nature of serious disturbance or bloodshed, was an achievement that cannot be dismissed lightly, particularly when one remembers the unsettled state of the country at that time. The possible outbreak of such troubles had been feared by some during the deliberations on the reform bill in the Diet, but the event showed our apprehension to have been groundless.

There occurred, of course, a certain amount of confusion in some districts; there were bound to be details in the reform plans that were open to criticism. But no one can deny that the reform contributed immeasurably towards raising the standards of living of the agricultural classes, or that the effects this stabilization and improvement of life in the rural areas had on the social unrest in Japan as a whole were profound. This was one of the immediate benefits of the land reform. And when we think of what that fact saved us from, we should also remember at the same time the sacrifice paid by the landowners and their uncomplaining attitude throughout. Had they been so minded, they could have expressed their discontent in political and social activities of no uncertain kind, that would not only have hindered the implementation of the reform, but have endangered still further the precarious state of our country. It is not too much to say that it is to the admirable behavior of the landowners that the success of the reform is largely due. The Japanese landowners were reviled during the planning of the reform as slave drivers and exploiters of oppressed tenants. But this is far from the truth. Unlike the situation in some other countries, the majority of Japan's landowners were men who made it their business to exercise a paternal regard for their tenants and to encourage the improvement of methods of agriculture. Many were generous benefactors to their villages and districts, and the manner in which they bowed out of existence as landlords was worthy of their past achievements.

Following the signing of the San Francisco Peace Treaty, there were those who demanded, and others who vaguely expected, that as the agricultural land reform had been enacted with the strong support and encouragement of the occupation authorities, some of its measures should be repealed. We decided, on the contrary, to incorporate the principles of the reform into the body of our national laws by combining them in one law, for which purpose a bill was introduced during the thirteenth session of the Diet held in 1952, while my third cabinet was in office, under the title of the Agricultural Land Bill. This was passed by both Houses by an overwhelming majority, including the Socialists, and became law on July 15, 1952.

The agricultural land reform thus enacted and enforced does not by any means solve all the problems which confront Japanese agriculture, if only for the simple reason that there is not enough farmland in Japan to provide our large rural population with a sufficiently high standard of living. But the aim of the reform lies in helping to increase total agricultural production in order to permit the raising of the standard of living of those engaged in agriculture. The reform is not an end in itself, but a means. And every other means should be employed, now as formerly, to obtain the maximum results from the reform.

# 20

# The Postwar Food Crisis

The question of the nation's food supply presented an even more pressing problem during the first postwar years than that of agricultural reform. Or, to be more accurate, food had been a pressing problem throughout the Pacific War, during which the daily allowance of rice per person in Japan was reduced from 2 gō 3 shaku (0.365 quart) in 1942, when food rationing was first introduced, to 2 gō 1 shaku (0.333 quart), including the equivalent amount of such other cereals as wheat, kaoliang, and maize, the edible portion of which came to considerably less.

This was one of the most serious matters confronting the Higashikuni cabinet upon its formation after the end of the war. The government succeeded in collecting the required quota of rice produced in 1944 from farmers, plus the utilization of existing army and navy stores, for relief purposes, thus enabling us to get past the immediate crisis. However, in the confusion and disorders that followed Japan's surrender, rather more of such reserve stores ended up in the black market than went into proper channels of distribution, and the rice crop of 1945 was a major failure.

In these circumstances, the Ministry of Agriculture calculated that unless the equivalent of 4,500,000 tons of rice could be imported many people would starve. It turned out that the amount actually needed to ward off starvation was only 700,000 tons, but the problem of obtaining that quantity from somewhere remained. The twin effects of war and bad weather were at that time causing food shortages in many parts of the world, and famines had already appeared in some areas of Asia and Europe. In February 1946, therefore, President Truman appealed to the American nation to assist in the relief of the countries affected and sent Mr. Herbert Hoover as his special envoy on a worldwide tour of inspection to report on the conditions actually existing. In May of the same year the International Emergency Food Conference was convened in Washington to inquire further into the matter and, as a result of this meeting, an International Emergency Food Council was created for the distribution of food, fodder, seeds, and agricultural implements to the stricken countries.

In such circumstances, the provision of relief for a defeated enemy such as Japan was bound to be deferred in favor of other applicants, and such a step as the planned import of foodstuffs was quite impracticable, so the government was driven to concentrating on collecting as large a quantity of rice produced in Japan itself as we could. However, despite strenuous efforts, the amount of rice harvested in 1945 offered for sale to the government amounted to only 77 per cent of the scheduled minimum, and official stocks had become dangerously depleted. By mid-1946 the distribution of rationed food was either being delayed or stopping altogether up and down the country. The resultant unrest was made use of by extremist elements for further agitation and on May 19 a "Food May Day" was held, during which a party of demonstrators forced their way into the imperial palace demanding to see the emperor.

Clearly, the initial task of my first cabinet when it was formed on June 13 of that year was to collect food in order to alleviate the situation. Rewards were offered to farmers for rice sold to the government above the official quotas set; all wheat and potatoes, apart from the amount needed by producers themselves for their families, were purchased by the government; and articles needed by farmers were released from government stocks in large quantities. Results still being far short of the minimum required, there was no other course left to us except to appeal to General MacArthur's headquarters for aid. During July and August, when the shortage of food was most acute, we managed to obtain the release of 510,000 tons of rice belonging to the Australian forces in Japan. This step enabled us to get through the two critical months, and from September onwards the further release of food by the occupation forces and the new crop of rice and sweet potatoes carried us into the next year. The 1946 harvest was good, and it was generally expected that the food situation would improve in 1947. However, by that time the price of rice on the black market had risen to a point at which farmers were reluctant to sell their rice to the government at the controlled price, and the total amount collected did not come up to our hopes. Moreover, rice-producing prefectures became fearful of not receiving their full government quotas and tended to delay sending their rice to nonproducing districts, so that delays of from five to nine days in the distribution of basic food became frequent towards the end of January even in Tokyo, in which city conditions had been relatively good till then.

General MacArthur's headquarters not only urged us on to further efforts to collect rice and remedy the situation, but instructed the provincial branches of the military government in all parts of Japan to spur on the work. On February 15 an American food mission that was in Japan at that time issued a statement appealing to the nation's farmers to turn over rice in excess of official quotas, and stressing that the country must first make every possible effort to produce all the food possible before it could expect to obtain help from abroad. On March 1 we were reluctantly forced to resort to compulsory measures for the collection of rice, coupled with a system of special awards; by March 6 the distribution of official food rations in Tokyo was being delayed from twelve to fourteen days.

On March 7, GHQ issued a report in the name of General MacArthur concerning the crisis, and on April 1 the supreme commander himself wrote to me personally, pointing out the gravity of the food situation and emphasizing the responsibility of the Japanese government in maintaining the food supply by judicious and efficient means. Simultaneously the Diplomatic Section of GHQ announced that the collection of sufficient rice to exceed the official quota by ten per cent was a necessary prerequisite to any plan for importing food into Japan. This statement reflected in part the unsatisfactory state of food production throughout the world at that time: during 1946–1947 there occurred an increase of ten per cent in world food production, but this was confined mainly to maize and oats grown for fodder, and little improvement occurred in the production of wheat and rye, particularly when the increase in the world's population was taken into consideration. There was, therefore, justification for the stand taken by GHQ that no food could be imported into Japan unless the nation first made every possible effort to increase its own food supply.

My first cabinet resigned in May 1947, and from that time until October 1948, when I formed my second cabinet, the food situation in Japan did not materially change; nor was it possible to increase the amount of the individual ration. From the point of view of the world as a whole, however, there was a definite turn for the better during 1948, due mainly to favorable weather conditions and the recovery of fertilizer production. The United States enjoyed good wheat and maize harvests, and the wheat harvest in European countries in many cases exceeded prewar levels. In addition, a change became apparent in U.S. policy towards Japan, which dated from the time when Mr. Kenneth C. Royall, then secretary of the army, made a speech at San Francisco in January 1948 concerned with the importance of building up Japan as a strong and stable democracy. Thus American aid to Japan began to take on a more positive aspect.

That fact was also reflected in U.S. policy regarding the import of food; from this point it became more a question of what was needed rather than to what degree imports could be kept down. Compared with a total of $392 million in 1948, American expenditures for aid to Japan increased to $429 million in 1949; in addition the GARIOA and EROA funds were established.

The GARIOA fund was limited to the provision of aid to prevent social unrest and sickness, but, American policy having taken a step farther in the direction of providing Japan with raw materials needed for economic recovery and the rehabilitation of her export trade, an additional $102,760,000 was allocated from the EROA fund for that purpose. In this way, food imports increased from 1,090,000 tons in 1947 to 1,770,000 in 1948. There no longer occurred any stoppages in the distribution of food, and much less delay than formerly. The amount of food found to be insufficient at the end of October 1948 came to only 14,000 tons as against 290,000 tons twelve months earlier. After the formation of my second cabinet we were able to increase both the normal rations and the additional rations provided for those engaged in heavy manual labor—the normal rice ration being raised to 2 *gō* 7 *shaku* (0.428 quart) per capita. This step called for further efforts on our part in the production and collection of rice, in which task we were assisted by the exhortations of General MacArthur's headquarters.

The world food supply began to show a surplus at about this time, so that Japan's imports of food for 1949, at 2,400,000 tons, showed an increase of 70,000 tons compared with the previous year. Of that amount, 40 per cent was purchased on a commercial basis and independently of any American aid, this representing the first sign that our food supply was no longer completely dependent upon American assistance. The rationing scheme no longer gave us any trouble, and with the derationing of potatoes and sweet potatoes in September 1949 Japan's food crisis as such was ended.

The time had now arrived to reconsider our food policy. The problem of maintaining a sufficient supply of foodstuffs for the people had become secondary to another question: the fact that it was an integral part of the program of the ruling Liberal Party to effect Japan's economic recovery by means of free competition. Wherefore the derationing of all staple foodstuffs became a matter for serious consideration. We announced this aim as part of government policy in March 1950, and in the same month a conference was held between government leaders and party members to discuss the means of bringing it about. The decision reached at that time, however, was to continue the rationing system unchanged until March 1951, when the question would be considered again in light of later developments.

Consideration of the question of derationing was connected with the fact that GHQ at that time was suggesting such a step in order to reduce government expenditure, for which reason derationing and the abolition of import subsidies were being seriously discussed within General MacArthur's headquarters.

With the outbreak of the Korean War in June 1950, however, the situation abruptly changed. The free price of rice markedly advanced, and compulsory measures to increase the internal food supply again became necessary, beginning with the official collection of the spring wheat crop for that year.

By autumn the situation had changed again, and we had once more to consider derationing and the abolition of import subsidies in connection with the compilation of estimates for the 1950 budget. We were, therefore somewhat surprised to be told by GHQ in November 1950 that rice was to be left out of the derationing plans; this was generally viewed at the time as meaning that the derationing of rice was considered dangerous because it might raise the price of the staple food at a time when the foundations of the national economy were still not secure. It seemed to me, however, that as the instruction coincided with the entrance of Communist China into the Korean War and U.N. bombing of the "privileged sanctuary" in Manchuria was being seriously discussed, what GHQ probably feared was the possible stoppage of all food imports into Japan. It was fortunate that the situation did not come to pass, but from that time we did not have another such favorable opportunity to deration rice in Japan.

The government accordingly prepared and introduced into the Diet a bill for the derationing of wheat only as from April 1951. This measure was vigorously opposed by agricultural bodies and members of the Diet from rural districts, and, although the bill passed the Lower House, the session ended before it could be approved by the House of Councilors. However, by that time the food situation had greatly improved, and free and official prices of wheat were practically the same. Wheat rations were constantly being refused, and the regulations for wheat control had become an anachronism. Further, the regaining of the national independence in April 1952 meant a substantial increase in government expenditure for the strengthening of our defense forces, reparations, and other reasons, the revenue to cover which was not immediately in sight.

Economy measures represented the only means available to us, and to this end the annual expenditure on food control, amounting to some 400 billion yen, seemed one of the most obvious and rational targets. We therefore decided to abolish food control from 1952, and negotiations were opened with GHQ to that end. But this time also, we were not able to obtain the consent of the occupation authorities, and so wheat only was scheduled for derationing in 1952.

A bill to implement this decision was introduced into the Diet in April 1952, and as this time the proposal was not to deration wheat completely, but for the government to purchase an unlimited quantity at a fixed price, the measure was enacted by both Houses without incident, and the modified form of derationing came into force in regard to wheat the following June. Only rice now remained rationed. Japan had a good crop that year, but cold weather and typhoons destroyed over 30 per cent of the expected crop for 1953, requiring our efforts to be directed towards maintaining the food supply at a satisfactory level by increasing imports, and so the derationing of rice was again relegated to some future date.

# 21

## Labor Reforms and After

Labor constituted another of the problems with which occupation policy was much concerned. In the eyes of the Allied powers, this freeing—from their point of view—of Japan's workers represented as necessary a step towards the democratization of Japan as the agricultural land reform and the benefits flowing from that measure to our farmers. The zeal of the occupation was never, however, more apparent than in connection with this question of the liberation of the nation's workers. And the evil effects of that fact are still being felt in my country today.

The labor situation in Japan following the Pacific War was a difficult and complicated one involving for workers, as for practically everyone else, hardships arising from inflation and food scarcities, agitation by newly liberated Communists, and the policy followed by the occupation authorities—each factor rendering any solution of the problem based upon any one of the factors concerned an impossibility. New legislation and labor customs born of experience during the past fourteen years have brought about a certain degree of improvement, but it now appears clear that a satisfactory solution of the questions involved can only emerge with the passage of time.

Looking back on the immediate postwar period, we were then faced with what looked very much like revolutionary conditions. In October 1945, only two months after the war ended, the premises of *Yomiuri shinbun*, one of Tokyo's largest newspaper companies, were occupied by Communist-led strikers in an avowed attempt to "democratize" the management. In February of the following year the executive staff of the Bibai coal mine in Hokkaidō were subjected by miners for over ten hours to what was called at the time a "People's Trial," modeled on similar proceedings conducted in

Soviet satellite countries. Not only strikes and demonstrations, but acts of downright terrorism, including intimidation in all its forms and the forcible detention of persons, were everyday occurrences; my first cabinet was formed at a moment when our headquarters were literally surrounded by a red-flag-waving mob.

Simultaneously with the holding in Tokyo, early in 1946, of a national meeting to welcome home Mr. Nozaka Sanzō, a native Communist who had been many years in exile and had cooperated with the Chinese Communists at Yenan throughout the Pacific War, these radical elements banded themselves together in a "People's Front." By August 1947 the National Congress of Industrial Organization (CIO) was formed under Communist leadership with some 1,600,000 members from trade unions in all parts of the country: this body for some time dominated the labor unions affiliated with it. The prewar General Federation of Labor (Sōdōmei), was also revived at about this time, but its affiliated membership only numbered some 850,000 workers, and there was little it could do to counteract the influence of the CIO.

Compared with this intensive organization of labor, the managerial side of industry only came together to form the Japan Federation of Employers' Associations (Nihon keieisha dantai renmei) in April 1948, the delay being due to the fact that so many of those formerly in executive positions in industry and business had been purged. Labor troubles having assumed such alarming proportions so early in the occupation as a result of these conditions, it may be worth remembering that on May 20, 1946, General MacArthur issued a statement prohibiting the use of collective force for purposes of terrorism at just about the time I was striving to form my first cabinet in the teeth of demonstrators armed with red flags. I myself also issued a statement shortly after the cabinet had been formed, emphasizing the intention of the government to punish according to the strict letter of the law any use of violence in labor disputes. Verbal instructions delivered on October 11, 1945, to Baron Shidehara, the then prime minister, concerning "reforms to be made in the social order of Japan" became the starting point of our labor policy immediately after the termination of the Pacific conflict, containing as they did a passage in which the supreme commander stressed the encouragement of the organization of labor, "that it may be clothed with such dignity as will permit it an influential voice in safeguarding the working man from exploitation and abuse and raising living standards to a higher level."

There were grounds for doubting the advisability of taking steps of that nature, which only too easily could, in such a time of confusion and disorder, become simply a means of furthering the aims of the radical elements within the nation. We were required to conform to occupation policy, however, and the result was what came to be known as the Three Labor Laws.

The Shidehara cabinet, in which I occupied the post of foreign minister, decided first of all to draft a Labor Union Law, for which purpose a Labor Law Deliberation Council was established, consisting of government representatives, labor experts, employers, workers, and members of both Houses of the Diet, to consider and report on the matter. On the basis of the council's report, a bill was submitted to the Diet and enacted, and became effective as the Labor Union Law on March 1, 1946.

We could have no knowledge at that time of the direction which the trade union movement in Japan was subsequently to take: in its discussions the council had only data furnished by the prewar trade union movement in Japan and the wishes of GHQ to go upon in framing its proposals. It therefore followed that the law as drafted by the council, and which the government adopted more or less in its original form, was based upon the conception that the unions would resemble the sensibly Socialist trade unions of prewar time, with the result that most of its clauses were directed against pressure of any sort being exerted either by the government or employers. Zeal to safeguard the legitimate rights of organized labor was such that in the original draft submitted by the council all acts forming part of trade union activity were declared unpunishable by law. This provision, at least, the government thought fit to alter, limiting such acts to "collective bargaining and other acts of a labor union which were appropriate," though even in this form the clause was to cause trouble later through the ambiguity of its phrasing.

The Labor Relations Adjustment Law, second of the three major labor laws enacted during the occupation years, was presented to the Diet in July 1946, during the term of my first cabinet, and became law on October 13 of the same year. In this case also the draft was prepared by the council, but GHQ supervised the work throughout, even going into the question of the degree of accuracy of the English-language translation, and the government was forced to adopt the draft without change. We desired, at least, to limit the extent to which schoolteachers could participate in labor disputes, but, in spite of repeated representations regarding the evils to which the unlimited participation of teachers in such activities might give rise, our protests were ignored. The result was a draft with which organized labor could certainly find no ground for complaint, but for some reason the Communists took exception to it and it became law without their support.

The Labor Standards Law was drafted under similar circumstances under my first cabinet and became law on September 1, 1947. This measure established the principle of the eight-hour day, equal wages for men and women, and so forth, and, being far in advance of Japan's labor laws in force until that time, produced protests from employers' groups that the raising of wages and other measures which the law made necessary would seriously hamper the nation's economic recovery, to avoid which development it was declared desirable that a period should be set during which the provisions of the law might gradually be put into effect.

We in the government were well aware of the fact that on many points the law was not in keeping with the impoverished state of the country, but it goes without saying that GHQ exercised the same close vigilance over the drafting of this law as it did in the case of the others. On the other hand, it should be said that the Soviet representative on the Allied Council for Japan, General Derevyanko, made particularly detailed demands within that body concerning the provisions of the Labor Standards Law, to which the reply was made by the American representative that they were already incorporated in the draft and there was therefore no need for the question to be debated by the council.

Following the issuing by General MacArthur of an order forbidding a general strike scheduled for February 1947, a change occurred in GHQ's policy of overlooking the excesses of the extreme Left and favoring the political activities of the trade union movement. The dismissal of some of the men within GHQ from posts connected with the handling of labor problems demonstrated that fact quite clearly. The Japanese labor movement, however, continued to develop in a direction that was not in line with what was envisaged by occupation headquarters. Shortly after the projected general strike in February, the government set up a Wage and Allowance Investigation Committee, with representatives of the workers included in its membership, to decide on a new basis of pay in industry. My cabinet having resigned as a consequence of the outcome of the general election of 1947, this task was inherited by the succeeding Socialist cabinet under the leadership of Mr. Katayama, but the committee failed to reach an agreement on the question. I had rather innocently imagined that there would be less labor trouble under a Socialist government, but it seems that Japan's trade unions do not operate on such a simple pattern, and I gradually came to realize that in the eyes of the native Communists the Socialists are as much their enemies as the conservatives like myself, so that so long as trade unions continue to be infiltrated and led by Communists there is no end to incessant labor disputes and unrest.

This fact was illustrated by a prolonged labor dispute which broke out under the Katayama and Ashida cabinets, between the government and government employees headed by the postal workers' union, and lasted for nearly a year. It was during this period that other groups of government employees whose terms of work made it illegal for them to strike came to devise tactics which just managed to keep on the right side of legality, such as taking holidays en masse and refusing to work overtime under any circumstances. The postal workers' union planned a national strike on the scale of the abortive general strike of February 1, and this too was called off by order of the occupation authorities.

The prolonged postal workers' dispute no doubt furnished GHQ with much food for thought, and in July 1948 General MacArthur wrote a letter to Dr. Ashida Hitoshi, then prime minister, suggesting a fundamental revision of the National Public Service Law and the placing of some legal check on the conduct of labor disputes by government and public corporation employees. The supreme commander pointed out in his letter that such employees in government enterprises were the servants of the people and their relationship with the state was different from that existing between workers and employers in private industry; and, further, that the right to organize and to strike should not be granted to government employees, while skilled workers in public corporations controlled by the government, such as employees of the national railways, should be accorded the right to organize and to bargain collectively, but not the right to engage in strikes.

The Ashida cabinet issued an imperial ordinance to that effect and was preparing to follow this with the introduction of the necessary legislation in the Diet, owing when, to a bribery charge having been brought against Prime Minister Ashida in connection with the Shōwa Denki case (of which Dr. Ashida was later cleared in the courts), the cabinet was forced to resign, and the task of arranging for the necessary legislation fell to my second cabinet, which then took office. The cabinet drafted the necessary amendments to the National Public Service Law and incorporated these in a bill which passed the Diet by a narrow majority towards the end of the year.

The main points of the measure were that both the right to organize and the right to strike were taken away from government employees, in compensation for which restriction a newly established National Personnel Authority was given full powers to deal with all questions connected with wages and conditions of employment as an agency functioning independently of the government in the interests of public servants and their welfare. A Public Corporations Labor Relations Law was prepared at the same time to deal specifically with the employees of the national railways, the Monopoly Bureau, and other public corporations. These were granted the right of collective bargaining, but not the right to strike, and machinery for settling any disputes was also set up in the measure. This bill also passed into law towards the end of 1948, and thus the principle was established that the position and trade union activities of government employees were of a different character and distinct from those of workers in private industry.

The postal workers' union, which together with the national railway workers' union formed the two largest trade unions affected by this revision of the law, ceased for some time thereafter to be prominent in labor disputes, while the activities of the national railway workers' union were similarly limited. I have already outlined the circumstances that made these restrictions necessary. But to the trade unions concerned, however, the new laws meant that rights enjoyed by them under the original postwar labor laws had been taken away. There was therefore some ground for the discontent which they were not slow to display. In following weeks and months they forfeited any public sympathy that might have accrued to them by launching a series of illegal work stoppages in an attempt to regain the right to strike, thus setting at naught the new legislation and replying by more strikes to measures taken against them.

The course of events thus demonstrated the fact that, at that time, Japan's trade unions were not so much concerned with the development of a healthy trade union movement in our country as with following the ideas of a limited number of leaders within the unions. This circumstance may have been a result of what one is tempted to term the feudalistic spirit, but at any rate the fact remained that many of the unions concerned were governed by a set of men who, in many cases, were not even professional members of the unions concerned and whose aim was to steer the youthful Japanese labor movement along a path ending in revolution. It was to combat that destructive tendency that General MacArthur had been obliged to forbid the carrying out of the general strike scheduled for February 1, 1947, and to write the letter advising the prohibition by law of strikes by government employees in July 1948.

The course of events thus demonstrated the fact that at that time there were no "unions" in the Western sense of that term, but workers' organizations controlled and run by political bosses, and it appeared that negotiations had already been in progress between GHQ and the Japanese government for a complete revision of the Labor Union Law before the formation of my second cabinet. That law had originally been framed to protect workers from all forms of outside pressure, but its provisions had increasingly been utilized by radical elements for political purposes: thus the object in revising the law was to limit the privileges granted to workers to the extent needed to bring these within a manageable scope and in line with their responsibilities, as well as their rights.

The Ashida cabinet having resigned before the necessary revisions could be made, the task of reforming the law was taken up first by Mr. Masuda Kineshichi, the labor minister in my second cabinet, and later by Mr. Suzuki Masafumi, who occupied the post in my third administration. Among the changes introduced was one legislating that, whereas formerly the acts of trade union members engaged in collective bargaining and other union activities were neither punishable under the penal code nor liable to damages in civil suits in the courts, the use of violence by any party should not be considered rightful or legal action. Further, it had under the old law been a crime for any employer to object to the formation of a trade union among his employees, or to refuse to enter into a collective bargaining: this provision was revised to give the Labor Relations Commission the power to order employers to withdraw such refusal or objections. The bill, as expected, met with violent opposition from the trade unions and radical parties, both within and outside the Diet. Following its introduction in the Diet towards the end of April 1949, debates on the measure were repeatedly disrupted by violent opposition demonstrations. However, it was duly passed before the end of the session and became law on June 1, 1949.

The Labor Relations Adjustment Law had for its prime purpose the smoothing out of difficulties in disputes between employers and workers and laid down rules of procedure in regard to conciliatory mediation, arbitration, and so forth. It had been enacted shortly after the formation of my first cabinet and has since been twice revised—the first time during the term of my third cabinet, at the same time as the revision of the Labor Union Law outlined above, and the second after Japan had regained her independence in 1952.

The second revision was of greater significance than the first, to explain which it is necessary to touch upon the general revision of all laws enacted during the occupation period, which had been instituted some time previously. I had already pointed out to GHQ on several occasions the need for taking such a step, when, in May 1951, General Matthew B. Ridgway, then Supreme Commander for the Allied Powers, issued a statement announcing the relaxation of controls hitherto placed upon the Japanese government and conferring upon the government the right to reconsider any and all laws and regulations enacted since the termination of the Pacific War. A Government Ordinances Consultation Council was accordingly set up, consisting of Mr. Nakayama Ichirō, then chairman of the Central Labor Relations Commission, and six other experts, to act as an advisory body to the prime minister, and the revision of the labor laws was among the subjects of their inquiry. Their subsequent report stressed that, while the laws formed the basis for the democratization of the Japanese economy and should, in that sense, be respected and strengthened where necessary, there were points in the laws which five years' experience of their working had shown to be unsuited to existing economic conditions in Japan, and that these required revision within the limits of keeping the nation in line with current international usage.

The next step was the creation of a Labor Relations Laws Deliberation Committee, composed of representatives of the employers, workers, and public welfare agencies, to discuss the labor laws further and to consider the question whether or not it was advisable to enact legislation to curb labor disputes which endangered the national economy and the livelihood of the people. The committee proved to be unable to reach a decision on the point. The government therefore undertook to draft legislation on its own responsibility and devised the system of emergency adjustment, now in force, as an amendment to the Labor Relations Adjustment Law. This conferred upon the prime minister the right to order the halting of such disputes and to refer them to the Labor Relations Commission for settlement.

The amending bill, together with a Subversive Activities Prevention Bill, was introduced into the Diet in May 1952, and, despite the usual noisy opposition from leftists, the two bills became law at the end of July.

The government's power of "emergency adjustment" was first exercised during a major coal strike during the closing months of that year when the safety workers in the pits abandoned the work of pumping, thus exposing the mines to the danger of flooding, after which no further occasion arose to make use of the provision of the law during my tenure of office.

The coal-mine strike was partly responsible for the taking of the next legislative step, aimed against the excessive misuse of the privileges previously granted to workers, which was the law to impose limits upon the extent and nature of labor's actions in industrial disputes. The revised Labor Union Law respected the justifiable actions of trade union members in disputes, but the definition of what actions were justifiable and proper had never been clearly stated, and the need had been increasingly felt that some legislative limitations should be imposed against actions which common sense indicated obviously went beyond the limits of what was right and proper in a civilized society.

One instance of this need was presented by a strike of members of the electrical workers' union, which occurred at about the same time as the prolonged coal stoppage, during which electric power frequently was disrupted as part of the tactics adopted by the union to coerce the employers. The annoyance and loss thus caused in various industries, and to the public in general, were widespread and costly, while the action of the coal miners' union in withdrawing the safety men and allowing the pits to become flooded furnished another example of irresponsible behavior. However, the framing of a law designed to curb such excesses on the part of striking workers was expected to meet with opposition of so violent a character from the trade unions and leftist elements that the government officials concerned displayed extreme reluctance to undertake the task. I accordingly consulted only with Mr. Totsuka Kuichirō, the labor minister, before stating in my policy speech at the opening of the fifteenth session of the Diet in January 1953, with reference to the coal and electricity strikes of the previous year, that, since it had obviously become necessary to protect the public from such manifestations of excessive zeal on the part of strikers, it was the intention of the government to introduce during that session a bill to deal with strikes in industries that vitally affected the public interest.

Our labor officials within the government were too conversant with the existing condition of affairs within the trade union movement and opposition Socialist Party to bring themselves to initiate such a step, but, once the cabinet had pledged action to remedy matters, their hesitation disappeared and they set to work on the drafting of a bill. This was duly enacted by the Lower House, but the Diet had to be dissolved on March 14 while the measure was still being debated in the House of Councilors. A general election followed, as a result of which I formed my fifth cabinet with Mr. Kozaka Zentarō as labor minister, and the bill was reintroduced in the sixteenth special session that convened following the appeal to the voters. The Labor Committees of both Houses were headed by Socialist chairmen, and their maneuvers aimed at prolonging the debates on the bill, coupled with the more active tactics pursued by the rest of the opposition members, increased our difficulties in enacting the measure. However, with the cooperation of the conservative opposition, an amended form of the bill was passed by the Lower House, and in the Upper Chamber it was withdrawn from the Labor Committee while still in the debating stage and put to the vote of a full session of the House of Councilors, where it was approved with the help of the votes of neutral members and the conservative opposition, to become law on August 5, 1953. I recall it as one of the bills which the government had the greatest trouble to get enacted.

The Labor Standards Law was an occupation-sponsored reform in connection with which the idealistic zeal of the progressive elements within General MacArthur's headquarters displayed more impatience over the actualities of Japanese economic conditions than most others. Of individual enterprises which came under the provisions of the law, 92 per cent employed fewer than one hundred workers apiece, and 70 per cent fewer than ten. On the other hand, violations of the law brought to the notice of enforcement officials during 1949 alone totaled 1,200,000 cases; nor did the fact that these cases were known mean that the provisions of the law were subsequently observed, since in most instances the employers concerned were in no condition to do so. Thus the exposure and punishment of such violations brought hardship and misery upon employers without achieving any improvement in the status of the workers concerned.

Something obviously needed to be done to correct this state of affairs, but in our approach to the problem we had also to remember that, in view of Japan's dependence upon exports, care had to be exercised not to arouse ill-feeling in countries that were not favorably disposed towards any increase in our exports. Such a step as the revision of the Labor Standards Law offered an all too obvious target for criticism from such quarters overseas. It was therefore decided first of all to seek to improve the methods of the law's application, and officials concerned were instructed to direct their efforts towards a greater understanding of the actual conditions in which individual employers were placed and to aid them to conform to the law instead of simply being intent upon punishing violations. At the same time I referred the law to the Government Ordinances Consultation Council, already mentioned, for discussion, and the revision of the law carried out in July 1952 was based upon the report of that body. Revision of the regulations relating to the application of the law had been effected before this—in October 1949—and further revision was made in June 1954.

# 22

## My Views on Japan's
## Labor Movement

I have already touched upon Communist activities in postwar Japan which did so much to retard the task of reconstruction in my country and to deflect our labor movement from a sound course of development. The change—in mid-stream as it were—in the labor policy of the occupation was certainly due in part to the need for the rectification of the New Deal idealism in evidence during the earlier stages and for taking more into consideration the actual conditions existing in Japan. But had our trade unions availed themselves more wisely of the protective policy of the occupation during the early days following the Pacific conflict, and been content to assert and safeguard whatever could properly be regarded as their rights, GHQ would not have been forced to adopt the sort of repressive policy to which it eventually was driven, nor would we have had to spend so much time and effort in trying to secure the revision of laws designed to protect the interests of the workers, or to revise them to the extent forced upon us. We may blame General MacArthur's headquarters for their initial policy of adopting the role of a too-indulgent mother towards the workers, but we should equally blame the Communists and leftist elements for leading the Japanese labor movement so far astray in the direction of pseudo-maneuvers aimed at promoting a problematical political revolution.

Still more regrettable is the fact that today, more than a decade later, we still see the tendency for our trade unions to be dragged by an extremist minority in a direction not necessarily desired or approved by the majority of the members concerned. I do not for a moment believe that the great majority of Japan's workers have any sympathy with the aims of these extremists: for that matter, neither did the militarists and ultranationalists form anything like a majority among our military men before the war. Many of those whom I knew were fine soldiers possessing a sound sense of what was expected of fighting men in the life of the nation. It was the extremist minority among them which finally brought both them and the entire Japanese people into a disastrous war. I hear that some of our more powerful trade unions are today being compared to the military clique of the old days. This is precisely what I myself feel.

The militarist groups had the habit of regarding themselves as constituting an elite within the nation, with everyone else considered a species on a lower level and below them. This is exactly what some of our trade union leaders are doing today: they consider that only they are in the right and brand all who differ in opinion from themselves as reactionary conservatives. There are also those among them who seem to regard the labor movement simply and solely as a vehicle for the achievement of quick personal success, and prefer declaiming at trade union meetings and heading protest demonstrations to doing what should be their real jobs of working as workers. To many teacher-members of the Japan Teachers' Union, the work of teaching children in the classroom is but a step towards standing as a candidate for the Diet, and so to feats of physical prowess in one or the other of the Houses. They may be termed professional agitators who prefer trouble to peaceful occupation with their work: thus the analogy between them and the militarists of former days becomes complete.

It has become an accepted habit in Japan that industrial unrest and strikes should occur at regular intervals each year: in spring for the next round of the workers' practically annual rise in wages; in summer to secure the maximum possible mid-year bonus; and in November or December to agitate for larger year-end bonuses. This extraordinary procedure does not occur in any other industrial nation and does not, as some might think, mean that Japan's capitalists and employers rank among the worst and most grasping in the world. It all seems to me to come down to one simple fact—that the theory and practice of a democratic society have not yet been sufficiently understood, so that in Japan too many think only of the interests of their own particular group without displaying any consideration for others, or for the interests of society as a whole. This causes them to become all the more easily the victims of the Communists, to whom strikes and unrest represent just so many steps towards the revolution of the proletariat which they seek.

It was the difference in labor psychology which struck me so forcibly when I visited West Germany, where I was told that the workers refrained from strikes because to them the reconstruction of their country came first. I am also reminded of what I was often told while I was ambassador in London—that British workers were at least always willing to consider the effect of wage increases in raising prices and to base their demands on a reasonably enlightened conception of what the national economy could stand.

Such examples, at least, permit me to think that, in view of what I myself have experienced of Japan's still youthful labor movement during my tenure of office, my country still has, by comparison, very far to go. I am well aware of the need for workers to unite and seek higher standards of living through collective bargaining with their employers, which might very well lead, at times, to strikes. But it is equally obvious that in a highly developed democratic society such as ours is today, employer and worker are no longer placed in the old relationship of the exploiter and the exploited. It is possible and necessary for capital, management, and labor to exist together: that seems to me the goal towards which the labor movement in Japan should also strive. And I hope to see the time when that objective is achieved and people no longer find any use for or meaning in any of the labor laws which I myself helped to enact.

I stated, early in this volume, that Prince Konoe said during an audience with the emperor towards the end of the Pacific War that, defeat then being imminent, one of the most serious results to be feared in the event of any mismanagement in bringing the conflict to a close was a Communist revolution. It is in a way ironical that, after we had surrendered to the U.S. forces in order to avoid such a disaster, one of the first acts of the occupation authorities was, if not actually to favor communism, at least to adopt an exceptionally lenient attitude towards Japan's Communists. It was, no doubt, a part of the policy of GHQ to make use of the native Communists so far as this could be done; it also is true that among the members of General MacArthur's headquarters staff there were those who, to say the least, were not unfavorably disposed towards our Communists and who promoted and urged measures of reform which, whatever the intended purpose may have been, served to aid the Communists in their extremist activities. We must also remember that at that time the Soviet Union was one of the major Allied powers and that hopes were even being entertained that the Russians might very well cooperate with the free countries in bringing democracy to Japan. The Americans are an unsuspicious race and, given such a background, may well have thought in those early days that the Russians— and therefore Japan's Communists, who were under the aegis of the Russians—were their friends.

It was not long, however, before both the U.S. government in Washington and GHQ in Tokyo were made aware of the price to be paid for this friendly attitude towards the Russians and our Communists; therefore it is perhaps appropriate to include here a few personal reminiscences of Mr. Tokuda Kyūichi, who was the first secretary-general of the Japan Communist Party after the Pacific War, more particularly as the feelings I still entertain towards his memory are not exactly unfriendly.

It was Tokuda who surrounded the official residence of the foreign minister with his men, and actually broke into it by climbing over a wall, while

I was engaged in the formation of my first cabinet. It was he who led the mob into the kitchens of the imperial palace during the national food crisis, and who resisted to the last the GHQ order to abandon the general strike planned for February 1, 1947. He was, therefore, a most objectionable character, and there was actually little love lost between us. Yet, somehow, compared with other prominent Japanese Communists, who were for the most part of the disingenuously scheming, stickily ruthless type, he gave one an impression of frankness which at times could be disarming.

I came to know him during the terms in office of the Katayama and Ashida cabinets, when my Liberal Party was in opposition: that fact placed us, so far as some Diet business was concerned, in the same camp as the Communist Party, and I would on occasion find Tokuda in our lobby. One day, when this quaint situation arose, I said to him in fun, "I'd no idea you had joined our party," to which he replied, "But I did, today." There was this strain of humor, unusual in a Communist, in him.

I recall one incident for which I shall always respect him. While the Liberal Party was in opposition, someone donated a million yen to the funds of our party and I was asked to write a letter of thanks to the giver in my capacity as president of the party, which I did. This communication later became a subject of discussion in the Diet, and I was called before some committee to answer questions concerning the circumstances in which the contribution was made. The chairman of the committee was a member of the Socialist Party, and Socialists on the committee asked the most detailed questions, concerned not only with the donation, but about my own personal affairs, which I refused to answer. Tokuda was also a member of the committee, but remained silent through the proceedings and showed by his attitude what he himself thought of the committee and the whole affair. Similarly, he would ask the most provoking questions when he took the floor of the House, but never intruded into the private affairs of the member on whom he was calling for the answers. It was a trait that I always admired in the man.

However, when it came to his activities as the leader of the Communist Party, it was, of course, a different matter. The reason why the occupation freed Tokuda and his fellow Communists from the prisons to which they were confined before or during the war was that the Allied powers considered Japan a police state in which the rights of man were not recognized and the freedom of citizens was trodden underfoot, and the Communists, therefore, were the victims of an inhuman regime. It is further possible that they entertained the idea that Japan's Communists might be utilized to break up and end the existing regime through their activities. Men who thought thus seem to have been particularly numerous in those sections of GHQ dealing with economic affairs, which constituted another point of difference between them and the officials of the U.S. army staff.

The Communists, for their part, at first termed the Allied forces "the Army of Liberation," and enunciated the doctrine that a peaceful revolution was possible, giving the impression that they were prepared to cooperate faithfully with the occupation authorities to the extent their basic doctrines permitted. And in view of the destitution and unrest which plagued Japan at that time, they may genuinely have believed they would be able to have their own way without resorting to arms or lawlessness.

That fact quickly resulted in placing them in direct opposition to the policy of General MacArthur's headquarters, which was to reestablish tranquility and order in the country as speedily as possible. This became apparent by the spring of 1946, by which time the May Day demonstrations and food riots sponsored and directed by the Communists had made their real intentions crystal clear. The U.S. representative on the Allied Council was then Mr. George Atcheson. He informed the council that, while the Japanese were free to act according to their political convictions, the U.S. government was no more disposed to favor communism in Japan than in America. This statement constituted the first definitely anticommunist declaration to come from any GHQ source, and was followed on May 22 by a special statement issued in the name of General MacArthur warning the Japanese people against the mass violence tactics of the Communists, declaring that GHQ would be obliged to take action if such extremist elements could not be induced to exercise more restraint, and adding that it was hoped that responsible Japanese public opinion would render any intervention by GHQ unnecessary.

I may mention here a personal reminiscence illustrating the disordered state of the country at that time. As I have previously noted, my first cabinet was formed to the accompaniment of revolutionary songs chanted by a mob massed around my headquarters. I had subsequently to tolerate more of the same sort of annoyance staged by the Communists. One day I was invited to lunch by General Eichelberger, then commander of the Eighth Army, just before I was leaving Tokyo on a political tour of Japan's western prefectures. During the meal I told the general of the journey on which I was about to depart, mentioning that it would not, by any means, be pleasant because I was a most unpopular prime minister. General Eichelberger appeared to take this to heart and stated—rather more forcibly than the tone of the conversation up to that point warranted—that while he was in command of the Eighth Army he would not let anything untoward happen to me. I did not then know what he meant, but the next morning I discovered he had sent two men in plain clothes to act as my personal bodyguard, and bearing a mountain of sandwiches with a message that they were to relieve the food situation! The two men accompanied me throughout the trip and whenever and wherever a mob threatened to assemble, their signals brought occupation troops who dispersed the crowd. It was welcome assistance, since in those days the police were impotent in such circumstances.

The trip took me to Osaka via the northwestern districts of the country, and when we alighted from the train at Toyama, groups of Communists who had come from Osaka especially to stage a hostile demonstration surrounded my car and would not let it start. They offered no violence, but just stood there, blocking all movement, and the police, as usual, were powerless. Then U.S. troops appeared and cleared a way for me. I was scheduled to address a meeting held in a theatre at Toyama, and local officials of my Liberal Party had displayed on the platform a large poster outlining the policy of the party. Communists in the audience raided the platform and tore the poster down, whereupon about ten American soldiers entered the hall and arrested the culprits.

In Osaka the site chosen for my meeting was a public park, and upon my arrival there I found several American soldiers loading their rifles. As I began to speak, these men moved forward so that they flanked me on either side, while from the platform I could see that a soldier was posted about every twenty yards around the perimeter of the crowd. I was, in fact, making my speech under an armed guard and, although there were no cheers, I did not hear any jeers either.

In those disturbed days no such thing as a settled public opinion existed. Or perhaps it would be correct to say that we had a public opinion, but it was subject to fluctuation since the Japanese newspapers were in the habit of taking the line that it was undemocratic for the police to enforce order when a crowd got out of hand. The atmosphere thus created was most favorable for the dissemination of Communist propaganda and standards of behavior, and after a period during which the extreme leftists operated in the open, concentrating on holding national "meetings of the people" and leading what they termed the "hardworking majority" of the nation in demonstrations, the Communists turned their attention towards infiltrating and capturing the trade unions. This change in tactics may have been partly due to the fact that GHQ took a stronger line against disorder in the streets, but the move in the direction of the trade unions was in keeping with approved Communist strategy. It was also tactically impeccable, since the trade union movement was under the protection of GHQ as an important influence making for the democratization of Japan, and encouraged to engage in political activities, so that almost anything was permitted if done in the name of the workers' movement. The Japanese press was equally eager to support the unions, and any interference by the police with them, unless union activities were of too lawless a nature, was apt to be criticized as an encroachment on the liberty of the citizen.

The initial attempt by the Communists to avail themselves of the opportunities thus offered them was the general strike scheduled for February 1, 1947. The entire group of trade unions of government employees was involved. There had previously occurred strikes and disputes involving men in the postal services, the national railways, and other branches of government service, but never a stoppage on the scale projected on that occasion, when members of all government workers' unions, involving a total of some 2,600,000 workers, were to stage nationwide walk-outs.

Had the general strike materialized, a situation of indescribable confusion would have been created, and the stoppage of all transport, food, and fuel alone might well have driven the Japanese people, already suffering from acute shortages of the necessities of life, into a state bordering on desperation. Despite the specious reasons for the strike given by the leaders, it was clearly aimed at producing just such a condition of affairs in order to serve Communist ends, and although the stoppage never happened, being banned by order of General MacArthur's headquarters, I still wonder precisely what was in the minds of that portion of the union leadership concerned who were not Communists. The government reply to the final demands of the unions was rejected as lacking in sincerity, and the intention to proceed with the strike was announced "to revive industry, save the Japanese nation from destruction, and so to liberate the workers who are the people." It is strange, in the calmer atmosphere of today, to read those words and to remember they were supposed to apply to the circumstances of the biggest attempt to disrupt the functioning of Japan's national life ever attempted by the Communists.

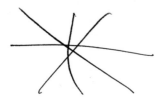

# 23

# The Communists
# as a Destructive Force

Most of the leaders of the Japanese Communist Party, as it was reconstituted after the Pacific War, were leftovers from the former Communist Party of prewar time. This was, perhaps, inevitable. But when we remember that the former party had something of the character of a religious secret society which had developed under the protection and direction of the International Communist Party to work for the promotion of revolution, it naturally follows that the new party also had for its design, from the first postwar days, the obstruction by every means of the economic recovery of Japan. It was this fact that placed the Liberal Party diametrically in opposition to the Communists throughout the years following the termination of the war.

The expulsion of Communists from government posts, the press, and industry, which was carried out later, involving the compulsory dismissal of Communists and their sympathizers, was attacked in those days as unconstitutional and an infringement of fundamental human rights. However, these people were not dismissed because of their ideas or the simple circumstance that they were Communists, but because the policies and activities of the Japanese Communist Party at that time were clearly of a destructive nature, menacing public safety. The Constitution had to be safeguarded at the expense of the Communists.

There can be no doubt that the projected general strike of February 1947 was instrumental in inducing GHQ to review and change its policy towards the Communists and adopt a sterner attitude. About a year earlier, during the period in office of the Shidehara cabinet, a government order had been issued prohibiting militaristic and other political bodies whose aims were opposed to those of the occupation, and requiring all political organizations to register themselves. But this order was mainly directed to curbing right-wing elements, and the Communists were not at that time the target of GHQ's anxieties. After the prohibition by GHQ of the projected general strike, however, the opinion gained ground within General MacArthur's headquarters that it had been a mistake to give government employees the right to strike. This fact, as I have previously noted, led eventually to the revision of the National Public Service Law during my second cabinet, and, although this step was not specifically aimed at the Communists, the purpose was, of course, to prevent them from obtaining control of the unions and so menacing the national economy. Since, in the case of government employees, the employers are the people, constituting the state, it was certainly strange that their trade unions should have been granted the same rights as those of workers in private industry. Nevertheless, had the trade unions, representing workers in public corporations, kept within the bounds of normal trade union activity, the need for taking legislative action to curb excesses would not have arisen. That they acted in the manner they did demonstrated the extent to which they had come under Communist influence.

It was shortly after the formation of my third cabinet in February 1949 that GHQ for the first time initiated steps aimed at legislative action openly directed against the Communist threat. This took the form of a directive ordering us to revise the government order, already referred to, issued at the time of the Shidehara cabinet. The revised order was issued in April of the same year under the name of the Organization Control Law, and prohibited all ultranationalistic and anti-democratic political associations whether of the Right or Left; required the registration of all associations engaging in activities likely to influence the political situation and the filing with the authorities of all periodicals issued by them; and reserved to the government the right to call in responsible officials of such organizations for questioning and to demand the presentation of data whenever such action was considered necessary.

This order served its purpose until the occupation ended, but after the coming into force of the peace treaty its validity, as a temporary order based upon a directive issued by the occupation authorities, ceased, and we were faced with the need for a new law. I had in mind at the time the setting up of a committee within the Diet along the lines of the U.S. House Committee to investigate Un-American Activities, the object of which would be to investigate Japanese suspected of engaging in pursuits contrary to the interests of Japan. But this project was found to present too many difficulties and had to be given up. The American Un-American Activities Committee itself was not too popular at that time, and we were not able to hit upon a means by which a similar Japanese committee would avoid giving the same unpopular impression.

When the Organization Control Law was promulgated, the Special Examining Bureau of the Ministry of Justice was charged with the task of implementing the order. The onerous task of registering the members of the Communist Party and its branch organizations was also undertaken by the bureau and completed the following year. Enforcement of the order bore other fruits as well. There existed a body called the League of Koreans in Japan, which was in those days even more addicted to acts of violence than the Communists and caused considerable trouble to the authorities; this body was dissolved and its property confiscated. There was also a National Liaison Council of Labor Unions, an association formed by Communists in March 1947 and composed of representatives of all trade unions in the country, a body through which a hold was maintained over the workers' movement. This council was affiliated with the World Federation of Trade Unions, a world organization of trade unions under the direct control of international communism, which implied that its purpose was to enroll Japan's workers in the cause of promoting world revolution. This organization too was therefore dissolved.

While such measures to check the lawless activities of Communists were being taken, opinion strengthened that the Japanese Communist Party itself should be declared illegal. General MacArthur's headquarters, particularly, frequently advanced such a suggestion informally. But although the idea itself had much to recommend it, neither of the two possible ways of banning the Communist Party seemed desirable. One would have been to declare the Communist Party illegal on the authority of GHQ; this would have offered no obstacles, but had the drawback that, once the occupation ended, we should be left very much where we were before. The other was to take regular legislative action, a course accompanied by so many difficulties that the contemplation of them alone made us pause.

The first formal suggestion coming from GHQ that the Japanese Communist Party should be declared illegal was contained in General MacArthur's Fourth of July message in 1949. In this the supreme commander pointed out the anomaly that Communists should be making use of the democratic freedoms which they enjoyed in Japan to destroy those freedoms, and went on to say that one might well doubt whether there existed any need to give legal protection to a political party advancing such political aims. The message was not so much an exhortation aimed at making the Communist Party illegal without delay, as a warning to the Japanese people concerning the nature of that party. But it also constituted a clear expression of occupation views as already foreshadowed in the directive concerning the Organization Control Law. As though willfully and deliberately to set the supreme commander's message at naught, a train of events added to the prevailing social unrest, including the death under mysterious circumstances, never fully cleared up, of Mr. Shimoyama Sadanori, president of the National Railways, and two instances of the derailment of trains in which drivers and passengers were killed. The exact nature of these incidents is even now not fully clear, so one may not be quite justified in viewing them as the work of Communists. But the fact that they had all to do with the operation of the National Railways, in which the largest number of workers were scheduled for discharge in line with the government's program for economic retrenchment—and in which feelings against the retrenchment program ran highest—did give us, and also GHQ, the impression that the Communists had been at work again.

The Japanese Communists became openly antagonistic in their attitude towards the United States the following year, the occasion for this development being furnished by Cominform criticism of Mr. Nozaka Sanzō, a leading Communist Party official. The Cominform, as most of us know, is in effect the International Communist Party in its resuscitated form since the Second World War and, whatever its avowed intentions, it is the organ through which the Soviet Union controls communists outside the borders of Russia. The gist of the criticism of the Japanese Communist Party policies seems to have been that Mr. Nozaka favored other means than force for bringing about a revolution in Japan, which in turn created a situation in which, from that time onwards, the Japanese Communist Party followed a course designed to bring about a revolution by force.

During the following weeks and months Communist acts of violence multiplied, increasing the social unrest. In such an atmosphere, General MacArthur stressed yet again, in a statement issued in May 3, the anniversary of the proclamation of Japan's postwar Constitution, the strange situation arising from the fact that the Communists were afforded the protection of democratic laws in order that they might carry out their subversive activities. The statement contained an even clearer expression than had his Fourth of July message of the previous year of the desire of the supreme commander to see the Japanese Communist Party declared illegal. Many other people in Japan felt the same way, and urged me personally to take that step, and I myself was almost disposed to agree. But finally I decided it would be a sounder course to rely upon the people's good sense to discredit the Communists in time, and I refrained from taking any action in the Diet. I was partly influenced in this matter by the fact that at the election of half the members of Japan's Upper House held in June that year the "direct action" tactics of the Communists had so disgusted voters that our Liberal Party gained enough seats to make us the first party in the Upper House, as is shown in the following figures:

| | |
|---|---|
| Liberals | 76 |
| Green-Breeze | 56 |
| National Democrats | 29 |

| | |
|---|---|
| Socialists | 62 |
| Labor-Peasants | 5 |
| Communists | 4 |
| | |
| Others | 16 |

In this election the Communists lost two seats. In the election of the House of Representatives held in October 1951, two years later, the Communists lost all the seats held previously, with no member returned; whereas in the previous election in January 1949 they had returned thirty-five members to the Diet.

One of the things that struck me most when I visited West Germany in 1954 was that I was told there existed no need for special legislative measures against communists, since the constitution of the West German Republic contained an article which laid down the principle that political parties whose aims and acts were inimical to a free and democratic social order, and endangered the existence of the republic, were unconstitutional. The Bundesverfassungsgericht decided whether any political party came under the article, and the West German government had already applied for a decision of the court concerning both the remnants of the former National Socialist (Nazi) Party and the Communists. A decision was handed down the following year concerning the National Socialist Party, declaring it to be an illegal organization, and in 1956 the Communist Party was also declared to be illegal on the grounds that the Communists, on their own admission, aimed at establishing a dictatorship of the proletariat and a Communist social order to be realized by means of a proletarian revolution; that history showed that it was necessary, in order to attain such ends, to resort to force, and armed uprisings were still the methods used by the so-called proletariat for obtaining power: and that, therefore, such aims were not compatible with the free social order existing in West Germany, and a party which professed these aims was unconstitutional. Acting on this decision, the West German government raided the Communist Party headquarters and confiscated its property.

The same brand of reasoning could be applied to Japan's Communists, but there exists no such article in our postwar Constitution, and from the legal viewpoint communism remains a matter of opinion—an opinion to which any person is free to subscribe. Moreover, there exists in Japan a widespread tendency to entertain a vague admiration for communism; even its excesses are condoned by many if they appear to be aimed against capitalism or imperialism. It is further quite usual for those Japanese who have visited the Soviet Union or Communist China, and leftist intellectuals who are considered sound judges in such matters, to excuse, praise, and idealize whatever they have seen or gathered of communism in practice. I often wondered why this should be so before I was told that by so doing those concerned were able to win the applause of large numbers of workers and students in Japan.

Instead of flattering those in authority as the same species did in prewar time, these modern sycophants truckle to present-day trends, and perhaps their poison is the more widely disseminated, given modern means of mass communication. That being the situation, the difficulties attending such a step as declaring the Japanese Communist Party illegal are too great to be ignored, and it still seems to me to be a wiser policy to leave the matter to public opinion for decision when public opinion shall come, as it does to an increasing extent, to express the genuine thoughts and feelings of the sounder elements among our people who even in those occupation days formed the actual majority. This view was also, perhaps, in the minds of those within GHQ when they refrained from pressing the question of banning the Communist Party.

As previously mentioned, the Communists came out into the open in opposition to the occupation and the United States after Cominform criticism of Mr. Nozaka Sanzō in 1950, which was also the year during which the Korean War began. On May 30 another of the so-called National Meetings of the People was held in the outer grounds of Tokyo's imperial palace, during which some U.S. officers who had come to witness the gathering and had taken some pictures were badly mauled by the mob. That was bad enough; worse was the propaganda against the occupation appearing in the *Akahata* (Red Flag), the principal organ of the Communist Party, and other Communist periodicals that had long overstepped accepted boundaries between political diatribe and downright libel. General MacArthur's headquarters had already, the previous February, warned the leaders that if the party persisted in violating the accepted limits of decent freedom of expression or otherwise performed acts which menaced the pursuit of legal aims in a free society, GHQ might be forced to suppress *Akahata* or even withdraw legal protection from the Communist Party. This warning failed to change the attitude of the Communists, and in June 1950 GHQ issued a directive in the form of a letter addressed to me by General MacArthur requiring us to purge twenty-four members of the party, including Tokuda Kyūichi and others on the central committee, and seventeen on the editorial staff of *Akahata*. The earlier directives on which the Organization Control Law and the Purge Law were based were cited as providing legal authority for this action, but nothing was said about taking any steps in regard to the party itself. Actual suppression of *Akahata* was purposely avoided, the reason given being that it would not be in conformity with the principles by which freedom of the press is guaranteed in postwar Japan and that such a step should not therefore be resorted to until all other methods failed. The letter was clear evidence that General MacArthur wished above all to refrain from having recourse to measures such as the banning of political parties and suppression of newspapers, which are not usually associated with the idea of democratic government.

The Communists were immune to all such cautionary gestures, and on June 25, when the North Korean forces began their invasion of the Republic of Korea, *Akahata* immediately published on its front page a large photograph of Kim Il Sung, the prime minister of North Korea, and began to print propaganda supporting the Communist invasion of South Korea. In retaliation, publication of *Akahata* was suspended by GHQ for thirty days, but it continued to disseminate pro-Communist propaganda through subsidiary publications and the printing of pamphlets, so publication of *Akahata* and all periodicals associated with it was suspended indefinitely from July 18, 1950.

The Special Examining Bureau of the Ministry of Justice and other police organizations were charged with the task of searching out and confiscating periodicals and pamphlets distributed through secret branches of the Communist Party, in the course of which work some were discovered calling upon the Japanese people to rise in arms, as well as orders of the party of the same nature. It was evident that the Communist objective was to do the best they could at that time, by such means, to prevent the U.S. occupation forces from being transferred from garrison duty in Japan to the Korean battlefront, and so, indirectly, to assist the North Korean invaders. The Special Examining Bureau also found evidence that plans were actually being formulated and pushed forward for the establishment of a secret organization designed to instigate and carry into effect the sort of armed revolution advocated in Communist periodicals, and summoned leaders of the party for investigation on this matter as the bureau had authority to do under the provisions of the Organization Control Law. Nine of those thus called, including Tokuda Kyūichi, refused to answer the summons, went underground, and remained undetected despite all efforts of the police to track them down. It was later reported that Tokuda had died in Peking. Everything the Communists did was always thus shrouded in mystery.

In addition to these measures taken against Communist leaders and the editors of *Akahata*, we instituted and enforced what was at that time popularly called the "Red Purge." This consisted of dismissing Communists and their sympathizers from government posts, press, and industries in order to prevent them from engaging in destructive activities within the organizations employing them. This was not done by order of the occupation authorities, but on the individual responsibility of our government agencies and the private firms concerned, but of course the step could not have been taken at that time had not GHQ suggested it and given us solid support. Enforcement was no easy matter, since, for instance, being a member of a trade union with marked Communist leanings did not in itself mean that the person concerned was a Communist, while in the case of genuine Communists it was their job to camouflage themselves and their opinions. In these circumstances, there was no other feasible course but to judge each case individually, a procedure which offered the soundest results because the objective of the purge was not to dismiss people for being Communists, but to defend organizations from the unwelcome political activities of those persons most likely to prove actual nuisances from the point of view of past experience.

The purge in private enterprises began with the press and radio and was gradually extended to industry in general. In July 1950 some Communist elements in a broadcasting station in Osaka were discharged and forbidden entry to the station where they had been working. This action gave rise to some public commotion, which, however, soon subsided, but its repercussions were sufficient to start a chain reaction of purges in press and radio quarters throughout the nation, followed first by the electric industry and others of national importance, and later by many other industries. The process was accompanied by a certain amount of friction in some areas, but on the whole it was carried out quietly—no doubt largely because it had the support of public opinion.

In this manner over six hundred men connected with the press and radio worlds, and over ten thousand in industry, were discharged, the total affected, including those in government offices, coming to some twenty-two thousand. Some eighteen months were needed to complete the purge, but it proved effective in removing at least some part of the Communist menace from government offices and key industries, and was the alternative chosen by us to making the Communist Party itself illegal. In regard to the question whether such a step represented a violation of fundamental human rights guaranteed by the Constitution, we took the view, as I have said before, that the men concerned were not deprived of their employment because they were Communists, or because of their belief in certain ideas which the government and public opinion did not share, but because the behavior of the Communists up to that time and during the purge period indicated that these men were potential menaces to the offices and industries employing them; so that in order to protect these from more trouble in the future, the government was justified in removing the men concerned.

After the signing of the San Francisco Peace Treaty in September 1951 and the return of peace and recognition of Japan's status as an independent sovereign nation by the world, apart from the Soviet bloc, the question of measures to be taken against the destructive activities of Japan's Communists again presented itself as a matter of urgency, more particularly as the decision had been taken to establish a system of defense for Japan in which the U.S. Security Forces would play a major role.

During the occupation era we could at least always rely upon the occupation forces in dealing with such issues as defense and the maintenance of order in the country, and initiate any legislative remedies necessary in the name of the occupation authorities. It now became the Japanese government's task to do all these things on our own responsibility. Something had to be supplied to take the place of the Organization Control Law (which had been a temporary occupation measure) as our legal authority in coping with the Communist problem, and this need brought us up against difficulties I have enumerated earlier. We could not ban communism as a political creed or do anything about the Communist Party itself without infringing our Constitution. We therefore had to frame a new law which dealt with illegal and destructive acts as means of achieving some political end; which would not be confined to Communists alone, but would cover subversive acts whether committed by those of the extreme Right or extreme Left. What was involved, in fact, was the question of transforming the Organization Control Law, which being legislated under the occupation was to become nullified with the termination of the occupation, into a permanent Japanese law—a project to which, so far as I could see, no one objected. However, when we settled down to determine the details, we found ourselves immediately exposed to criticisms and apprehensions that this or that point in the draft proposals threatened restrictions on freedom of speech, or represented an unwonted intrusion into the private lives of citizens. The debates which followed the presentation of the bill to the Diet during the same year centered on these questions, and it was not finally enacted until July 1952, under the title of Subversive Activities Prevention Law.

The fact that a new government agency, called the Public Safety Investigation Agency, was to be established to supervise the work connected with the application of the law also invited the criticism that this was a revival of the old secret police, and there occurred some fierce debates on the subject. Some years have already passed since all this happened and the measure became law: in the meantime none of the evils that were then alleged by the opposition have materialized. It seems to me that any law that has to do with any kind of police control inevitably entails, to a certain extent, the restriction of individual freedom. Nevertheless such laws have to be enacted where the need for them exists, and it finally becomes a question of what kind of freedom we most prize. A proper understanding of the question by everyone concerned would, of course, make all such laws unnecessary.

# 24

## The San Francisco Peace Treaty

Whether the peace treaty between the Allied powers and Japan signed on September 8, 1951, in San Francisco was really the just and generous treaty that it was then generally considered to be or not is a matter only history can decide. But, for our part, we at least did our best to ensure that the treaty should be an advantageous settlement for Japan, and also that the document should be signed and go into effect at the earliest possible date in order that Japan might regain its independence.

As I look back at the events that led up to the treaty, two Americans stand out prominently, so that without reference to them it would be impossible to speak about the treaty itself, for without these two it might never have materialized. One is General Douglas MacArthur, the first Supreme Commander for the Allied Powers in Japan; the other is Mr. John Foster Dulles, then adviser to the U.S. secretary of state. We Japanese must remember with gratitude General MacArthur for his consistent advocacy of an early peace treaty, and Mr. Dulles for making the terms of the treaty of such advantage for Japan, and thus producing a treaty based—in Mr. Dulles's own words—upon trust and understanding.

At the outset of the occupation, prospects regarding the drafting and signing of a peace treaty were remote. While the Potsdam Declaration stated that the Allied forces would be withdrawn from Japan upon the objectives of the occupation being accomplished and a peacefully inclined and responsible government established in my country, it was up to the Allied powers to decide whether the objectives of the occupation, such as the democratization of the country, had been accomplished, and whether the government in office was, in fact, responsible and peacefully inclined or not. Thus, should the Allied powers so desire, they could go on occupying the

Japanese homeland indefinitely. There were actually some in the United States, and in the U.S. forces in Japan, who favored an indefinite occupation. After the surrender the Japanese had received the incoming Americans with more than ordinary kindness. The climate of the nation was pleasant; the scenery famous for its beauty. Add to these attractions the strategic advantages accruing to the United States by reason of the occupation, and one can understand that the Americans, and particularly some of their military men, should want to stay on.

It is to the credit of General MacArthur that, in such an atmosphere, he never for a moment ceased contending that an early termination of the occupation was desirable. It was his firm belief that it should be ended in three years, or not much longer, since history records no instance of a successful military occupation lasting more than five years. As a soldier, General MacArthur well knew that the longer an army of occupation remained in a defeated country, the more would discipline be relaxed, and the greater the threat of corruption, thus leading to alienating the people of the occupied country. And he must have feared such a development in Japan more than anything else. The supreme commander often spoke in this vein to me personally, and did not hesitate to point the same moral in his public statements. His views on this matter were a source of great encouragement to us during the years he was in Japan. To have, as the government of an occupied nation, to negotiate with GHQ daily on every minor point of government that required attention, constituted an intolerable burden. The situation was even worse in the provinces, where friction was continually arising between the people and the occupation authorities. Weighing upon us even more heavily was the thought that a prolonged occupation of the country might take away from our people all spirit of independence, after which it would not greatly matter any longer when the occupation ended. Thus, although our reasons may have been different, we in the government were at one with General MacArthur in desiring that the period of occupation should be as short as possible.

Only eighteen months after the termination of hostilities, in March 1947, General MacArthur expressed the opinion, at a press conference for foreign correspondents in Tokyo, that the time had come to conclude a peace treaty and end the occupation. However, we could not feel so optimistic. At that time, the peace treaty between Italy and the Allied powers had not yet come into effect. And no one could say when such a treaty between Germany and the victorious powers would be signed. Moreover, relations between the United States and the Soviet bloc had been steadily deteriorating since the end of the Second World War, and it was widely anticipated that growing tensions would inevitably produce differences of opinion between the two camps in regard to the question of peace with Japan. This turned out to be only too true. When in July of the same year that the supreme commander made his statement to the press, the U.S. government proposed holding a preparatory conference to discuss the question of a Japanese peace with the eleven nations composing the Far Eastern Commission, the Soviet Union immediately countered by proposing instead a foreign ministers' conference between the United States, Great Britain, the Soviet Union, and China. Thus the first deadlock occurred over the question of procedure, an issue that was not resolved until several years later.

At that time the U.S. government itself was still uncertain whether it should press the question of concluding peace with Japan or not. Mr. Robert Lovett, the U.S. undersecretary of state, declared that the peace conference would be postponed for a while, and Mr. Kenneth C. Royall, secretary for the army, speaking of making Japan a bulwark against the totalitarian menace in the Far East, gave the impression that the Americans intended to stay on in Japan. It is clear therefore that the antagonism between the United States and the Soviet Union had the effect of delaying peace talks. General MacArthur persisted in his opinion, however, and in his statement on the occasion of the third anniversary of the conclusion of the Pacific War he declared the Japanese people had done all that had been required of them and the time had come for a peace to be concluded. I knew that he meant what he said, and remember telling a press conference that the supreme commander favored an early peace—a statement that I made deliberately in order that the Japanese people should not be depressed by the thought that peace would never come.

The delay was not without its advantages for Japan. What is most to be feared by a defeated nation is that severe terms such as would endanger future freedom and independence may be imposed upon it as the price of peace, and this is precisely what could very well have happened in the case of Japan if peace had been concluded shortly after the surrender, while hostile feelings were still strong among the Allied nations and their peoples. As things turned out, feelings became more restrained with the passage of time, bringing better understanding of my country, while we, for our part, were given more leisure to prepare the ground for an acceptable peace.

The basic factor that guided our approach to peace was that, unlike the Portsmouth Conference that ended the Russo-Japanese War, and the Versailles Peace Conference following the First World War, the conference that would be held this time would not be one in which victor and vanquished came together to discuss the terms of peace on a more or less equal footing. The demand for unconditional surrender advocated by President Roosevelt, and the Potsdam Declaration, made that much clear. This implied that what the Allied powers would do would be to build up—during the occupation—the kind of conditions in the vanquished country that would be demanded at the peace conference, and then present such conditions as an accomplished fact at the conference itself. This interpretation of the situation meant further that, in effect, the terms of peace were gradually being made clear throughout the duration of the occupation, so that our daily negotiations with GHQ were so many negotiations for peace.

With this thought in mind, we regarded such negotiations as something more than mere routine work imposed upon us by the occupation, and strove to see those in the upper ranks of GHQ as frequently as possible to give them a wider understanding of the situation than the actual matter in hand perhaps demanded. Whenever prominent Americans, whether officials of the U.S. government or private citizens (or other men from the Allied countries), visited Japan, I myself did my best to meet them and explain the real state of affairs in my country. I still think this policy which we adopted was not without its effect. There was another point to be considered, which was that, if the terms of a peace treaty were to be discussed between the Allied powers alone and then simply imposed upon Japan at a conference, we should have to choose some country to plead our cause for us in our absence. That country, obviously, had to be the United States, for since that was the nation most directly concerned with the occupation of Japan, it would naturally be expected to play a leading role in the framing of a peace treaty. Furthermore, in contrast to some of the Allied powers, which still at that date entertained feelings of hatred and distrust towards Japan, the United States had arrived at a better understanding of conditions in my country and so had become more sympathetic towards our hopes and claims. Also working in our favor in that respect were the friendships that had sprung up between Americans who had been stationed in Japan and the Japanese people, and the goodwill and generosity that are outstanding characteristics of the American nation. It was clear therefore that there existed little hope of a peace acceptable to Japan unless the United States spoke for us during the preliminary talks among the Allied powers concerning the convening of a peace conference.

For the United States to assume this role, however, it was necessary for her leaders to be put in possession of all the facts concerning postwar Japan, and for those facts to be presented in a form that would make them comprehensible to the U.S. authorities in Washington, who were still ignorant of many problems on which GHQ in Tokyo needed no briefing from us. We therefore began in the autumn of 1946 compiling such data in English, starting with a review of economic and political conditions in the country at that time. Special pains were taken in compiling data concerning our territories: we set forth the facts concerning such integral parts of Japan as Okinawa and the Bonin Islands, the Kuriles, and Sakhalin, alike from the historical, geographical, racial and economic points of view, and—in the case of the Kuriles—explained in detail the circumstances that made them an integral part of Japanese territory. The material thus presented in regard to the territorial question alone filled seven volumes.

We were uncertain at first whether the U.S. government would accept such material from us, but, through the kind offices of the Diplomatic Section of GHQ, a way was found whereby, from 1948 onwards, the papers were presented informally by the Japanese Foreign Office to the Diplomatic Section and thence transmitted to Washington. We were subsequently informed that the papers had been very well received there as being valuable material for study. Encouraged by that fact, we set to work, with other ministries cooperating with the Foreign Office, and compiled material concerning the population problem, war damages, standard of living, shipping, fishery, and so on, amounting to several hundred thousand words and filling between fifty and sixty volumes. By 1950 we had covered practically every question that might be expected to come up in connection with the terms of a peace treaty, so that U.S. government officials in Washington must have had all the material needed at their disposal when they began drafting the treaty.

# 25

## Preparatory Negotiations for Peace

By the spring of 1950 the U.S. government had set to work in earnest on the problem of paving the way for a peace with Japan. In April of that year Mr. John Foster Dulles, a member of the Republican Party, was appointed adviser to Mr. Dean Acheson, then secretary of state, and specifically charged with the drafting of a peace treaty. The fact that the Democratic Truman administration had named a prominent Republican senator to undertake the task showed that it was determined to treat the question from a national, non-partisan standpoint, and clearly marked a step forward in the direction of a peace treaty.

In June 1950, just before the outbreak of the Korean War, Mr. Dulles made the first of three trips to Japan. On that occasion he must have come simply to acquaint himself with conditions in Japan, and to hear the views of GHQ and the Japanese government before beginning his task of framing a draft peace treaty. Or so it seemed, for the talks we had with Mr. Dulles were confined to general topics. At that time the U.S. government still appeared undecided regarding which solution was to be found for the defense of Japan after the coming into effect of a peace treaty, and Mr. Dulles himself sounded us on the possibility of Japan's agreeing to a measure of rearmament.

On June 25, 1950, shortly after this first visit of Mr. Dulles to Japan, the Korean War began, and first reports from Washington indicated that this development was likely to add to the difficulties of arranging the signing of an early peace treaty, which certainly did not encourage optimism. However, in the autumn of the same year we learned that Mr. Dulles had been empowered by the U.S. government to initiate negotiations with the countries concerned in preparation for the formulation of a treaty and had begun talks with representatives of Great Britain, the Soviet Union, China, the Philippines, India, and other nations to that end.

Mr. Dulles visited Japan again towards the end of January 1951—this time in the capacity of special envoy of the American president. I had several talks with him, and he also met many leaders of our political, economic, and labor groups, showing himself ready to listen to their views. In my talks with him, I stressed that Japan desired a peace which its people could accept without loss of national pride; that we wanted a peace that would enable us to complete the democratization of our country and our national economic recovery, in addition to regaining our independence; and that after this had been accomplished, Japan would do her best to contribute towards the strengthening of the free world and the building up and maintaining of a close and solid relationship with the United States. I further stated that there were many aspects of the reforms enacted during the occupation which failed to take fully into account actual conditions existing in Japan, and it was my intention to ask the supreme commander to remedy this situation without waiting for the signing of a peace treaty.

Mr. Dulles indicated his view that if a peace treaty had been signed three years earlier, its terms would inevitably have been much more unfavorable to Japan, but that now the aim of the United States was to frame a treaty which would not be a document to be signed between victors and vanquished, but a peace signed between friendly nations. The point in which America's special envoy was chiefly interested, it seemed, concerned in what way a Japan without any armament to speak of could accept her share of responsibility as a member of the free world. I shall refer to this point later in connection with the U.S.-Japan Security Treaty; at the time, I told Mr. Dulles that such matters could only be considered and debated after my country had once again achieved economic independence.

During these talks with Mr. Dulles a document was handed me outlining the principles on which the U.S. government proposed the peace treaty should be based. The contents of this, dealing with the disposition of our territories, Japan's position in the world after the signing of the treaty, and so on, were of a far more generous nature than we had been led to expect, and greatly heartened us. The proposals were examined in detail by our Foreign Office and further discussed with Mr. John M. Allison and others in Mr. Dulles's suite. In this way we were able to review the issues thoroughly in advance of the beginning of the actual task of framing the treaty, and both sides were satisfied with the results achieved. Before departing from Japan, Mr. Dulles told me he expected to complete the blueprinting of the treaty within three or four months, but that in the meantime he anticipated meeting with a good deal of opposition from the Philippines and some of the British dominions.

The basic principles, as originally disclosed to us, underwent a certain amount of revision and alteration during the subsequent negotiations between the United States and other countries concerned, but were in the main incorporated in the final treaty. The question of security, while not actually included in the provisions of the peace treaty, represented an important problem for Japan after the signing of that document, and was included in the principles set forth. A basic understanding on this point was also reached between Japan and the United States during Mr. Dulles's second visit, and later was formalized in the U.S.-Japan Joint Defense Arrangement. In addition to reaching decisions on the framework of the final peace treaty, Mr. Dulles's second visit led to other important gains for us. We asked that the reforms enacted under the direction of the occupation authorities should not be made permanent by being written into the treaty; that war reparations should take the form chiefly of payment in kind, in order that Japan should not be drained of her foreign currency reserves; that there should be no further additions to the list of war criminals, and the case of those already condemned and sentenced as such should be reconsidered where possible. On all these points an understanding was reached between the Americans and ourselves.

Mr. Dulles came to Japan for the third time on April 16, 1951—the same day that General MacArthur left to return to the United States. I met Mr. Dulles on April 18, and was immediately reassured by him that the dismissal of General MacArthur did not in any way affect American policy in the matter of the conclusion of peace with Japan. Mr. Dulles then briefed me concerning his recent visits to the Philippines, Australia, and New Zealand. One country had advanced strong demands in respect to reparations, while another had urged that limitations be placed on Japanese rearmament. Mr. Dulles stated that he had experienced considerable difficulties in winning these countries over to the American point of view, but that he had, at any rate, drawn up a draft peace treaty on his return to Washington, which had been circulated to fifteen countries for consideration. Among the fifteen was the Soviet Union, and Mr. Jacob Malik had already issued a statement announcing the intention of the Soviet government to have nothing further to do with the proposed peace treaty. Mr. Dulles also disclosed that Great Britain had submitted an alternative draft of her own framing.

It was at this meeting that I gave General Matthew Ridgway, the new supreme commander, who was present, a written request for permission to review and reconsider such of the reforms carried out during the occupation period as did not fit in with actual conditions existing in Japan. This had been prepared for submission to General MacArthur, but he had departed from Japan before I could hand it to him. Before concluding his third visit, Mr. Dulles told me that many problems had already been overcome in regard to the framing of a peace treaty, and that he felt confident that the remaining obstacles could also be overcome, adding his assurance that the U.S. government and people would not rest until a real peace had been secured.

After his return to Washington, Mr. Dulles again visited Great Britain in June further to discuss treaty matters with members of the British government. Distrust of Japan was still strong in that country, in which, moreover, very real fears were entertained of Japan's again becoming a serious rival to Great Britain in the shipping and trade spheres. The Commonwealth countries also had their views: one was demanding the limitation of Japanese armaments, and another restrictions on the activities of Japanese fishermen. It was natural, therefore, that the draft of the peace treaty prepared by the British should have been rather more severe towards Japan in its provisions than that proposed by the United States. We had already communicated our own views on the British draft to Mr. Dulles, and he did his best for us during his stay in London. He left for Paris to discuss the treaty with the French government and returned again to London for further consultations, after which, on June 14, we received news that complete agreement had been reached between Great Britain and the United States on all questions concerned with the peace treaty.

Mr. John M. Allison came to Japan, in the capacity of minister, to report to us the results of the London talks, and stated that the draft as agreed between the two parties was based upon the American draft and that, although some alterations had been introduced from the British draft, making the final document a little less advantageous to Japan than the original version, we should not, by any means, find the terms unacceptable. Mr. Allison further informed us that, in regard to the question of China's being represented at the peace conference, the United States had insisted that she would not on any account sign a treaty in company with Communist China, which was at that moment actually engaged in hostilities in Korea, while Great Britain, on the other hand, had maintained that of the two Chinese governments, the one that should be seated and sign at the peace conference was the regime which two-thirds of the countries represented on the Far Eastern Commission recognized. In the end, it was agreed that China should not be represented at the conference, and that Japan could sign a separate peace treaty later with whichever of the two Chinese governments she chose to recognize.

We again outlined our own views in detail concerning the amended draft, and also expressed to Mr. Allison our desire that the inhabitants of Okinawa should continue to be treated as Japanese subjects and economic and other relations be maintained as before; that measures be instituted to hasten the repatriation of Japanese still held in captivity abroad; and that buildings and equipment then in use by occupation authorities in Japan be returned as soon as possible after the coming into effect of the peace treaty. The U.S. government then set to work to frame the final draft of the treaty.

# 26

# The San Francisco
# Peace Conference

On July 12, 1951—five days after it had been communicated to the Japanese government by Mr. W. J. Sebald, then in Japan with the rank of ambassador—the U.S. government published the text of the draft peace treaty with Japan.

This was the fruit of a full year's hard work by Mr. Dulles, who had visited Japan on three occasions to study actual conditions and to listen to what our leaders had to say, and in the meantime had visited the other countries concerned to prevail upon their governments to accept the treaty he was preparing. In the past, treaties of peace had usually been arrived at with representatives of the vanquished side being summoned to a conference at which their claims were ignored by the victors, whose demands then became the terms of the treaties concerned. The peace treaty concluded between Japan and the Allied powers marked a radical departure from this tradition in that Mr. Dulles had taken upon himself the responsibility of shouldering all the difficulties of negotiation, and thereby won for Japan the most important concessions from other Allied governments that we ourselves at that time would have been in no position to secure. As soon as I heard that the draft had been completed, I wrote a letter of thanks to Mr. Dulles, which was the least I could do under the circumstances. He replied in a letter dated July 9, in which he was most insistent that I myself should attend the forthcoming peace conference as a delegate. On the occasion of his last visit to Japan he had asked me who would be included in the Japanese delegation, but I had refrained at that time from being explicit in my answer.

On July 20 the U.S. government formally invited the nations concerned to the peace conference, to be held in San Francisco, and the Japanese government accepted on July 24. I decided to attend myself. And, in order that our delegation should be as representative of Japan as possible, I invited Mr. Tomabechi Gizō of the Democratic Party, Mr. Tokugawa Muneyoshi of the Ryokufūkai Group in the Upper House, and Mr. Ichimada Naoto, president of the Bank of Japan, to join the delegation, in addition to Mr. Ikeda Hayato, the minister of finance.

The Japanese delegation arrived in San Francisco on September 2. The conference, which lasted from September 4 to 8, was held in the San Francisco Opera House, the historic building where the United Nations Charter had been signed. Fifty-two countries were represented, with Mr. Dean Acheson, the U.S. secretary of state, in the chair. President Harry Truman opened the proceedings with a speech in which he stated, "Let us be free of malice and hate, to the end that from here on there shall be neither victors nor vanquished among us, but only equals in the partnership of peace," and the conference was certainly conducted in the atmosphere desired by the president. It was friendly throughout, without any manifestation of hostility towards us; the conference itself taking the form of adopting the draft of the peace treaty jointly proposed by Mr. John Foster Dulles, the U.S. delegate, and Mr. Kenneth C. Younger, the British delegate. It is true that the Soviet Union, Poland, Czechoslovakia, and other Communist nations represented attempted to delay the discussions by making difficulties on points of procedure; by raising the question of the absence of Communist Chinese representation at the conference; and by proposing amendments to the draft; but they were outvoted at every step by the free countries. Mr. Acheson was admirable in his management of the proceedings.

It was particularly gratifying to us to hear both the American and British delegates, in their exposition of the draft treaty, make it quite clear that the sovereignty over the Okinawa Islands rested with Japan. Delegates of other countries represented then made their speeches, and, although some expressed dissatisfaction in regard to the provisions of the treaty concerning reparations, none said anything that could be construed as anti-Japanese. Finally, at 8:17 p.m. on September 7, after speeches by other delegates had concluded, I was asked to make a speech accepting the treaty on behalf of Japan.

The evening session began with my speech, and in the course of my remarks, I laid particular stress on the territorial question, rebutting the Soviet delegate's statement that the Kuriles and southern Sakhalin had been wrested from Russia by force, and showing that Japanese sovereignty over the southern Kuriles was a fact accepted even by imperial Russia, while the Habomai and Shikotan Islands that formed an integral part of Hokkaidō, Japan's northernmost home island, were still under the occupation of Soviet forces in violation of international law. Needless to add, my emphasis on these points was intended to serve for future reference.

The peace treaty was signed the following day, on September 8, 1951. Venezuela was the last of forty-eight countries signing on the Allied side in alphabetical order, and then, upon Mr. Warren Kelchner, the secretary-general of the conference, calling out "Japan," I went to sign, followed by the rest of the Japanese delegation. Mr. Acheson then made a closing speech, in which the phrase "our friend Japan" stands out in memory. Looking at my watch, I saw that it was 11:44 a.m.

As I shall mention later, the U.S.-Japan Security Treaty was also signed at 5 p.m. that day. It was almost exactly six years since the documents of surrender had been signed on the deck of USS *Missouri* in Tokyo Bay in September 1945. The years between had been both long and short. To the Japanese government, daily transacting business with the occupation authorities, they were certainly six long years, but when we look back to the days immediately following the termination of the Pacific War, when Allied forces were landing in quick succession in our country and it was the concern of every Japanese to know when the occupation would end and national independence be regained, six years was a rather shorter period of time than we had then generally expected. To me personally, those years had been spent in such a confusion of work that, although it does not seem that much time has passed since those days, there are many things which I can only recall when reminded of them by others. However, objectively speaking, we cannot be said to have taken too much time in achieving our prime objective, which was the regaining of our national independence.

In this connection, Japan was undoubtedly fortunate in the circumstance that the United States was the country primarily responsible for the occupation of our homeland. At the same time, the efforts made by the Japanese people in speeding national recovery during those six years must also be remembered. The results achieved did not fail to impress the Allied governments and had finally led to the peace treaty. These were the thoughts uppermost in my mind as I signed that document, which again made my nation sovereign and independent.

The evening I arrived in San Francisco, I had paid an official call on Mr. Acheson and Mr. Dulles at the headquarters of the American delegation at the Palace Hotel and conversed with them for about an hour. In the course of our talk Mr. Acheson assured me that the United States wished to welcome Japan back into the society of nations no matter what attitude the Soviet Union might adopt at the conference, and, further, that since the draft of the treaty had been thoroughly discussed by all the countries concerned for a year past, it was the intention of the American delegation not to accept any amendments that might be proposed to the draft treaty; to make this point clear in the rules of procedure governing the conference; and to limit the time allowed for speeches by any delegate to one hour. Mr. Acheson went on to say that, apart from the objections of the Soviet Union and its satellites, Pakistan, Ceylon, Indonesia, and the Philippines were not satisfied with Article 14 of the treaty—dealing with reparations and Japanese property abroad—and it was even conceivable that one or more countries might refuse to sign; that being the case, it would be most unwise for Japan herself to express dissatisfaction with the article. Mr. Acheson urged me to make it clear to other countries before the conference opened that they could rely upon Japan's good faith in fulfilling the provisions of the article in question.

I record this conversation because it shows how wholehearted were these two American statesmen in their desire to smooth Japan's path at the conference. True to his word, Mr. Acheson met all protests and amendments advanced by the Communist countries with firmness and tactfully disposed of them. It was all done with such skill and adroitness that I was filled not only with gratitude but also with admiration. I myself had of course followed the advice given me by Mr. Acheson and Mr. Dulles concerning the attitude of Asian countries such as the Philippines and Indonesia, and had visited their delegations before the conference opened in an effort to prevail upon them to sign the treaty. Whether as a result of my visits or not, all of them signed, and the delegate from Ceylon made a speech which was, to me, profoundly moving as a sincere expression of friendship towards Japan. I was approached by the delegates of some other countries also in connection with questions not specifically covered by the terms of the peace treaty. The Dutch delegate asked the U.S. delegation to act as intermediary in demanding the payment of an indemnity to Dutch nationals imprisoned in Indonesia during the war, and, as this was a question affecting other countries as well, we had to be cautious in our reply. However, through the good offices of the American delegation, we were able to reach a solution by securing the agreement of the Dutch delegate to an official exchange of notes mentioning future measures to be taken by Japan on her own initiative. The Indonesian and Australian delegates wanted us to impose restraints on our fishing operations, and the Norwegian delegate on our whaling operations. It was agreed that subsequent negotiations on these matters should take place as provided for in the treaty, and we parted on that understanding.

It had been my original intention to make my speech to the conference in English. However, Mr. Acheson suggested it was preferable to make it in Japanese, since the Russian delegate had made his in the Russian language, and I saw no reason why I should refuse. It was not until I mounted the rostrum and began delivering my speech that the thought came to me that among the three thousand persons in the audience, probably less than one in every hundred understood Japanese. It was very much like talking to a group of deaf persons, and during the twenty minutes that were required to complete my remarks, I was sorely tempted more than once to abandon it unfinished. Later I was told that the speech was not only broadcast directly to Japan, but simultaneous translations of it in English, French, and other languages were being transmitted to the earphones with which the audience was provided, so that it was fortunate both for myself and my translators that I persisted to the end.

After the signing of the treaty, it was naturally the policy of the Japanese government to take all necessary steps for its ratification without delay, and to complete the measures required to enable Japan to operate again as an independent state. To that end, the Diet was convened on October 10, 1951, and bills for the ratification of the peace treaty and the U.S.-Japan Security Pact were introduced into the House of Representatives on the same day.

The position confronting my administration and the Liberal Party within the Diet on the ratification issue was somewhat confused. There had already been some trouble within the Democratic Party over the inclusion of Mr. Tomabechi as one of the Japanese delegates to the conference, and that rival group was not expected to vote unanimously in support of the two treaties, although the general expectation was that a majority of the party would vote with us. The case was different with the Socialists, the right and left wings of which group had come to differ more and more on points of policy, so that in the matter of the two treaties the right-wing Socialists and "neutrals" within the party favored ratification of the peace treaty but were against the Security Pact, on the grounds that the first restored the nation's independence but the Security Treaty would transform Japan into an American colony; while the left-wing Socialists were opposed to both treaties, arguing that the two could not be separated. This conflict of views eventually led to the Socialists splitting into two separate parties, with the Left Socialists and the Right Socialists going their own ways until they re-merged in 1955.

Such was the position when the Diet convened on October 10, and I made my opening speech two days later. In this, I explained the nature of the two treaties and placed particular stress on the fact they were one and indivisible. The vote was taken in the Lower House on October 26, when both treaties were approved. We experienced more difficulty in the Upper House, in which a great deal of discussion occurred regarding the relationship between the treaties and the postwar Constitution and the question of military bases. The session was due to end on November 18, and it was feared that we might not succeed in bringing the treaties to a vote in the Upper Chamber before that time. This prospect posed a rather serious problem, since any failure on the part of the Japanese Diet to ratify the treaties would inevitably have repercussions in other countries concerned, and might well retard the ratification of the peace treaties elsewhere, and the Security Treaty in the United States. In the event, we managed to secure the passage of both agreements on the final day of the session. They were then presented to the emperor for His Majesty's attestation, and so ratification was completed.

# 27

## The Territorial Question

Japanese national territory after the Pacific War was limited by the Potsdam Declaration to the four main islands of Honshū, Hokkaidō, Kyūshū, and Shikoku, and unspecified outlying small islands. In regard to the latter, we had no course open to us but to accept the ruling of the Allied powers as to the extent of the outlying islands included in this definition. But since this point would be determined at the peace conference, it was important that we should make every effort to have the treaty framed with a minimum of disadvantage to us, and particularly to ensure that the definition of territory gained by aggression was not stretched to include territory that did not fall into that category.

I have already mentioned our efforts to inform the Allies on this point. We continued such efforts after the treaty had been drafted in the spring of 1951, and when Mr. Dulles came to Japan for a third time after prevailing upon the other Allied powers to approve the terms of this original draft, we requested him to make clear in the treaty that the southern Kuriles, which had always been a part of our possessions, were not included in the Kuriles which were to be handed over. Mr. Dulles appreciated our point, but indicated that if this were done it would involve going afresh into the wording of the document with the other countries concerned, which would delay the peace conference and so the signing of the treaty. He therefore asked us to waive the point, suggesting instead that we express our own view on the matter in our speech accepting the terms of the treaty, which we did.

In contrast to Article 2 of the peace treaty, in which we were required to relinquish all rights and claims over Sakhalin, the Kuriles, Formosa, and so on, no such restrictions were placed on Japan's claims in Article 3 governing the disposal of our island possessions in the southwest and south. Our claims to sovereignty over these islands were not abandoned; they were simply turned over to the Allied powers in anticipation of their being placed under the mandatory rule of the United States after the coming into effect of the peace treaty. This means that the Article leaves room for the possibility, at some future date when the international situation may permit, of measures being taken in line with the wishes of the inhabitants in regard to their status, communication facilities with the Japanese mainland, and other such points. Meanwhile, the potential sovereignty over these islands rests with Japan.

During our preliminary negotiations with the United States over the terms of the peace treaty, the Japanese nationality of the inhabitants of Okinawa Islands was to have been recognized. We had re-emphasized the desire that they should be treated as Japanese subjects, and economic and other relations with Japan maintained as formerly, during the actual drafting of the treaty. It transpired, however, after the treaty had been signed that the conditions obtaining in these islands could not be made to conform to what we had wished and envisaged. Nevertheless, it is quite clear that the United States harbors no territorial ambitions over these islands, the control of which by that country continues for purely military reasons. It is, therefore, still my belief that, given an improvement in the international situation, a time will come when matters will be adjusted in accordance with the desire of the majority of the island inhabitants concerned.

# 28

# The U.S.-Japan Security Treaty

The San Francisco Peace Treaty was signed on the morning of September 8, 1951, and at 5 p.m. the same evening we met the American delegates at the headquarters of the U.S. Sixth Army in that city to sign the U.S.-Japan Security Treaty. It was a simple ceremony, with only the United States and Japan participating. Mr. Dean Acheson, representing the U.S. delegation, made a speech in which he characterized the new treaty as the first step towards security in the Pacific, and I replied by saying that the treaty safeguarded a Japan deprived of her own defenses. The four members of the American delegation signed, and then I signed representing the Japanese delegation. This was because one of our delegates, Mr. Tomabechi, was unable to sign the Security Pact, although he had signed the peace treaty, opinion within the Democratic Party to which he belonged being divided in regard to the security arrangement.

Following acceptance of the terms of the Potsdam Declaration, Japan had been required to disarm completely, while renunciation of war formed one of the articles of the postwar Japanese Constitution. It was thought at one time that this stipulation might also be included in the terms of the peace treaty: in the event of such a development, the conclusion reached by our Foreign Office was that Japan should ask for a collective guarantee of her security from Great Britain, the United States, the Soviet Union, China, and other countries, while at the same time declaring her permanent neutrality. But we were not, of course, at all sure that this could be arranged, or, if done, that it would be sufficient to guarantee Japan's security. With the growth of tension between the United States and the Soviet Union, and its effects upon the international situation, the prospect underwent a change, which materially altered the attitude of the Western Allies towards us. In his

New Year message of 1947, President Truman stated that Japan and Germany could not be left forever in a condition of uncertainty in regard to their future, and it was in March of the same year that General MacArthur stated at a press conference that the time had already come for concluding peace with Japan. By May of that year both Mr. Dean Acheson and Mr. Herbert Hoover were advocating the immediate conclusion of a separate peace with my country.

The atmosphere was now favorable for the opening of private and unofficial talks between the United States and Japan concerning a peace treaty and the related question of Japanese security. The Americans were ready and willing to listen to us, and we on our side were able to learn the trend of American opinion on these matters. It seems that at first, however, the Americans themselves were not quite sure as to what should be done in regard to the question of security. Mr. George Atcheson, the American representative on the Allied Council for Japan, once told officials of our Foreign Office privately that he thought it quite possible that the United States might suggest Japan's referring the question of her security to the United Nations, to which our men replied that, unless the organization of the United Nations was one upon which absolute reliance could be placed, there did not seem to be any way for Japan to defend herself against foreign invasion except by an alliance with a third power. This sort of informal exchange of opinion was followed by more official efforts on our part to convey our views to the Allied governments, which were continued under the Katayama and Ashida cabinets. In our own Foreign Office circles it was thought at first that if the Allied forces were going to remain in Japan after the signing of a peace treaty the purpose would be to ensure that the terms of the treaty were carried out, much in the manner of what occurred in Germany after the signing of the Versailles Treaty at the end of the First World War. As U.S.-Soviet relations became ever more strained, however, we could sense that the American view was changing to that of the need to guarantee Japanese security as part of world security. Our own ideas began to tend in the direction of having the United States reinforce our defenses, rather than relying upon what was then the still problematical organization of the United Nations to assist us in the event of need.

This development in our thinking was made clear in a written statement entrusted to the care of General Eichelberger, the commander of the U.S. Eighth Army, to be delivered to Washington when he departed from Japan on leave in September of the same year. The document was drawn up by Dr. Ashida Hitoshi, then foreign minister in the Katayama cabinet, and Mr. Nishio Suehiro, the chief secretary of the cabinet, and written in the name of Mr. Suzuki Tadakatsu, who was then head of the Central Liaison Office. Its purport was that, while Japan was in a position to deal with internal disturbances without outside aid, the best means of safeguarding her independence in the present condition of international stress was for Japan to enter into a special pact with the United States against external aggression by a third country, while at the same time reinforcing her own land and sea forces, and that, further, it was thought that, so long as the United Nations was not yet capable of fully enforcing the terms of its charter, the Japanese people desired the security of their country to be guaranteed by the United States. The statement did not specifically request the continued stationing of U.S. forces in Japan, but its conception was the same as that on which the U.S.-Japan Security Treaty was later to be based. There did not seem to me to be any other possible policy, and after I had resumed the position of prime minister again in October 1948 it was adopted by my cabinet without change, although actually there were no further developments in that direction until the coming of Mr. Dulles to Japan in January 1951.

Upon the occasion of Mr. Dulles's first visit to Japan in June 1950 the question of security was discussed only in general terms, although Mr. Dulles did suggest the desirability of Japan's rearming—a proposal against which I protested strongly for economic and other reasons, which I have mentioned in earlier pages. But when Mr. Dulles came to Japan again in January 1951 the armies of Communist China had intervened in the Korean conflict, while we ourselves had formed a National Police Reserve to supplement our police force. Conditions having thus drastically changed since his first visit, Mr. Dulles had progressed from ideas on Japanese rearmament to more definite views on the conclusion of a mutual security pact between the United States and Japan. And in talks which we had during that visit we may be said to have reached substantial agreement on the basic principles governing a U.S.-Japan security treaty, as well as a peace treaty. We came to an immediate understanding at that time not only on the necessity for the two treaties to be framed and concluded separately, but also in thinking that the two were essentially inseparable. In other words, there could be no peace treaty and independence unless Japan's security was guaranteed. At the same time, however, the peace treaty and independence to follow represented what was most earnestly desired by the Japanese people, while from the viewpoint of the United States also they were objectives to be realized at the earliest possible opportunity. Such was the background to the framing of the two treaties.

One point very much in my mind in regard to the treaty of mutual security was that the United States and Japan should be signatories to an agreement on an equal footing, and the extent of the obligations undertaken by each country clearly laid down in the terms of the security treaty. Obviously, since Japan possessed next to nothing in the way of armament, there could be no equality in that respect: the nation whose security was to be guaranteed was Japan, while that country herself could do nothing to guarantee the security of the United States. But if the United States, with her immense economic and military power, and Japan, by all the means at her disposal, were to cooperate in the defense of Japan as part of the defense of the free world, it would be for the benefit of both countries and of the entire free world also. That was the conception on which any security treaty would have to be based and, as such, Japan and the United States had to approach the project as independent countries on an equal footing. This point I stressed to Mr. Dulles, and, in addition, the further point that we could not agree to the inclusion in the terms of the treaty of anything that was contrary to the terms of Japan's new Constitution.

We desired the United States to show clearly in the treaty that she accepted the responsibility for safeguarding the security of our country. In other words, since we were accepting the obligation of having U.S. forces stationed in the Japanese islands, we considered it proper that that country should recognize an obligation to defend Japan. The American view, however, was that this could not be done: Japan did not possess the power to defend herself, and that fact precluded any idea of a pact between the two nations guaranteeing mutual security. This contention we had perforce to accept as irrefutable, and the American argument that if Japan were invaded while U.S. forces were actually stationed in that country they could hardly adopt a neutral attitude also seemed to us quite reasonable. These considerations meant that the Americans were anxious that Japan should take steps to reinforce her own defensive power after the regaining of her independence. The question naturally came up for discussion during my talks with Mr. Dulles on his second visit, and he stressed the fact that the United States could not be expected to extend military assistance to Japan indefinitely; that it was necessary to reduce that assistance gradually as Japan's own defensive power increased; and that although he quite understood the difficulties in the path of Japanese rearmament, such an increase would have to be envisaged if only to contribute by so much towards the collective defense of the free world.

Rearmament was for Japan out of the question at that time, and it was our idea to entrust the defense of the country to the U.S. forces, while we cooperated in the task to the best of our power with the reinforced police force. But even for that limited purpose it was clear that our National Police Reserve was very far from adequate, alike in numbers and equipment, and in any case this situation needed to be remedied as soon as possible. Furthermore, we could not discuss the treaty with Mr. Dulles without committing ourselves to some effort to reinforce our defensive power, and as we were invited to indicate some plan representing at least a first step in that direction, we outlined to him a project, long under consideration, for increasing both our land and sea forces and placing them under the control of an embryonic Ministry of Defense. This disclosure appeared to satisfy Mr. Dulles to a certain extent, and it was finally decided to give expression to such defense efforts on our part by stating in the preamble to the security treaty that:

> The United States of America, in the interests of peace and security, is precisely willing to maintain certain of its armed forces in and about Japan, in the expectation, however, that Japan will itself increasingly assume responsibility for its own defense against direct and indirect aggression, always avoiding any armament which could be an offensive threat or serve other than to promote peace and security in accordance with the purposes and principles of the United Nations Charter.

The points on which we had reached agreement during our discussions were then put into written form, and on the understanding that they bound neither government and were designed merely to mark a stage reached in our general peace negotiations, were signed on February 9, 1951, by Mr. John Allison, the American minister, and Mr. Iguchi Sadao, our vice minister for foreign affairs. Another document, by which Japan committed itself to continued cooperation with the U.N. forces in Japan for the prosecution of the Korean War, was similarly signed at the same time. Mr. Dulles came to Japan on his third visit in April 1951, by which time all major points of the U.S.-Japan Security Treaty arrangements had been discussed and agreed upon, although certain phrases were altered or amended to clarify meanings. In June of the same year Mr. Allison arrived in Tokyo with a fresh draft of the Security Treaty incorporating amendments proposed by the Allied powers. We found nothing unreasonable in these amendments, and others that we ourselves proposed were also discussed and accepted. The final draft reached us on August 14. In the case of this treaty, as in the negotiations preceding the drafting of the peace treaty, we found the Americans were always prepared to listen to our views and to comply with our wishes whenever feasible. I still recall with appreciation the goodwill extended to us by them throughout the long-drawn-out negotiations.

# 29

# The Administrative Agreement

The Administrative Agreement was concerned with the details not included in the Security Treaty, which, being concerned only with principles, consists of just five articles—Article 3 of which stipulates that "the conditions which shall govern the disposition of armed forces of the United States of America in and about Japan shall be determined by administrative agreement between the two governments." Originally, upon our presenting our own views concerning the question of security guarantees during Mr. Dulles's second visit to Japan in January 1951, the Americans handed to us in return a detailed plan dealing with all points connected with the stationing of U.S. forces in Japan. This was, in effect, a combination of the original U.S.-Japan Security Treaty and Administrative Agreement, and its contents did not differ very much from those documents, but there were some points which diverged somewhat from what we ourselves were envisaging. The points concerned were mainly of a purely technical nature, which meant, however, that a considerable amount of time would be lost if we were to go over them with the Americans, point by point. And we could not afford to let slip the opportunity presented to us to conclude an early peace treaty merely for the sake of discussing such minor points. The fundamental question was whether or not we should agree to have the U.S. forces stationed in Japan: once that had been decided, there existed precedents governing such stationing of foreign forces in a country. In addition to which, it was clear from the attitude shown by the Americans in all previous negotiations that they would not be likely to demand of us terms that we should find difficult to accept. All these considerations led us to leave technical details out of the Security Treaty and to leave them to be included in an Administrative Agreement to be discussed and agreed upon after the signing of the other treaties.

Another reason why we thought it wiser to postpone negotiations for the conclusion of an Administrative Agreement was that the same sort of talks were then in progress between the United States and the nations of Western Europe for the stationing of U.S. forces in those countries in accordance with the North Atlantic Treaty signed in April 1949, and it seemed to us an advantage for both parties if the terms eventually to be agreed upon between the United States and the countries of Western Europe were available for reference, and such a procedure was likely to prove advantageous to us. The terms and conditions governing the stationing of U.S. forces in Western Europe were in due course embodied in what came to be called the "Agreement between the Partners of the North Atlantic Treaty regarding the Status of their Forces," which was signed in London in June 1951, but not ratified by the United States until much later. This delay was expected by us, but by the time the debates in Japan's Diet on the San Francisco Peace Treaty and the Security Treaty were nearing their close, it was felt that further delay in taking up the question of the Administrative Agreement would be inadvisable, particularly as it had become clear that the peace treaty would be ratified by the countries concerned in time to come into effect by April 1952.

At that time I combined the post of foreign minister with that of prime minister, and in order that the negotiations for an Administrative Agreement should be conducted with dispatch, I arranged for Mr. Okazaki Katsuo, then chief secretary of the cabinet, to be named minister of state without portfolio towards the end of 1951 and assigned to deal exclusively with the question. The Americans, on their side, named Mr. Dean Rusk, then assistant secretary of state for Far Eastern affairs, ambassador, and special representative of the president, and sent him to Japan with Mr. U. Alexis Johnson, director of the Office of North-East Asia Affairs in the Department of State, and other experts in his suite.

Negotiations were begun on January 28, 1952, and concluded one month later. There were three points of policy which Mr. Okazaki, with my entire approval, was determined to keep before him throughout the negotiations: these were (1) that, with the regaining of our national independence, the occupation forces, as such, would cease to exist, and in their place U.S. forces would be stationed in Japan in accordance with the terms of the Security Treaty; but it was highly undesirable that either the Japanese people or the U.S. forces stationed in our country should have the impression that the occupation was being continued, wherefore the changeover in status must be given such form as would make that fact clear to all; (2) that there existed a wealth of precedents for foreign forces being stationed in a country, including those set by Japan herself before the Pacific War, among which the agreement between the parties to the NATO Pact regarding the status of their forces was undoubtedly the example to be followed; and (3) that since the negotiations were concerned with an agreement to take effect after Japan had regained her independence, and begun while that country was still under occupation purely from motives of expediency, they should be conducted by both sides on an absolutely equal footing.

Turning to some of the issues that arose, discussions were conducted, in general, in an atmosphere of friendliness and goodwill. Article 6 of the peace treaty provided for the withdrawal of foreign forces from Japan within ninety days of the coming into effect of the treaty. This provision conformed to international usage, but was not intended to apply in the case of those portions of the U.S. forces in Japan that were to remain after the coming into effect of the treaty. However, it was agreed that these detachments, too, should be redeployed from the centers of the larger cities to bases provided by the Japanese government in rural districts, and that the removal should take place within ninety days. We also requested the immediate return after the regaining of Japan's independence, of the Dai-Ichi Sōgo Building facing the moat of Tokyo's imperial palace, which had served as the general headquarters of the occupation forces and come to be regarded as the symbol of the occupation itself, a request promptly agreed to by the Americans. In the case of other prominent buildings requisitioned by the occupation forces in Tokyo, Osaka, Yokohama, and other cities, their return was agreed to in principle, but some time was needed before our national budget permitted us to offer substitute accommodation for such establishments as the headquarters of the U.S. air and naval forces.

A point which raised considerable difficulties was the question of jurisdiction. In Europe during the Second World War all offenses committed by members of the U.S. forces were dealt with by American military courts, which was natural since the Americans had crossed the ocean in order to take part in the battle to free Europe from the menace of Nazism. After the end of the war, however, the situation had changed, and in the agreement between the NATO partners already referred to it was laid down that an offense committed while the offender was on official duty should be judged by U.S. military courts, while an offense committed when off duty should be judged by the courts of the country in which the offender was stationed. But this provision met with violent opposition in the U.S. Senate on the ground that the American forces were remaining in Europe in order to preserve the freedom of Europeans, and that such a ruling would be bound to affect adversely the morale of the men in the forces, with the result that at the time of our own negotiations on this question the NATO agreement still awaited ratification by the United States, although it had already been ratified by its European signatories.

We in Japan also wanted a similar clause included in the agreement under negotiation between us and the United States, but the Americans were
firm in maintaining their point that they could not agree to the inclusion
of a clause which at that time the U.S. Senate was debating with such vehe-
mence. The political power wielded by the U.S. Senate was well known to
us, and we realized that we were asking the Americans to make an impossible concession. We therefore contented ourselves by inserting in Article 17
of the U.S.-Japan Administrative Agreement the provision that, when the
agreement between the NATO partners should be ratified by the United
States, the U.S.-Japan Administrative Agreement would be revised to bring
it into line with that document. Ratification finally took place in 1953, and
our Administrative Agreement was revised accordingly.

Most of the problems arising in connection with the Administrative
Agreement were discussed and dealt with in the course of informal talks between Mr. Rusk, the chief American negotiator, and our Mr. Okazaki, and
the most difficult of all those encountered during the negotiations was concerned with Article 24, which was concerned with the procedure to be
adopted in the event of Japan being exposed to the danger of foreign invasion. The European signatories of the North Atlantic Treaty had framed that
pact with the primary object of having U.S. forces stationed within their
borders, so that on the question of command and organization, as with
other issues, Great Britain, France, Belgium, and the other countries concerned had taken an unshackled view of things and made no objection to
their own armed forces being consolidated into one large force, which on
occasion could be commanded by an American. President Dwight D. Eisenhower, as all the world knows, was for a time the supreme commander of
the NATO forces. Now the point arose as to what should be done in regard
to the same command question in Japan.

The Americans, not unreasonably, took the view that, since the U.S.
forces in Japan might in time of need be called upon to cooperate with our
own defense forces, the procedure to be adopted in such an event should
follow the lines of the North Atlantic Treaty: that is to say, as the American
and Japanese forces could not be expected to act independently of each
other, a unified headquarters should be established. Nor was there anything
strange in the Americans demanding that there should be one. This brought
up the question of who was to be in command, and it appeared obvious
that, alike from the relative strengths of the two forces and actual experience
of modern mechanized warfare, the choice would inevitably fall on an
American commander. This, however, in view of the peculiar ideological
conditions obtaining in Japan at the time (and perhaps, to a certain extent,
persisting even now), was calculated to give the impression that our defense
force was being made the tool of the Americans. Questions were already

repeatedly being asked in the Diet whether or not a secret understanding to that effect had been reached with the Americans. This ideological, and largely fanciful, preoccupation with the question of who was going to be first and uppermost in the defense arrangements presented a far more serious political obstacle to the conclusion of an agreement than American common sense could grasp, and on several occasions brought the negotiations close to a deadlock. The efforts of Mr. Okazaki, however, and even more perhaps the understanding displayed by Mr. Rusk, who appreciated our predicament and did his best to explain it to Washington, resulted in the U.S. government's intimating that our position was fully understood and that they had no intention of making it more difficult, and suggesting the following wording for Article 24: "In the event of hostilities, or imminently threatened hostilities, in the Japan area, the Governments of the United States of America and Japan shall immediately consult together with a view to taking necessary joint measures for the defense of that area, and to carrying out the purposes of Article 1 of the Security Treaty." This wording was quite acceptable to us, and the problem was solved. The agreement was signed by Mr. Okazaki and Mr. Rusk on February 28, 1952, and came into effect on April 28 of that year, at the same hour as the Peace Treaty and Security Pact.

Thus Japan, having regained her national independence by the coming into effect of the San Francisco Peace Treaty, was guaranteed against foreign aggression by the Security Treaty and Administrative Agreement. To summarize my own views concerning these measures, it has always been my firm belief that Japan should associate and cooperate closely with the free nations in planning her future course. I do not deny the eventual possibility of friendly intercourse with the Communist countries, but a recognition of facts as they now stand, and my abiding faith in liberalism, made me welcome the peace treaty as it emerged as a result of the San Francisco Conference. However, the independence thus regained was political in nature, consisting mainly in the reassumption of sovereignty. Economic independence remained to be regained, and Japan is far from that goal, even today. To concentrate upon the attainment of that objective required that our national security be guaranteed from both internal and external aggression and threats, which, in turn, raised the question of rearmament. But our economic condition debarred any such development, in addition to which circumstances we needed to remember that many of the countries with which we had been at war still held Japan in distrust, a distrust which could easily be fanned into active hatred. And, above all, we had to consider the fact that rearmament is expressly forbidden by our postwar Constitution.

Despite such obstacles, however, our regained independence had to be defended, and, most fortunately, the position of the United States in regard to the Soviet Union made the defense of Japan and that country's economic recovery a necessary part of the policy of the United States in the Far East. The interests of the two nations were as one, and that fact led to the present system of collective defense of the Japanese home islands. The further fact that the Soviet Union is a neighbor of both countries helped to bring that situation about. The resulting ties, however, required to be cemented by friendship and, in spite of our ideologists, it is my firm belief that the friendship is there.

# 30

## Postscript

Before concluding these memoirs, I desire to say a few words more concerning the late Mr. John Foster Dulles, former U.S. secretary of state. From the earliest days of the predominantly American occupation of the Japanese homeland, the U.S. State Department had borne in mind the eventual conclusion of a peace treaty with Japan when the time was ripe. However, the interests of the various Allied powers were at variance in this matter; nor could agreement be reached regarding the precise organization of the peace conference. The outbreak of the war in Korea, which eventually saw the United Nations forces ranged against the Chinese Red Army, made any approach to a solution of the problem still more difficult, and when the exercise of the right of veto by the Soviet Union continued to retard the conclusion of peace treaties between the Allied powers and Germany, and the same powers and Austria, the signing of a peace between Japan and the Allies appeared for the time being to be well-nigh out of the question.

The U.S. State Department could do little in the face of these obstacles, and four years had passed without any definite progress beyond the work of blueprinting a draft treaty, when President Harry Truman appointed Mr. John Foster Dulles special adviser to the Department of State charged with conducting the negotiations for the conclusion of peace with Japan.

As a first step towards breaking the deadlock, Mr. Dulles, instead of calling immediately for an international conference, adopted the policy of discussing the draft treaty with each country concerned in turn, making a series of trips for this purpose first to Great Britain and other European countries and subsequently to countries in Asia, including Japan, Korea, Formosa, the Philippines, and Indonesia, and lastly revisiting Great Britain.

Mr. Dulles visited my country three times in the course of his mission for peace, and in all covered a distance of over 12,500 miles on these trips. An entire year was devoted to such preliminary discussions, and when in September 1951 the Peace Conference convened in San Francisco, he personally played a leading role in the proceedings, taking the floor himself on several occasions specifically to rebut charges made against the treaty by Mr. Gromyko, the chief Soviet representative, and sparing no effort to smooth the path to the attainment of a satisfactory settlement of the questions involved. The success of the conference was largely due to his endeavors, for which the Japanese nation must always remember him with gratitude. He accomplished the work he did with the aid of that fervor that comes from religious conviction. Ill health took him from us, and both Japan and the United States are the losers.

As I have outlined at length in earlier chapters of this record, the imperial Japanese Army began increasingly to interfere both in the internal and external affairs of Japan about the time I returned to my country from my post as ambassador to the court of St. James in the winter of 1938. Because of that fact, we were drawn more and more into the camp of the Axis powers, and finally entered the Second World War on their side in 1941—a tragic event that occurred despite the fact that both the throne and those responsible for the government of the country up to that time (besides the imperial navy, with its traditional associations with the British Royal Navy) were opposed to such a step, while the Japanese people as a whole never really envisaged the possibility of Japan's entering the war at all.

The reasons for this change of front must be sought for in the events of Japan's immediate past. We had emerged as a first-class power in the Far East in a matter of a mere fifty years or so since the Meiji Restoration in 1868. On the factors that made such a transformation possible there is not space here to dwell, but the result thereby achieved did not place us in too happy a position. Though my country had become industrialized, it possessed no natural resources to speak of. We had turned our nation into a modern state, but the rest of Asia was still composed of countries which, through wars and famine attendant upon misgovernment, remained in that stage of development which was barely sufficient to enable them to maintain their independence, so that, whatever we ourselves might have become, their backward condition acted as a drag on us, which prevented Japan from putting itself on anything like the same level as the other major world powers. In addition to this, the worldwide depression of 1929 caused the precariousness of our position to be still more acutely felt, while at the same time the vitality of our people, which had been responsible for our national development, continued to seek some further outlet—and it was only natural that this should have been found in China, from Manchuria southwards, and in the Pacific area.

The Anglo-Japanese Alliance had originally come into being at the suggestion of the British to curb the eastward expansion of the Russian Empire. It had been made the keynote of our diplomatic policy, and had come to be regarded by us as the foundation of peace in the Far East. Japan's growing influence in China, however, brought us into collision with British interests; later the Americans—who at the time had taken on themselves the task of educating the Chinese and opening their minds to more modern ideas, swayed no doubt by the tireless propaganda of the so-called Young Chinese—began to look askance at my countrymen as potential aggressors and disturbers of the peace in the Far East, a development that led eventually to an outburst of anti-Japanese feeling in California and other states of the Union. Finally, the Anglo-Japanese Alliance was dissolved, at the instance of the U.S. government, after the Disarmament Conference held in Washington in 1922, thus causing a marked cooling off in popular sentiment in Japan towards both Great Britain and the United States.

Japan's uniformed politicians in the ranks of the imperial army took full advantage of this fact to steer my country into close relationship with Germany and Italy, and there appeared on the national scene extremist elements who openly demanded war against our former allies. Neither the imperial navy nor the majority of the Japanese people were ever of that opinion—particularly the navy, which had been modeled on British lines and well knew what such a war would mean. The people remained indecisive to the last, and it certainly provides food for thought that our body politic up to that climactic time was so constituted that such crucial national decisions as entering a world war on the Axis side could be reached largely as the result of agitation by what was after all strictly a minority group. Our initial successes in combat, achieved during the early stages of the Pacific War, did not continue, and in the end Japan was forced to capitulate.

Quite apart from the psychological effects of the nation's defeat in war and the occupation of our territory by foreign troops—both of which were events the nation had never before experienced in its long history—the actual ravages sustained before the termination of hostilities were literally incalculable. When I was called upon to form my first cabinet in May 1946, the extent of the devastation within the boundaries of Tokyo, our capital, was such that its restoration to anything like what it had formerly been was something I found hard to envisage. Hunger stalked the streets, and inflation menaced those who still lived, while the red flags carried by demonstrators were everywhere to be seen. The miracle of Japan's national recovery was accomplished, however, in the short space of ten years, and when I recall the speed and thoroughness of that event, I am reminded first of all of the obvious fact that this modern miracle would not have been possible without the aid extended to us in every way by the United States, and then of the further fact that recovery could not have been achieved, even with that abundant aid, but for the vitality and pertinacity of our people.

I hope that I am justified in recounting here, with a certain pride, some of the different stages and aspects of that recovery. One of the items we found in short supply after the termination of the war was coal. In order to meet the shortage of labor during the Pacific conflict, the Japanese government had arranged for large numbers of Koreans to be employed in our coal mines; upon the cessation of hostilities, these Korean workers all deserted the pits on the pretext that they were now citizens of an independent nation and as such need no longer undertake work for Japan. Output of coal promptly and sharply declined to some 10 per cent of the maximum production attained during the war, confronting the nation with a fuel crisis unprecedented in its history. U.S. aid, and the combined efforts of the Japanese government and people saw us through the emergency, but five years passed before coal output had recovered to the prewar level of the year 1934–1935. After the lapse of another five years, however, in 1956, output had again reached the wartime maximum of fifty million tons annually, so that the problem now is to adopt measures so as to avoid producing more coal than is needed.

The food situation in 1946 was perhaps even more critical. It also contributed directly to simmering social unrest, and riots occurred about the time when my first cabinet was formed, when some elements of a mob forced their way into the imperial palace itself. Here again, however, the American occupation forces were most helpful, enabling us to ride over the worst period with the aid of the imported food they released to the Japanese authorities and also the food stored in different parts of the country during the war—stocks that most fortunately proved to be far more abundant than was expected. By 1949 the inflation had passed its peak and, parallel with this improvement, an increase in fertilizer production, a more even supply of agricultural labor, and improvement in farming methods produced a situation in which from 1950 onwards the food shortages evaporated. From 1955 to the present time, favorable weather conditions experienced in the Japanese islands and other factors have contributed to the attainment of an extraordinary increase in the yearly production of foodstuffs, not only rice and wheat but other agricultural products also. In the case of rice, Japan's staple food, the year 1955 showed an increase amounting to 24.5 per cent over the year 1950–1951, while further increases over that year of 9.8 per cent and 15.4 per cent were achieved in 1956 and 1957 respectively.

This wholly unprecedented increase in rice production has, apart from weather conditions, been widely attributed to an improvement in seed and agricultural methods. This is not to be denied, but in my opinion there exist two other factors that should not be overlooked in seeking the causes for recent record crops in Japan. The first of these is the agricultural reform which was introduced during the period in office of my first cabinet, whereby agricultural land in my country came to be owned for the most part by smallholders instead of great landlords who rented out their land to tenant farmers. This reform has acted as an incentive to greater production. The second was the adoption of the present system of stabilizing agricultural prices—not only of rice and wheat but of agricultural crops in general. The relevant law, termed the Staple Food Management Law, was originally framed at the time of the acute food shortage with the object of fostering the cheap and even distribution of available foodstuffs. With the steady increase in the volume of agricultural production, the law has come to be operated increasingly in the direction of preventing an undue fall in the prices of agricultural products, with the consequent effect of encouraging food production.

The increase in home-produced foodstuffs has resulted in a corresponding decrease in imported foods, so that, in the case of rice, whereas over one million tons had to be imported yearly between 1953 and 1955, the amount declined to 700,000 tons in 1956 and to 340,000 tons in 1957, the latter figure representing rather less than one quarter of the maximum volume of rice formerly imported in a single year.

Electric power suffered least from war damage, comparatively speaking, and was among the quickest of all our basic industries to recover. Even so, however, 44 per cent of Japan's coal-fired electric power plants had been destroyed in wartime air raids and, together with other equipment, the total loss of property was estimated to have been over 20 per cent of the whole industry. Added to this, the absence of repairs during the war years and the superannuation of machinery, as well as lack of coal and the poorness of the quality of what coal was available, caused a serious shortage of electric power in the early years following the Pacific conflict. Japan's output of electric power, which had totaled 27,300,000,000 KWH in 1936, and 38,600,000,000 KWH in the peak year of 1943, fell to 23,100,000,000 KWH in 1945, the year of our surrender. Repairs and additional equipment were urgently needed, but it was considered unwise to increase electricity rates, a step that would have had an adverse effect on industry and depressed national living standards in general. And it was not easy to discover other means of raising the necessary funds with which to rehabilitate the industry. Nevertheless, such obstacles were overcome in time and by 1954, nine years after Japan's defeat and surrender, output of electrical power had risen to over 60,000,000,000 KWH, and in 1957 it reached 81,300,000,000 KWH, or twice the maximum attained in prewar years.

With the improvement in output of coal and electric power, recovery of other industries was rapid. According to the Economic Planning Agency, production in 1946 fell to as low as 30.7 per cent of the 1934–1935 level, but rose to 83.6 per cent in 1950, the year the Korean War began, spurted to 114.4 per cent one year later, and has since steadily expanded. The index figure was 180.7 in 1955, and 257.2 in 1957, or two and a half times the prewar level. The increase has not, of course, been evenly distributed among all branches of industry. According to official statistics for 1956, the chemical industry stands highest with 442.9, while the textile industry—which before the Pacific War had led the world in exports—had recovered only to prewar level, with the textile index figure only 109.2 in 1957. That figure, however, concerns the textile industry as a whole: although silk no longer occupies its former place of importance in textile exports, Japan's overseas sales of cotton goods have once again risen to first place in the trading world and in 1957 accounted for 33 per cent of the world total.

The nation's postwar overseas trade has far outstripped all records set in that field in prewar time. Many changes have naturally taken place both as regards monetary values and the destination of our exports, but the fact that, whereas in the fiscal year 1934–1935 neither exports nor imports totaled more than $1 billion, Japan's exports in 1957 amounted to $2,858,000,000 and imports to $4,283,000,000 is sufficient to demonstrate the extent of the national recovery. During the period immediately following the conclusion of hostilities our overseas trade was under tight occupation control; we had lost the natural resources which Japan formerly possessed in Korea and Formosa; China, which had been one of our best customers, was closed to Japan as a market; silk, formerly the mainstay of our exports, had been ousted from the international market by the development of chemical fibers. Moreover, Japan needed to import a large volume of goods to hasten the repair of the ravages of war, and the nation had no ships in which to carry those cargoes, nor money with which to pay for them. Nor, at that time, did we have any export production with which to earn the necessary funds—in fact our overseas trade had ceased to exist. It is in view of these manifold handicaps under which my country was placed that I am dwelling here with something approaching complacency on the vast changes achieved during the past decade.

The rapid expansion of Japan's overseas trade in the postwar era has inevitably caused friction in many of the markets into which our goods have gained an entry. In particular, exports of cotton goods have been the subject of complaints alike in the United States and Europe, it being argued that Japanese cotton goods are in most cases quoted at far below current prices for similar items manufactured elsewhere, and so tend to flood the market. Similar complaints are now being heard concerning other Japanese goods, ranging from chinaware, veneer, and umbrella-ribs to precision items such as cameras, sewing machines, and transistor radio sets. Such complaints may very well result in legislative measures being taken against the import of these goods in some countries concerned. And, apart from that contingency, such a situation is to be deplored as calculated to foster unfriendly feelings towards Japan. The cause of such criticisms may certainly lie in part in a lack of an adequate understanding of commercial morality among some sections of Japanese businessmen. But that such a rapid expansion of Japan's overseas trade, by which my nation must live, should have been possible does seem to demonstrate that our people have begun to recover their technical ability as economic conditions within Japan have become more stabilized.

In no other field is this recovery better illustrated, or more in evidence, than in the case of shipbuilding. That industry was created and expanded in prewar days to meet the requirements of the Japanese Navy and merchant marine. Our shipyards and other equipment were earmarked for drastic reduction under the terms of the Potsdam Declaration, but the transformation in the international situation that occurred in the early postwar years saved them from this fate, and the nation's still extensive ship-building facilities were preserved intact in the condition from which these emerged from the war years. That fact made possible the rapid recovery of our shipbuilding industry which, after re-creating our merchant marine, turned for the first time to the building of ships for export. The result, aided by the modernization of facilities and methods, was spectacular: figures issued by Lloyd's disclose that ships built in Japanese yards totaled 1,746,000 gross tons in 1956 and 2,433,000 gross tons in 1957, thus putting Japan in the lead among the world's shipbuilding nations by a considerable margin.

This industrial recovery has made possible a definite improvement in the general living conditions of our people. In assessing the extent of that improvement, it is necessary to take into account the drastic change that has occurred in monetary values in considering the actual increase in individual incomes in Japan. But there can be no question that the improvement in rural incomes due to the policy of stabilizing the prices of agricultural products on which I have already dwelt, and the increase in the income of city workers resulting from the improvement in labor-capital relationships, have contributed greatly to the stabilization of the national economy and the expansion of the purchasing power of the people. The dire effects of depression have menaced Japan's national economy on three occasions since the termination of the war, but in no instance did they result in panic as would most certainly have been the case in prewar days, and recovery was effected after a short period in each case. The two stabilizing factors mentioned above undoubtedly helped in creating this steadiness, which indicates that Japan's economic recovery since the Pacific War has been one of quality as well as quantity.

The nation's health has similarly improved. Japan's death rate never fell below 20 per thousand before 1926, and was still 16.8 per thousand in 1935. In 1951 it fell to 9.9 per thousand, and in 1957 to a record low of 8.3. This achievement was clearly due not only to recent advances in medical science, but also to a sharp decrease in the infant death rate, which declined from 106.7 per thousand in 1935 to 40.1 per thousand in 1957. There can be no question that the Japanese people are today better protected against sickness and death, as well as the ill effects of extreme poverty, than was the case in the years before the war.

All of which is a just cause for congratulation. But apart from the nation's recovery in the economic sphere, there still remains a long way to go before we are in a position to consider that Japan and its people have achieved a reasonable standard of safety in the troubled world in which we now live.

The cabinet system in Japan dates only from the time of Prince Itō in 1885, when the work of the Meiji Restoration began to assume tangible form. The party system was introduced into Japan early in this century, but it was not until the twenties, at the time of the tenure of office of the Hara cabinet, that the new political system could really be said to have begun functioning normally. Any new system of government requires at least twenty years before it becomes soundly established, and it is still less than ten years since Japan regained its independence after the coming into effect of the peace treaty, while the changes that occurred in our national institutions as a result of Japan's defeat have been as momentous and far-reaching as any experienced in our past. The so-called democratic form of government is still in its infancy in my country. And though its outlines may now seem to have been determined, so far we see little indication that its spirit has come to live amongst us. The state of our political world has probably never been more unsettled; public opinion fluctuates constantly; laws are enacted and later abolished, without much regard from the first as to whether they can be observed. Years must pass before what is now new and strange to us in democratic politics becomes common-sense procedure and the muddles and frustrations at present in evidence in the political sphere are straightened out.

Unfortunately, Japan's outward prosperity, and the vitality of our people which made this possible, have attracted the notice of Communist lands, and their efforts to draw Japan into their own camp and away from the free world have redoubled in persistence of late. The rivalry existing between the two world camps today may make this seem a natural state of affairs, but the Japanese people appear to me to be dangerously complacent in regard to the possible effect which Communist propaganda might come to exercise in our country. Communism is still widely thought of as something vaguely good and progressive. Our intellectuals flaunt their sympathies for it, and few express doubts concerning their travelers' tales from Communist China and the Soviet Union. The Japanese government has constantly declared that friendship with the United States forms the keynote of our diplomatic policy, yet some Japanese politicians can go on visits to Communist China and there express the opinion that the United States is the common enemy of Japan and China. Neither the lesson of Hungary nor, more recently, of Tibet—nor that of the Soviet Union itself for that matter— seems to convey much to these people; and if Hungary and Tibet are states bordering on Communist nations, so is our own country. A time will surely come when we shall be confronted with the test, not in terms of being well enough thought of as a progressive intellectual by one's neighbors, but in those of cold reality.

In approaching and solving these and other problems, Japan must ulti- mately rely upon the hard-won wisdom of its people, gained in the course of the struggles of their daily existence. Vitality in trade and industry does not go alone. Experience backs it and it is the kind of experience which, in a democracy, also has the last word in politics. And we have at least un- locked and opened the door to democracy—or rather, opened the door to those democratic concepts that have always been latent among our people. It is a question of time, though time may well prove the deciding factor in that matter. And here I am reminded once more of the manner in which my nation came through the tragic episode of our defeat.

There can be no question to which of the two world camps—free or Communist—we are committed. And it is not the mass of our people who entertain any doubts on that point. Politicians may have to begin thinking of politics in terms of statesmanship before too long, when many problems will become clearer to them, as they are already clear to any thinking per- son. Included in those problems is that of Communist China, which need not be Communist; of an Asia at present offered only the choice between communism and the starkest poverty. Here is a field, it seems to me, where much can and needs to be done, and will have to be done, by the three "old China hands" who are the United States, Great Britain, and Japan.

There is still room left for hope.

It is not my intention to draw up a balance sheet of the achievements of the occupation. I am too deeply involved in its drama: an actor is ill suited to be a critic of his own acting. Moreover, sufficient time has not yet elapsed to provide the necessary perspective for a fair assessment. However, I may, I believe, safely vouch for future historians that in a large measure the occu- pation will be judged as a successful venture. I hardly think it necessary to remind the readers of these pages that it was an extremely difficult and del- icate task, requiring, as it did, far-sighted vision and consummate tact. It was fortunate for Japan that the occupation was guided by a person of Gen- eral MacArthur's caliber and conviction, a man who was an idealist and yet a realist endowed with a keen sense of history. He is not only a good sol- dier, but also a great statesman.

I have stated elsewhere in this book that the basic aim of the occupation was identical with ours. The supreme commander endeavored hard to re- form and recast Japan into a peaceful and democratic nation. We too wanted to reconstruct and reinvigorate our country on a basis of peace and democracy. But it was sometimes unavoidable that the views of the SCAP ran counter to ours. Ensuing negotiations were often difficult, but divergences were generally settled through amicable compromise by wise decisions of the supreme commander. That would have been utterly impossible if we had been under the occupation of, say, the Soviet Union.

As a matter of fact, the occupation began its work amid chaos and confusion. Japan was bled white by a protracted war, and our people were on the verge of starvation. Food was scarce, communications were disrupted, foreign trade remained at a standstill, and hunger stalked the streets. To aggravate the situation, some seven million soldiers and military personnel were to be repatriated from various theatres of war, adding to the already unbearable strain. Experts estimated the deficiency of the staple grains at some 3,500,000 tons, a staggering figure for a destitute government. Millions might have perished if it had not been for the speedy relief given by the U.S. Army. Similarly, our industry was completely at a standstill for lack of materials essential for its operation. It was only with the assistance of the United States that it was revived and restored. For all this, our people will ever remain grateful. In fact, our gratitude constitutes one of the main factors that ensure a constantly growing friendship between Japan and America.

At the same time, candor demands that we admit that there was another aspect of the occupation which is less commendable. Quite understandably, the occupation commenced its work of reforming Japan on the erroneous assumption that we were an aggressive people of ultra-militaristic tradition to be castigated thoroughly in order to be refashioned into a peace-loving nation. Moved by such a prejudice, the occupation vigorously condemned all the existing institutions—political, economic, and cultural—as an embodiment of the militarism which it sought to eradicate. This was more marked in the early stages of the occupation, when overzealous members of the GHQ, dedicated to "new-deal" idealism, often went to extremes, in complete ignorance of the complex realities then prevailing in our country. I have already described at length how a purge was enforced which deprived our nation of a trained body of men at a crucial moment; how the financial concerns were disintegrated through the complete breakup of the *zaibatsu* and by the institution of severe antimonopoly measures, gravely retarding our economic recovery; how notorious Communist leaders were released from prison and praised for their fanatical agitation, causing untold injury to our body politic; how organized labor was encouraged in radical actions thus endangering law and order; how education was reformed, sapping the moral fiber of our bewildered youth. Besides, our politics were so disorganized that militant unions, heavily infiltrated by communism, ran amok in defying the authority of the government. It was

ironical, to say the least, that the Communists took advantage of democratic freedom accorded them by law and yet were actually indulging in agitation to undermine it.

I do not wish to condemn the occupation now, since the zealous excesses
were a result of a spirit of enterprise for which Americans are justly famous.
But we cannot deny the fact that the result was only to multiply the confusion which had already existed. How can it be otherwise when the established order was destroyed overnight? Indeed, the occupation spared no effort in drastically altering the old order, from the imperial house to village
shrines and temples. Even a cursory study of our history will make it abundantly clear that our imperial reign has, since ancient times, been characterized by an earnest solicitude for the welfare of people in general. In fact,
our nation has been spared despotic sovereigns and rulers, despotism not
being indigenous to our soil. Our record is also almost untainted by atrocities, as our people are essentially gentle and dislike brutal strife. It was only
under a tremendous pressure exerted by the powerful military clique that
our people were finally dragged into the war against their will. Therefore
distinction must be made between the militarists who misled the nation,
and the people at large who are peaceful by nature.

However, the legacy of the ruthless regimentation of the war years cannot
be swept away at a stroke of the pen, however ingeniously the SCAP directives were phrased. It takes time for democratic practices to reassert themselves in the life of a nation. Such, I submit, is the background of the recent
turmoil that occurred in Tokyo—more precisely in June 1960—which unfortunately led to the cancellation of President Eisenhower's visit to these
shores. That is an incident which I deplore most keenly.

An organized minority of leftists had mobilized chaos with spectacular
success, under effective leadership of the militant Communists with the
half-hearted cooperation of shallow-minded Socialists. The mob dominated the streets day after day, freely resorting to violence and completely
immobilizing the police. Labor unions and radical student associations
swelled the ranks of the mass demonstrators, instigated by the so-called
progressive intellectuals, who unwittingly but unremittingly served the
cause of communism. This was, indeed, a shocking revelation to our people, and as they never approved of the lawless deeds of demonstrators the
unrest subsided gradually and soon ceased completely. Recent lawless
demonstrations make me fear that our people are not really aware yet of
the menace of communism and they hardly realize the magnitude of the
danger to which they are exposed. I shudder to think that if General
MacArthur had not, with his usual foresight, prevented the occupation of
Hokkaidō by the Russian forces, the recent disturbances caused by leftist
students and workers might well have been seized upon as an opportunity
to stage a revolution.

During the occupation my policy was to cooperate sincerely with the supreme commander so as to obtain the most advantageous results for my country, which in turn was, so I believed, also beneficial for the promotion of friendly relations between our two nations. It never occurred to me to scheme for the thwarting of the implementation of the occupation policies. I tried my utmost to urge a reconsideration of these policies whenever I deemed it necessary for the good of the country. I often succeeded in my efforts. I also failed just as frequently. So I had to wait patiently for opportunities which would present themselves after the peace treaty was signed. It is a pity that I could not use these opportunities, as I soon relinquished my office. Successive cabinets all lacked opportunities to embark upon an early rectification of the policies, and their aftermath, of the occupation.

I frankly admit that the recent disturbances in Tokyo have dealt a severe blow to the prestige of my country. I am fully aware of the necessity of rehabilitating our reputation as a reliable ally of the free nations, especially the United States. I believe the necessity to be quite urgent in view of the deterioration of the international situation. The free nations must close their ranks in face of the growing menace of international communism and cooperate more and more closely to defend the peace and liberty of this part of the world.

Such a view is fully shared by the overwhelming majority of our people. I know that some of the foreign journalists who witnessed the recent disturbances feared that Japan was on the eve of a bloody revolution engineered by the Communists. They were wrong. Events have since disproved this hasty impression. I, for one, did not entertain any doubts as regards the transitory nature of the mob violence. The solid good sense of our people, as I expected, soon came into play, thereby facilitating a quick restoration of tranquility. Public opinion has consistently opposed fanaticism, both of the Left and Right, and the larger body of our nation is anxious that a stable government should exercise a strict control over the extremist elements which agitate in collusion with foreign Communists. I am certain that most of these misguided elements will in time be cured of their juvenile radicalism as our country continues to advance steadily towards a true democracy. At the time of writing, the Socialist Party, which contains a number of Communist sympathizers, is declaring itself publicly in favor of a policy of increased friendship with the United States. This is certainly a volte-face, since that party had previously attacked the United States as an archimperialist power, and therefore an enemy of Japan. They were, it seems, obliged to make this turn about because our people have remained immune, and even hostile, to their anti-American campaign and, moreover, are reacting strongly to their efforts, making them increasingly unpopular.

At this critical juncture when communism is making heavy inroads in many parts of the world, I earnestly hope that Japan will continue to serve as a bastion of peace and liberty in Asia and, consequently, in the world. Accurate information and its proper assessment regarding the long-term designs of the Communist powers are most necessary for this end, and I urge our allies to join efforts to meet this requirement.

History attests to the fact that we are a resilient nation, quick to recover. We have recovered rapidly from the disastrous defeat, thanks largely to the assistance of the United States. We are thoroughly convinced that our future lies in the fullest possible cooperation with the free nations. If my administration has contributed anything towards the welfare of our people, it may lie in the fact that the majority of our thinking public fully subscribe to this conviction.

# II
## NEW TRANSLATION

# 31

# Korean War, Peace, and Independence

Because of the Korean War, the Japanese economy made a quick and complete transformation. People began to speak of "special procurements." Emergency orders for goods from the American forces stationed in Japan first stimulated the economy, and the economy was spurred by the continued climbing of consumer prices abroad. Psychologically, too, a certain sense of frustration was felt, stemming from an anticipated boom in the economy or perhaps from a feeling that there was a lack of goods. This was followed by a rise in pay and an increased money supply, all taking shape as a type of inflation. I began to worry, especially after having spent a considerable amount of time and effort on stabilizing the economy. Now that the economy was just beginning to shrink back to normal, I worried that it might backslide. However, Mr. Ikeda Hayato, minister of finance, reassured me, explaining that the conditions that resulted in the current situation were fundamentally different from the inflation we had experienced immediately after the war, despite the fact that the economy appeared to be inflationary, judging from higher consumer prices and higher pay. He further explained that this boom in the economy was caused by increased demands and high consumer prices abroad; thus, we should conform to the prevailing economic trend of the world, think about taking advantage of this opportunity to enlarge the economy, and encourage our factories to become more efficient. Consumer prices in Japan, too, were intimately connected to consumer prices in the rest of the world—now that the exchange rate of 360 yen to the dollar had just been established—so that the consumer prices in Japan would surely be affected by those in the rest of the world. Preventing consumer price changes in the rest of the world from affecting the domestic economy by means of altering the exchange rate would be out of the question. It was also difficult to adjust consumer prices at home and abroad by means of levying an export tariff on each of the export items or by subsidizing imports. In the end, Mr. Ikeda suggested that the only way would be to take steps domestically so as not to cause inflation and to follow changes in consumer prices abroad.

It was decided then that we would push a policy for increasing imports. The idea was to balance the economy by importing more, while helping to create a better foundation for increased production activity, which would then bring consumer prices, which had been on the rise excessively, under control. To this end, we implemented a policy to establish a system in which importing goods could be done freely and actively. This decision entailed adjusting the budget allocated for foreign currencies, expanding imports, giving automatic approval for import of a wide range of goods, and so forth. At the same time, the government allowed private trade companies longer periods of time to reconcile accounts-payable in foreign currencies in order to promote the cash flow for these companies.

The most debated question around this time was that of whether or not we should resurrect control over economic activity. When it appeared that the outcome of the Korean War would not favor the United Nations forces, some felt that if the United Nations lost the war, Japan would become isolated in the middle of the Pacific Ocean and would no longer be able to import food or natural resources. The argument went that, if this scenario were to take place, it would put Japan in an extremely difficult situation. Thus, we must have a controlled economy; the United States, too, had already implemented measures to control their economy to a degree. Japan should follow suit. The proponents of this view made it sound as though consumer prices would not rise and the balance between demand and supply would somehow be achieved, as long as control was in place.

Of course, we are speaking of a Japanese economy which then lacked strength and resilience; its foundations were by no means solid. This meant that it was probably necessary to control its direction to a certain degree. The office in charge of these affairs was of the opinion that this control would be limited to general measures to adjust the economy, such as manipulations of capital through financial policies and foreign currency trade. The opinion was that the road to strengthen the Japanese economy would be to take advantage of this opportunity to expand its size by promoting imports and exports. In order to achieve this goal, Japan should aim to control its consumer prices at a level just below global consumer prices. By doing this, even if the global economy were to stall, Japan should be able to manage its economy so as to be able to respond to this change rapidly. In order to do this we needed to become a bit fiscally more conservative on the domestic front.

Amid all these discussions, we decided to work on the supplementary budget for FY 1950 and the budget for FY 1951 as quickly as possible, since Dr. Carl S. Shoup (an economics professor at Columbia University, who, at the request of the U.S. government, headed up a team of economists that advised Japan on the tax and budget system) was visiting Japan to reexamine Japan's taxation system, not to mention a visit by Mr. Joseph Dodge in early October. Since I had wanted to ensure that campaign promises made at the last election took concrete form as a matter of a domestic policy as quickly as possible, I made a decision on the general policy of the budgets by mid-July. By the time these visitors came to Japan, it was not difficult for me to give some shape to these budgets. In fact, by September 20, the day before Dr. Shoup was to make a second set of recommendations, the cabinet, fully mindful of the impending visit of Dr. Shoup, made a rough outline of the 1951 budget. On October 7, Mr. Dodge arrived in Japan and began negotiating with Mr. Ikeda, minister of finance. Most of these negotiations ended on a positive note. For instance, the new budget contained a provision for a tax cut. Japan was able to establish an export bank. There was less burden of the cost of adjusting consumer prices, and more funds were allocated to public works. The salary system was improved, and we were no longer liable for the restitution of war bonds. Negotiations were arduous—commonplace during these days. For instance, the financing of the operation of special accounts, a matter which had not been a source of much discussion up until this point, was taken up for debate in considerable detail. GHQ strongly called for abolishing the current practice of borrowing funds for special accounts from the Bank of Japan, and, instead, insisted on bringing the funds from the general account. A release of deposits and collateral funds also attracted a fair amount of discussion. In the end, we moved in the direction of less governmental restrictions, such as abolishing public corporations and some price subsidies, and we reached the point of discussing such questions as the following: What would we do with the rice subsidy? Would we make it possible to sell and buy rice freely after it was delivered to the government? What about wheat? Should the government stop purchasing all the rice produced from the farmers and instead purchase it on an as-needed basis? These questions were discussed at length when drafting the budget.

When a new situation arose in which China decided to intercede in the Korean War, a plan of sorts to abolish the price control on rice was drafted. Due to this new political development, Mr. Dodge began to take a cautious stance about abolishing the system altogether. In the end, the plan was scrapped. As for the price control of wheat, there was a problem—GHQ demanded that the government should make a promise about how much wheat it was willing to buy. If this policy were not established, GHQ said, it would be difficult to estimate the cost of the purchase and to decide if the food account would have sufficient balance from a transfer of funds from the general account, or, if the government would have to borrow money to make the purchase. Mr. Hirokawa Kōzen, minister of agriculture, thought that honoring such a request would be all but impossible and that we should resolve to stand our position. He was reluctant to make such a promise. Since GHQ would not approve the supplementary budget until this question was settled, Mr. Hirokawa's opinion put Mr. Ikeda in a very awkward position. These two ministers discussed this issue but held to their respective opinions to the end. I recall that I finally resolved the situation by asking Mr. Hirokawa to sign off on the budget. The budget for 1951 passed the House of Councilors on March 28. For the first time after the war, this was a budget that was approved before the end of the fiscal year of March 31.

In the spring of 1951, the world economy showed signs of slowing down, and talks for a truce in the Korean War were about to take place. These two developments caused a reaction in the Japanese economy, which had enjoyed a boom owing to the Korean War. Trade companies that had lost money defaulted on bank loans. From around this time on, much was discussed about extending credit too easily to companies and about how unhealthy this practice was to the Japanese economy. One more thing about banks—soon after the export bank went into operation, we decided to create a development bank, by means of reorganizing the financial bank for reconstruction. This decision revived the financial bank for reconstruction, which had been dormant for some time. The idea was to inject it with a new soul. If memory serves, there were many such discussions about financial matters, but in the arena of financial policies, things were much quieter. GHQ cautioned the government, and the public also complained, that there were too many outstanding loans and loans for the construction of unnecessary buildings. It was not until the fall of that year, as I recall, that banks began to voluntarily set up more stringent standards for loans.

In terms of financial policies, as a result of the end of American financial support at the end of July, we were faced with the issue of asking the United States to bear the financial burden of occupying Japan. This issue was part of a series of developments—the end of financial support, which had been under discussion for some time, and the issue of U.S.-Japan economic cooperation. There had been a number of ideas and studies within the Japanese government on the topic of U.S.-Japan economic cooperation, especially as it related to the issue of the San Francisco Peace Treaty, from about the time Mr. John Dulles visited Japan in January of 1951. There were similar developments in the private sector as well. In mid-April, if my memory is correct, General Marquat, chief of the Economic and Scientific Section of GHQ, paid me an unexpected visit and informed me that he would go to

Washington himself on behalf of the Japanese government to sound out the American government with regard to this economic initiative. It was after he and his staff left Japan for Washington on this trip that the issue began to come to the fore.

I always thought that Japan, where natural resources were scarce and the population was large, could not maintain a healthy economy unless its people were resourceful. But our pride as citizens of a nation would not permit Japan to be the puppet of a more influential country. In my thinking, it was quite acceptable, however, to join our hands in economic endeavors, if Japan could achieve this as an independent nation on an equal footing with the other. In order to do that, we might consider the possibility of closely linking the two systems for regular trade and business transactions. Alternatively, I believed that we might also consider allowing foreign investments to develop Japan and promote industry, which would lead Japan to prosper. With this thinking, I generally favored economic cooperation and foreign investments. Politically, too, this was attractive, as the American and Japanese economies would be more closely linked together, helping Japan to make its footing more secure. Japan would continue to interact with other Asian countries and they would help each other prosper. I thought to myself that it would be ideal if something like this could be achieved.

General Marquat returned to his post in Japan on May 16 and made a statement about the issue of U.S.-Japan economic cooperation. Most of his statement was abstract and somewhat preachy in places. Since the Japanese government had been asked to state its position about economic cooperation, we did so about a month later. We stated that we wanted to join the world market as an independent nation as quickly as possible, join the International Monetary Fund, promote foreign investments, and reap fruit from economic cooperation, to name a few items. We wanted to demonstrate our strong interest and enthusiasm in economic cooperation. As a practical matter, however, economic cooperation and foreign investments did not proceed smoothly; it was not until after 1952 that we saw results on these fronts.

Mr. Ikeda, who went to San Francisco as one of the members of the Japanese delegation vested with full authorities of the Japanese government, discussed economic and financial policies of the future with Mr. Dodge. Mr. Ikeda began working on the supplementary budget for 1951 as soon as he returned to Japan. From what I understand, Mr. Dodge tried to persuade Mr. Ikeda to come around to his point of view, arguing that managing the Japanese economy after independence was no easy task, so one must be vigilant at all times; tax cuts at this point should be reconsidered; Japan should maintain sufficient financial flexibility, considering such costly items as war damages, foreign debts, foreign aid, self-defense, issues surrounding the bereaved families of the war dead, and so forth; and finally, it was absolutely necessary to make sure that the Japanese economy would not become inflationary due to investments. I heard that, even after he returned to the United States, General Marquat wrote Mr. Ikeda lengthy letters expressing these worries repeatedly. Mr. Ikeda indicated to him that he would take the responsibility for the tax cuts, and, before Mr. Dodge arrived in Japan for another visit, he had mapped out the rough form of the supplementary budget.

GHQ did not protest as vociferously as before and, without waiting for Mr. Dodge to arrive in Japan, approved the budget. The timing of the budget was immediately after the San Francisco Conference, and GHQ must have decided not to meddle with details only a few days before Japan's independence. With Japan's independence as a foregone conclusion, the Japanese government's eagerness to think on its own feet about its future and take responsibility for its actions might have reflected positively on GHQ. Hence the supplementary budget was sent to the Diet before Mr. Dodge arrived in Japan.

A more difficult item was the 1952 budget. We were going to push through the tax cuts, since we had already agreed to do this in the supplementary budget. There was, however, the looming question of abolishing price controls on rice. There were various problems on the domestic and international fronts that accompanied the return of peace. The question was how to consolidate and unify these diverging interests. No sooner had Mr. Dodge arrived in Yokohama, than he questioned the wisdom of the tax cuts. Commenting on the rice issue, he said that the Japanese government was too optimistic about its outcome. These statements piqued the interest of the newspapers as well as a variety of public opinions. In the end, however, we decided to go ahead with the tax cuts as planned.

We ran out of time to act on the rice issue, due partly to the fact that there was a considerable amount of debate at a conference of prefectural governors on the government purchase of the rice crop and partly because there were divergent opinions within the government itself. I thought this outcome was regrettable, especially because we had set a direction in which we thought we should proceed with this issue. This was to become an issue that would consume us for a long time during the following year. From this time on, it seems that the essence of this issue changed from a control that was "harsh to the farmers" to one that was "indulgent of the farmers."

The most arduous negotiations with GHQ appeared to have been with regard to how to consolidate the various costs relating to the peace treaty, with the defense cost at the center. The cost, including the cost for the support of the bereaved families of the war dead, was large, estimated first at ¥200 billion, which represented a considerable increase over the year before. Even after taking care of this payment by transferring a sum to a special account, more money was needed from the general account. This situation caused a spirited debate in cabinet meetings when we discussed budgets. Mr. Amano Teiyū, minister of education, was quite beside himself with anger, arguing that too many funds were cut from education. Mr. Hashimoto Ryūgo, minister of welfare, was very dissatisfied with the budget allocated to the support of the families of the war dead. My party, too, was adamant that the government should increase the amount of public spending. Some of these agenda items had to be tabled until the next meeting, since we were unable to reach a decision in the first meeting.

When listening to the various points of view in budget meetings, I became aware of the complexities of issues and the difficulties of solving them, making me wonder how one could ever reach a decision. Peace and independence—we would be able to finally win these, after a long, painful wait. Wonderful though it would be, how difficult it would be to join the international arena and fulfill our responsibilities as a nation. Paying for damages, paying foreign debts, guaranteeing national security, and ensuring domestic peace are issues that an independent nation must consider in order to reconcile with the past and live in the future. We also need to develop our domestic economy and investments in industries and public works to encourage development. The more we can concentrate our resources on these areas, the better the future will be. At the same time, the more we allocate for social work, such as social security and the support for families of the war dead, the better life will be. Of course, it would be best if the tax rate were light. The fact was that we could not satisfy every one of these competing interests fully. How to apportion the funds sensibly and bring together these interests had to be ultimately decided by the minister of finance. I therefore trusted Mr. Ikeda and supported his decisions. On behalf of Mr. Ikeda, I persuaded any cabinet members who did not agree with his decisions to come around to this view.

Because the political situation between this time and the dissolution of the Diet at the end of August was messy, I do not have specific recollections of events relating to finance and monetary policies. I do recall, however, some major events—Japan would join the International Monetary Fund and Mr. Ikeda would attend the annual meeting representing Japan. It came to pass that Japan would discuss foreign debts with the United States and Great Britain and, to this end, Mr. Tsushima Juichi was kind enough to accept the position of ambassador plenipotentiary to represent Japan, when he traveled to the United States.

# 32

# My View on the
# Imperial Household

I believe that the Japanese people hold the view that the imperial household and the people of Japan are one and indivisible. In my understanding, the wording in the Constitution that "the Emperor is the symbol of the State and the unity of the people" clearly points to the fact that the people and the imperial household constitute a single and indivisible whole. People who descend from the same parents constitute a family; likewise, those who descend from the same ancestors constitute a people, a nation. The ancestor of the imperial household is the ancestor of the Japanese people, and thus I believe that the imperial household is the sovereign family of the Japanese people. In other words, the group of families centered around the imperial household constitutes the Yamato people, the Japanese; and this comprises Japan as a nation. From ancient times, the sovereign emperor and his subjects have come to the aid of one another in the formation of the country. Due to this history and tradition, the principle of ancestor worship was born, nurtured, and developed into a characteristic of Japan, eventually constituting the very foundation of the Japanese nation. Without viewing it this way, it is impossible to explain the unwavering admiration and reverence of people towards the imperial household. Some scholars have argued that the public's attitude towards the imperial household has been used for political purposes since the Meiji era. If I may say so, this analysis is laughable and superficial. If we hold to that position, how are we to explain our increasingly strong and profound affection and reverence towards the imperial household, even in the aftermath of the war? The only possible answer then is that the Japanese people regard the imperial household as their ancestral source.

In any country with a long history, ceremonies have been equivalent to political actions. The same can be said about ancient Japan. The central stage for ceremonies and politics was the imperial household, a fact unchanged from ancient Japan to modern Japan. Imperial ceremonies and political activities undertaken by the imperial household were one and the same; that is, the imperial household was the nation. In other words, the history of the imperial household is the history of the Japanese nation. The religion of the imperial household as well as of the Japanese people is Shinto. Although, during the long history of the imperial household, some members converted to Buddhism, imperial ceremonies rooted in Shintoism were still conducted without interruption. True, during the occupation after the war, a policy was implemented to separate religion from politics, but this made no difference—imperial ceremonies continue even today with little change from ancient times.

We cannot deny that the Allied forces held very strict views about the imperial household at the end of the war. I heard that many opinions were expressed concerning how to deal with the imperial household, some extreme. Fortunately for us, General MacArthur dealt with it with compassion and understanding, enabling us to retain the imperial household as it is today, as the center of Japanese unity. We should remember the general's farsightedness for generations to come.

When I consider the historical background of the imperial household, the public's respect and affection towards it mentioned earlier, and how it is sanctioned in the Constitution, I feel strongly that the imperial household should continue to remain active as the spiritual and moral center of all sectors of society, including politics, religion, and culture. For instance, imperial ceremonies, which had borne official significance until the end of the war, should not be observed by the imperial household alone; instead, I propose that they be treated as ceremonies of the people, to which not only cabinet members and other invited guests but also representatives of the Japanese people in general be invited to attend. This seems to be in accordance with the general thinking of the public; at the same time, this maintains a historical tradition, and serves as an act for spiritually unifying the Japanese people.

The foregoing is just an idea of mine, and let me suggest some more—it would be desirable if the imperial household could voluntarily protect and encourage education, culture in general, and social and welfare projects. I would suppose that this is also what the Japanese people wish as well. Of course it goes without saying that the government should do its part for social and cultural projects, and, as our society becomes more advanced, it would be natural for the government to solicit help from the private sector to bring success to these initiatives. I think that if the imperial household would encourage projects the government and private sector are yet unable to undertake, it would serve the public's interest by increasing the visibility of these projects. The only way, I believe, to create a great nation both in name and in substance would be to make use of this conviction, rooted in Japanese tradition, that Japan is a nation of families—with the imperial household at the center, which in turn unifies the people and inspires co-operation and mutual assistance among its citizens.

Since the end of the war, a very small number of people—however small that number might be—have proposed the idea that, ignoring our history and tradition, democracy means to sever the imperial household from the people as much as possible. Some scholars, who bill themselves as "progressive," ignore the fact that, throughout history, emperors have always shown affection towards the farmers, and the farmers themselves have also returned their loyal devotion to the emperors, forming a great, harmonious family of people of all ranks. These scholars, who I believe should be condemned as unpraiseworthy extremists, go so far as to believe in a type of Marxism that holds that "human history is a history of class struggles," and they apply this view to Japanese history, thinking that this represents "a new perspective on history." If they are interested in a perspective, let me say this—to apply today's yardstick to interpret the entirety of hundreds and thousands of years of history is just as harebrained as looking at a naked Adam and Eve and condemning them for violating today's manners and etiquette. There has been no class struggle of any type whatsoever between the Japanese imperial household and the people; rather, we should say instead, from the point of view of world history, that the Japanese people enjoyed idyllic, peaceful rule for a good part of their many thousands of years of history.

Moving on to another topic, if we were to look for a royal family that is the most similar to our imperial household, it would be the British royal family. Needless to say, its origin and history are not the same as the imperial household, but it is quite similar to ours in that the British royal family is the object of national respect and great affection. It is also similar in that it upholds the principle with regard to politics that the royalty "reigns but does not govern." If we look at British history, during its infancy, that is, when the royal family was equivalent to the nation itself, all actions for exercising sovereign rights were concentrated in the royal family and the government and finances were all under the royal family's power and control. As the parliamentary form of government came into existence, the political duties of the nation were transferred to the parliament, and the remaining portion, that is, the function not transferred to the parliament, such as the issue of succession, was retained by the royal family as its prerogative. In this way, the Privy Council, an organization whose power belongs exclusively to the royal family, came into existence. This system is sanctioned by the peculiarly British customary laws, but nowadays the function of the

Privy Council is to act on behalf of the royal family in maintaining a close relationship between the royal family and the people of Great Britain and to handle matters regarding politics, economics, culture, and religion when working towards national prosperity, cultural development, and the enhancement of social welfare.

In my view, if we create a new organization that corresponds to the British Privy Council and run it in accordance with the needs of our country, it would contribute greatly to the achievement of a monarchical democracy that is specific to Japan. The Privy Council, translated into Japanese, becomes *sūmitsuin*, but this word reminds one of the same name in the past, a word that might invite an unfortunate misunderstanding. If we were to create a privy council, it would be better to select another term for it in Japanese. Regardless of what such a mechanism might eventually be named, if we were to follow suit and create a system similar to Great Britain's, I would place the system of awarding honors under the imperial household, which will then make the decision about honors. If these honors are not awarded with absolute fairness to recipients, who have made laudable contributions to the country, turning a blind eye to politics, political parties, and any other interest, their value will be nil. In order to achieve a just system, the imperial household, which holds no interest in politics, should consider candidates in areas of philanthropy, justice, humanitarianism, culture, and such, having received the advice of the government and unbiased deliberation by the "Privy Council." The awardees will be suitably honored if they are to be recognized in the name of the imperial household. This system would also be received well abroad and go far to elevate the significance of the awards as well. It would also be all the more impressive if the highest of the honors could be awarded by the emperor himself at the palace. I wonder if the current system does not give us the impression that awards are not handled with due dignity and pomp and that receiving those honors is not entirely without annoyance.

If we were to create a system in the imperial household much like the British Privy Council, we should make a most careful selection of its members, selecting those who are both learned and respected by the public. Awards become meaningful only if these highly respected people deliberate on candidacies and select the awardees in response to the emperor's inquiry. This mechanism will ensure that we give due respect and meaning to the honors so awarded, which in turn will make the recipients all the more appreciative.

In this connection, I would also like to propose a method of bringing the imperial household and the public closer together; that is, we should try to make wider and more frequent use of the custom of inviting guests—individuals and representatives of organizations that have made significant contributions in the service of the nation, in all fields including the political, financial, and scholarly arenas—to receptions in the imperial household on a regular basis, on such occasions as the birthday of the emperor, or once in the spring and once in the fall. When foreign dignitaries are visiting Japan and are invited to the palace for dinner, I would think that guests should include not only the concerned ministers but also those who have given distinguished service to the state in a field of endeavor.

During the Meiji era, Emperor Meiji often required senior advisers and ministers to dine with him. On such occasions, His Majesty would banter with them in a booming voice, making comments to which the advisers scrambled to come up with suitable answers, whereupon His Majesty would also laugh gregariously; such frank exchanges seemed to have made him quite contented. It was during one of these occasions that a humorous event took place. His Majesty asked Prince Matsukata Masayoshi how many children he had. Unable to come up with an answer swiftly, the prince replied, "I ask His Majesty to please allow me an opportunity to look into it." The relationship between the emperor and his senior subjects was quite congenial, not unlike water and fish.

In the early years of Shōwa, I often observed at dinner parties held for foreign dignitaries that Japan was fortunate to have such a stately imperial household, when I would see in the far distance His Majesty's senior ministers, such as Prince Saionji, Count Makino, Mr. Ichiki, the minister of imperial household, and Mr. Yuasa, the grand keeper of the imperial seals, flanking His Majesty in a dignified and graceful manner. My dream would be to establish a system like the British Privy Council, choose the best people Japan offers for the task, have the members enjoy the honor of participating in ceremonies in the imperial household, as well as state ceremonies, and dinner parties for foreign dignitaries. This would bring back the splendor of the imperial household of the past.

What would also be welcome in order to bring the imperial household and the people together would be to appoint members of the imperial family to important positions in organizations for religious, cultural, and social work. I would think that accepting these posts willingly is only befitting of the roles of the imperial family. In this sense it was my genuine pleasure to hear that the crown prince had gracefully agreed to an appointment to the position of vice president of the Japan Red Cross. It was also gratifying to hear that the crown prince had accepted as well the nomination to the presidency of an international sports event to be held in Tokyo in 1958, at which, as I understand, His Majesty has consented to appear in person to open the event.

If we look at Great Britain and other royal families in Europe, I often reflect on the fact that society is healthier if the relationship between the public and the royal family is amicable. I have heard reported that, fortunately, since the war, an increasing number of people visit the imperial palace or stand in line to wish His Majesty well on his birthday and on New Year's Day. I privately enjoy hearing this as it is proof to me of the health of public thought. I pray that the government and the imperial household agency will make every effort to respond to the public's respect of and affection towards the imperial household. Only in this way, I believe, will the imperial household be able to become the object of adoration of Japanese families, be able to protect and develop the unity of the people, and then in turn enable us to become upstanding citizens of the family of nations of the world.

Now that I have aired my private views on the matter of the imperial household, let me touch on a speech of mine. On November 10, 1952, the imperial household held a ceremony to mark the twentieth birthday of Prince Akihito and to formally install him as crown prince. I gave a congratulatory speech on that occasion. This speech later became a center of debate in various quarters. Critics took issue with the fact that I called myself the "Imperial subject Shigeru," a phrasing that was construed as being antidemocratic and unforgivable from the point of view of the new political ideology. I merely followed my own belief and I added the word "Imperial subject" myself to the name Shigeru when I read the congratulatory remarks. I remember that I was quite infuriated by this criticism and even contemplated abusing the critics verbally in order to encourage them to rethink the matter, but I held back and remained silent, thinking that virulent remarks would not befit a nation in celebration. If I may be allowed to say a few words on this, the fact that critics regarded my calling myself an "imperial subject" as going against the idea of democracy shows how superficial their understanding of the essence of democracy really is.

Regardless of how our society develops, we cannot maintain order nor stability of the country if we are disrespectful to our parents or siblings; negligent of seniority in family and workplace; or indifferent to appropriate behavior suited for social ranks. Our view of history and tradition holds that the imperial family is the ancestral home and the sovereign family of our people. This is not mere theory; it is a fact and tradition. Respecting the imperial family is our moral duty and has formed the foundation of our social order. Hence democracy in Japan must be based on this idea and spirit. I have observed a tendency among the so-called progressives, whereby they automatically consider anything imperial or royal to be feudalistic and harbor the notion that these institutions are therefore unfitting for democratic governance. This sorry lot is uninformed about the history of our own nation and ignorant of the histories or current states of foreign countries.

In Great Britain, where democracy and parliamentary governance originated, the notion of loyalty to the royal family is considered even today to be the basis of all morality. The queen honors people who have made significant contributions to the nation by giving them the title of "Sir." Even the head of the Labor Party, when his services are completed, is included among the ranks of nobles. The parties in opposition to the ruling party, whether the Conservative or the Labor Party, are generally referred to as "His Majesty's Opposition." When the military yielded great power, someone in Japan used this very British phrase and referred to the members of the Diet who were in disagreement with a particular policy as "His Imperial Majesty's Opposition." What was comedic about this was that this reference enraged the military; they complained, bawling loudly that "Opposing His Majesty the Emperor is treachery." In fact, "His Majesty's Opposition" refers to a party that watches over governance for or on behalf of His Majesty. The idea is that even the actions of opposition parties are considered to be carried out for His Majesty. "His Majesty's Opposition" is also understood to mean "for the people of the nation." Accordingly, the British do not think that such reference to His Majesty is at all feudalistic. It is well known the world over that Great Britain has the most advanced system of governance based on a parliament and political parties.

In addition to Great Britain, three northern European countries—Sweden, Norway, and Denmark—are countries in which democratic governments run smoothly, though these countries are by no means superpowers. These countries, where a socialist party or a party similar in political inclination to socialism is in power, have implemented well-developed systems of social security and have long enjoyed political stability and peace. These are all monarchical countries, where the royal families are objects of national admiration and respect. In addition to these northern European countries, the Netherlands, Belgium, Luxembourg, and Greece are either monarchies or marquisates, where the people also can boast of peace and enjoy freedom. Canada, Australia, and New Zealand, British commonwealths where social facilities and welfare are highly advanced, uphold the queen of England as their own with no suspicious feelings whatsoever.

From this point of view, it is evident that welfare states, in the new sense of the word, and those nations where democracy is most developed today are frequently monarchical nations. True, this may not mean that monarchy brings about these advantages, but one clearly cannot argue from the standpoint of reality that the customs and practices surrounding imperial or royal families are feudalistic and that they diametrically oppose the notion of democracy. Some so-called progressives in our country seem to be uninformed of these facts.

Every country, then, has its proud history and tradition. A country should cherish its history and traditional character as best it can, and on this basis build a government organization and economic system that are suitable for the times. I cannot help but wonder about the lucidity of someone who considers a country to be ideal, however wonderful its national system and social structures may be, both in terms of ideology and form, if a child of such a country reports a wrongdoing on the part of his parents to the national police, and that act then forces the parents to criticize themselves publicly or to be brainwashed. I firmly believe that our long-standing tradition of parent-child and sovereign-subject relationships must be the center of Japanese ethics and the source of national order for a long time to come. Given this, why did it then become an issue when I called myself "an imperial subject"? I submit that the very idea of criticizing the term "imperial subject" should be disavowed. I should add that in democratic nations in the Americas and Europe, the use of the title "Majesty" when speaking to a foreign emperor or monarch or the use of "Sire" raises no eyebrows; rather, one who avoids their use will be despised as unmannered and ignorant.

Now that I have voiced some of my personal thoughts on the imperial household, I would like to say a few words about some matters concerning the current emperor and empress. I think no other emperor has experienced as much hardship as the current emperor. In the mere twenty years, between November of 1921 and December of 1941, that is, between the time when the current emperor was appointed prince regent and when the Pacific War broke out, four prime ministers—Mr. Hara Takashi, Mr. Hamaguchi Osachi, Mr. Inukai Tsuyoshi, and Mr. Okada Keisuke—were either murdered in office or experienced murder attempts on their lives. Further, more than ten influential figures in politics and other fields were gunned down or knifed to death. What makes me shiver in horror was the utterly shocking, disgraceful event of December 27, 1923, when an assassin made an attempt on the life of the emperor in Toranomon, Tokyo. This was followed by the 5.15 and 2.26 Incidents, and by the Manchurian and the China Incidents abroad, and ultimately by the outbreak of World War II. I still feel chills down the spine when I look back at this period, when the situation Japan put itself in was truly tumultuous.

Even during those times of raging political unrest, the emperor held fast to the principle of monarchy to the end—"reign but not govern." The governmental practice was that the cabinet would deliberate on a policy, make a decision and submit this as a proposal to the throne for consideration. The decision rendered by the emperor was by no means a mere formality—this was obvious since His Majesty would often ask questions that touched on the crux of the proposal, questions to which the cabinet members often could not furnish ready responses. I myself was frequently obliged to reply to some of the emperor's questions with the promise that I would look into them right away. Every time I answered in this way, I shuddered from the fear that the emperor must be surprised to find the prime minister to be such an ignoramus. But His Majesty was kindhearted; he never once reproved me. He treated me with compassion, a quality that made me feel all the more respectful towards him.

The emperor seldom expressed his opinion about proposals submitted by the cabinet, even when we thought that some aspects of these proposals would not please him. The emperor, however, was endowed with excellent memory and I heard that if someone happened to state something that was different from an earlier proposal, His Majesty would point it out or question him closely for an explanation. When the leaders of the military, such as the minister of the army or the chief of the general staff, drafted a proposal to the throne during the war, the emperor reportedly demanded explanations on some points and scolded them, which made these officers leave his presence in terrible shame.

Such was the case with any grave matter that concerned the nation as a whole. Usually the emperor did not express his opinion, but when he deemed the matter at hand represented an important policy, he would not hesitate to hand down a resolute decision. During the 2.26 Incident, the leaders in the military were in confused disorder in the beginning and then they were not only extremely indecisive as to how to treat the insurgents but hesitant in deciding about how to punish the rebels. The emperor was not. Calling them "rebel forces," he offered to take a personal role in putting down the insurrection. This galvanized the military to produce a force to bring the rebellion to an end.

The same can be said about his decision to end the war. When the military was wielding power, it was the emperor who was able to bridle the military's desperate attempt to wage the final contest on the mainland. Without this decision, Japan would have become nothing more than a scorched land, where the people would not have had a place to call home. Thus the emperor made the announcement of the end of the war on the radio. In this imperial edict, he said that he held "a desire for peace throughout the ages" and that he "always stood with his subjects," a message that revived the Japanese people, who by this time had moved to the edge of abysmal desperation. Frankly, I cannot read this proclamation that ended the war without tears welling up in my eyes.

One foreigner who genuinely welcomed the emperor's decision to end the hostilities was the Supreme Commander of the Allied Powers, General Douglas MacArthur. Judging from the ferocious battles the Allied forces fought against the Japanese in Guadalcanal and elsewhere, the Allied forces were prepared to make an extraordinary sacrifice in the imminent, final face-off on the mainland. Despite this, the Allied forces landed in Japan and occupied our country without losing even one soldier, a turn of events that took everyone by surprise. When General MacArthur learned that the emperor's imperial edict had made this bloodless occupation possible, he then understood that the emperor yearned for peace and the people held deep affection towards the emperor. General MacArthur studied the emperor carefully, and although I have no way of knowing what he discussed with the emperor in the first meeting after the occupation, it seems to me that General MacArthur was deeply impressed by the emperor as a person, a sense which no doubt solidified his beliefs about the Japanese people. Indeed General MacArthur commented to me time and again about the emperor's benevolence, that he had never met anyone so irreproachable and devoid of personal interest as the emperor.

I suspect that General MacArthur took to the emperor, holding more affection and respect towards him, as he held more meetings with the emperor, a development that I believe affected the occupation policies considerably. When bidding farewell to Japan, General MacArthur made a special visit to the emperor to report in person his intention to return to the United States, and this, I think, was prompted by his reverence for the emperor. After the war, the Shidehara cabinet, in which I served as foreign minister, received the proposed constitution drafted by the general headquarters. All the cabinet members spiritedly debated Article 1, which stated that the emperor was the symbol of Japan. After ten days of discussion we still could not reach a decision. Then we heard a report that the emperor assented to the wording and he considered it unnecessary for the cabinet to spend more time on this topic. Hearing this, the cabinet members felt as if a new horizon opened up in front of them and immediately came to an agreement.

The emperor showed considerable interest in foreign affairs. When the emperor gave audience to foreign envoys and state guests, I thought he was quite well versed in foreign matters, which made me think about how considerate he was to others. I have an account of my own to relate. The emperor, then crown prince, traveled on the warship *Katori* to England in May 1921, flanked by the warship *Kashima*. As a diplomat stationed at the Japanese embassy in Great Britain, I went to the British colony of Gibraltar to meet the emperor in person for the first time. Naturally I was able to see him during his stay in England. What is vivid in my memory even to this day is the night of a royal dinner party at Buckingham Palace hosted by George V in honor of His Highness. More than a hundred guests, including the royal families of England as well as high government and court officials, sat dignified and solemn, like stars, in their full formal attire. The crown prince was seated between King George V and the queen. A short speech the crown prince made in response to the king's welcoming remarks rang through the hall resonant and clear, seeming to overwhelm everyone present. Even some of us who sat in a corner of the large hall were able to hear his every word with perfect clarity. We had been more accustomed to the crown prince's gentle look; therefore, seeing him in a commanding presence at this formal, international reception aroused a deep and somber emotion in all of us.

After more than ten years since the defeat in the war, Japan has reconstructed itself and now enjoys a measure of stability and prosperity. Since the crown prince ascended to the imperial throne and became the reigning emperor, he has faced a number of national exigencies and unprecedented crises. I have no doubt in my mind that it was due to his benevolence that the nation has been able to come this far towards prosperity. For many aeons to come, I hope that we will not ask the emperor alone to worry about the nation's path. The Empress Nagako's attendants constantly speak of her kindheartedness, although particulars are not easily known to those of us outside of the palace. When my cabinet members and I visited the palace to pay our respect to His Majesty, we would be given seasonal gifts. On one such occasion, I received cigars. The thought of His Majesty's learning that I took pleasure in smoking cigars made me feel very much honored. At another time, when I once made a visit to the Hayama palace, I received a *waka* poem composed by His Majesty, which was handed to me through a chamberlain.

> A humble door fashioned from tree branches
> brought me to wonder how the old man was
> I have not seen him for an aeon

The emperor's care to even the smallest of his subjects moves me to tears.

# 33

# Recollections of
# My Days as a Diplomat

I graduated from the law faculty of the University of Tokyo in July 1906, passed the diplomatic examination in September, and joined the Ministry of Foreign Affairs. This was the period of the first Saionji government and the minister of foreign affairs was Count Hayashi Tadasu. The choice of becoming a diplomat was more coincidental than deliberate. When I was preparing for the entrance examinations to higher school, I caught conjunctivitis. I went to Hakone to convalesce, and missed a year of school. When I had fully recovered, I returned to Tokyo and discovered that Gakushūin University had openings for students, and I somehow managed to get in. My thinking was that I would be able to go on to the University of Tokyo from there. Shortly thereafter, the superintendent of Gakushūin, Prince Konoe Atsumaro, decided to add a university-level curriculum to the school in order to provide specialized training for future diplomats. So when I finished the higher school curriculum at Gakushūin, I naturally proceeded to the university in the same system, a development that somehow nurtured me to become a diplomat. I had no inflated desire to become the likes of famous diplomats such as Count Mutsu Munemitsu or Marquis Komura Jutarō and contribute to the nation's progress here and abroad through diplomatic parties and negotiations.

When I was in the third year at Gakushūin University, Prince Konoe died suddenly. This event prompted the closing of the university and forced the students to enroll in other universities. I went to the University of Tokyo. Among the men who went to the Ministry of Foreign Affairs in the same year as I and are still living are Mr. Ozaki Nobumori, Prince Mushanokōji Kintomo, Mr. Fujii Minoru, and Mr. Hayashi Hisajirō. The late Mr. Hirota Kōki joined the ministry at the same time but he was my senior by one year at the university. For health reasons, I took lessons at an equestrian school in Koishikawa for about ten years, or almost all my school days. I completed the school's curriculum and received a diploma, an accomplishment of which I am quite proud although I cannot say the same about my academic abilities. I would have been able to make a livelihood as a horse trainer, however, if I had failed the foreign service examination.

The Ministry of Foreign Affairs operated with a budget of about four million yen at that time. In addition to the main ministerial office, it housed two important offices, the Political Bureau and the Bureau of Trade and Commerce, the main duties of which related to China. That is, issues and policies dealing with China comprised Japanese foreign policy during those days. Before the Sino-Japanese War (1894–1895), the ministry's main duties consisted of correcting inequalities in treaties. Immediately after the conclusion of that war, Russia, Germany, and France exerted pressure on Japan to cede control of the Liaodong Peninsula. Dealing with this was the ministry's first diplomatic assignment with European nations.

After this incident until the end of the Russo-Japanese War (1905–1906), the major diplomatic charges of the ministry were to sign the alliance with Great Britain and help with occasional discrimination problems that plagued Japanese emigrants to California. The alliance with Great Britain, concluded in 1902, was very significant, and played an important role in the subsequent development of Japan. If I may be frank about the power relationship when the alliance was signed, it was Great Britain that courted Japan to join in this alliance, an offer to which Japan decided to consent. Japan, a small island nation in the Far East, joined hands with Great Britain, a country that ruled the seas. It was a bit of a stretch for Japan, but the Anglo-Japanese Alliance was concluded with each partner standing on equal footing.

When I started out at the Ministry of Foreign Affairs in 1907, I was assigned to the Fengtian Consulate General as an assistant to the consul general. After I finished the assignment at Fengtian, I spent the majority of the following twenty years abroad in consulates and consulate generals in China, and my years in Italy, France, and Great Britain amounted to only a few years. The main focus of Japanese foreign affairs in the Meiji, Taishō, and even Shōwa eras concerned China, as I mentioned above, but what was interesting was that the elite course for career advancement in the ministry was not, curiously, "China service" or looking after Japan's interest in China, and definitely not holding posts in Japanese consulates in China. The sunniest road to success in the ministry had traditionally been assignments in capitals and large cities in Europe and the United States, such as London; Paris; Berlin; Washington, D.C.; and New York. Thus, however snobbish I might want to be with regard to how my career advanced in the ministry, I cannot say that I was ever in the elite, fast track. I do not want to sound like a sore loser, but, looking back, I am convinced that I gained a great deal of knowledge and experience from working in China during my earliest days in the ministry.

China in those days was in transition from the Ch'ing (Qing) dynasty to the early days of the 1911 Revolution. China's domestic situation, particularly internal politics, was complex and constantly changing. Added to this was the full complement of diplomatic maneuvers on the part of foreign countries. To take Japan as an example, the Ministry of Foreign Affairs and the military, especially the army, each operated its own intelligence service. Acting on their own volition, the operatives separately approached local government officials and military leaders. Making this scene more crowded were private Chinese citizens, party members, and politicians who acted as if they were seasoned political masterminds. Being able to see all this firsthand was not a waste for me. I also learned that before a man complains about the situation he is in, regardless of what situation or position in which he might find himself, he should make his very best effort.

After serving for about one and half years at the Fengtian Consulate General, I was assigned to the Consulate General in London. After only a month there, I was transferred to the Japanese embassy in Rome. I served two years in Rome, then quite unexpectedly, I was called back to Japan. My new assignment was to go to Manchuria, as the consul of Andong Prefecture. It was August of 1912. At this time, the governor general in Korea was General Terauchi, but the Ministry of Foreign Affairs thought that he was rather a difficult person to deal with for reasons then unknown to me. I had become acquainted with this man during my days at Fengtian, when I was an assistant to the consul general, so it turned out that the reason I was assigned to this post in Andong Prefecture was to work with the general to smooth things over. For this reason, I also served as a secretary for the Government-General for Korea. During the general's assignment in Korea, I was naturally unable to move from the post in Andong.

In November of 1916, General Terauchi left Korea to form a cabinet in Japan, succeeding the Ōkuma government. My four-year assignment at Andong Prefecture came to an end at the same time. My new assignment was at the Japanese embassy in Washington, D.C. However, as I was making preparations for the transfer, I was told that the appointment was cancelled; instead, I was assigned to the post of acting chief of the Document Section, the most undistinguished position in the ministry. The reason behind this assignment was as follows. One year prior to this shameful turn of events, during my days in Andong Prefecture, the Ōkuma government had presented the Twenty-one Demands to China, causing serious political repercussions. Being young and a mere consul in Andong Prefecture, I opposed this move and tried to mount an opposition initiative by rounding up support for my viewpoint from various consulates in Manchuria. This movement did not materialize in the end, but someone among my colleagues reported my activity to the ministry later, causing a great amount of frustration at the ministry. The ministry no doubt thought that an inexperienced consul like me had no business opposing its grand plan, and blacklisted me from then on. When my assignment to Washington, D.C., came about, a highly placed ministry official must have remembered this incident in China, and promptly put an end to this transfer. I gathered that what I did would have cost me my job under normal circumstances, but the punishment was commuted to an unglamorous assignment, probably because they felt obliged to keep me on staff in deference to my father-in-law Count Makino Nobuaki.

After serving as chief of the Document Section for several months, I received an assignment in February of 1918 to the post of consul of Jinan. My duties included work in the Civil Administration Department for the Qingdao Defense Army, where Director Akiyama was serving as the head of the Department of General Affairs of the Qingdao Defense Army Headquarters. I had been an acquaintance of his since my Korea days, and I suspect that he had a hand in rescuing me from the Document Section, probably with the private encouragement of Prime Minister Terauchi. Soon thereafter, I heard that Count Makino Nobuaki was making a trip to the Paris Peace Conference, with Prince Saionji Kinmochi, as a plenipotentiary member. I volunteered my services and succeeded in accompanying him in February of 1919. This was the first time I ever lobbied for a post. By this time, I had served the ministry for more than ten years, with assignments in backwater posts. I decided that attending the conference was a chance in a lifetime and felt an urge to work myself into the diplomatic mission, even though I would be among the lowest ranked diplomats there.

The diplomatic mission to the Paris Peace Conference consisted of Prince Saionji Kinmochi, head of the mission and ambassador plenipotentiary, Count Makino Nobuaki, Mr. Chinda Sutemi (ambassador to Great Britain), Mr. Matsui Keishirō (ambassador to France), and Mr. Ijūin Hikokichi (ambassador to Italy); the last four in this group also had authority to speak on behalf of Japan. Assisting these diplomats were the elite of the Ministry of Foreign Affairs, making the entire entourage more than one hundred and fifty at one time. Since this conference was held to mop up the aftermath of World War I, the topics of discussion ranged far and wide, including war restitution, territorial settlements, economy, and industry. Even with the multitude of talent in the entourage, however, it was difficult to look after all details.

I will not go into the details of the conference since a large number of documents about this conference are available, but I would like to make a few observations. Ambassador Saionji studied in France when he was a young man and lived in Paris for a long time. During that period, he had stayed in the same Paris apartment house as Georges Eugene Benjamin

Clemenceau, a close friend who was later nicknamed the "Ferocious Tiger," and who wielded formidable power in French politics of the day. This same Clemenceau served as chairman of the conference. Since many years had passed since Prince Saionji's student days in Paris, his French was a bit shaky, necessitating assistance from Mr. Katō Tsunetada, minister posted to the Belgian embassy and one of the best French speakers in the ministry (he would later become the mayor of the city of Takayama). Prince Saionji consulted Mr. Katō whenever he needed specialized vocabulary, for example, "How does one say 'trust territory' in French?"

According to newspaper reports, Prince Saionji kept his silence throughout the conference, thus earning the unflattering nickname "Ivory Mask." True, he was not given a chance to make eloquent speeches. However, the fact that an old friend of the chairman of the conference headed the Japanese mission undeniably impressed other missions, making them more aware of our presence, and opportunities favorable to Japan were brought about as well.

I remember as well about Count Makino's proposal at the conference for equal rights for all races. He proposed that a principle guaranteeing all races would be treated as equals be included in the peace treaty and in the covenant of the League of Nations, which was to result from the conference. This proposal for equality, I believe, was an idea that came from Count Makino himself, for the following reason. When he was the minister of foreign affairs under Yamamoto Gonbei's first government, Makino worked quite a bit on anti-Japanese movements in California and elsewhere that attempted to purge Japanese students and to prohibit Japanese from owning land. In my estimation, he wanted to advance the principle of racial equality at this conference in order to influence indirectly the anti-Japanese discrimination in the United States. Major nations, such as Great Britain, the United States, and France, were agreeable to this proposal, but Australia— which discriminated against nonwhites under the "White Australia" policy—opposed this vociferously. Australia's argument was received with some sympathy by the American public, enough to make the United States switch its position abruptly. This created an ominous atmosphere and threatened a serious fallout. In the end, with General Jan C. Smuts of the South African Federation working as an intermediary, a compromise was finally worked out, which called for tabling the discussion of the Japanese proposal, and in its stead, granting Japan most of its claims concerning the Laizhou Bay. Considerable successes were attributed to Count Makino at this Paris conference. There was some thought that his proposal for racial equality was created as a bargaining chip in order to bring the Laizhou Bay issues to an agreement in Japan's favor, but such an analysis focuses on how negotiations ended, and it misses, I believe, the count's desire to defend the Japanese from the aforementioned anti-Japanese sentiment in the United

States. In view of today's sense of how the world operates, it might strike us as puzzling to learn that the principle of racial equality came out in the open at an international peace conference of grave importance and that it caused all sorts of debate in favor of and against the proposal. Racial discrimination still exists today, for example, against blacks in the southern United States, but it is generally regarded as a domestic issue, of which the root cause is ultimately found in the nation's sentiments. The principle being upheld now among nations of the world is that all nations participate as equals in international conferences, such as meetings at the League of Nations, regardless of how a country is racially made up or how powerful a nation is. No one doubts that a nation is entitled to cast one vote when a proposal comes up for vote. But only forty years ago, this type of equality was not yet regarded as an international standard. Considering these circumstances, the Japanese proposal for racial equality at the Paris conference could be called far-sighted or perhaps progressive, an event that played a leading role in history. Some people have pointed out that, as a result of the Pacific War, Japan promoted independence movements in a number of South-East Asian nations. In this connection, some people use Count Makino's proposal for racial equality in the Paris conference as an example of the Japanese contribution to the world. These views highlight the end result, however; I tend to regard these as events that transpired without lofty foresight or awareness. As I related earlier, the proposal for racial equality was born from the Japanese experience with hardship, and was then probably brought to the open when Japan saw its international status rise.

These considerations do not mean we can make light of the contributions of Prince Saionji and Count Makino, because I am second to none in acknowledging their contribution. In any case, in the Paris conference, Japan ranked among the five great powers, and was asked to serve as a member of the Permanent Council in the League of Nations, which was created subsequent to the conference. The effort of numerous Meiji statesmen to make Japan an equal to other nations of power, that began from the opening of Japan, finally bore fruit.

When the Paris conference concluded, I was assigned to the Japanese embassy in London in May 1920, where, for the next year and a half, I worked under Ambassador Hayashi Gonsuke. Then, in March of 1922, I was again assigned to a post in China as consul general of Tianjin. When I had spent approximately three years there, I was called back to Japan. Rumors in the ministry then had it that I would be sent to Sweden or Norway as a minister, which half made a believer out of me. One day, I was called to a meeting with the minister of foreign affairs Baron Shidehara Kijūrō (under the Katō Takaaki government). He said, "I am very sorry but we have not been able to come up with the right person to head up the Fengtian Consulate General. Will you take that post?" "In return," he continued, "I will do my best to ensure you a brighter future." I pressed him about what he meant by that. He replied that he would make me a higher official first rank. Since I was to be promoted to higher official first rank, the ministry determined that Mr. Hirota Kōki (chief of the European and American Bureau), who had entered the ministry at the same time as I did, had to be accorded the same chance for advancement. The ministry therefore recommended promotion for both of us. Our cases came up for discussion at the cabinet's promotion committee but it was decided that, although Mr. Hirota could be promoted, I could not, since I did not have sufficient years of service. Mr. Hirota had been working at the ministry headquarters; he therefore satisfied the requirement for the years of service more quickly, but I had not, since I spent more of my years in service abroad. So Mr. Hirota, whose career had advanced at the same rate as mine up to this point and whose promotion was only an afterthought, turned out to pass the promotion review, while I, who was promised a brighter future, was passed up. Thus, the only plan to give me a brighter future, as promised by Minister Shidehara, did not materialize. Since I had not received a promotion, I put in a request for a transfer to Manchuria after securing a letter of introduction from Prime Minister Katō. I remember most vividly what happened when I went to the prime minister's office to receive the letter of recommendation. Prime Minister Katō looked at me intently over his eyeglasses and handed me the letter, intoning, "Will this do?" Behind those glasses were, as I recall, very cynical eyes as if to say that the letter did not quite stay true to the facts and contained undeserving accolades. I took this letter of recommendation written by the prime minister himself and went to Fengtian. I made full use of it and had a good time knocking people over with it.

I returned to Japan after serving in Manchuria for a year and a half, and towards the end of 1928, I was appointed vice minister of foreign affairs, succeeding Mr. Debuchi Katsuji. The duties of the minister of foreign affairs at the time were also performed by the prime minister General Tanaka Giichi, who, in my entire life of civil service, was by far the easiest superior to work for. He was magnanimous and openhearted, a generous person who never got caught up in detail. He delegated all clerical work to the vice minister and he seldom came to his office. On those rare occasions when he personally made an appearance to his office, I would take all authorizations requiring his official stamp into his office. He would hold up the official stamp inked and at the ready and, looking at a document, ask, "Is it all right?" When I replied, "I think so," he would authorize it with a stamp, without even reading one line. "Is it all right?", "I think so", stamp—this was all that was required to act on a mountain of documents, making office work quick and easy.

In July of 1929, the Tanaka government, which was supported by the political party Seiyūkai, fell apart, making room for a government led by

Hamaguchi and the political party Minseitō (Liberal Party). The post of the minister of foreign affairs was again occupied by Baron Shidehara, and I remained in the vice minister post. Tanaka's temperament and personality were diametrically opposed that of Mr. Shidehara's. Mr. Tanaka was somewhat cursory and delegated work to others; in contrast, Mr. Shidehara was always a meticulous, cautious administrator. Since Mr. Shidehara's background was in the Foreign Ministry, he knew everything about the ministry, like the back of his hand. He was an expert in writing diplomatic documents in English, perhaps even more skillfully than native-speaker specialists. So, much of the ministry's work was done very expediently by him, leaving the vice minister with nothing to do. Seeing this, some loudmouths in the ministry rudely quipped, "Vice Minister Shidehara and Foreign Minister Yoshida."

After about a year and a half serving under Foreign Minister Shidehara, I was assigned a new post of ambassador to Italy in November 1930. During my year and a half in that post, I attended the conference in Lausanne to discuss war restitution and also an extraordinary meeting of the League of Nations in Geneva that discussed the issue of Manchuria. I attended both as a plenipotentiary member of the Japanese mission. I had very little to say at those meetings. In the fall of 1932, I was called back to Japan. When I returned to Japan and reported to the Ministry of Foreign Affairs, Minister and Count Uchida Kōsai asked me if I wanted to succeed Mr. Debuchi Katsuji as ambassador to the United States. I had a distaste for the type of foreign policy Uchida had implemented, which forced Japan to leave the League of Nations, so it took only a moment to decline the offer. Uchida must have recommended me to the post out of goodwill, so when I said "no" straight to his face, he looked quite taken aback. I was sorry that I was not able to respond to his good intentions, but I had determined that I would not be able to serve a post to anyone's satisfaction under a minister whose fundamental policies I did not agree with.

So, I spent the end of the year waiting for an assignment. Soon, I was asked to make the rounds of inspecting Japanese foreign missions in Europe and the United States. I suspect that the vice minister of foreign affairs, Mr. Shigemitsu Mamoru, gave me this chance as a friendly gesture. I was grateful for this opportunity to leisurely visit these missions abroad from the end of 1932 to the spring of the following year. In November of 1935, still waiting for an assignment, I retired from the Ministry of Foreign Affairs.

Soon after the 2.26 Incident of the following year, when I was reflecting on the end of my diplomatic career, the Hirota government was formed and I was appointed ambassador to Great Britain. I had been slated for an appointment as a member of the cabinet in the Hirota government but the military opposed this move; as a consolation, Mr. Hirota gave me the post in London. Considering the domestic and international situation, not to mention the thorny Anglo-Japanese relationship, I thought that taking this assignment might result in unpleasant experiences here and abroad. At the same time, something in my heart told me with pride that, in the autumn of life, someone with my experience should take on the challenge. So I accepted this very substantial assignment.

Arriving in London, I found that old friends, not to mention officials in the British Government, welcomed me with unchanging kindness and friendship. The sentiment of the public towards the Japanese was, overall, not bad. The truth of the matter appeared to be that the government and the people tacitly agreed that they should be friends of Japan, or at least try to avoid putting Japan out of humor and becoming its enemy. As I observed the attitude of the British people of all social classes at that time of international anxiety, I was deeply impressed by the excellent sense of judgment the British had. Indeed, the two years spent as the ambassador to Great Britain count as the most memorable among the many years of my service as a diplomat.

About a year after my arrival in London, in May of 1937, the Chamberlain government came into power. In July of that year, the so-called Rokōkyō Incident (Lugouqiao Incident) took place and triggered the Japan-China War. In November, Japan signed an anticommunist agreement with Germany, making more apparent the threat of the so-called Axis to world peace. Messages were delivered to me through military attachés—Mr. Tatsumi Eiichi at the embassy in Great Britain and Mr. Ōshima Hiroshi at the embassy in Germany—urging me to endorse the treaty, but I steadfastly opposed it. Despite this very difficult situation, the Chamberlain government maintained composure and patience, even with the Japanese military's anti-British provocations, and never reacted to them, trying their utmost to placate the adversaries.

The best example of this philosophy is seen in the Chamberlain government's decision to send as ambassador to Japan Mr. Robert L. Craigie, an accomplished diplomat who had been assigned to the task of studying British policies relating to the United States up to that point. Ambassador Craigie, who is perhaps still fresh in the reader's memory, toiled tirelessly to avert the war, just as the American ambassador Joseph C. Grew did, until moments before it broke out. Mr. Chamberlain placed his complete trust in Ambassador Craigie. In other words, the fact that Mr. Chamberlain sent the most trusted man to the post of ambassador to Japan indicates how seriously Great Britain followed Japan's moves and how earnestly they wanted to appease Japan. In retrospect, I think Japan should have taken Britain's hand in their peacemaking effort—after all, the British and the Japanese once joined hands in a treaty for a common goal in 1902—and should have taken advantage of their friendship to mollify Japan's domestic political issues.

Prime Minister Arthur Neville Chamberlain was exceedingly patient with the indiscriminate threats and violence carried out by the Japanese military and Nazi bullies. He conciliated them and did his best to seek peace so that we might avoid a calamity. This policy of appeasement appeared to have failed when World War II broke out, but the principle of it was peacemaking, which anyone who plans to serve in international politics and diplomacy should keep in mind. Further, I think we should be inspired by and learn from the British public's steadfastness and patience with Mr. Chamberlain's appeasement policy, wherein the public applauded and encouraged his policy for at least a short period of time, instead of criticizing it.

After about two years of service in London, I was called back to Japan. I returned to Japan at the end of 1938 and finally entered into retirement. In Japan, an anti-Anglo and anti-American sentiment was sweeping the political landscape. Two factors probably determined my return to Japan. First, someone with my background—they labeled me a "liberal Anglophile"— was the target of much loquacious criticism and, secondly, the Foreign Ministry then was headed up by a general of the army, Ugaki Kazushige. In only about six months after my return to Japan, World War II broke out on September 3, 1939, and from there, as we all know, Japan swiftly leapt into the war.

Let me relate a bungle I made while I was in the ministry. In 1908, I was assigned to London. Before departing, I went to see Mr. Hagiwara Morikazu (father of Ogiwara Tōru, current ambassador to Canada) to bid him farewell. Mr. Hagiwara told me this. "Katō Takaaki is being sent to London as Ambassador and he is looking for a secretary. If you travel on the same boat as his, I will bet that he will ask you to be his secretary. You shouldn't think that you are just an ambassador's apple-polisher. So, take the next boat to London." I thought Mr. Hagiwara was someone with backbone and decided to go along with his advice. In 1916 when the Terauchi government was formed, I was called back to Japan. Within a few days after returning, I went to the prime minister's office, when the prime minister was having lunch with someone from his hometown. I was taken in to see him anyway and, suddenly, the prime minister popped a question to me. "Hey, Yoshida, do you want to become my secretary?" On the spur of the moment, I said, "I may be able to do the Prime Minister's job, but I don't think secretarial work suits me." The guest rejoined, laughing, "He is right, you know." Prime Minister Terauchi countered, as if to reprimand me, "Don't be so cocky. I haven't even offered you the job yet." Of course, I said this in jest, but it is also true that the situation reminded me of Hagiwara's maxim, which I learned before I took the London assignment.

I have already related the episode about how I lobbied for a job, so that I could be a member of the plenipotentiary diplomatic mission to the Paris Peace Conference in 1919. "A member of the plenipotentiary mission" sounds grand, but I was merely a secretary of my father-in-law, Count Makino. Count Makino was quite busy while the conference was in session, as his presence was wanted everywhere. This kept me fiendishly busy but did not bother me since the work was related to my assigned duty and the conference. When the conference ended and Count Makino finished his official duties, it was time for us to return to Japan. At this point, the duties of the secretary included more work of a personal nature than of an official nature.

Prince Saionji and Count Makino decided to stop by England and then board a ship in London for Japan. The secretary of Ambassador Saionji was Mr. Saionji Hachirō, the son-in-law of the ambassador. This man was no slouch; as soon as he learned that the ambassadors would be returning to Japan via England, he went to the Paris office of the Thomas Cook travel agency and made all travel arrangements for the stopover in England and return to Japan. He made arrangements in advance for not only the train and ferry tickets, but also the lodgings, which made travel go quite smoothly for the ambassador. In contrast, the secretary of Ambassador Makino, which was I, was not exactly quick; carefree by nature, he naturally did not have the wits to ask Thomas Cook for travel arrangements. As a result, while the Saionjis received attentive and cordial service throughout their trip back to Japan, Ambassador Makino suffered pitiful and wretched treatment. Count Makino, usually a gentle soul who abhorred criticizing others, finally became impatient with this nonsense, and as a result he seldom talked to me during the month-long voyage from London to Yokohama.

As mentioned earlier, I was given a chance to become a secretary for Mr. Katō, who was ambassador to Great Britain, or secretary to Prime Minister Terauchi, but I wanted to follow Mr. Hagiwara's advice and my own sense of who I was and decided not to take up those offers. The one time that I volunteered to be a secretary because I wanted to attend the Paris conference ended with a pathetic note. I learned that I was not made to be a secretary. No man should volunteer to accept a job if he is not meant for it.

When I look back at the more than thirty years of service, from the first day of service in the ministry in 1906 to the last assignment as ambassador to Great Britain in 1939, myriad thoughts and emotions come to me. I want to relate a few of these. Counting only those who did not also do double-duty in another post, the ministers of the Ministry of Foreign Affairs during the Meiji and Taishō eras were Mr. Hayashi Tadasu, Marquis Komura Jutarō, Mr. Uchida Kōsai, Count Makino Nobuaki, Mr. Katō Takaaki, Mr. Ishii Kikujirō, Mr. Motono Ichirō, Mr. Gotō Shinpei, Baron Ijūin Hikokichi, Baron Matsui Keishirō, and Baron Shidehara Kijūrō. Although I might have formed this opinion because of my youth and inexperience, this list of ministers sounded to me men of considerable caliber. Incidentally, General

MacArthur often commented to me how much he respected Generals Tōgō and Nogi, not to mention the other generals in the Russo-Japanese War. Just like myself, his view may have been colored by his youth, because he met these generals when he was a young man, perhaps as a first lieutenant. In any case, it appears to me that diplomats during the Meiji and Taishō eras saw and acted in the interest of the state. Many of them could be said to have possessed the temperament of a samurai. Only a few diplomats were self-centered or interested in career advancement. Of course, Japan had more leeway in those days, very different from the hard times of today. In those days, the pattern was that if anything happened to Japan as a nation, public opinion would readily come to a consensus to address the problem. This naturally compelled politicians and diplomats to act in the interest of the state.

The ministry used to retain foreigners on staff as consultants. These are the so-called foreigners for hire. Mr. Henry Willard Denison, an American, and Dr. Thomas Baty, a British citizen, were well-known in Japan. Dr. Baty made tremendous contributions to Japan, so much so that the British government took away his citizenship during World War II. After the war he died in Japan. In addition to these, French and German consultants were also retained. Not only did these foreigners help write diplomatic documents but some of them also participated in policy decisions at considerably high levels in the ministry. Since we thought that foreigners' points of view were often different from ours, whenever a diplomatic problem arose, we learned how they felt about it or how they might react to it, and that was very useful in interpreting the situation and in solving the problem. I think we tend to become complacent if confined within the narrow spectrum of Japanese thinking. Take reading in a foreign language for example. Regardless of what it is—documents, newspapers, magazines—native speakers of the language can read two or three hundred pages in an evening, with speed and accuracy of understanding that has no comparison to that of a Japanese. I therefore think that we should retain this system of using foreign consultants. To think that we can do it ourselves or to feel xenophobic about using foreign consultants is both small-minded and asinine.

I have a few things to say to the young people of Japan about the importance of foreign-language learning. Learning a foreign language is not limited to diplomats, and mastering a foreign language, especially English, is an essential skill in any discipline. Some hold the opinion that the Japanese are bad at foreign languages by nature no matter how much they study, but this is nonsense. True, we may have more difficulty learning English in comparison to a European, but with discipline and study, we can overcome this difficulty and use the language just as skillfully as a native speaker of English.

The man who was an expert in English in the ministry was Baron Shidehara. Everyone knew that his English was good, but he had made a tremendous effort in studying the language since his youth, a sustained task that a man of ordinary endowment might not be able to replicate. One of Baron Shidehara's daily activities when he was posted in London shortly after joining the ministry was to translate the editorial of the *London Times* into Japanese. He then rewrote it in English, compared it to the English and studied the difference. This was a well-known episode in the ministry. When he was assigned to the ministry in Tokyo, he befriended Mr. Denison—the aforementioned consultant—in order to study the writing of diplomatic documents. He would get up early, stroll a while with Mr. Denison, and then go to his office at the ministry. There he would set up a desk next to Mr. Denison's and study English under Mr. Denison's tutelage from morning until evening. In terms of making use of a foreign consultant, Baron Shidehara topped them all in the ministry. Mr. Denison also thought very highly of Baron Shidehara's English skills. Baron Shidehara studied the language for a long time and I suspect that he did not stray too far from a Webster's dictionary until the day of his death. When we young diplomats got together, we cynically commented that anyone who studied that much was bound to improve, but I know this was just sour grapes.

Since Baron Shidehara was such an expert in English, there were many episodes that related to his English skills. I may have touched on this earlier, but when he became prime minister, I, then foreign minister, went to GHQ headquarters to pick up an agreement. Out of the blue, General MacArthur asked, "This Baron Shidehara, how old is he?" "He is seventy something," I replied. "An old man, is he?" Then he continued, "How is his English?" probably thinking that an old man in his seventies undoubtedly would be unable to speak the language. I, of course, assured him that Shidehara was quite good in English, and took back the agreement. The general's question of whether Baron Shidehara could speak any English struck me as deliciously ironic when I knew that he and all his peers thought that he was second to none. When I returned to the office, I did not tell the baron about this part of my exchange with General MacArthur, because I wanted to save it for another occasion to tease him. It is a pity that I did not have a chance to do so before he died. In reality Baron Shidehara and English were synonymous. Someone once asked him to sign something. He measuredly produced an inkstone and a brush from a desk drawer. Astonished, the man exclaimed, "Do you write Japanese, too?" He must have expected Baron Shidehara to sign in English with a fountain pen.

The topic of English makes me think of two other people, both now deceased, Mr. Saitō Hiroshi and Mr. Shiratori Toshio. Mr. Saitō died in office in Washington, D.C., when he was ambassador to the United States. As a sign of the highest respect from the United States government, his body was returned to Japan on an American warship. Mr. Shiratori served as ambassador to Italy. After the war, he was named a war criminal, and later he died of an illness. These two diplomats were also regarded as among the best English speakers in the ministry.

Both of these men attended the Washington Armament Reduction conference as assistants to Japan's plenipotentiary mission, and were assigned to record the proceedings of the conference. That is, they were charged to record all the discussions by and proposals from the diplomats and specialists of Japan, Great Britain, and the United States. When the day's conference ended, they went straight to a hotel room and organized and rewrote all the records, and delivered them to the Japanese mission that night—a truly Herculean effort. Of course each country had its own secretary to record the proceedings, but British and American missions discovered during the conference through the grapevine that the Japanese records were more accurate and complete than those done by their own people, so much so that, in the end, they came to Mr. Saitō and Mr. Shiratori to ask for the minutes of the conference. This episode speaks to these two men's remarkable gifts, as well as their skills in English. Both of these men were born in Japan and graduated from universities in Tokyo, having never had a chance to study abroad. They gained their expertise in English by studying on their own. This is an example of how, if Japanese put their minds to it and keep their noses to the grindstone, even Japanese, who think that they are poor at learning foreign languages, can perform just as well as Americans and British in a job that requires English.

Recently, I have often been asked if nonprofessional diplomats might not be better than veteran diplomats. When there are important diplomatic issues with a foreign country, the argument goes, appointing an influential politician or industrialist with negotiating authority might be more effective than using career diplomats from the Ministry of Foreign Affairs. Nowadays there has been much talk about economic diplomacy, and some have proposed that financiers should be considered for ambassadorial posts in countries that have strong economic ties with Japan. Proponents of this view cite examples of ambassadors to Japan from Great Britain and the United States, who were formerly industrialists, lawyers, and newspaper publishers.

I cannot go along with this line of reasoning as a matter of principle. That is, given our current state of affairs, it is still best to send diplomats from the Ministry of Foreign Affairs to these diplomatic posts abroad. Although it might sound quite ordinary, the foremost reason is that such a person must be someone who has acquired long years of training in the international arena. Beginning with when he is young, a diplomat receives training and experience in international sensibility, etiquette, protocol, and lifestyle. Regardless of how achieved and talented a man might be, it is by no means taken for granted that the man would be able to work effectively among foreigners. I might say that there are domestic models and export models even among these people. In this connection, I cannot deny that, generally speaking, Europeans and Americans are more international than the Japanese. This is why many among the industrialists and self-employed professionals in Europe and the United States can become ambassadors and ministers at a moment's notice. This is a natural consequence of their climates and lands, customs, and languages. I say this only about peoples that are more naturally suited for diplomatic work; I do not wish to imply that Japanese counterparts to European and American industrialists and self-employed professionals are somehow inferior to them in talent and cultivation. In today's world, where transportation and communication are more developed, it is unavoidable that we will have increased contacts with foreign countries, with the result that the Japanese will become more internationalized in time, like Europeans and Americans. So it appears to me that it will be still some time in the future before we can post respectable ambassadors and ministers with backgrounds in areas other than the Ministry of Foreign Affairs.

Except for posts in established diplomatic missions abroad, the question still remains of whether or not influential politicians or financiers with specialized knowledge might not be more appropriate than usual career diplomats to represent Japan in large international conferences and negotiations that take place from time to time. I can see a certain advantage in this approach. In the past, Japan sent the prime minister and admiral of the navy, Katō Tomosaburō, and former prime minister Baron Wakatsuki Reijirō to arms reduction conferences in Washington, D.C., and London as ambassadors plenipotentiary, and they accomplished their duties admirably. It is not unusual for industrialists to head up a mission abroad in smaller conferences dealing with economic negotiations and successfully complete their missions. We must be careful to point out that in all these cases the teams of negotiators empowered to speak for Japan have always included high-level officials from the Ministry of Foreign Affairs as members, and these officials served as assistants to the others. Although my views might be a bit prejudicial since I spent my entire career in the Ministry of Foreign Affairs, it totally misses the mark to attribute all the glory of the outcome to the main players and to use this to say that nonprofessional diplomats outperform career diplomats without noting the unsung efforts of the assistants. To sum up in another way, I urge leaving kettle making to kettle makers because they do the best work.

# 34

## Recollections of Friends

I spent a long time abroad and did not have anything to do with politics until the end of the war, so I may not have as many acquaintances and friends about whom I have specific recollections as one might think. But during my long service, I received guidance, some directly and some indirectly; favors; and good wishes from a number of predecessors and colleagues. I would like to relate a few of the thoughts as they come to me in the next few pages. I will be genuinely pleased if readers find something to gain from these episodes, and that will make a serendipitous addition to the personal feeling I have towards these friends.

I came to know Prince Saionji Kinmochi for the first time in January of 1919, at the peace conference held at the palace of Versailles. As the reader may recall from a previous chapter, I became intimately acquainted with him when I was a member of the plenipotentiary mission to negotiate the settlement for World War I. Prince Saionji was not only a great statesman with distinguished service spanning the Meiji, Taishō, and Shōwa eras, but also the last senior adviser from the Meiji era. After the Paris conference, I came into contact with Prince Saionji from time to time when I worked as an emissary for Count Makino. Ordinarily, the prince was a man of magnanimity and gentle manners, but he could sometimes be quite harsh. Prince Saionji happened to notice a newspaper article on little-known facts about living in Paris, which was filled with innuendo and half-truths written by one of the newspaper reporters who accompanied the Japanese mission to the Paris conference. He became furious: "How can anyone write this kind of article at this most important juncture in the Franco-Japanese relationship? This may seem minor, but it is egregious." His assistants tried to mollify him but to no avail. The reporter was finally banned from the headquarters of the Japanese mission.

In the early spring of 1933, the day before Mr. Matsuoka Yōsuke was to depart to Geneva to attend a general meeting of the League of Nations, I paid a visit to him and asked him not to take the thoughtless, hot-headed action of resigning from the league. Mr. Matsuoka agreed with me wholeheartedly. In my opinion, Japan's status within the league as a member of the General Council of the League of Nations was earned due to Japan's contribution during World War I. Being a member of the council was the only privilege that enabled Japan to speak as a major power about issues in international politics, diplomacy, and economics. Nothing was more costly for Japan than to relinquish this power. Soon after Matsuoka led the Japanese mission to Geneva, newspapers started to report rumors that Japan might resign from the League of Nations. It occurred to me that I should perhaps see Prince Saionji to discuss this matter. It so happened that I read a newspaper article that said that Prime Minister Viscount Saitō Makoto had called on Prince Saionji at his villa in Okitsu, Shizuoka, an event that gave me the impression that it was all over for Japan. I wanted to see Prince Saionji myself to voice my opinion that Japan should not resign from the League of Nations.

The old man listened to me intently. After hearing me out, he said in a measured, careful manner that he agreed with my position in abstract terms, but he did not in practical terms. I was wondering what he meant by this, when the prince continued, suddenly in a more uncompromising tone of voice. "To contravene on a matter of such grave importance to our nation as this, one must be willing to sacrifice oneself to that cause. Do you have that courage?" To this comment, I could not but straighten myself up. While I had stated my belief on the issue a bit impertinently, I had, needless to say, no intention of placing my life on the line for the cause. I learned from this incident that if I could not resolutely follow through with my conviction on issues affecting a nation, I did not have any business expressing a conviction or acting on it. The old man's solemn and assured poise still comes back to me, as if alive, in front of my eyes.

It is probably very obvious that I would include my memories of my father-in-law, Count Makino, among the episodes about people who preceded me in the ministry. I can only say that this senior ministry official and father-in-law inspired me in myriad areas, including foreign policy, politics, and industry. The count was a man who never lost his Satsuma traits and temperament. As I have touched on earlier in several places, General Terauchi Masatake, another person to whom I owe a great deal, spoke frequently about the difference in temperament between Chōshū and Satsuma men. Chōshū men, he said, would not easily admit someone through the front gate, but once the person was in, he had unlimited access to the donjon of the castle. In contrast, he commented, men from Satsuma would let anyone through the main gate, but would not allow just anyone to come near the donjon. The meaning of this is that Chōshū men are at first difficult to get to know, but once one succeeds in becoming a friend to them, they will open up their hearts. Satsuma men befriend easily, but do not readily allow others in their inner sanctum. I am, of course, indebted to Count Makino in countless ways, since I am his son-in-law and followed his steps in the Ministry of Foreign Affairs. Despite this, he treated me like a foreigner; to borrow General Terauchi's words, I was not allowed into his donjon. Even when I attended a gathering of his relatives, whenever Count Makino talked about Satsuma, he would always preface his comments with, "Perhaps I should not say this in the presence of Yoshida."

The count also possessed one of the virtues of Satsuma men, typical of the Satsuma temperament during the Meiji Restoration. As is well known, the count was born in Meiji as the second son of General Prince Ōkubo Toshimichi and married into the Makino family. During his early years, he studied in the United States and followed a successful career track in the Ministry of Foreign Affairs. He then served as a minister to Italy and Austria, became the minister of education for the first Saionji government, minister of agriculture and commerce for the second Saionji government, and foreign minister for the Yamamoto government. In 1920, he was appointed to the position of grand keeper of the imperial seals, where he served for sixteen years until 1935. After one look at his pedigree and career, we may be led to think that he lived a life of affluence and excess and left a handsome estate to his heirs; this cannot be farther from the truth.

During the infamous 2.26 Incident, he was attacked by the rebels in Yugawara, where he was convalescing. He luckily escaped without injury. Afterward, he spent some time in secluded retirement in Kashiwa in Chiba Prefecture. His lifestyle was extremely simple, and I learned that especially during the post–World War II inflation he had to sell many of his possessions. None of these inglorious turns of fate was ever mentioned to me, the son-in-law. In the general election held in 1949, the Jiyūtō (Liberal Party)— the party I belonged to—won the absolute majority. Quickly, I made a trip to Kashiwa to report the results of election to the count. Though bedridden from an illness, he was elated to hear my report. This turned out to be my last meeting with him. He must have known that his time was coming. His last words, spoken as if they were meant for himself but said to his grandson at his bedside, were "I have never done anything that tarnished my conscience." No man can be happier if he comes to the end of his life with the secure knowledge that he has never done anything against his conscience. After the count's death, few items of value were left in his estate. He owned a small tract of land in a section of Shibuya in Tokyo, about three-quarters of an acre in size, sale of which was perhaps earmarked for his declining years. Knowing firsthand that he never lived a life of luxury as a young man and that he led a simple life in his senior years, our hearts were touched all the more by the count's upright and honest way of life.

One of the men who accorded me friendship and guidance when I was young was General Terauchi Masatake. Terauchi had been governor-general of Korea, prime minister, and a senior official of the army, not to mention an influential statesman. I was first posted in Manchuria in the beginning of 1907, when the cleanup of the Russo-Japanese War still had not been completed. This was the time when Japan had to negotiate with China's Ch'ing (Qing) dynasty and Russia concerning how Japan should return occupied Manchuria to the Chinese. There was also constant friction between the governor-general's office in Lushun and the consulate in Fengtian as to who had authority on which matters.

The minister of the army, Terauchi, was sent to Manchuria to solve these problems. When General Terauchi arrived in Manchuria, Consul General Hagiwara Morikazu of the Fengtian Consulate General was in Japan, having been called back to the ministry for consultation. So during Hagiwara's absence I took care of General Terauchi, as a representative of the consulate. In retrospect, the difference in our ranks—minister of the army and a lowly assistant to a consul—was as large as any imaginable, but because I was young and reckless or perhaps because I did not fully realize who he was—as the old proverb says, "Ignorance is bliss"—I did not treat him any differently just because he was an army general or a minister of the army. I am certain that he thought that I was a strange chap, especially considering how he, as minister of the army, must have been more accustomed to being treated with kid gloves. The manner in which I interacted with him somehow made an impression on the minister. From that time on, he was very good to me.

General Terauchi was the type of man who would encourage and support anyone once he took him under his wings. He would let the man know if he slipped up or bark at him for a mistake. He did not berate his subordinates emotionally; it was clear to all of us who were young diplomats that his lashings were rooted in his kindness, intended to teach a lesson and channel younger diplomats in the proper direction. So when we were dressed down, we would make ourselves scarce in fear of him, but within a few days, we would go back to him for guidance.

I once did double duty as the consul of Andong Prefecture while, at the same time, serving as an aide to Terauchi for the Ministry of Foreign Affairs when he was the governor-general of Korea. One day during this period, a reporter from *Jiji shinpō* by the name of Kamei came to see me. He said that he was planning to start a movement to oust Yuan Shi-kai and asked me to introduce him to General Terauchi. I obliged him by writing a letter of introduction to the general. Kamei must have given General Terauchi an earful of what he believed. He said something like, "Yuan Shi-kai is up to no good. As long as this fellow is in Beijing, we will have no chance for good China-Japanese relations. He needs to be neutralized somehow." When I met General Terauchi later, he scolded me roundly, "Conspiring to assassinate a head of state is outrageous. On top of that, you wrote a letter of introduction for this conspirator, which is even more inexcusable."

General Terauchi's personality had this very draconian side, but also showed a very lovable, childlike innocence. Once I went to a dinner party at the residence of the governor-general of Korea in Seoul. General Terauchi brought a live baby tiger to the dining hall and let it roam around on its own. It was a very young tiger, only a few weeks old, but a tiger is still a tiger, not at all like a domestic cat. We feared it might take a fancy to our feet under the table and take a big bite, so we were all very vigilant, unable to taste anything. The lady guests in particular, not to mention the gentlemen, were ill at ease and at a loss as to what to do. The only person smirking with content, as he watched this scene of consternation, was the bald-headed, child-faced general. I cannot forget this wicked but humorous incident.

Now that I have said a few things about a general of the army, I cannot help but remember an admiral of the navy, Count Yamamoto Gonbei. Count Yamamoto was one of the most senior officers in the navy and served as prime minister on two occasions. I met him for the first time when I was vice minister of the Foreign Ministry during the time the ministry was led by Baron Shidehara. The occasion was an armament reduction conference held in London in early 1930, to which Japan sent a plenipotentiary mission. The diplomatic corps consisted of former prime minister Wakatsuki Reijirō, minister of the Navy Takarabe Takeshi, and Mr. Matsudaira Tsuneo and Mr. Nagai Matsuzō from the foreign ministry.

The agenda of the London conference was the reduction of naval armament, a topic about which the Ministry of the Navy and the Ministry of Foreign Affairs still had not ironed out their differences. We therefore thought that we should ensure that the Foreign Ministry's position be made abundantly clear to Count Yamamoto—who was the most influential person in the Ministry of the Navy—so as to forge a unified Japanese position. Without this, we thought, we could not hope for satisfactory results, no matter how arduously the mission worked in London.

Foreign Minister Baron Shidehara was quite passionate about tinkering with the wording of the treaty, but did not show much interest in the planning and negotiating of the treaty with the Ministry of the Navy. This meant that I, as vice minister of the Foreign Ministry, was placed in a position to do the work for the ministry. Count Yamamoto was a good friend of Count Makino, for they both hailed from Satsuma. I seldom asked Count Makino to write a letter of introduction for me but I had him write one in order for me to see Count Yamamoto.

So I went to meet Count Yamamoto. Before I had finished my greeting, he began to speak about the forthcoming armament reduction conference in impassioned eloquence, despite the fact that I had taken the trouble to visit him in order to explain the Foreign Ministry's position on the matter. He did not even once let up on his rhetorical comments, so much so that I did not have a chance to get a word in edgewise. As I sat there listening to him, I thought that he was never going to hear even one word that I had to say unless I took drastic measures. I adopted the strategy of disagreeing with him openly; when I saw a chink in his eloquence, I said something like this to him. "General, you are a man of considerable influence in the navy and a senior adviser on matters that concern the nation. If I may be frank, what you are saying sounds as if the navy was the top rung of the ladder and a man is not a man unless he is a naval officer. In contrast, a man like Prince Saionji is immeasurably fair; he listens to those of us who are young diplomats and offers indispensable guidance."

At this, he glared at me sharply, his famous falcon eyes shining brilliantly, as if to say I was a conceited fool. Fueling his eloquence, he began to make reference to the Foreign Ministry's handling of the Amoy Incident, and said: "During the Fuzhou Incident, a rumor was circulated that the army was going to attack Amoy. The navy thought this was a preposterous violence and we resolved to not only refuse to cooperate with the army, but to sink army supply ships. We finally persuaded the army not to attack Amoy. When we face an international problem, the decision should have nothing to do with the army or the navy. The problem should be dealt with unwavering decisiveness for the good of the nation. Civilians have never been shown to have this kind of courage." Yamamoto expounded on and on in this manner, arguing this way, disputing that point, totally impermeable to any arguments I presented. Thus the meeting turned out to be a soliloquy, and at the end of this performance, he quietly intoned, "I am saying this because I think you will soon take a post of considerable responsibility. My friendly advice to you is 'Don't miss the right timing for a decision.'" For a relatively short period of time, between this meeting and the end of 1933 when the count died, I met him again several times. I always discovered some things that were immensely instructive behind his fierce disposition and eloquent delivery of words and ideas.

Both General Terauchi and Count Yamamoto were generally feared, because they were thought to be cantankerous, stubborn curmudgeons. Their looks and mannerisms in speech seemed to give credence to their truly fiery tempers, but one of the characteristics consistently observed in the accomplished politicians of the Meiji and Taishō eras is that, when they reproached or bawled at the younger men, they invariably did so with the purpose of nurturing and guiding them. I cannot help but feel a deep sense of appreciation when I compare this approach with politicians of today who busy themselves with trying to make and preserve a name for themselves.

The first minister of foreign affairs with whom I became acquainted during my career in the ministry was Count Katō Takaaki. He not only was a superb diplomat but also led the government later (from June of 1924 to January of 1926). He was intimately acquainted with a number of senior governmental advisers, and had a special friendship with Marquis Ōkuma Shigenobu. Count Katō was not only tough but also very careful. As is well known, the wife of Count Katō was a former Mitsubishi (Iwasaki family) and Mrs. Baron Shidehara Kijūrō was a younger sister of hers, so Count Katō and Baron Shidehara were brothers-in-law. When Count Katō was the minister of foreign affairs, Baron Shidehara was his immediate subordinate; when Count Katō was prime minister, Baron Shidehara was the minister of foreign affairs. Baron Shidehara once held a garden party in Hongō at his residence. Count Katō commented on a phrase in the invitation for this party which read "at my humble home." "What does he mean by 'my humble home'?" Count Katō remarked, "He lives in a house that belongs to the Iwasaki; he is just renting it." So, unbeknownst to many, Count Katō was sometimes a man with a cynical streak. At the same time, he was very supportive of his subordinates. For instance, as mentioned earlier, when I was posted as consul in Fengtian, he was kind enough to furnish me with an unduly complimentary letter of recommendation.

Minister of Foreign Affairs Viscount Motono Ichirō, who served in this position from November of 1916 to April of 1918, was better known abroad than in Japan. He served in Germany and elsewhere in the cities of Europe as a diplomat for many years. He was a natural for languages and his command of French was near-native, which enabled him to cultivate friendships with a large circle of people. This made Viscount Motono one of the very few among Japanese diplomats in Europe whose name was instantly recognized by the French, a distinction rarely achieved by any diplomats from other foreign missions. Viscount Motono was well-versed in modern European history. This was the time when people in diplomatic circles often spoke of "cooperative trade" as in "cooperative trade between Great Britain and France." He was also very knowledgeable about this topic, so much so that when he was ambassador to Russia, other foreign missions in Peterograd would come to see Viscount Motono to ask about "cooperative trade" whenever problems about this arose between European nations. His knowledge was highly sought after. He was one of the very few, truly international men.

Many young people may not know much about Count Chinda Sutemi, who was the grand chamberlain at the beginning of Shōwa, perhaps because he was a man with a reserved nature. He was one of my predecessors in the ministry. Count Sutemi was a courteous, sincere gentleman, with the tenacity typical of someone who had roots in Tōhoku. Count Sutemi, then ambassador to Great Britain, was one of the plenipotentiary members of the Japanese mission to the Paris Peace Conference. At one juncture during this conference, Count Makino, a member of the Japanese mission, and Mr. Ku Weijun, a member of the Chinese plenipotentiary mission, could not come to terms on how Japan should return the Laizhou Bay in Shandong Province, which Japan had occupied during World War I. Mr. Robert Lansing of the American mission supported the Chinese position, that Japan should declare again publicly that it would allow all the rights and interests in China's Shangdong Province that Germany had held to be returned directly to China, without passing through Japanese hands.

Lansing must have tried very hard to persuade Count Makino. One day during the conference, he telephoned the office of the Japanese mission to set up a meeting with Count Makino. The count was reluctant to oblige at first, but finally agreed to call on Lansing in his quarters. For some reason, Count Makino was inadvertently led into a waiting room for the general public. Count Makino waited, but Mr. Lansing never appeared. Taking advantage of this error, Count Makino promptly returned to the Japanese quarters. Soon thereafter, a secretary at the U.S. mission telephoned the room where Count Chinda and I were. "We are terribly sorry for that dreadful mistake, but I wonder if it would be possible for the Count Makino to make a trip over to the American mission again," the caller inquired. After talking it over briefly, we replied, "Count Makino has gone out and is unavailable. In his stead, Count Chinda will be happy to oblige." So, Count Chinda went to see Mr. Lansing and talked many hours with him. In the end Count Chinda's tenacity must have defeated Mr. Lansing; Japan did not have to make the concession that would have abandoned its rights to Shandong Province.

We thus experienced firsthand and for the first time Chinda's gift for steadfastly striving to achieve a goal, but there was another incident that illustrated his skill even more aptly. After the Paris conference, Prince Saionji and Count Makino decided to visit Great Britain. During their stay in England, they were invited to meet the royal family. His Majesty King George V was quite forthright and gave them a welcome much as if his own family members were visiting. In conversing with the king, Prince Saionji and Count Makino were told that the royal family owned land in Scotland. Potatoes and wheat harvested on the land were an important source of income for the family. Prince Saionji and Count Makino learned of a rather private situation as well, that potatoes had not done well that year and this affected the finances of the family significantly. Somewhat troubled, Count Makino related this episode to the embassy staff when he returned, and one of them telegraphed all the details to the Foreign Ministry in Tokyo. This story was then carried in a magazine that circulated among the ministry employees.

Someone at the British embassy in Tokyo noticed this article, whereupon a telegram was quickly dispatched to England. That Japan had made the royal affair available for public consumption outraged Lord Curzon, then foreign minister and a man known for his fortitude of character. He lodged a strong complaint with Ambassador Chinda, to the effect that, from that this time on, no matter how highly ranked a Japanese official was, the British government would never again invite him to meet the royal family or another British official. To this, Count Chinda, known for being genial, explained to Lord Curzon, who was fuming in anger, that this unfortunate incident harbored not a grain of malice whatsoever. Two hours later, he finally persuaded Lord Curzon to undo the phrasing about Japanese visitors not being able to meet British counterparts. This was a famous episode in the ministry. Everyone praised Count Chinda's tenacity, but it also taught us a valuable lesson, that international protocol necessitates that we should refrain from directly quoting dignitaries even if they are speaking about topics of a personal nature.

I also have some recollections from my younger days about Prime Minister Hara Takashi. Mr. Hara was arguably one of the greatest of the prime ministers. When he was a young man, he studied in France and then began to work for the Ministry of Foreign Affairs. I met him only once, when Emperor Taishō gave a dinner party for the Japanese diplomatic mission to the Paris Conference. I was also invited to this party and sat in a far corner in the dining hall.

Mr. Hara was the prime minister then. "I saw from a far distance" is more precise than "I met him." Of course, he did not speak to me. When the dinner conversation turned to the topic of how poor the Japanese are at foreign languages, His Majesty made the comment, "Prime Minister Hara, your French must be excellent, since I hear that you spent some time in France as a student." Hara replied, "My French, Your Majesty, is completely bogus." He said this in a loud voice that could be heard even where I was. I do not have any specific recollection of the party, but I remember this quite clearly. I heard a story about the prime minister that Count Makino told me. There was an occasion when Count Makino and Mr. Hara were both invited to a dinner party at the Belgian legation. Before retiring for the night after the party, Mr. Hara, Count Makino, and the host Belgian minister sat talking in the receiving room. The Belgian legation was then housed at the former house of Prince Ōkubo Toshimichi, the father of Count Makino, and the conversation that night naturally touched on the demise of Prince Ōkubo. As the reader is surely familiar, Prince Ōkubo was slain by Shimada Ichirō in a section of Tokyo called Kioichō in May 1878. The day after the party, fate had it that Hara was attacked and killed by Nakaoka Kon'ichi in front of Tokyo Station.

No service was more pleasurable than working as vice minister during the period that the government was headed by Mr. Tanaka Giichi, who also did double duty as the minister of foreign affairs. I touched on this earlier, but how I became vice minister itself owed a great deal to Mr. Tanaka. While I was a consul at the Fengtian Consulate, Mr. Tanaka held a conference entitled *Tōhō kaigi* (or Conference on East Asia) from June 27 to July 7 of 1927. Mr. Mori Kaku, then the deputy director of foreign policies of the ministry, proposed the conference. He wanted to bring together all the ministry's establishments in China and Manchuria in order to forge close cooperation between the government and political parties and to use this opportunity to take diplomacy out of the reach of political struggles. This conference was thought to showcase the proactive China policies of the so-called Tanaka Diplomacy. It was a focus of attention and we heard many rumors and speculations about what it might entail. In any case, after this conference Mr. Mori and I became quite good friends. In the spring of 1928, I was assigned to the post of the minister extraordinary and plenipotentiary to Sweden, and shortly thereafter, I was told to serve Norway, Denmark, and Finland simultaneously as well. Then, Mr. Debuchi Katsuji, who had held the post of vice minister of the foreign ministry, was sent to the United States as ambassador. Before he left, he recommended a man to replace him in the ministry, while Mr. Mori recommended me for the same post. Mr. Debuchi was a relative of Foreign Minister Tanaka, so it looked as if his recommendation would carry more weight. Around this time, a friend of mine was being transferred to an overseas position. When I went to Yokohama to see him off, I ran into Mr. Mori. He said, "I don't think you have much of a chance for the vice minister post. Take the job in Sweden." "In that case, I want to talk to Mr. Tanaka directly. Can you set up a meeting with him?" I inquired. "Are you sure you want to do that?" he asked, a bit worried, though he was known to be fearless. "I don't know," I said, "but if it doesn't work, I will know at least I tried." Mr. Mori agreed. Soon thereafter I went to see Prime Minister Tanaka.

When I saw the prime minister, he started the meeting with a question. "How is Zhang Zuolin doing these days?" "Prime Minister," I said, "I am not here to discuss Zhang Zuolin. I myself think very strongly that I am the best person for the post of vice minister of foreign affairs." I continued, "From what I understand, you do not seem to think so, so I will take the assignment to Sweden. Before doing that, however, I thought I would tell you what I would do at this juncture if I were the foreign minister." With this introduction done, I gave him an earful about what I would do in foreign policies towards Manchuria and China. The prime minister did not say a word while I was speaking and gazed quietly towards the garden. Later I found out that when Mr. Tanaka was told something he did not like to hear, he would remain silent and quietly look at the garden. Therefore this was a sure sign that he did not relish hearing a long-winded explication of my foreign policy. A short while after I returned home, I received a telephone call from the prime minister's office asking me if I could come to the prime minister's cottage in Koshigoe, Kanagawa Prefecture. I called on him at the appointed time. Prime Minister Tanaka emerged from the back of the house to greet me, smiling broadly, and said, "I am going to ask you to take the post of vice minister of foreign affairs, if it is agreeable with you, that is." "If it is agreeable with you, that is" struck me as a bit odd, because he said it to someone who, only the day before, had gone to see him to lobby for the position. Mr. Tanaka would feign innocence inexplicably like this. After that, I came to like the man and served under him for a long time. During my long life of service to the ministry, I lobbied for my position only twice, once when I wanted to join the Japanese plenipotentiary mission to the Paris peace conference and another time when I wanted this post of vice minister.

I had one experience that very much vexed me when I worked for Mr. Tanaka. A minister from an eastern European country called on the prime minister. This diplomat was not only repetitious, but continued on and on about topics that only tangentially related to Japan. Prime Minister Tanaka was known for cordiality but he was getting impatient. Interrupting the minister's impassioned discourse, he said in Japanese, "This man must be a fool." The speaker might not have been good at Japanese, but anyone who has spent any time in Japan would know the Japanese word for "fool." I was serving as the interpreter, and thought for a moment he might catch on. Though Mr. Tanaka was a man who was inattentive to detail, he had quite a sense of humor.

I would like to relate a brief story about Mr. Zhang Zuolin, since his name has been mentioned. The years from the end of the Taishō era, when I was a consul of the Fengtian Consulate General, until the beginning of Shōwa, were a time when the so-called Baron Shidehara foreign policies were at their apogee. These policies were designed to make the claim to China that Japan did not want to interfere with its domestic policies. The problem was that directives from the Ministry of Foreign Affairs to Manchuria and China went unnoticed or frequently ignored, especially by the army and the South Manchuria Railway Company. This was a cause of constant trouble for various Japanese interests and offices there.

For instance, when the Guo Songling Incident took place in November of 1925, the Ministry of Foreign Affairs held fast to the policy of not interfering with China's internal politics. Officially, the ministry was neutral about the outcome of this battle between Guo Songling and Zhang Zuolin. But, Mr. Zhang colluded with the Japanese Army to strengthen his position. Although it looked as if he was about to flee at one point during this conflict, he was able to turn the tide with Japanese assistance. It stood to reason that Mr. Zhang was very much obligated to the Japanese Army, but he did not warm up to the Japanese Foreign Ministry. I saw him often around this time, but I cannot say that we were close. One day, Lieutenant Colonel

Machino Takema, military adviser to Mr. Zhang, came to see me and asked if I could join Mr. Zhang for a meal. I replied, "I cannot simply say 'yes' just because someone asks me to come. I am not his servant." A few days later, a formal invitation arrived. Lacking a good reason to decline, I accepted the invitation. At the dining table, Mr. Zhang said, "If we wanted to get along with each other, I think we could. How about it? Just give me the word." "I don't know what you mean by that," I replied. "We are getting along just fine now, are we not?" He seemed unable to conjure up a good comeback. So, in this way, we never really got along. When the Guo Songling Incident ended, Mr. Zhang delivered gifts of tiger pelts to all concerned, probably as tokens of gratitude for the assistance he received from the Japanese. I later found out that I received the smallest tiger pelt.

As some readers perhaps know, Mr. Zhang Zuolin was a man from Lulin, formerly a leader of bandits on horses. He was a man of idiosyncratic traits, in a sense, an interesting man. He led a checkered life; in the end, he met his death violently at the hands of the Japanese military, the very people with whom he had colluded for many years.

I think the first time we began to attach the name of the foreign minister to Japan's foreign policies, as in "such-and-such foreign policies," was in the case of the Shidehara foreign policies. Baron Shidehara Kijūrō epitomized the Foreign Ministry in its most quintessential sense. He served more than five years as the minister of foreign affairs under four governments, led first by Count Katō Takaaki, then the first Wakatsuki, Hamaguchi, and the second Wakatsuki. It goes without saying that Baron Shidehara was one of the few men who knew every inch of the ministry.

It seemed that the Foreign Ministry was a very comfortable place for Baron Shidehara. When he attended a cabinet meeting as the minister of foreign affairs, other ministers would remain with the prime minister for luncheon after the meeting, but Baron Shidehara would come back to the ministry and enjoy taking his meal with the bureau chiefs in the ministry's dining hall. On these occasions, he would usually be in an especially jovial mood, and this stern-looking man would tell jokes. If I may be so bold as to say what I really thought of his jokes, they were no more than puerile wordplays. An example. His name is, of course, "Baron Shidehara" but some people mispronounce it as "Hidehara." When asked which one was correct, he replied, "Of course, I'm 'Hidehara' [he] and my better half is 'Baron Shidehara' [she]." This type of wordplay that made use of English was typical of him. Baron Shidehara was synonymous with English since he was such an expert at it. But I think sometimes his expertise in English excessively influenced other aspects of his work. For instance, the major posts in the ministry were once occupied by his friends and associates. One thing that was consistent about his personnel was that they were all excellent at languages. When I looked at Baron Shidehara's personnel, I wondered if

Baron Shidehara did not mistake language ability for administrative capability. That is, when I looked at his personnel style, I was convinced that men with highly developed language skills tended to be scouted out for high posts, while those with mediocre aptitude for language were thought to be incompetent and left behind. Needless to say I was in the latter group.

I was accorded a special friendship with Baron Shidehara in his senior years, but during my younger days I was by no means a man of Baron Shidehara's liking. Not only were my language abilities not up to par, but also I tended to say things that came to mind dauntlessly and express my disagreement, traits that probably annoyed Baron Shidehara. There is an episode that still makes me break out into a cold sweat. I related an episode earlier that, when I was in a rank called second secretary at the embassy, my assignment to Washington, D.C., was cancelled, endangering my career. I was salvaged as acting chief of the Document Section. I was quite beside myself since my pride had received a humbling injury, so much so that even when Vice Minister Baron Shidehara rang a bell to summon me to his office, I would not budge from my desk in protest.

As the end of the year neared, it became impossible for me to stubbornly continue this insolence, for it was essential for me to appear in person in the vice minister's office. That is, if I refused to appear in person to see Vice Minister Baron Shidehara, he would not give me the envelope containing the year-end bonus for my staff. If this had been only a personal vendetta, I might have continued my policy of noncooperation longer, but given that the staff could lose the chance to receive their bonus, I could not help but cave in to the pressure. I reluctantly presented myself at the vice minister's office, bowed deeply to Vice Minister Baron Shidehara, and received the bonus for the entire staff.

At the end of the year that World War II ended, that is, when Baron Shidehara was the prime minister, he suffered from pneumonia. At that time, it was not easy to obtain penicillin in Japan, so it was decided that we should contact GHQ. I called on General MacArthur and he quickly consented to help and, although I would have been happy just to receive the antibiotic and leave, he insisted on calling his personal physician so that the physician could look over Baron Shidehara. The doctor, perhaps thinking that Japanese physicians were still learning how to use a stethoscope, said, "I am not sure if Japanese doctors know how to administer penicillin, so let me see Baron Shidehara in person." Unable to decline this kind offer, we ended up accepting the invitation of MacArthur's personal physician. When I showed up for the second time for more antibiotic, the doctor was again eager to help. His confidence in Japanese doctors was nil, I surmised. I did not feel sanguine about taking advantage of an American doctor, so I contacted Dr. Takemi Tarō, a relative of Count Makino, and asked if he would do the injection. The doctor vehemently declined. "How can a famous Japanese doctor like myself give an injection when some backwater doctor from the United States is watching me over my shoulder?" So the American doctor had to see Baron Shidehara several more times until he recovered completely.

At the end of the Terauchi Masatake government (October 1916 to September 1918), Minister of Foreign Affairs Viscount Motono Ichirō died, so Count Gotō Shinpei, who had been the minister of the interior, succeeded Viscount Motono. Count Gotō was the doctor who had tended Count Itagaki Taisuke when he was attacked by an assailant with a knife in Gifu Prefecture on April 6, 1882. Later, Count Gotō became the director of civil affairs under Kodama Gentarō, governor-general of Taiwan and general of the army. Japan had obtained this island of Taiwan as a result of the Sino-Japanese War. When Southern Manchuria became a Japanese territory after the Russo-Japanese War, Count Gotō became the president of the South Manchuria Railway Company because he agreed with General Kodama about how to run it. The South Manchuria Railway Company was not only a railway company, but operated coal-mining, steel-making, and many other businesses, and extended its influence to the politics and foreign policies of Manchuria. It had the power and authority of a large national policy concern in colony management similar to the East India Company in British India.

This was roughly the background of Count Gotō when he came into the Ministry of Foreign Affairs from the Ministry of the Interior. The vice minister of the ministry then was Baron Shidehara. As noted before, Baron Shidehara spent most of his public service life in the Ministry of Foreign Affairs and considered the ministry his home. Baron Shidehara told me later that, when he heard that Count Gotō would head up the ministry, he feared that Count Gotō might spend the ministry's funds for confidential purposes as if he were still with the South Manchuria Railway Company. Baron Shidehara therefore made up his mind that, as his solemn duty as vice minister, he would resolutely cite any unjustified expenditures on the minister's part and keep a tight reign of the coffer. But when Count Gotō began his tenure at the ministry, his only request to use the funds was to hire someone to read foreign newspapers and magazines on his behalf, so that he would be able to stay abreast with current affairs, and that the salary should be drawn from the ministry's secret funds. Baron Shidehara told me that during Count Gotō's short tenure of about six months as minister he did not make any more requests for money from these funds, which disappointed Baron Shidehara by upsetting his grand plan to call attention to any unreasonable expenses.

Later, Baron Shidehara and I talked good-naturedly about the large scale of things that Count Gotō worked with. As governor-general of the South Manchurian Railway Company, he was used to huge expense accounts, and he probably did not even notice the meager funds for secret affairs in the ministry. The part of this episode that made me smile was the delightfully uncanny contrast between Vice Minister Baron Shidehara, an honest, meticulous administrator who tracked even pennies, and Minister Gotō, who was always part of some grand scheme that ordinary people could not even comprehend and for which he would not have hesitated to invest massive sums of money.

I served as vice minister of the ministry under both Tanaka and Baron Shidehara. People referred to foreign policies under these ministers as Tanaka Diplomacy and Baron Shidehara Diplomacy and regarded the former as passive and the latter as proactive. Looking back, these days were when liberalism in Japan was at its peak. Government based on political parties was quite developed as well, even by today's standards. The two opposition parties were the Seiyūkai Party, which traced its roots back to the Jiyūtō (Liberal Party) of the Meiji era, and the Minseitō Party (Liberal Party), which goes back to Kaishintō (Progressive Party). Governmental power changed back and forth between these two parties. These parties also sported clearly contrasting policies. In financial and monetary policies, Takahashi Korekiyo's proactive policies, which the opposing party called the free-fall policy, and Hamaguchi Osachi's austerity policy, which the opposition party called a passive policy, contrasted to a certain degree, both in philosophy and concrete policies.

The Baron Shidehara and Tanaka foreign policies were unlike each other in nature, although not to the same degree as the monetary and economic policies. This was evident in policies directed towards China. The China policy of the Minseitō government, in short, was, at least in appearance, that of noninterference in Chinese internal affairs and of international cooperation. In contrast, the Seiyūkai government led by Tanaka had its eyes on Japanese interests in Manchuria and Mongolia and proposed to act diplomatically within that parameter. If one asked how much difference there was between these policies in reality, the truth would be that it was negligible, and all the more so in retrospect. In the end the distance between these policies amounted to the slightly different ways each was designed to handle problems in China and this dissimilarity, if any, did not derive from divergent bases in political philosophy, but reflected instead differences and changes in the internal politics of Japan and the international state of affairs.

The Baron Shidehara foreign policies neither made light of the Japanese interests in Manchuria and Mongolia nor proposed to abandon them altogether. Although the Tanaka foreign policies were said to be autonomous, they were not so independent that Japan would disregard treaties and agreements with the U.S. and European countries and assert its interest stubbornly to the end, a characteristic that made Tanaka's policies different from the military's some years later. To wit, the slaying of Zhang Zuolin was a maneuver that Tanaka would not have condoned; as we all know today, he must have racked his brains about how to deal with this issue. It is basically meaningless for us to call one policy weak and the other strong, except when attacking one policy in preference of another.

Among my memories of foreigners, my friendship with Mr. Chamberlain was one of the most memorable. It is now well known that he followed a policy of appeasement towards Germany, but as I indicated earlier in this chapter, he did not spare any effort to mollify Japan until the very last moment. Soon after Mr. Chamberlain formed his government in May of 1937, he invited me to a luncheon; this was when I was posted in London as the Japanese ambassador. It was not infrequent for heads of government to invite foreign diplomats and emissaries to state dinners and parties on national holidays, but it was quite rare for the leader of a country to privately invite a foreign diplomat to take a meal together. This, obviously, represented an extraordinary gesture of goodwill on his part. When I arrived, I found that he had invited only three or four close friends of his, in addition to me as the guest of honor. This was a quite informal, unreserved gathering, which delighted me. Conversations at the table, too, were therefore relaxed and open, typical among the closest of friends. At one time, Mr. Chamberlain confided, "My father thought nothing of spending good sums of money to send my eldest brother Austin to school in France or Germany, but other sons did not get any such luxurious treatment. As soon as we got out of school, he sent us to work in a bank or made us businessmen. I was sent to the West Indies to run a farm." Without missing a beat, an old friend of his chimed in. "Ah, all right. So it was about that time when you also ran a general store peddling chemises to native women!" "Oh yes," replied Mr. Chamberlain, "I lost a lot of money on the store and, because of it, I was called back to England. So I ended up getting into politics." Teasing banters and hearty laughs of all present made this meeting all the more lively and friendly. I gained a very good sense of the English character revealed through this chitchat. As we can detect from the episode, Mr. Chamberlain related stories unpretentiously, even a family as prestigious as his did not spend much money on its sons, except for the eldest one. So if a son wanted to go into a costly profession like politics, the eldest one would be allowed to pursue it; other sons were put in more productive professions. Accordingly, Mr. Chamberlain, as well, was supposed to devote himself to opening up of a land for farming. I think this is very typical of English families in a fine family tradition of steadfastness. When I traveled to England a few years ago, I had the pleasurable opportunity of seeing Mrs. Chamberlain, then widowed, and reminiscing about Prime Minister Chamberlain.

Now that I am speaking about English prime ministers, I must say a few words about Mr. Churchill. I met Lord Winston when I was in London as ambassador. Mr. Churchill was not even a member of Chamberlain's cabinet, although he had a distinguished record of service to the state as the minister of the navy during World War I. He was at odds with Mr. Chamberlain on some matters, constituting, in a manner of speaking, an opposition element within the same political party. He was not at the forefront of the political arena and public opinion about him was not exactly flattering; he was thought to be an ambitious, opportunistic man. In addition to this, I was more closely associated with Prime Minister Chamberlain, naturally reducing my chance to become acquainted with Mr. Churchill. It was not until the fall of 1954, when I went to visit London, that I had practically the first chance to speak to Lord Winston frankly. When we met, I was quite impressed by the attentive and courteous welcome he gave me, as if he were seeing an old friend of many years. The time the crown prince visited Great Britain, an event that took place shortly before my visit, was a volatile period, when anti-Japanese sentiment arising from the cruelty to English war prisoners was still felt very strongly by the British, so much so that anti-Japanese demonstrations were held in Newcastle and articles about Japanese war atrocities were carried in London newspapers. Prime Minister Churchill summoned the newspaper representatives and admonished them by reminding them that English civility called for everyone to afford equal courtesy to all foreign dignitaries. This settled the whole matter. In fact, as is well known from news photographs, Prime Minister Churchill hosted the crown prince in his official residence with unparalleled courtesy and warmth as if His Highness were his own family.

Although we generally have the opinion that Mr. Churchill was a prominent statesman and the embodiment of toughness, whose true value was felt in the two wars during the autumn of national crises for Great Britain, my first impression of Mr. Churchill was that he was a man full of genuine goodwill. On one occasion, he made a speech to welcome me at the dinner table. "From what I understand, Prime Minister Yoshida is known in Japan to be rather a tough politician. When I see him in person, however, I find that he has proven himself to be quite genial." I wanted to return this assessment of me to him, as I found it to be a very fitting description of the man himself, but not of me. While I was talking to Mr. Churchill, we happened to touch on his very famous memoirs about the war. He asked me why I was not writing a memoir. I responded, "I once read in a magazine or something that if an idea occurred to you when you were writing a memoir, you would jump out of bed even in the middle of the night, rouse up the secretary, and make him take dictation, while you sat back and sipped brandy. I can never bring myself to do that. I feel very fortunate that I was not your secretary." "No, no, nothing is further from the truth," he vehemently protested, "what I drank at night was not brandy, it was whisky." I thought he would discount the whole story, but he only corrected the drink selection with a straight face, which struck me as very unconventional and highly witty.

I do not guarantee the authenticity of the following story attributed to Mr. Churchill. It goes like this. One year, Mr. Churchill went to a resort on the Mediterranean to convalesce. He was enjoying a day of swimming and relaxation, when a newspaper cameraman approached to take a photograph of him in a bathing suit. All of a sudden, Mr. Churchill splashed the man with water from the Mediterranean. This episode made me chuckle mirthfully, for I learned that I was not the only man who splashed a cameraman with water. In my case, it was a glass of water; in his case it was Mediterranean seawater, of which he had plenty at hand.

Mr. Churchill related to me a story that his mother once had visited Japan and told young Mr. Churchill about how beautiful Japan was, especially Mt. Fuji, and that made an indelible impression on him. Hearing this, I promised him that I would get a first-class painter to make a painting of Mt. Fuji for him. Returning to Japan, I called on the painter Mr. Yasuda Yukihiko, who also lived in Ōiso, to ask if he would do the painting. "I have not studied Mount Fuji. I think Yokoyama Taikan is the best man to do it," declined Mr. Yasuda. I finally prevailed on him, however. Mr. Yasuda painted a wonderful work, which I sent to Mr. Churchill last year. Mr. Churchill wrote me a very gracious letter thanking me for the painting.

As we know, Mr. Churchill was not only an eminent statesman but also a talented man of letters, an eloquent orator, and he produced a number of apt sayings and witticisms, which are known the world over. The expression "iron curtain" is one of his phrases. In his memoirs, too, there are some beautiful turns of phrase that are bound to impress the reader. One of the phrases I particularly like concerns goodwill and patience. Admonishing shortsighted, shallow foreign policies, Mr. Churchill cautioned that history shows that, because of the existence of goodwill and patience, a number of conflicts did not come to pass; when there is a lack of these things, many unfortunate international incidents have occurred. Foreign diplomacy must always utilize goodwill and patience. This is indeed an important lesson to the younger generation from this accomplished, renowned statesman.

Nineteen sixty-one will be the ten-year anniversary of the San Francisco Peace Treaty, which also gave independence to Japan. I made a proposal that we should invite all foreign nationals who contributed to Japan up to this point, so that they might witness the reconstruction of Japan firsthand. If this plan is adopted, the place of honor in the list of guests will no doubt go to General Douglas MacArthur, Supreme Commander of Allied Powers. I wrote about his contributions to Japan during the occupation's days in various places in this memoir, but I don't think it would be useless to say a few more words to summarize General MacArthur's contributions. From the Japanese point of view, General MacArthur's foremost contribution was that he gave the utmost goodwill and support within his discretionary power to maintain the imperial system in the format that exists today. By this I do not mean of course that we can forget the efforts of pro-Japanese figures such as Mr. Castle (former American ambassador to Japan) and Mr. Grew, who were both very knowledgeable about Japan and supported the continuation of the imperial system. It was General MacArthur, however, who made a preemptive move to adopt a new constitution and went to great pains to implement a well-thought-out, farsighted plan to protect the imperial system, being well aware of the ominous air surrounding the Far Eastern Commission and the Allied Council for Japan and sensing what they might recommend in the end. For this reason, General MacArthur deserves a great amount of our respect and gratitude.

Another notable deed of General MacArthur was that he denied the proposal from the Soviet military, a member of the Allied forces, to occupy Japan's northern island Hokkaidō. Think about what would have become of Japan if the Soviets had occupied Hokkaidō—it would not require many words to describe how great General MacArthur is in terms of his contribution to the happiness of the Japanese people. General MacArthur also put the brakes on the idealistic occupation policies of the so-called New Dealers who filled GHQ offices for a brief period of time, placing a check on their activities; this all occurred thanks to General MacArthur's power and good sense. The general also strongly advocated an early withdrawal of the occupation forces, a position that of course promoted other countries to conclude peace treaties with Japan. These are just a few items from a long list of the general's contributions to Japan. It makes me wonder often why it is, then, that Japanese people do not recognize or express gratitude to this great benefactor's contributions.

I would imagine that the general was a man of solitary existence and he was not easily marketable to the public for that reason. There are a large number of worshippers of General MacArthur, but it is probably fair to say that he was not the most popular general. During the occupation, he would go back and forth between the embassy, where his official residence was, and GHQ, housed in the Dai-Ichi Sōgo Building, and seldom left these familiar surroundings, except to check on the Korean front. He never made an appearance to any place for socializing, such as clubs and entertainment districts. At the end of the day, he would spend quiet time reading the Bible. I am almost certain that a general who lived such a solemn and pure life as General MacArthur's is a rarity in all of man's history. General MacArthur is a human being after all; some criticized him, saying that he was snobbish, high-flown, and the like, but the fact that we had General MacArthur as the commander of the occupation forces was indeed a fortuitous turn of events.

Since the general was difficult to approach, only a few glimpses of his personal life are known to the public. For Christmas one year, I gave a present to his only son, Arthur—who was about ten then—a toy donkey. I don't remember exactly where, but when a part of the donkey was pushed, it would raise its legs, move its head, or swish its tail. A few days after Christmas, I had a chance to visit the embassy, where I ran into the general's wife. "Thank you for the Christmas present," she said. "I should tell you that the General"—she always referred to him as "General"—"has taken the toy away from Arthur and won't let him play with it. The General himself plays with it every day, though, making it move its legs and raise its tail, and so forth. So that's why Arthur has not thanked you; but I can say that the General is quite smitten with it." I thought that this was an interesting story that told me one aspect about the general. The general now lives with his son, Arthur, in an apartment in the Waldorf-Astoria Hotel in New York and serves as chairman of the board of Remington Rand—a famous company that produces typewriters. I paid a visit to him last year and saw him for the first time in many years. When I told him about the current conditions in Japan and reported how the reconstruction efforts were going, he seemed genuinely pleased and gave me his blessings on the future of Japan.

We know quite a bit about Prince Konoe Fumimaro. I also added a few episodes of my own elsewhere in this volume, but I wanted to take this opportunity to tell some stories about my misadventures that relate to him. One of my schemes that ended in failure was a plan to go to Europe with Prince Konoe towards the beginning of the war for peacemaking maneuvers; it failed because the plan did not come to pass at all. Another was the time when I became involved in Prince Konoe's plan to draft a letter to the emperor, which resulted in my spending forty days in the custody of the military police. In addition to these two stories, I have a few more of the silliest episodes. Some time ago, I wanted to hire a man for domestic help, instead of using a live-in student as in the past. The maid recommended her cousin. This man was a faithful, reliable man, with whose service all of my family members were quite happy. But moments before I was taken into custody by the military police, the man disappeared. At about the same time, the woman, who had vouched for the man, also disappeared. We thought this was strange, but did not think any more about it. When we began to look into this incident, it turned out that the man was a spy working for the military police, who reported to them all the goings-on in the house. We also discovered that the maid had colluded with this man and had him hired into the household. This man was no ordinary character. As soon as he finished his mission at my house, he crawled under the floor of Prince Konoe's villa in Odawara, set up a microphone, and recorded all the conversations in the receiving room. I was connected to Konoe even through this spying incident.

This is not the end of this story. Out of the blue, this man came to see me after the war. "I am very sorry for what I did during the war," he began. "I was ordered to spy on people and I could not say 'no.' I am very sorry for all the trouble I have caused," he apologized. I was feeling magnanimous and praised him, saying, "You followed orders and you needn't apologize." Later, he asked me to write a letter of recommendation for a job, so I vouched that he performed all his duties faithfully. I am sure he is doing very well even as I write these words.

This episode took place during the Higashikuni government after the war. One day Prince Konoe, then minister of the interior, contacted me to ask me to inquire what Count Makino thought about a certain issue. I called on Count Makino, who then lived in Chiba, for consultation, and stopped by the prime minister's residence in Nagata-chō in Tokyo on the way back. I was planning to go straight home after reporting, but Kobata Toshishirō, minister of state and former lieutenant general of the army, whom I had not seen for a long time, happened to find me in the room. One thing led to another, and all of us set out to have dinner at the prince's temporary residence in the Ogikubo section of Tokyo. The prince's wife was delighted to receive us there. Topics ranged far and wide, including stories about the war, as we enjoyed the woman's cooking and champagne that Konoe had saved for special occasions like this, far into the night. When I finally thought better of myself and wanted to take a leave, I could hardly stand straight. The woman of the house tried to persuade me to say overnight, but I insisted that I had to be in Ōiso the next day and bid good-bye to their hospitality. Prince Konoe was justifiably worried and had a boarder take us to the Shinbashi Station by car.

I was quite inebriated and to this day do not remember how I boarded the train. I woke up with a start in the train several hours later. Something was not right. I could clearly see mountains on the right and the ocean on the left—there was no such place with these features between Shinbashi and Ōiso. I had no idea where I was. Soon the train stopped and I quickly got off, where I discovered that I had come as far as Atami. I wanted to take a train in the other direction as soon as possible but it was already after the last train of the day had departed. I resolved to stay overnight in the waiting room at the station. I did not realize until then that I had been carrying around a bottle of champagne Prince Konoe had given me, as if it were a treasure. The weight of the bottle probably did not bother me since I enjoyed libation in any and all forms. When I woke up in the morning in the waiting room, there was a crowd queuing up. I soon found out that I had to stand in line to get a train ticket home, so I joined the line, but, as luck would have it, tickets sold out when there were only a few people left ahead of me in the line. This made me seriously perturbed, but there was nothing I could do about it. They announced that tickets for the next train would be put on sale more than two hours later. I was getting hungry but there was no restaurant open so early in the morning. I searched in my memory for someone who lived in the city. I remembered Marquis Hachisuga Masashi, who had been a student when I was posted ambassador in London. I boldly decided that he did not need advance notice, so I walked to his home, carrying the champagne in my hand. I invited myself in for breakfast at their home and explained the situation. When the breakfast was over, Hachisuga said, "I have something for you," producing a new pair of shoes. "They are made in England," he said. I thanked him for the gift and offered the champagne from Prince Konoe in exchange.

The next time I saw Konoe, he asked me if I was able to return home all right that night. I told him the whole story, which made him laugh uncontrollably. "We sure had a lot to drink that night," he said. We must have. I never said a word, however, about how the champagne he gave me turned into shoes.

# Glossary

*1911 Revolution.* Begun in 1911 as an uprising in a western province of Sichuan and quickly spreading to other provinces, it marked the end of imperial rule in China. The country was first unified under Sun Yat-sen in January of 1912 and the Republic of China came into existence. After the emperor abdicated, the government was handed over to Yuan Shi-kai in the following month.

*2.26 Incident.* An attempt, on February 26, 1936, by young military officers to overthrow the Japanese government. With the help of fifteen hundred troops, army officers killed high-ranking government officials and occupied key government buildings and areas in Tokyo. The rebellion was suppressed within a few days, and the conspirators were put to death.

*5.15 Incident.* An attempt, on May 15, 1932, to overthrow the Japanese government. Ultraright young navy officers, helped by students in the army officer training school, attacked the official residence of the prime minister, the Bank of Japan, the National Police headquarters, and a number of other places, killing Prime Minister Inukai.

*Battle of Mukden.* A battle (May 1905) between Japan and Russia fought outside of Mukden (a.k.a. Fengtian, now called Shenyang), capital city of Manchuria. This was the last major battle of the Russo-Japanese War, which ended with Japan as the victor.

*Boxer Rebellion, The.* A rebellion by a religious group, "the Boxers," against the foreign powers in China (Russia, France, Germany, Japan, Great Britain). Beginning in 1899 members of the group, who believed that sorcery rendered them invincible, attacked foreign outposts, missions, and the like, killing a number of foreigners. The Westerners responded by capturing Beijing and making the Chinese government succumb to humiliating demands.

*Ceylon.* An old name for the country of Sri Lanka prior to 1972.

*China Incident.* An English translation of the name in Japanese for Japan's war against China, which began in July 1937 with the Lugouqiao Incident.

*Ch'ing Dynasty* (also Qing dynasty). The last Chinese imperial dynasty, which ruled China from 1616 to 1912. See also *1911 Revolution*.

*Chōshō.* The name of a fief and province in Japan occupying the northern and western part of the present prefecture of Yamaguchi at the western tip of the main Japanese island of Honshū. Satsuma and Chōshō samurai joined their forces to bring about the Meiji Restoration and, for this historical reason, many officials from these two provinces served in the Meiji government.

*EROA.* The abbreviation for the Economic Rehabilitation in Occupied Areas Fund, a program of the United States to help rehabilitate countries affected by the Second World War.

*Formosa.* The former name for Taiwan, from the Portuguese *formosa*, "beautiful."

*Fuzhou Incident.* An incident in Fuzhou, the capital of Fujian Province, China, where about one hundred Japanese youths clashed with Chinese students in November 1919. This event was emblematic of the anti-Japanese sentiment then prevalent in China.

*GARIOA.* The abbreviation for the Government Appropriation for Relief in Occupied Areas Fund, an assistance program of the United States to help ease the occupied areas ravaged by the Second World War.

*GATT.* The acronym for the General Agreement on Tariffs and Trade, an international agreement that came into existence in Geneva in 1947 in order to reduce and seek equity of tariffs among twenty-three signatories. Japan joined the group in 1955.

*Great Kantō Earthquake.* A large earthquake that hit the Tokyo area on September 1, 1923, in which about a hundred thousand people died.

*Guo Songling Incident.* In November 1925, Guo Songling, a Chinese warlord, openly opposed another Chinese warlord, Zhang Zuolin, who received much covert support from the Japanese military. In the end, Guo's resistance failed. He was captured and put to death by a firing squad.

*Hull Note.* A memorandum from the United States government to the Japanese government in November 1941, which urged Japan to withdraw from China and Indochina and to make other military concessions. The note was taken by the Japanese government as the ultimatum for war.

*Imperial Rescript on Education.* Issued in October 30, 1890, in the name of the Meiji emperor, the rescript spelled out the basic principles of moral behavior and education. It was recited daily in Japanese schools. It was abolished in 1948.

*Korean War*. A war between North and South Korea that began in June 1950, lasting for about three years. South Korea was supported by the United States and United Nations troops, while North Korea was assisted by the Chinese.

*League of Nations*. An international organization founded after the First World War to promote disarmament, prevent war through collective security and diplomacy, and improve global welfare. The United Nations effectively replaced it after World War II.

*London Conference*. A conference held in London from September to October 1954 to discuss the international status of West Germany, resulting in the Paris Agreements. It was attended by representatives of Belgium, Canada, France, Great Britain, Italy, Luxembourg, the Netherlands, the United States, and West Germany.

*Lugouqiao Incident*. A military incident that triggered Japan's war against China. On July 7, 1937, Japanese troops stationed at Lugouqiao, a river bridge on the outskirts of Beijing, attacked Chinese troops, believing that one of the Japanese soldiers had been shot by the Chinese. Although the two sides decided not to enlarge the scale of the conflict, and signed an agreement to that effect on July 11, this incident intensified the anti-Japanese sentiment in China, leading the countries into a full-scale war.

*Manchukuo*. A Japanese puppet state established on March 1, 1932, in present-day northeast China, which then included three provinces and a part of Inner Mongolia. Pu Yi was installed as emperor. The country dissolved at the end of the war in 1945.

*Manchurian Incident*. A series of maneuvers taken by the Japanese military in northeast China that was met by China's strong resistance. Also known as the "Mukden Incident," it is regarded as the precursor of the full-scale war between China and Japan. On September 18, 1931, the Japanese military staged a bombing of its own Manchurian Railway, a few miles north of Fengtian (a.k.a. Mukden, present-day Shenyang), using the incident as a pretext for the occupation of the whole of Manchuria.

*Meiji Restoration*. A series of political events in Japan spanning 1867–1868 including the returning of the government from the Tokugawa shogunate to the emperor and the installation of the emperor as the head of state, as well as a formation of a new nation-state.

*Meiji*. The name of a Japanese imperial era spanning 1868–1912.

*NATO*. The abbreviation for the North Atlantic Treaty Organization, an organization of nations designed to secure mutual security, enacted in 1950.

*Paris Agreements*. Refers to the four agreements signed in Paris on October 23, 1954, which, among other things, restored West German sovereignty and provided for the entry of West Germany into the Western European Union, limited armament of West Germany, and membership in NATO.

*Paris Peace Conference.* A peace conference held in Paris in January 1919 to conclude World War I. As a result, the Versailles Treaty was signed, which spelled out, in part, the end of the Russian, German, Austro-Hungarian, and Ottoman empires.

*Potsdam Declaration.* A joint declaration made by the United States, China, and Great Britain to Japan on July 26, 1945, in Potsdam, Germany. The statement concerns the conditions of Japan's surrender, treatment of war criminals, and territorial questions, among other things. Japan accepted these terms, thereby ending World War II.

*Russo-Japanese War.* A war in 1904–1905 between Russia and Japan, over control of the Korean peninsula and northeast China (so-called Manchuria), in which Japan emerged as the victor.

*Satsuma.* The name of a fief and province in Japan during the Edo period (1603–1867), occupying the western part of the present-day Kagoshima Prefecture, located in the southern tip of the island of Kyūshū. Satsuma and Chōshō samurai joined forces to bring about the Meiji Restoration and, for this historical reason, many officials from these provinces served in the Meiji government.

*Shōwa.* The name of an imperial era spanning 1926–1989.

*Sino-Japanese War.* A war (1894–1895) between Ch'ing (Qing) China and Japan over control of Korea, which resulted in a victory for Japan. China agreed to pay a large amount of money to Japan, to cede control of Taiwan and the Liaodong Peninsula to Japan, and to recognize the independence of Korea.

*Taishō.* The name of an imperial era spanning 1912–1926.

*Twenty-one Demands to China.* Refers to the twenty-one demands the Japanese presented to the Chinese in 1915. They included, among other things, demands for political and commercial privileges in Shandong Province, northeast China, and Inner Mongolia, which fueled anti-Japanese sentiment in China.

*Yuan Shi-kai.* A Chinese politician (1859–1916) who became the head of the Republic of China after the fall of the Ch'ing (Qing) dynasty in 1911.

*Zaibatsu.* Family-controlled banking and industrial conglomerates that started in the Meiji era. Famous *zaibatsu* include Mitsui, Sumitomo, Mitsubishi, and Yasuda. Prior to the end of World War II, *zaibatsu* controlled enormous capital and gained much influence on government policies in Japan and colonies abroad. *Zaibatsu* were dissolved after the war but reemerged as *keiretsu* (groups of related companies) in the 1960s.

# Index

China, 15–16; Grew's dislike of
extremists, 19; Guo Songling and
Zhang Zuolin, 282–83; interference
in government, 225–26; political
influence of, 11–12; against
Potsdam Declaration, 19–20; radical
elements in, 19–20, 23; war
prisoners, 98; against Yoshida,
13–15; Yoshida's arrest and release,
23–26; Yoshida's dislike of, xii. *See
also* Self-Defense Force; 2.26
Incident
army of occupation, 27; administrative
structure of, 28–30, 37–38; change
in early occupation policies, 31;
disposal of Japanese Army assets,
29; food aid, 233; Japanese police,
146–47; morale, 44; about
resistance of Japanese Army, 31–32;
role of Russian army in occupation,
44; two contrasting groups in,
37–38; unrest in Kobe, 145. *See also*
MacArthur, General Douglas A.;
Occupation; U.S. Eighth Army
Arnold, Dr. Karl, 89–91
Ashida Hitoshi, Dr.: Democratic Party,
69; labor reform, 176–77; Liberal
Party, 58, 62; as prime minister,
71–72, 118; revising Constitution,
115; Shōwa Denki case, 176
Atcheson, George, 185, 214; diplomatic
adviser to SCAP, 47
Attlee, Clement, 97
Australia, 27, 28; aids in food crisis,
168; as a British commonwealth,
252; new Constitution, 110, 111;
San Francisco Peace Conference,
209; "white Australia" policy, 261

Baba Tsunego, and educational reform,
140
Ball, W. Macmahon, 163
Baty, Dr. Thomas, 268
Bertoin, Jean, 87
Bisson, Thomas Arthur, 125
Black, Eugene R., 101
black market, 167–68

Bonin Islands, 200
Boxer Rebellion, 10, 294
Burgess and Maclean case, 81
Butler, R. A., 99

Canada: as a British commonwealth,
252; Far Eastern Commission, 27;
trade with, 85; Yoshida's trip to,
83–87
Castle, William Richards, 101, 290
Central Liaison Office (Japanese): new
Constitution, 109; organization and
function, 30–32, 48; purges, 122,
124, 134; Security Treaty, 214
Chamberlain, Mrs. Neville, 98, 287
Chamberlain, Neville, 15, 265, 266;
averting war, 98, 255–65, 287;
Yoshida visits, 287–88
Charter Party Agreement (Japan-U.S.),
154
China, Republic of: Boxer Rebellion,
10, 294; as cause of war, 15–16;
China, Communist, 192, 232;
China Incident as basis for purges,
127; delegate from, at peace
conference, 207; intellectuals and,
231–32; Japan's expansion in, 3–8;
in Korean War, 171, 215, 241;
occupation of, by Japan, 50;
propaganda of, and Japan, 231–32;
questions about, in British
Parliament, 96–97; San Francisco
Peace Treaty, 199, 205; Sino-
Japanese war, 5, 7, 258, 285;
Twenty-one Demands, 6–7, 259
Chinda Sutemi, Count and ambassador
to Great Britain, 260, 278–80
Churchill, Sir Winston Spencer, 15, 16;
receives Yoshida, 97, 287–89
CIO (Japanese), 173
Clemenceau, Georges Eugene
Benjamin, 260-61
Cominform, 191, 193
Communist Party (Japanese): action
against, 193–94; anti-American
propaganda, 77–78; education,
140–41; effect of Peace Treaty on,

# About the Editor

**Hiroshi Nara** is professor of Japanese and chair of the Department of East Asian Languages and Literatures at the University of Pittsburgh. In addition to Japanese language pedagogy and linguistic semantics, his research interests include intellectual history of Japan during the interwar years. His most recent books are *The Structure of Detachment: The Aesthetic Vision of Kuki Shūzō* and *Inexorable Modernity: Japan's Grappling with Modernity in the Arts.*